W9-DDN-210

STOP!

This is the back of the book.
You wouldn't want to spoil a great ending!

This book is printed "manga-style," in the authentic Japanese right-to-left format. Since none of the artwork has been flipped or altered, readers get to experience the story just as the creator intended. You've been asking for it, so TOKYOPOP® delivered: authentic, hot-off-the-press, and far more fun!

DIRECTIONS

If this is your first time reading manga-style, here's a quick guide to help you understand how it works.

It's easy... just start in the top right panel and follow the numbers. Have fun, and look for more 100% authentic manga from TOKYOPOP®!

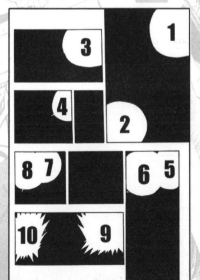

ALSO AVAILABLE FROM  TOKYOPOP®

MANGA

.HACK//LEGEND OF THE TWILIGHT
@LARGE
A.I. LOVE YOU February 2004
AI YORI AOSHI January 2004
ANGELIC LAYER
BABY BIRTH
BATTLE ROYALE
BATTLE VIXENS April 2004
BIRTH May 2004
BRAIN POWERED
BRIGADOON
B'TX January 2004
CARDCAPTOR SAKURA
CARDCAPTOR SAKURA - MASTER OF THE CLOW
CARDCAPTOR SAKURA: BOXED SET COLLECTION 1
CARDCAPTOR SAKURA: BOXED SET COLLECTION 2
   March 2004
CHOBITS
CHRONICLES OF THE CURSED SWORD
CLAMP SCHOOL DETECTIVES
CLOVER
COMIC PARTY June 2004
CONFIDENTIAL CONFESSIONS
CORRECTOR YUI
COWBOY BEBOP: BOXED SET THE COMPLETE
   COLLECTION
CRESCENT MOON May 2004
CREST OF THE STARS June 2004
CYBORG 009
DEMON DIARY
DIGIMON
DIGIMON SERIES 3 April 2004
DIGIMON ZERO TWO February 2004
DNANGEL April 2004
DOLL May 2004
DRAGON HUNTER
DRAGON KNIGHTS
DUKLYON: CLAMP SCHOOL DEFENDERS:
DV June 2004
ERICA SAKURAZAWA
FAERIES' LANDING January 2004
FAKE
FLCL
FORBIDDEN DANCE
FRUITS BASKET February 2004
G GUNDAM
GATEKEEPERS
GETBACKERS February 2004
GHOST! March 2004
GIRL GOT GAME January 2004
GRAVITATION
GTO

GUNDAM WING
GUNDAM WING: BATTLEFIELD OF PACIFISTS
GUNDAM WING: ENDLESS WALTZ
GUNDAM WING: THE LAST OUTPOST
HAPPY MANIA
HARLEM BEAT
I.N.V.U.
INITIAL D
ISLAND
JING: KING OF BANDITS
JULINE
JUROR 13 March 2004
KARE KANO
KILL ME, KISS ME February 2004
KINDAICHI CASE FILES, THE
KING OF HELL
KODOCHA: SANA'S STAGE
LAMENT OF THE LAMB May 2004
LES BIJOUX February 2004
LIZZIE MCGUIRE
LOVE HINA
LUPIN III
LUPIN III SERIES 2
MAGIC KNIGHT RAYEARTH I
MAGIC KNIGHT RAYEARTH II February 2004
MAHOROMATIC: AUTOMATIC MAIDEN May 2004
MAN OF MANY FACES
MARMALADE BOY
MARS
METEOR METHUSELA June 2004
METROID June 2004
MINK April 2004
MIRACLE GIRLS
MIYUKI-CHAN IN WONDERLAND
MODEL May 2004
NELLY MUSIC MANGA April 2004
ONE April 2004
PARADISE KISS
PARASYTE
PEACH GIRL
PEACH GIRL CHANGE OF HEART
PEACH GIRL RELAUNCH BOX SET
PET SHOP OF HORRORS
PITA-TEN January 2004
PLANET LADDER February 2004
PLANETES
PRIEST
PRINCESS AI April 2004
PSYCHIC ACADEMY March 2004
RAGNAROK
RAGNAROK: BOXED SET COLLECTION 1
RAVE MASTER
RAVE MASTER: BOXED SET March 2004

10103

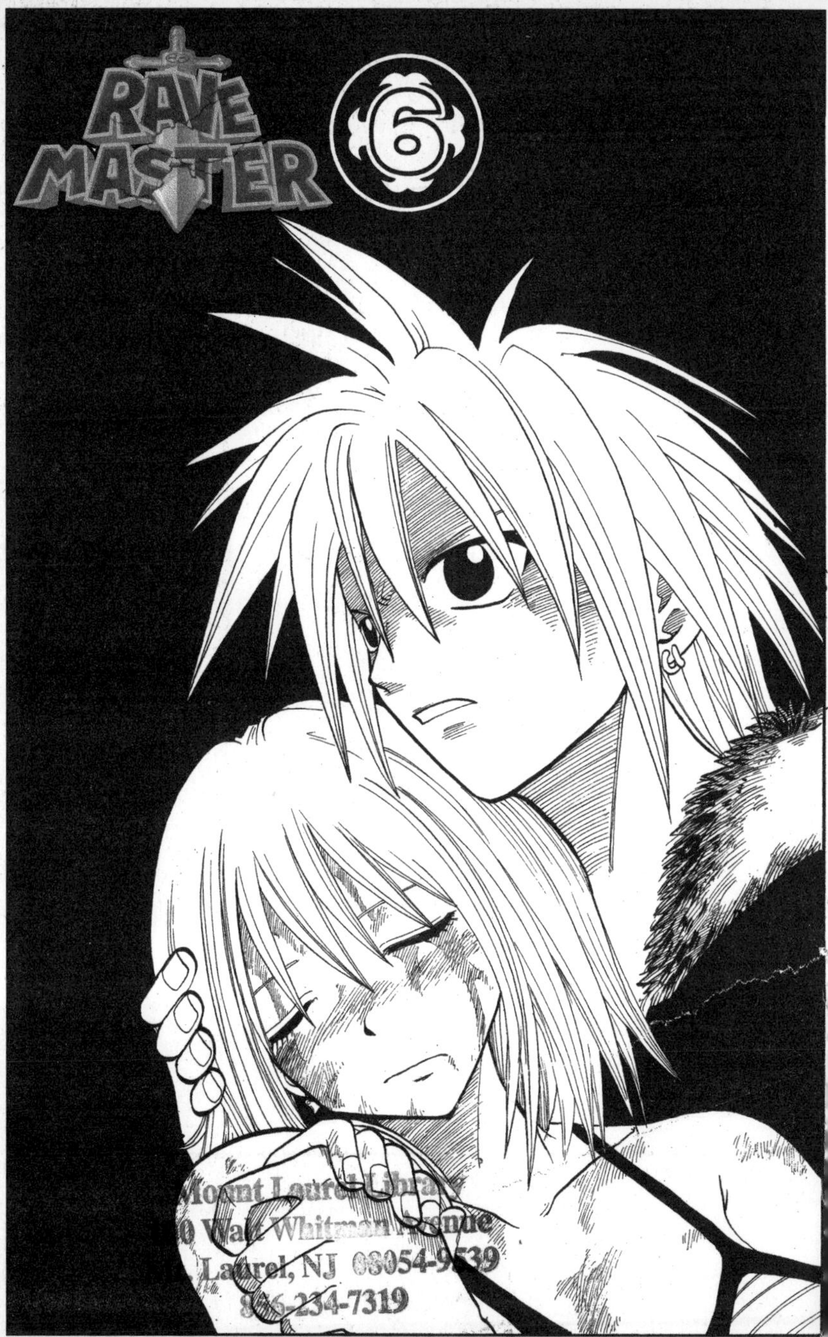
RAVE MASTER
6

Translator - Amy Forsyth
English Adaptation - James Lucas Jones
Copy Editor - Carol Fox
Retouch and Lettering - Marnie Echols
Cover Colors - Pauline Sims
Cover Design - Raymond Makowski

Editor - Jake Forbes
Managing Editor - Jill Freshney
Production Coordinator - Antonio DePietro
Production Manager - Jennifer Miller, Mutsumi Miyazaki
Art Director - Matt Alford
Editorial Director - Jeremy Ross
VP of Production - Ron Klamert
President & C.O.O. - John Parker
Publisher & C.E.O. - Stuart Levy

Email: editor@TOKYOPOP.com
Come visit us online at www.TOKYOPOP.com

A  Manga

TOKYOPOP Inc.
5900 Wilshire Blvd. Suite 2000
Los Angeles, CA 90036

Rave Master Vol. 6

ISBN: 1-59182-213-0

First TOKYOPOP® printing: December 2003

10 9 8 7 6 5 4 3 2 1

Printed in the USA

VOLUME 6

Story and Art by
HIRO MASHIMA

Los Angeles · Tokyo · London

RAVE MASTER™

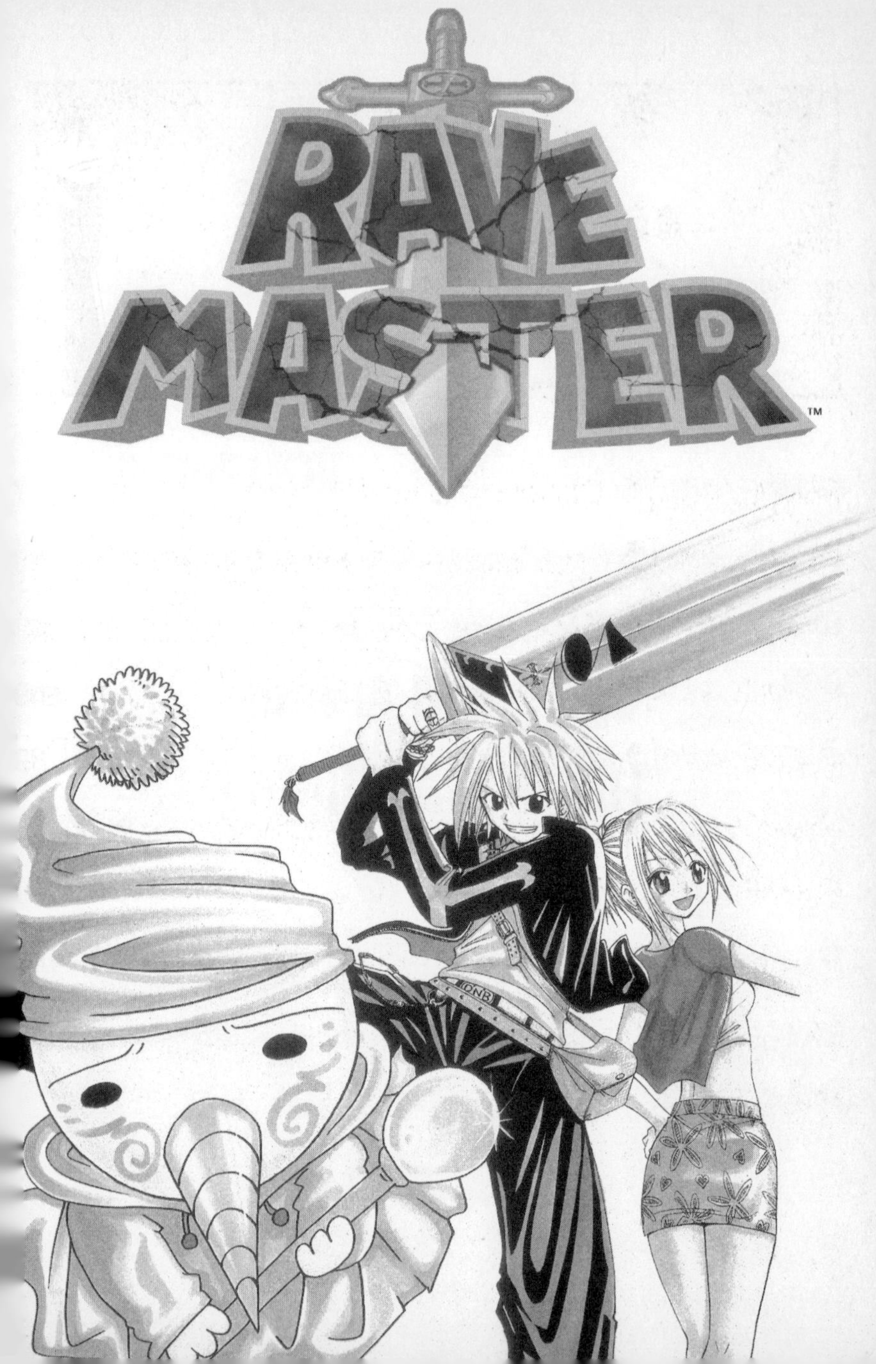

RAVE MASTER 6
CONTENTS

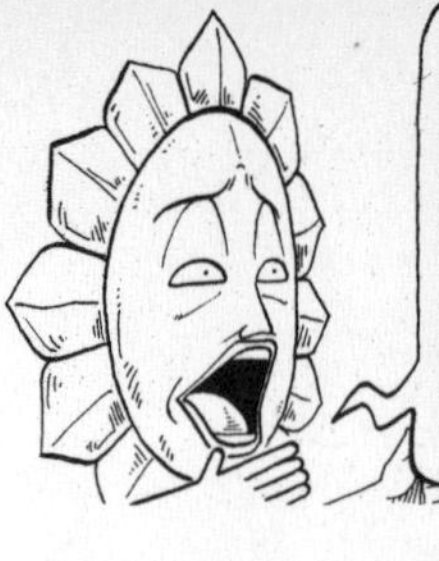

The Story So Far...

Haru Glory and his friends have obtained the first missing Rave, the Rave of Knowledge, and now they have journeyed to Experiment, the largest city on the Continent of Song. After a quick stop at the beach, they visit Symphonia Museum, where hundreds of artifacts related to the Symphonia Kingdom, including records of the first Rave Master, are kept. But even as our heroes search for clues, they are being hunted by Seig Hart, an Elemental Master, with orders to kill the Rave Master. While Elie stumbles upon more clues to her own past in the museum, Haru visits a fortune teller and hears a most disturbing prediction-Elie will die right before his eyes!

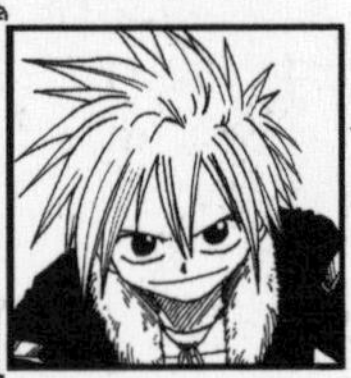

HARU GLORY: The Rave Master. Haru is the heir to Rave, the only one capable of wielding it and destroying Dark Bring. Impulsive and headstrong, he's not afraid to put himself in danger to do what is right. His father disappeared in search of Rave when he was very young.

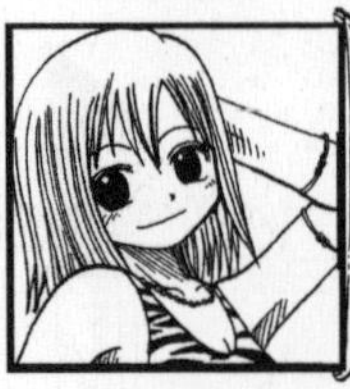

ELIE: A Girl with no past. Elie travels the world in search of the key to her forgotten memories. Outwardly cheerful, she hides a great sadness from her past. She's hot-headed, so when she pulls out her explosive Tonfa Blasters, bad guys watch out!

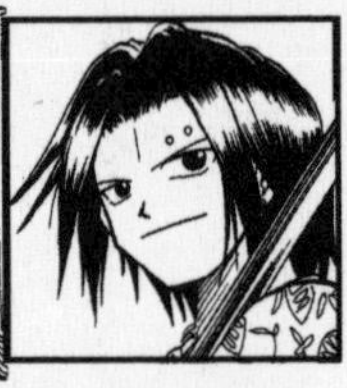

MUSICA: Leader of the Silver Rhythm Gang. An orphan whose family was slaughtered when he was a baby, Musica became a street-fighting petty thief, but he has a good heart.

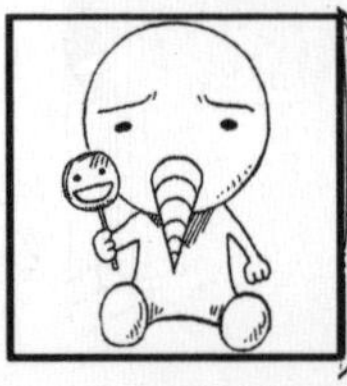

PLUE: The Rave Bearer. Plue is supposed to be Haru's guide in finding the Rave Stones, but so far he's just gotten him in and out of trouble. No one knows exactly what Plue is, but he seems to have healing abilities and is smarter than your average...whatever he is.

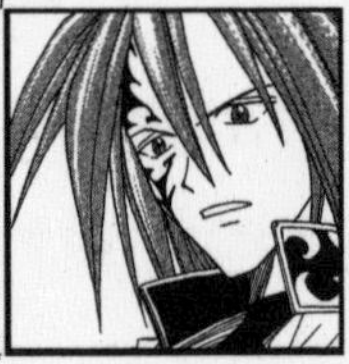

SEIG HART: The Elemental Master Seig Hart has a tenuous relationship with Demon Card. He's been ordered by King to kill the Rave Master, but his own quest is to kill woman 3173.

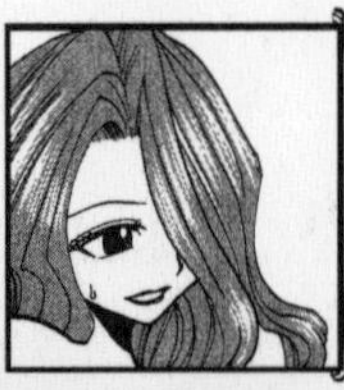

REINA: Don't be fooled by Reina's sexy exterior-she's one of Demon Card's Oracion Six, reporting only to the supreme leader, King. She's flirtatious and devious but her true power has yet to be seen.

RAVE MASTER

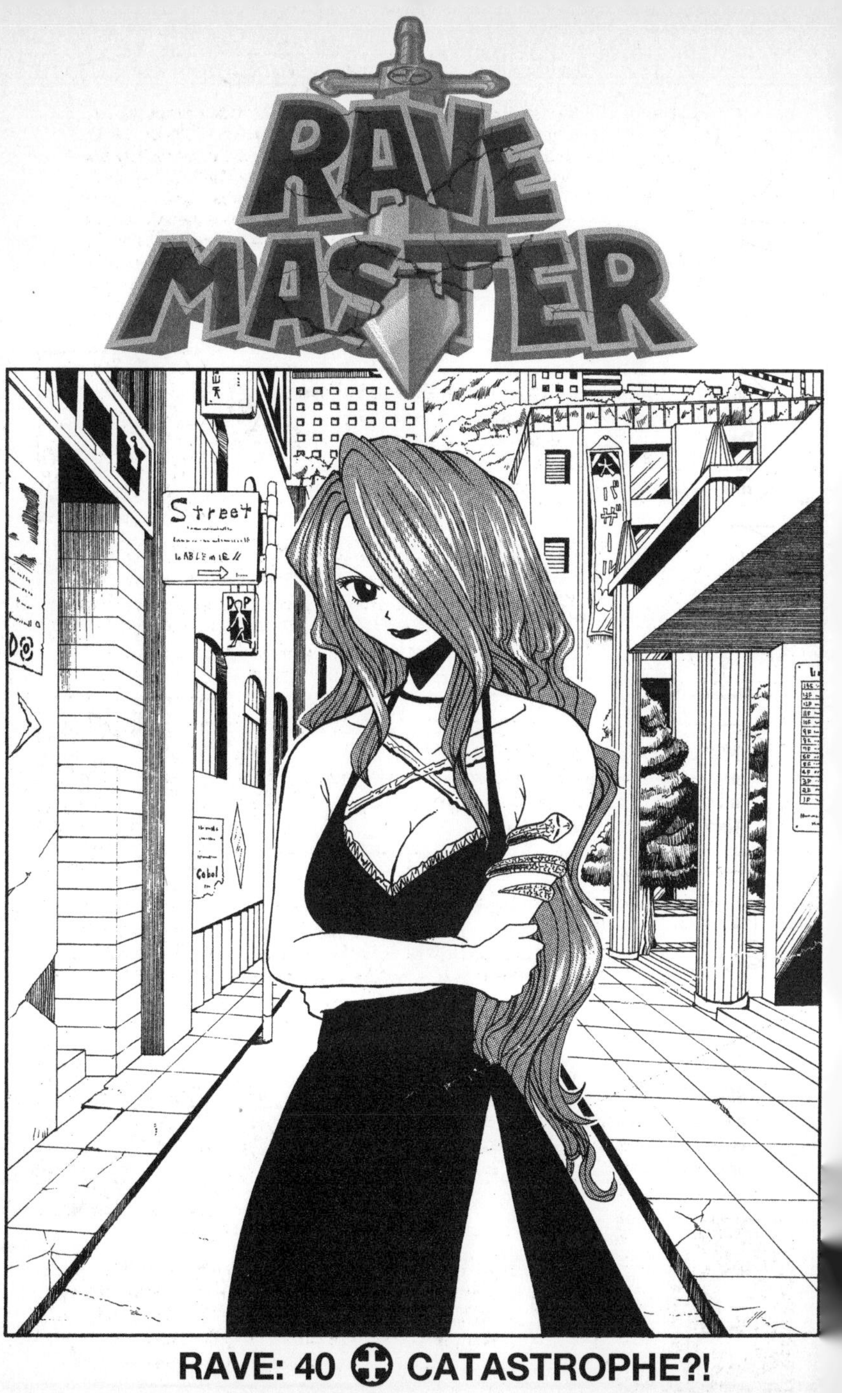
Street
Cobol

RAVE: 40 ✠ CATASTROPHE?!

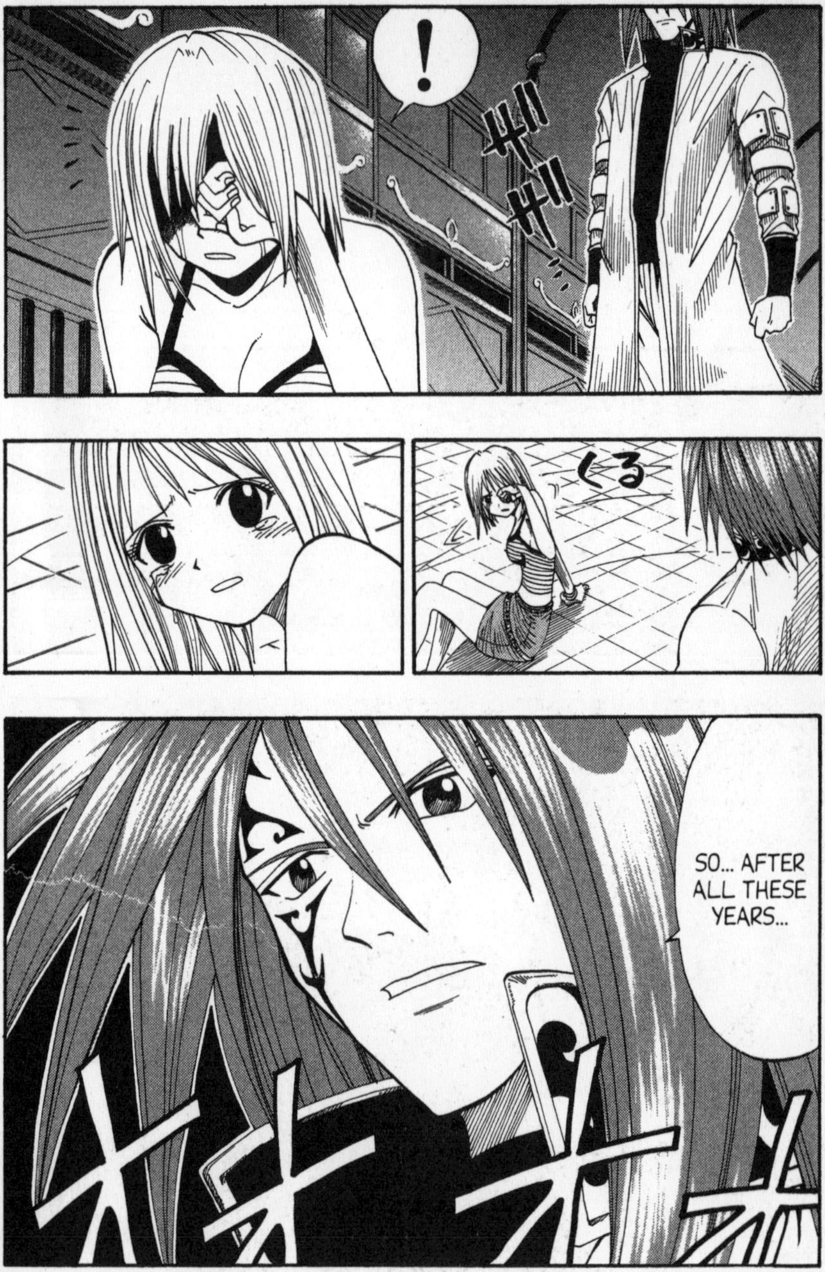
!
くる
SO... AFTER ALL THESE YEARS...

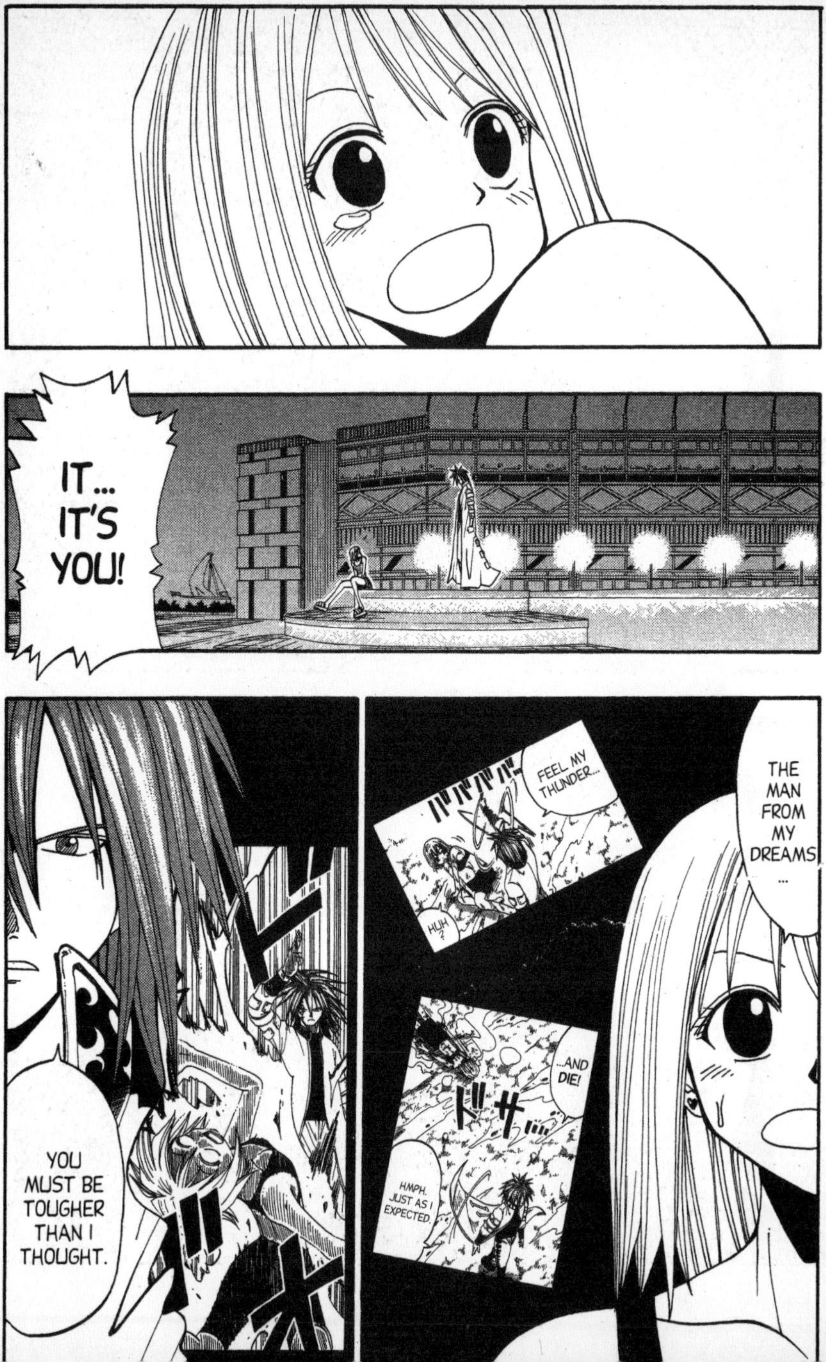
IT... IT'S YOU!
THE MAN FROM MY DREAMS...
FEEL MY THUNDER...
HUH?
...AND DIE!
HMPH. JUST AS I EXPECTED.
YOU MUST BE TOUGHER THAN I THOUGHT.

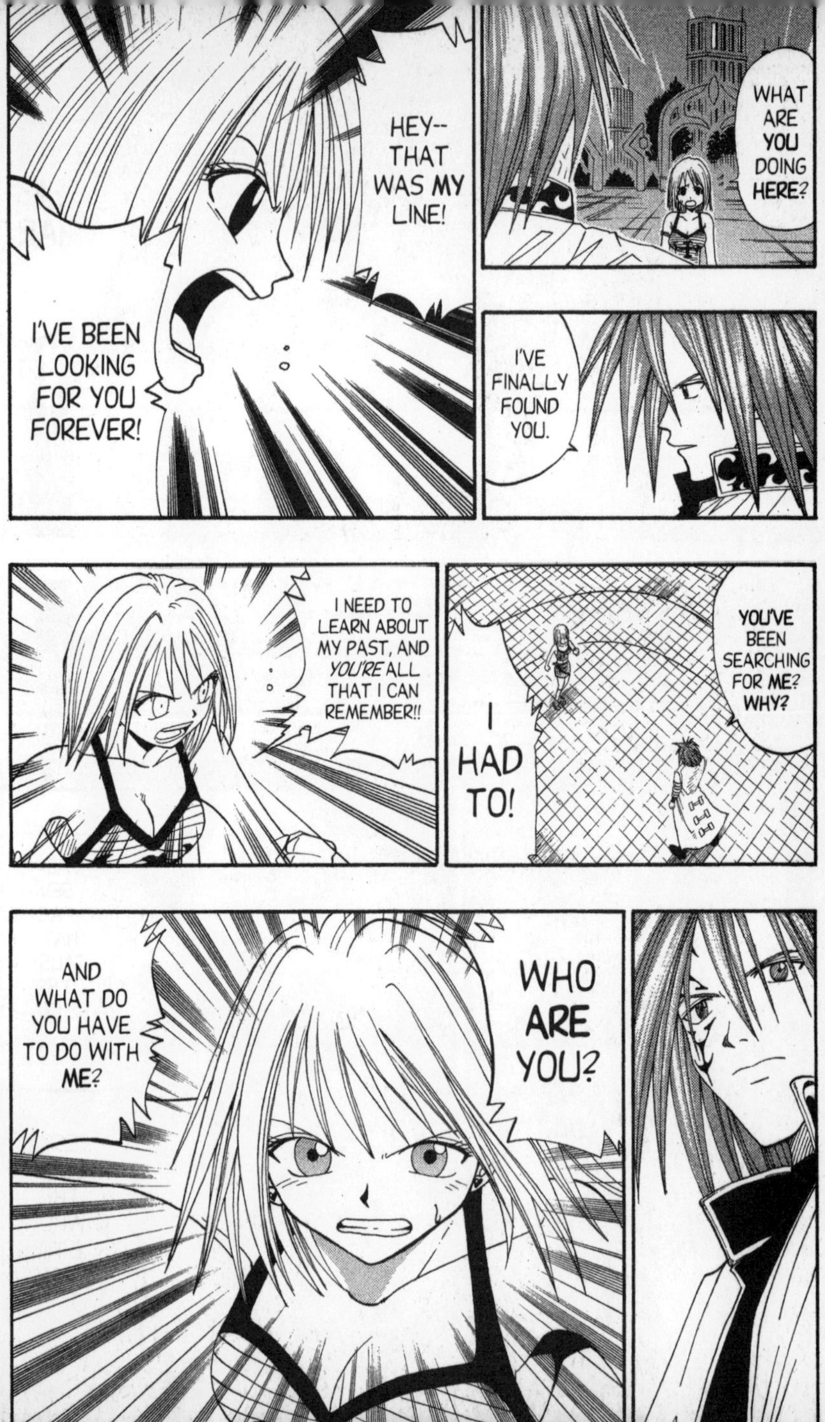
WHAT ARE YOU DOING HERE?
I'VE FINALLY FOUND YOU.
HEY-- THAT WAS MY LINE!
I'VE BEEN LOOKING FOR YOU FOREVER!
YOU'VE BEEN SEARCHING FOR ME? WHY?
I HAD TO!
I NEED TO LEARN ABOUT MY PAST, AND YOU'RE ALL THAT I CAN REMEMBER!!
WHO ARE YOU?
AND WHAT DO YOU HAVE TO DO WITH ME?

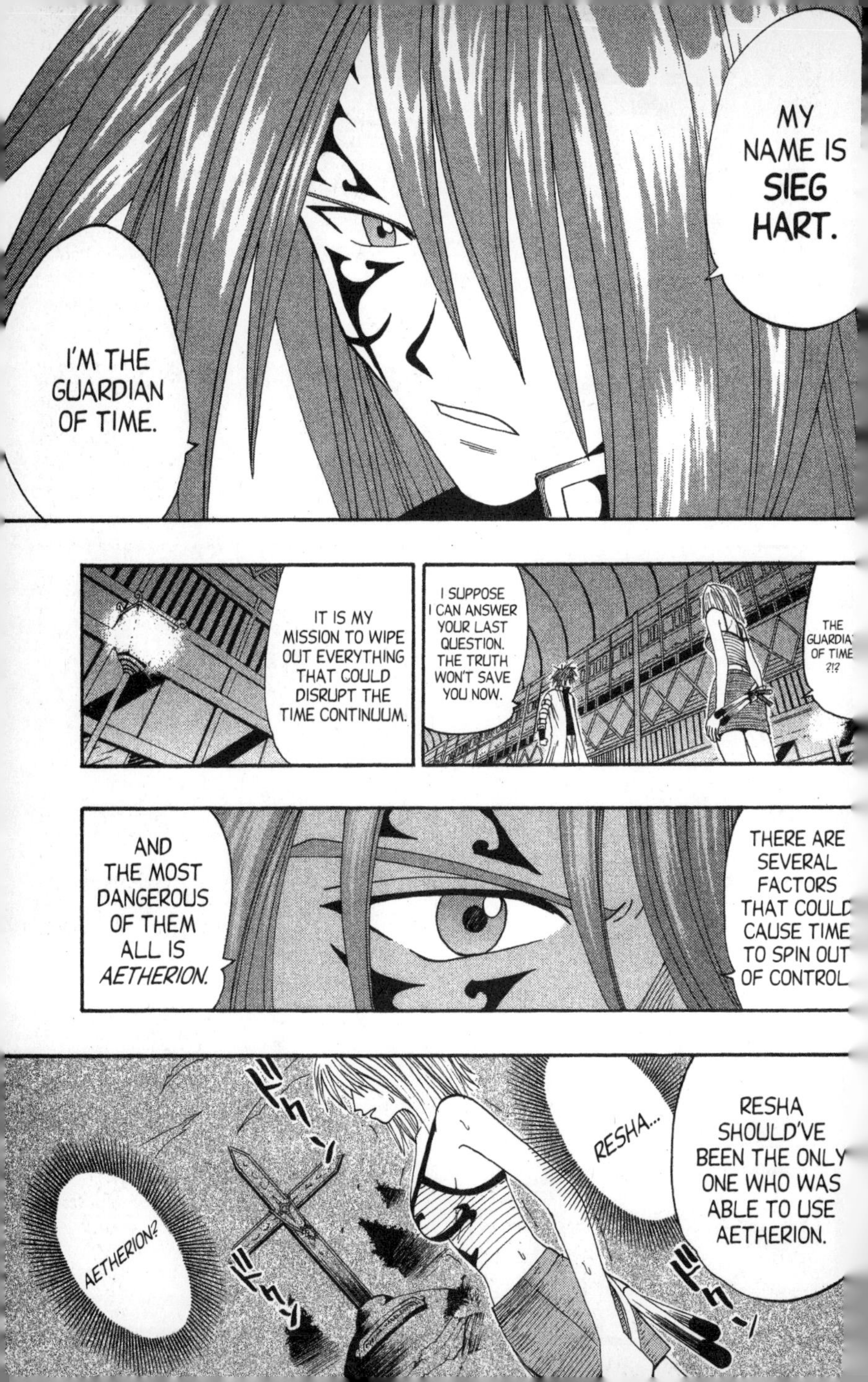
MY NAME IS SIEG HART.
I'M THE GUARDIAN OF TIME.
THE GUARDIA OF TIME ?!?
I SUPPOSE I CAN ANSWER YOUR LAST QUESTION. THE TRUTH WON'T SAVE YOU NOW.
IT IS MY MISSION TO WIPE OUT EVERYTHING THAT COULD DISRUPT THE TIME CONTINUUM.
THERE ARE SEVERAL FACTORS THAT COULD CAUSE TIME TO SPIN OUT OF CONTROL.
AND THE MOST DANGEROUS OF THEM ALL IS *AETHERION.*
RESHA SHOULD'VE BEEN THE ONLY ONE WHO WAS ABLE TO USE AETHERION.
RESHA...
AETHERION?

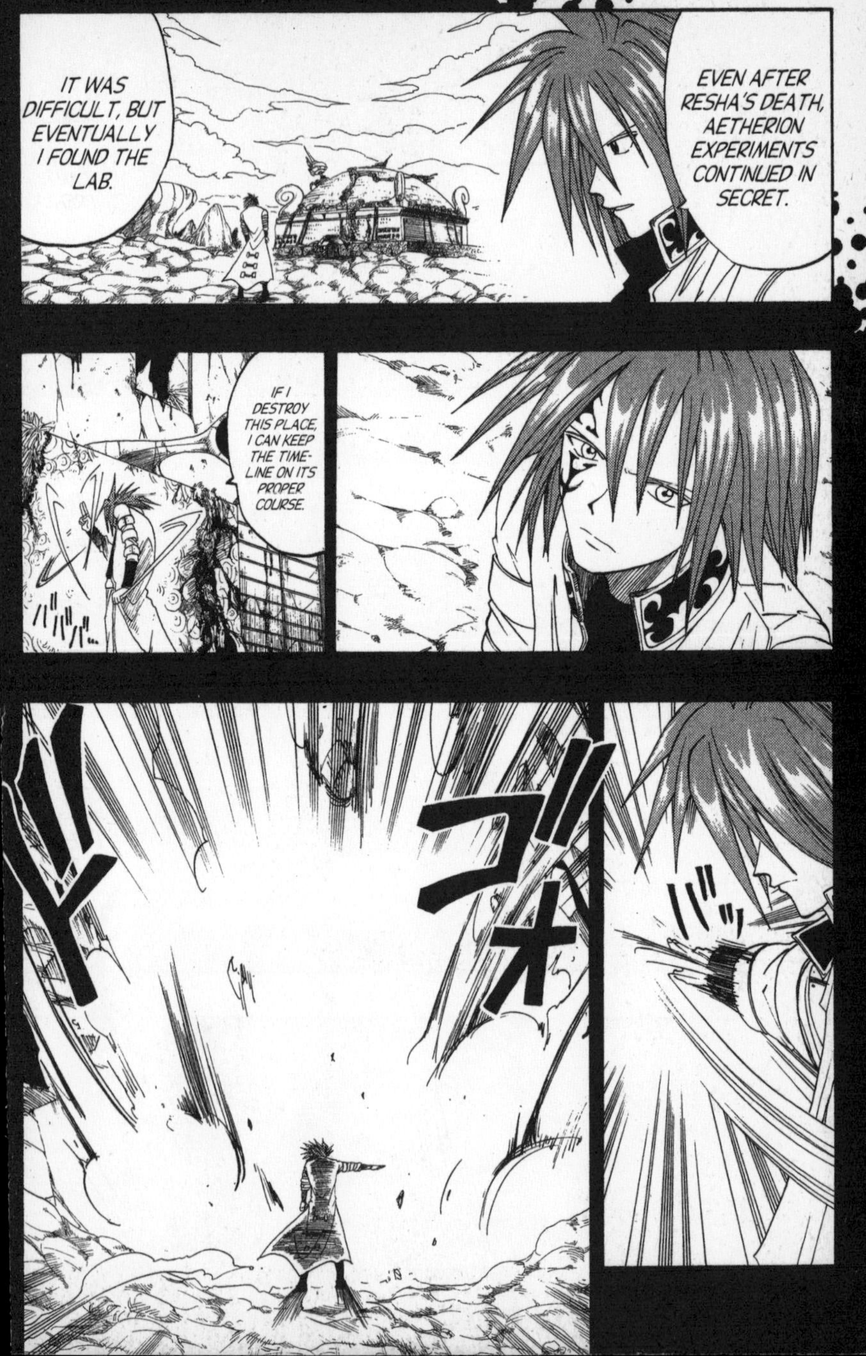
EVEN AFTER RESHA'S DEATH, AETHERION EXPERIMENTS CONTINUED IN SECRET.
IT WAS DIFFICULT, BUT EVENTUALLY I FOUND THE LAB.
IF I DESTROY THIS PLACE, I CAN KEEP THE TIME-LINE ON ITS PROPER COURSE.

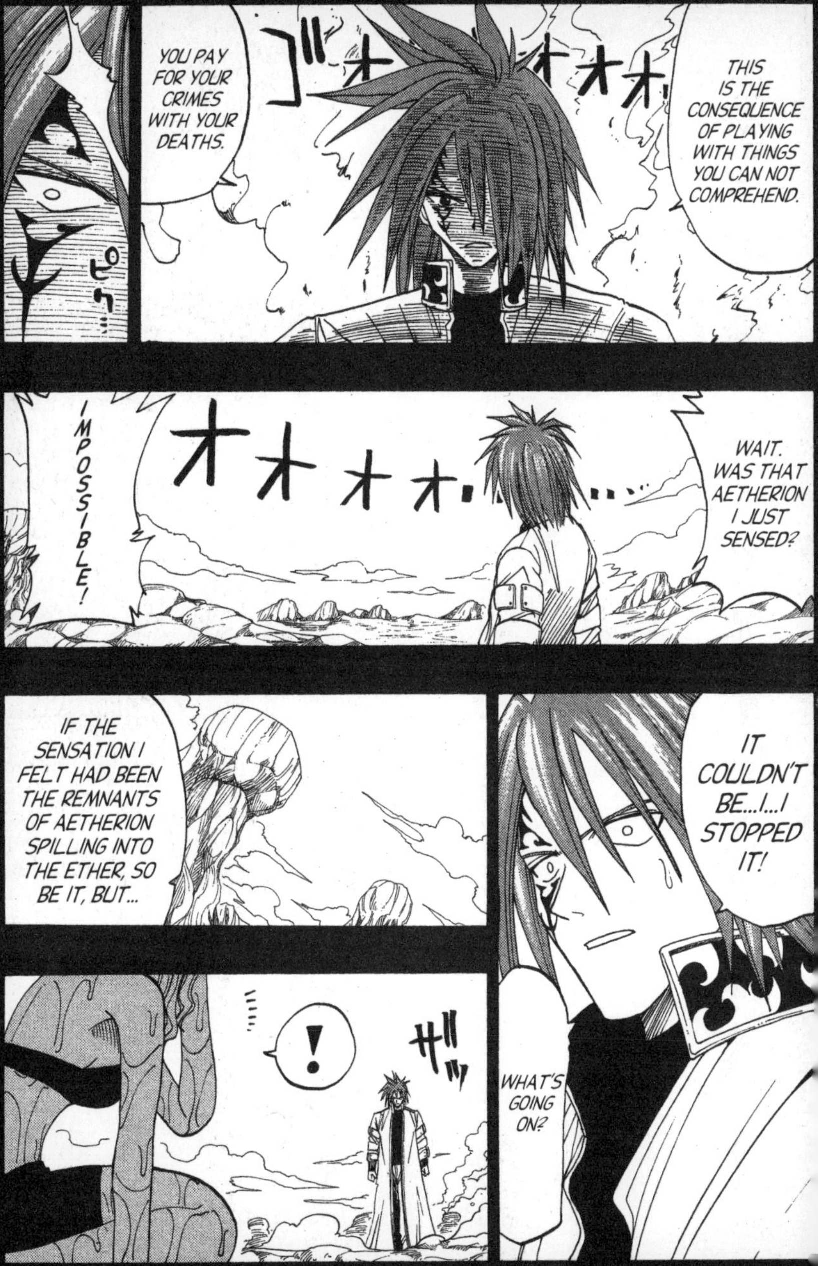
ゴオオオオ
THIS IS THE CONSEQUENCE OF PLAYING WITH THINGS YOU CAN NOT COMPREHEND.
YOU PAY FOR YOUR CRIMES WITH YOUR DEATHS.
オオオオ……
WAIT. WAS THAT AETHERION I JUST SENSED?
IMPOSSIBLE!
IT COULDN'T BE...I...I STOPPED IT!
WHAT'S GOING ON?
IF THE SENSATION I FELT HAD BEEN THE REMNANTS OF AETHERION SPILLING INTO THE ETHER, SO BE IT, BUT...
ザッ
!

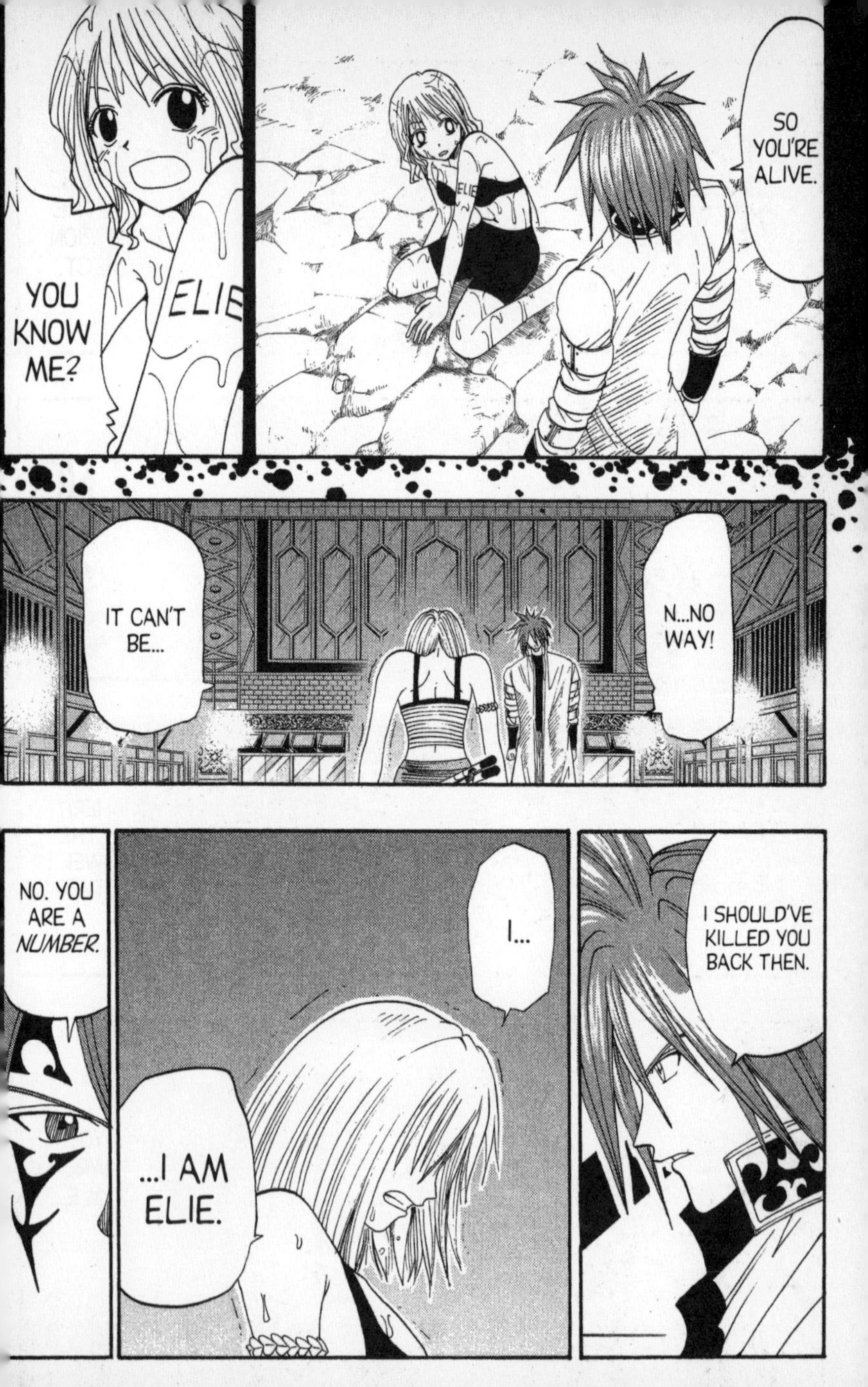
SO YOU'RE ALIVE.
YOU KNOW ME?
N...NO WAY!
IT CAN'T BE...
I SHOULD'VE KILLED YOU BACK THEN.
I...
...I AM ELIE.
NO. YOU ARE A *NUMBER.*

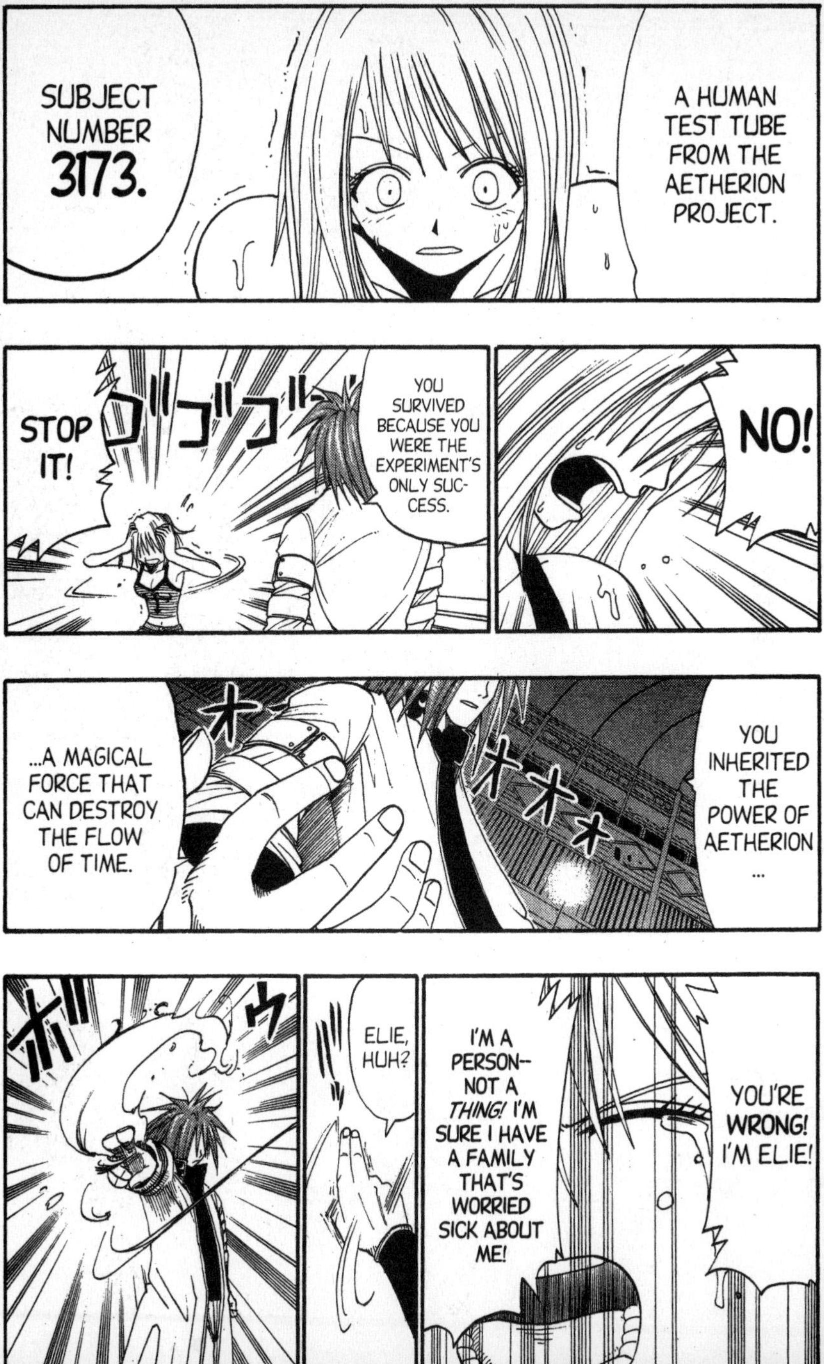
A HUMAN TEST TUBE FROM THE AETHERION PROJECT.
SUBJECT NUMBER 3173.
NO!
YOU SURVIVED BECAUSE YOU WERE THE EXPERIMENT'S ONLY SUC-CESS.
ゴゴゴ
STOP IT!
YOU INHERITED THE POWER OF AETHERION ...
オオオオ
...A MAGICAL FORCE THAT CAN DESTROY THE FLOW OF TIME.
YOU'RE WRONG! I'M ELIE!
I'M A PERSON-- NOT A *THING!* I'M SURE I HAVE A FAMILY THAT'S WORRIED SICK ABOUT ME!
ELIE, HUH?
ボウ

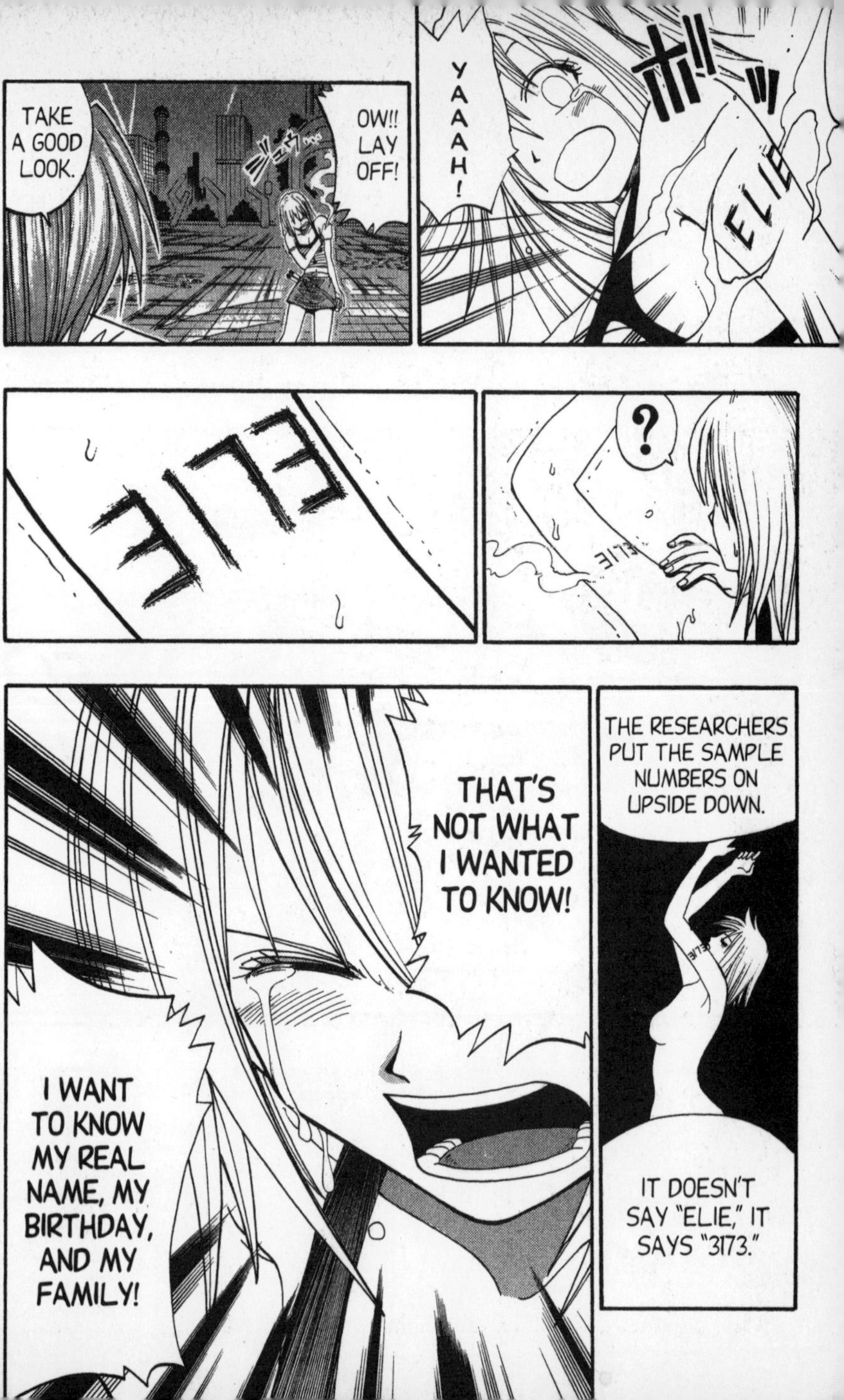
YAAAAH!
ELIE
OW!! LAY OFF!
TAKE A GOOD LOOK.
?
ELIE
THE RESEARCHERS PUT THE SAMPLE NUMBERS ON UPSIDE DOWN.
IT DOESN'T SAY "ELIE," IT SAYS "3173."
THAT'S NOT WHAT I WANTED TO KNOW!
I WANT TO KNOW MY REAL NAME, MY BIRTHDAY, AND MY FAMILY!

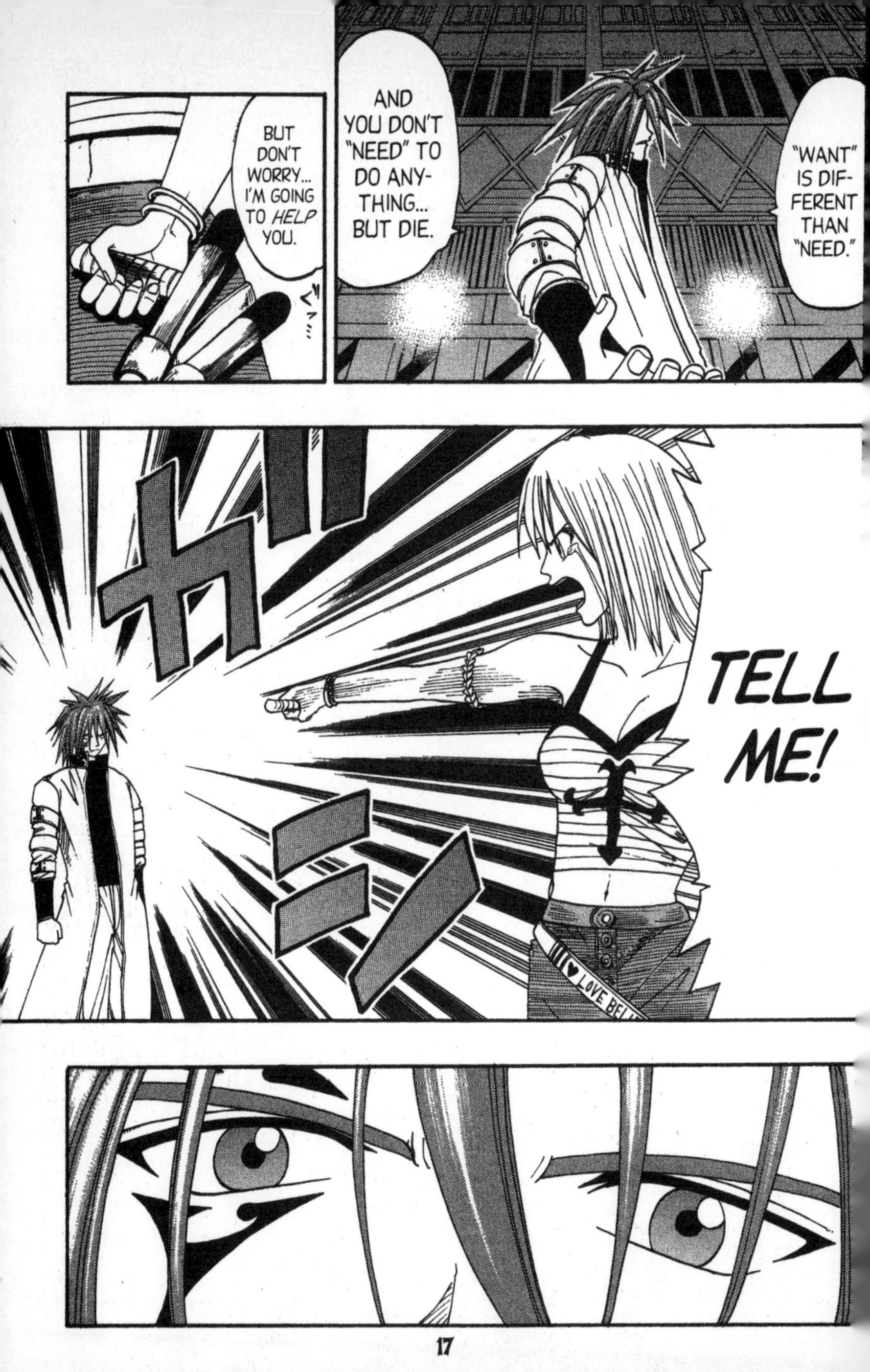
"WANT" IS DIFFERENT THAN "NEED."
AND YOU DON'T "NEED" TO DO ANYTHING... BUT DIE.
BUT DON'T WORRY... I'M GOING TO *HELP* YOU.
TELL ME!
LOVE BEL

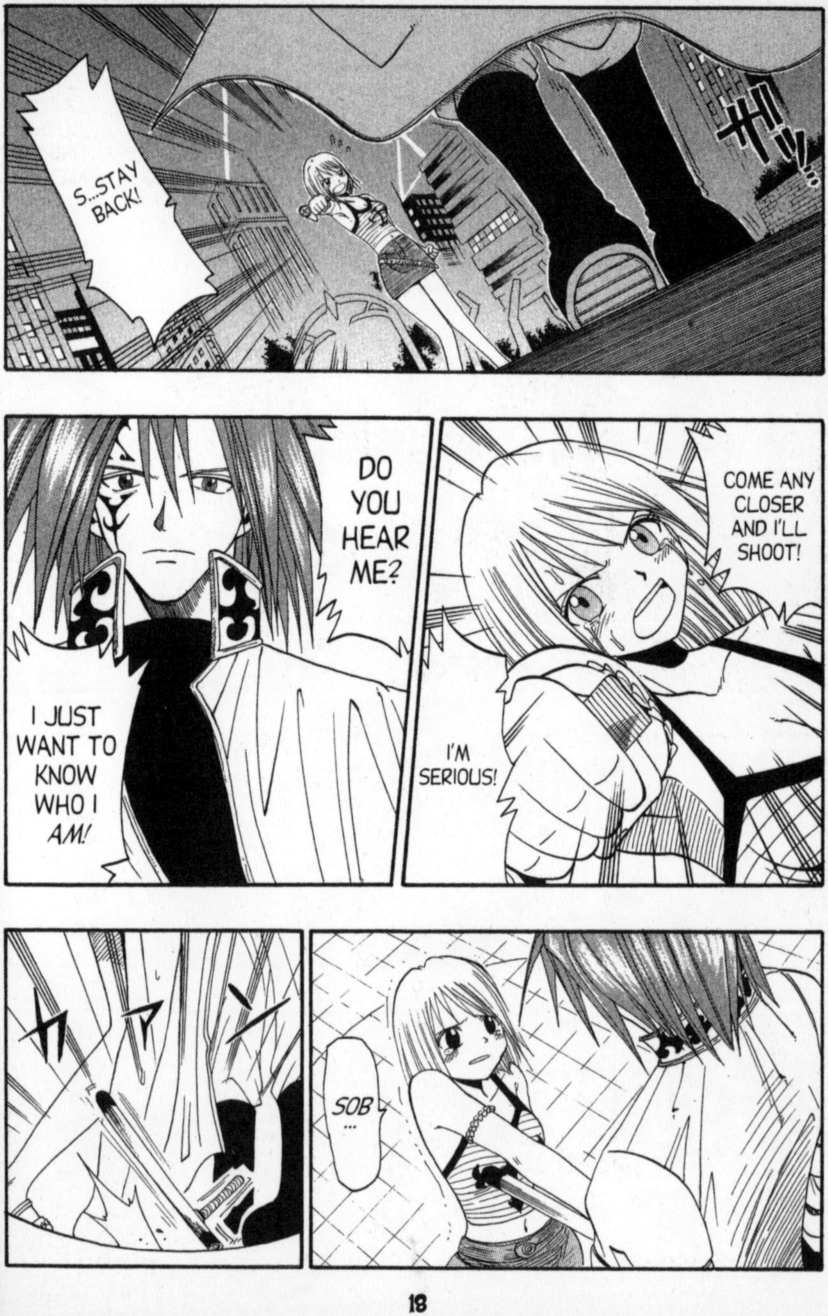
S...STAY BACK!
COME ANY CLOSER AND I'LL SHOOT!
I'M SERIOUS!
DO YOU HEAR ME?
I JUST WANT TO KNOW WHO I *AM!*
SOB...

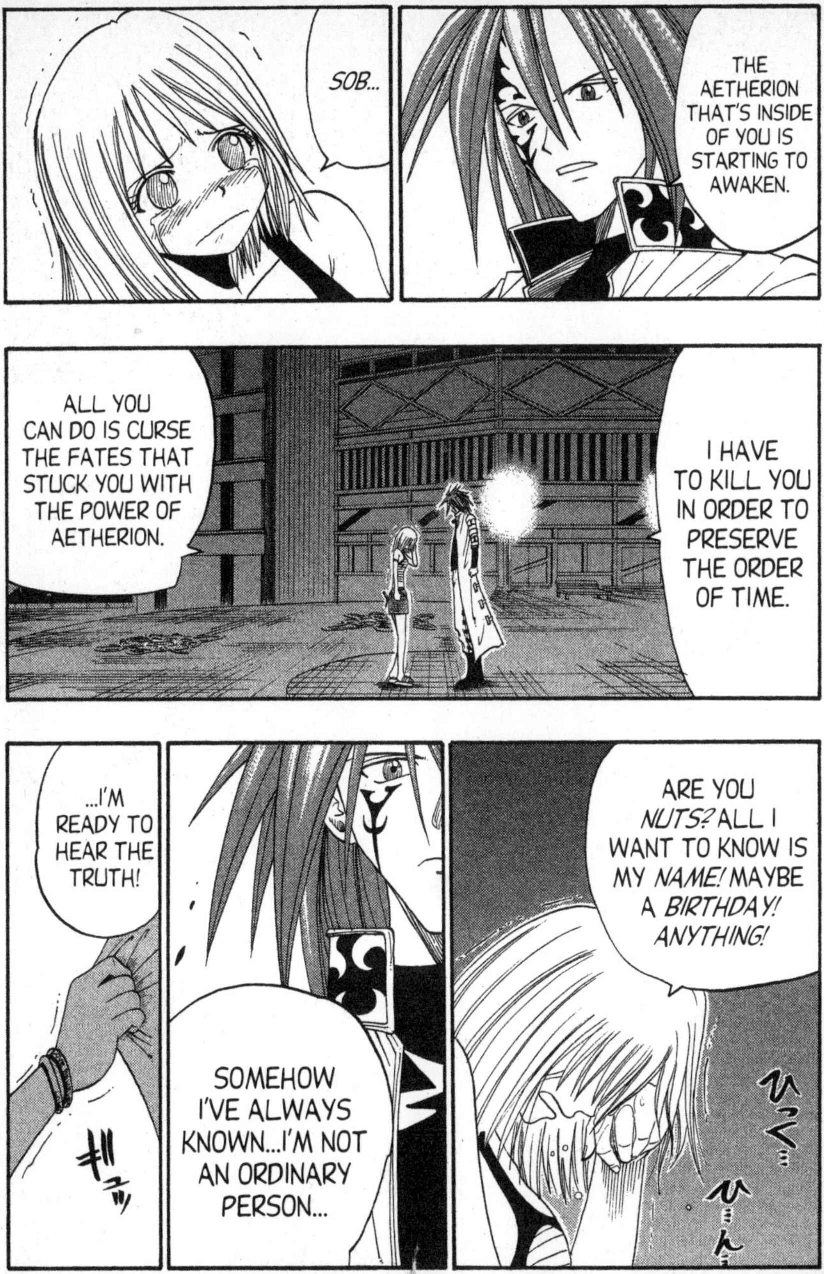
THE AETHERION THAT'S INSIDE OF YOU IS STARTING TO AWAKEN.
SOB...
I HAVE TO KILL YOU IN ORDER TO PRESERVE THE ORDER OF TIME.
ALL YOU CAN DO IS CURSE THE FATES THAT STUCK YOU WITH THE POWER OF AETHERION.
ARE YOU NUTS? ALL I WANT TO KNOW IS MY NAME! MAYBE A BIRTHDAY! ANYTHING!
ひっく…
ひ…ん…
SOMEHOW I'VE ALWAYS KNOWN...I'M NOT AN ORDINARY PERSON...
...I'M READY TO HEAR THE TRUTH!
ギュッ

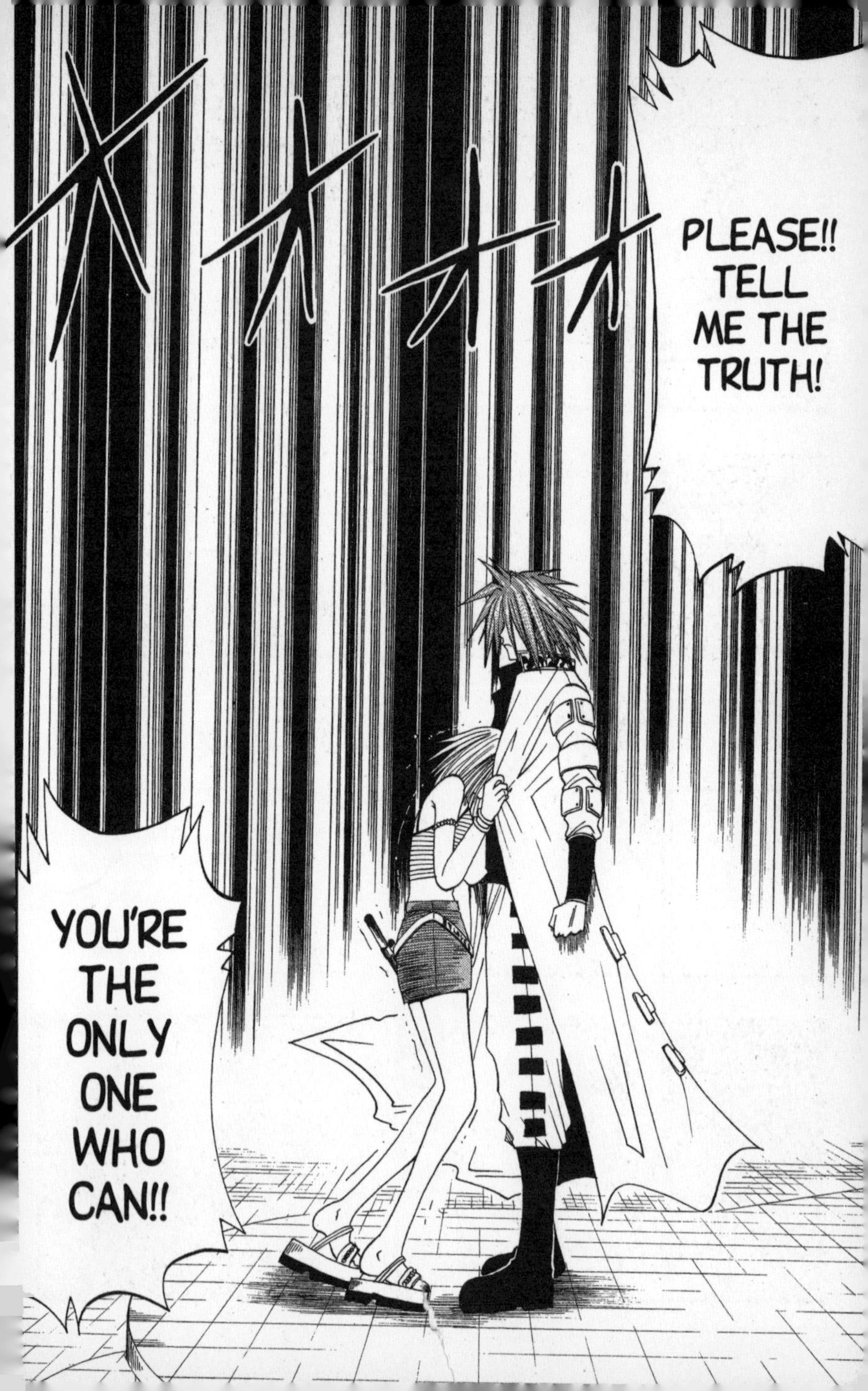
PLEASE!! TELL ME THE TRUTH!
YOU'RE THE ONLY ONE WHO CAN!!

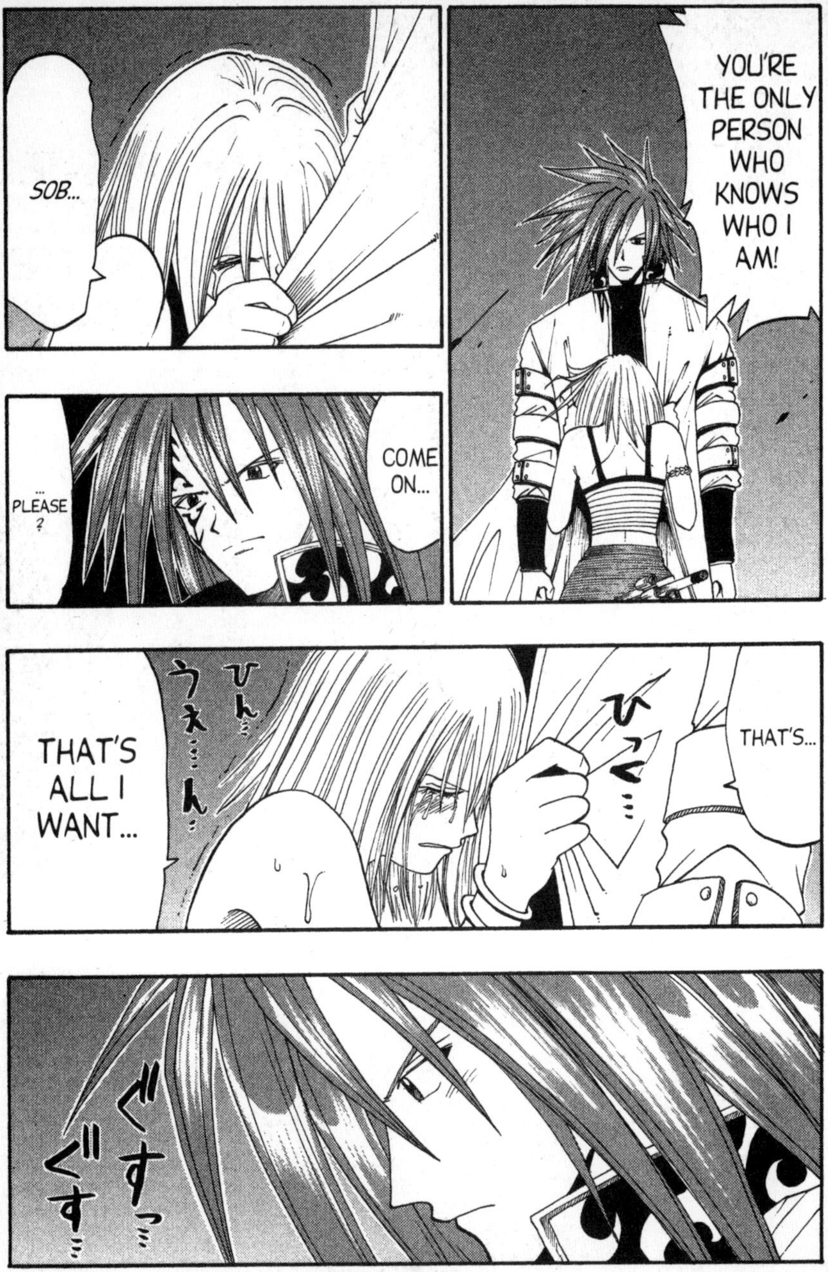
YOU'RE THE ONLY PERSON WHO KNOWS WHO I AM!
SOB...
COME ON...
... PLEASE?
THAT'S...
ひっく…
ひん…
うえ…ん…
THAT'S ALL I WANT...
ぐすっ
ぐすっ

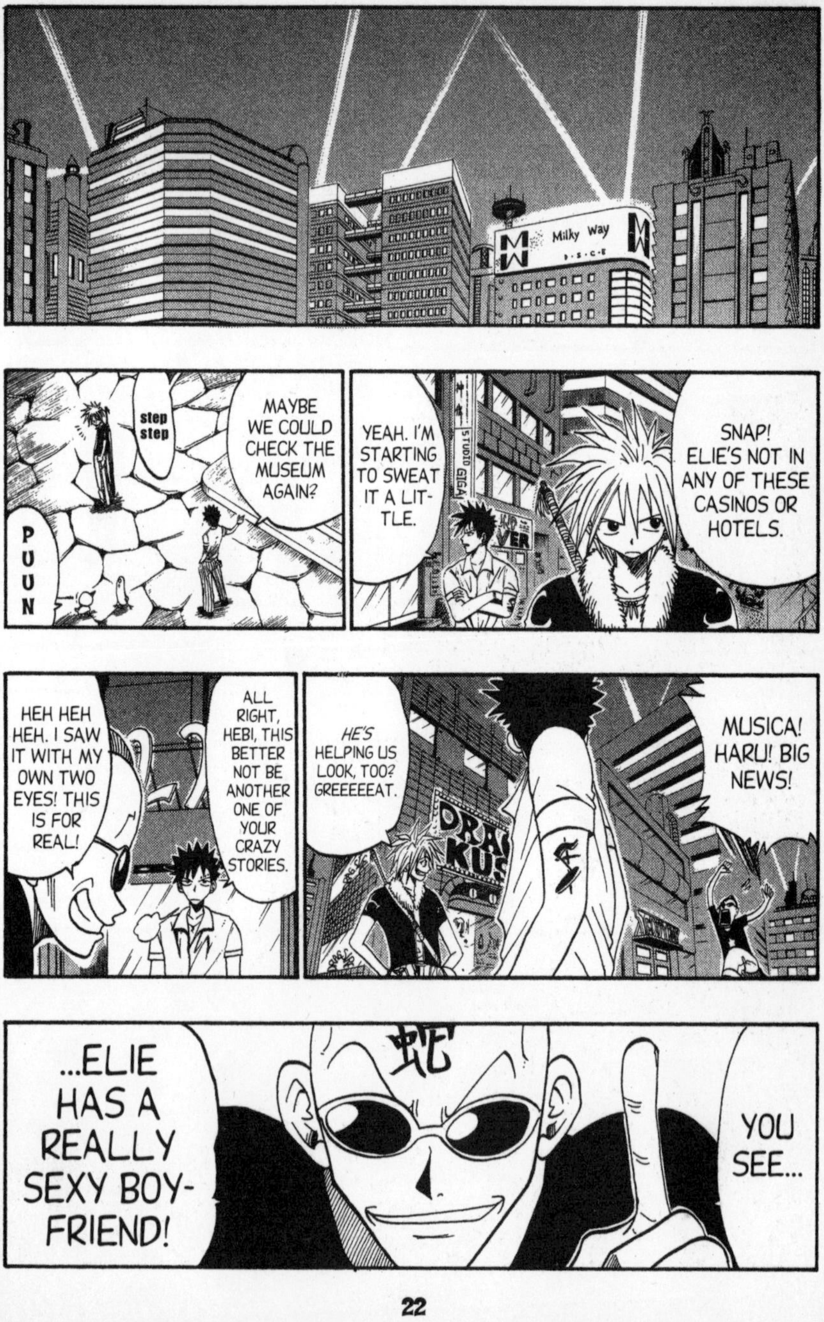
Milky Way
SNAP! ELIE'S NOT IN ANY OF THESE CASINOS OR HOTELS.
YEAH. I'M STARTING TO SWEAT IT A LITTLE.
MAYBE WE COULD CHECK THE MUSEUM AGAIN?
step step
PUUN
MUSICA! HARU! BIG NEWS!
HE'S HELPING US LOOK, TOO? GREEEEEAT.
ALL RIGHT, HEBI, THIS BETTER NOT BE ANOTHER ONE OF YOUR CRAZY STORIES.
HEH HEH HEH. I SAW IT WITH MY OWN TWO EYES! THIS IS FOR REAL!
YOU SEE...
蛇
...ELIE HAS A REALLY SEXY BOYFRIEND!

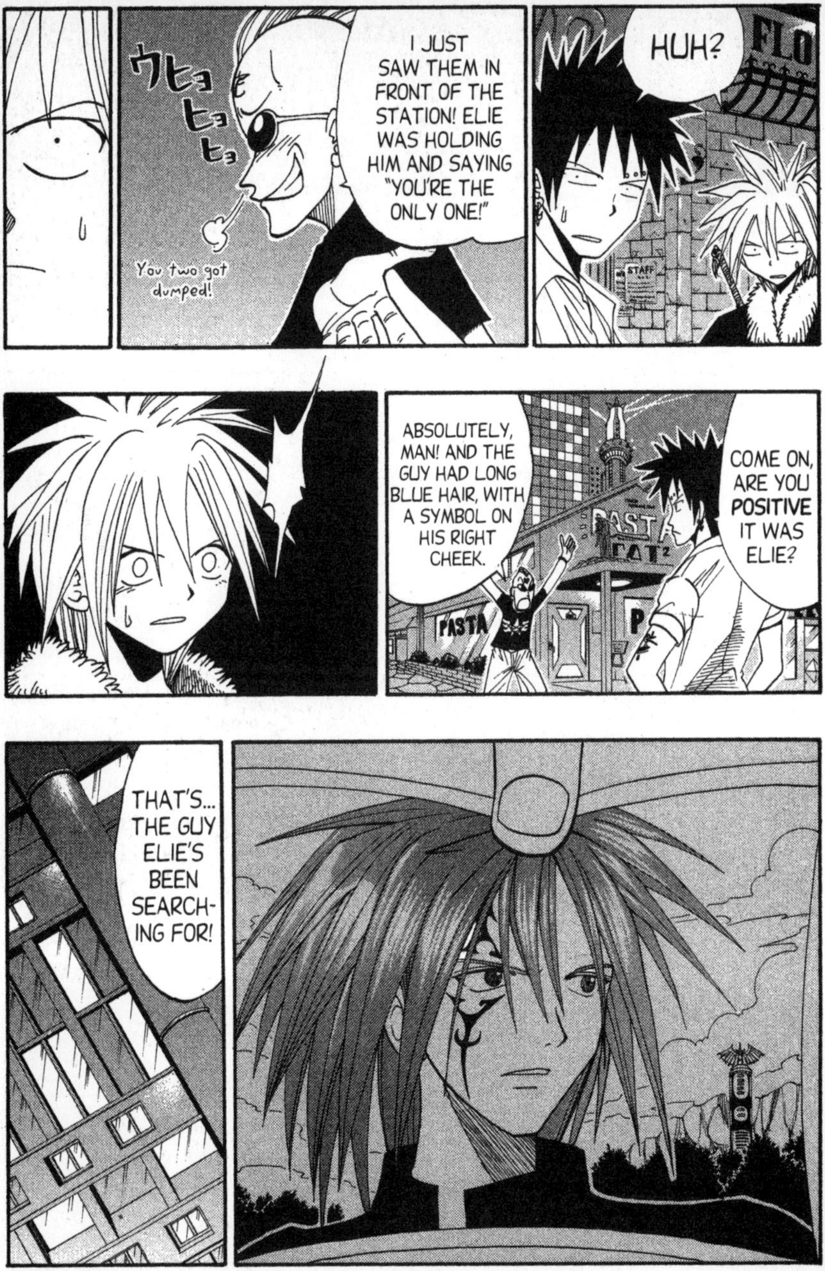
HUH?
FLO
I JUST SAW THEM IN FRONT OF THE STATION! ELIE WAS HOLDING HIM AND SAYING "YOU'RE THE ONLY ONE!"
ウヒョヒョヒョ
You two got dumped!
STAFF
COME ON, ARE YOU POSITIVE IT WAS ELIE?
ABSOLUTELY, MAN! AND THE GUY HAD LONG BLUE HAIR, WITH A SYMBOL ON HIS RIGHT CHEEK.
PASTA
PASTA
THAT'S... THE GUY ELIE'S BEEN SEARCHING FOR!

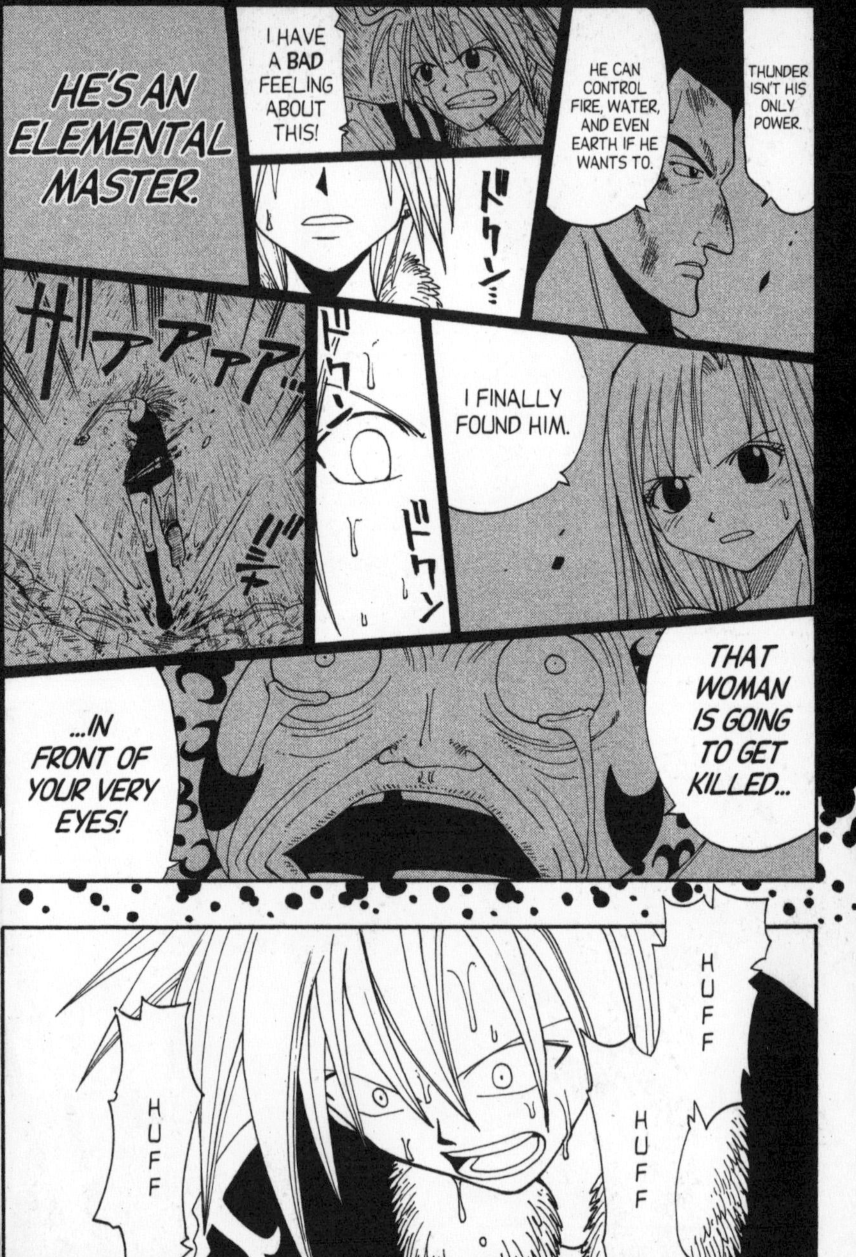
THUNDER ISN'T HIS ONLY POWER.
HE CAN CONTROL FIRE, WATER, AND EVEN EARTH IF HE WANTS TO.
I HAVE A BAD FEELING ABOUT THIS!
ドクン…
HE'S AN ELEMENTAL MASTER.
I FINALLY FOUND HIM.
ドクン
ドクン
ドクン
THAT WOMAN IS GOING TO GET KILLED...
...IN FRONT OF YOUR VERY EYES!
HUFF
HUFF
HUFF

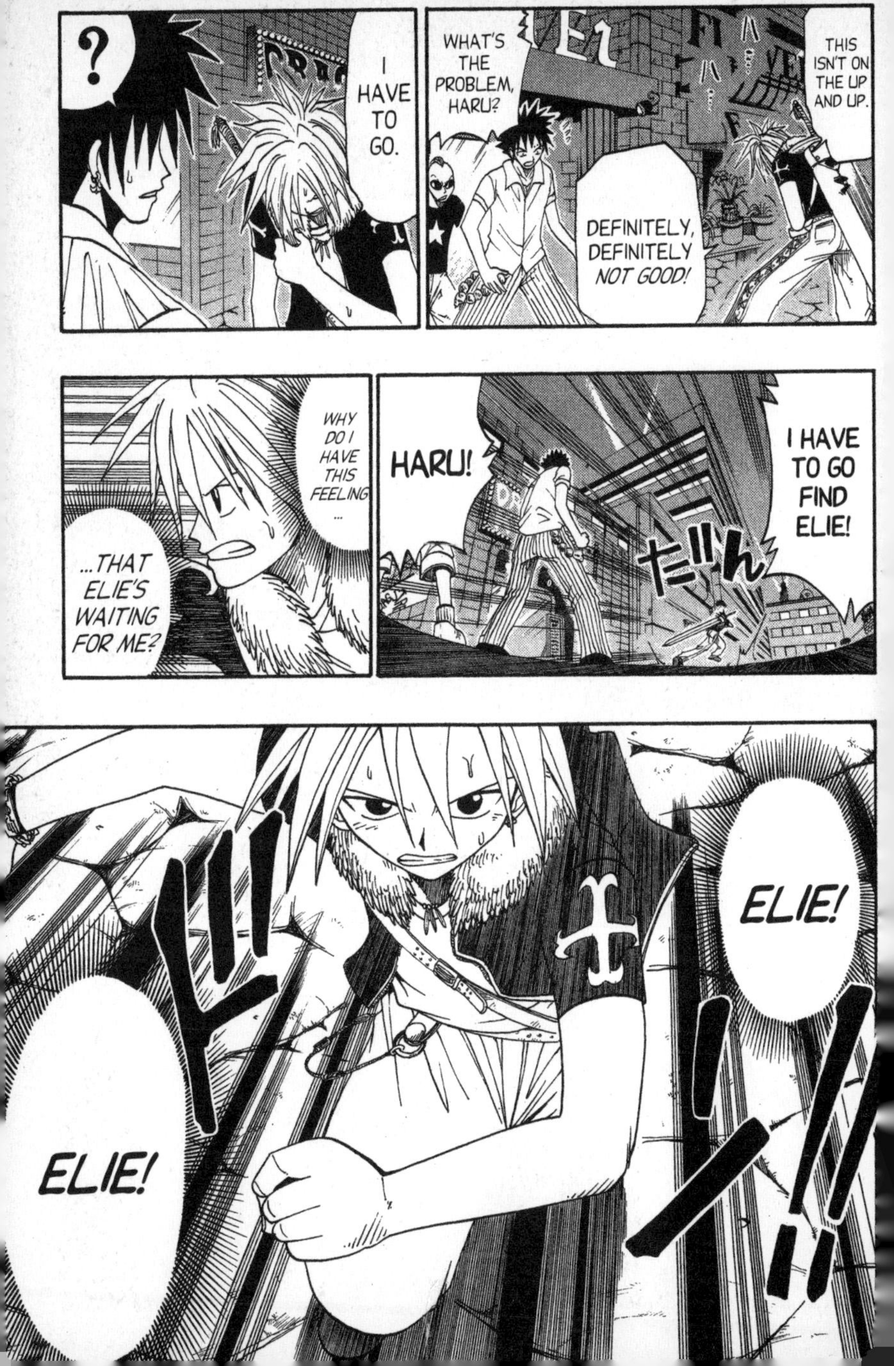
THIS ISN'T ON THE UP AND UP.
WHAT'S THE PROBLEM, HARU?
DEFINITELY, DEFINITELY *NOT GOOD!*
I HAVE TO GO.
?
I HAVE TO GO FIND ELIE!
HARU!
WHY DO I HAVE THIS FEELING ...
...THAT ELIE'S WAITING FOR ME?
ELIE!
ELIE!

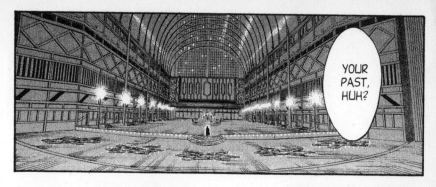

YOUR PAST, HUH?

NO!

AREN'T YOU A LITTLE MORE CONCERNED ABOUT YOUR *FUTURE?* THE ONE *I'M* ABOUT TO *END?*

!

NO!

WHO IN THE WORLD *AM I?*

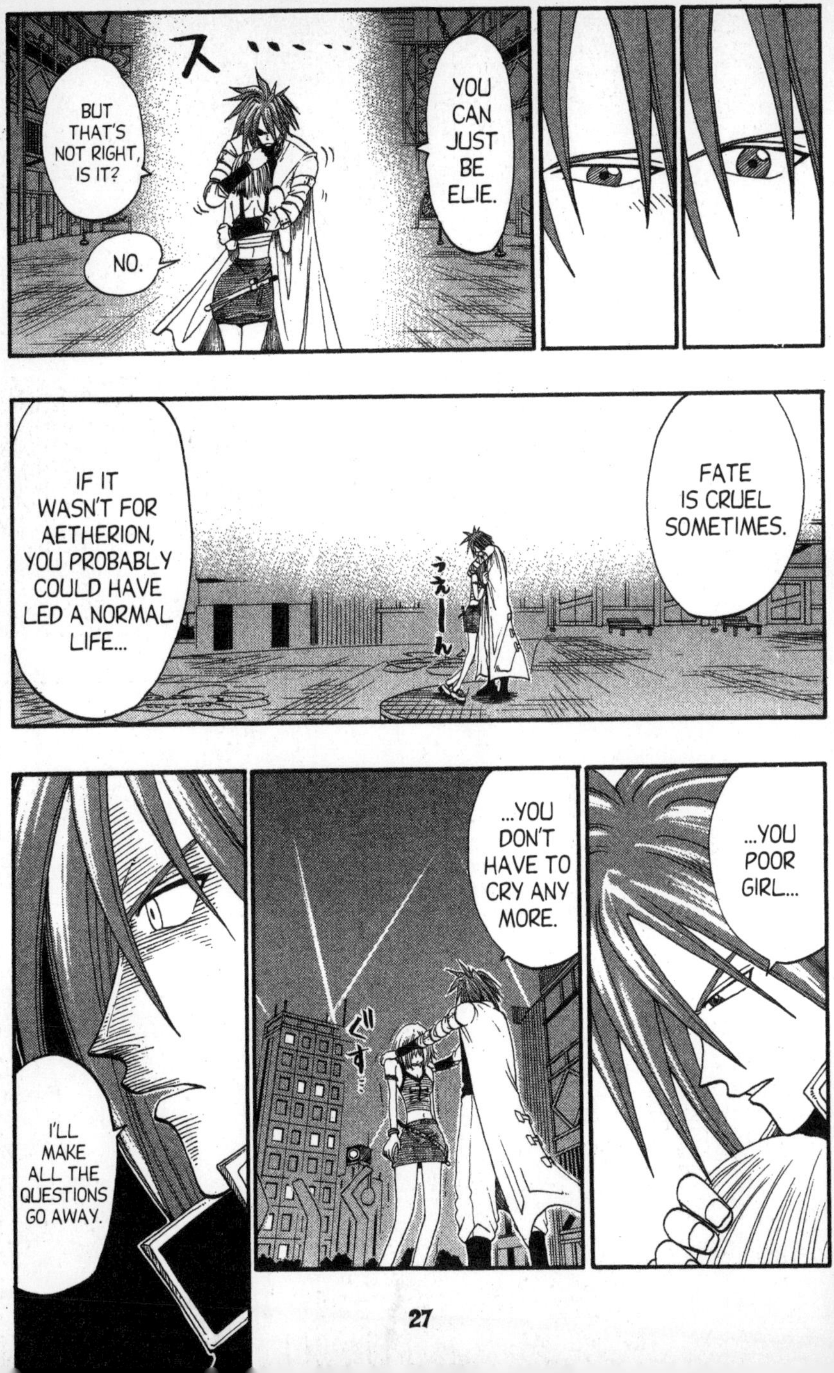
YOU CAN JUST BE ELIE.
ス……
BUT THAT'S NOT RIGHT, IS IT?
NO.
FATE IS CRUEL SOMETIMES.
うえーん
IF IT WASN'T FOR AETHERION, YOU PROBABLY COULD HAVE LED A NORMAL LIFE...
...YOU POOR GIRL...
...YOU DON'T HAVE TO CRY ANY MORE.
ぐす…
I'LL MAKE ALL THE QUESTIONS GO AWAY.

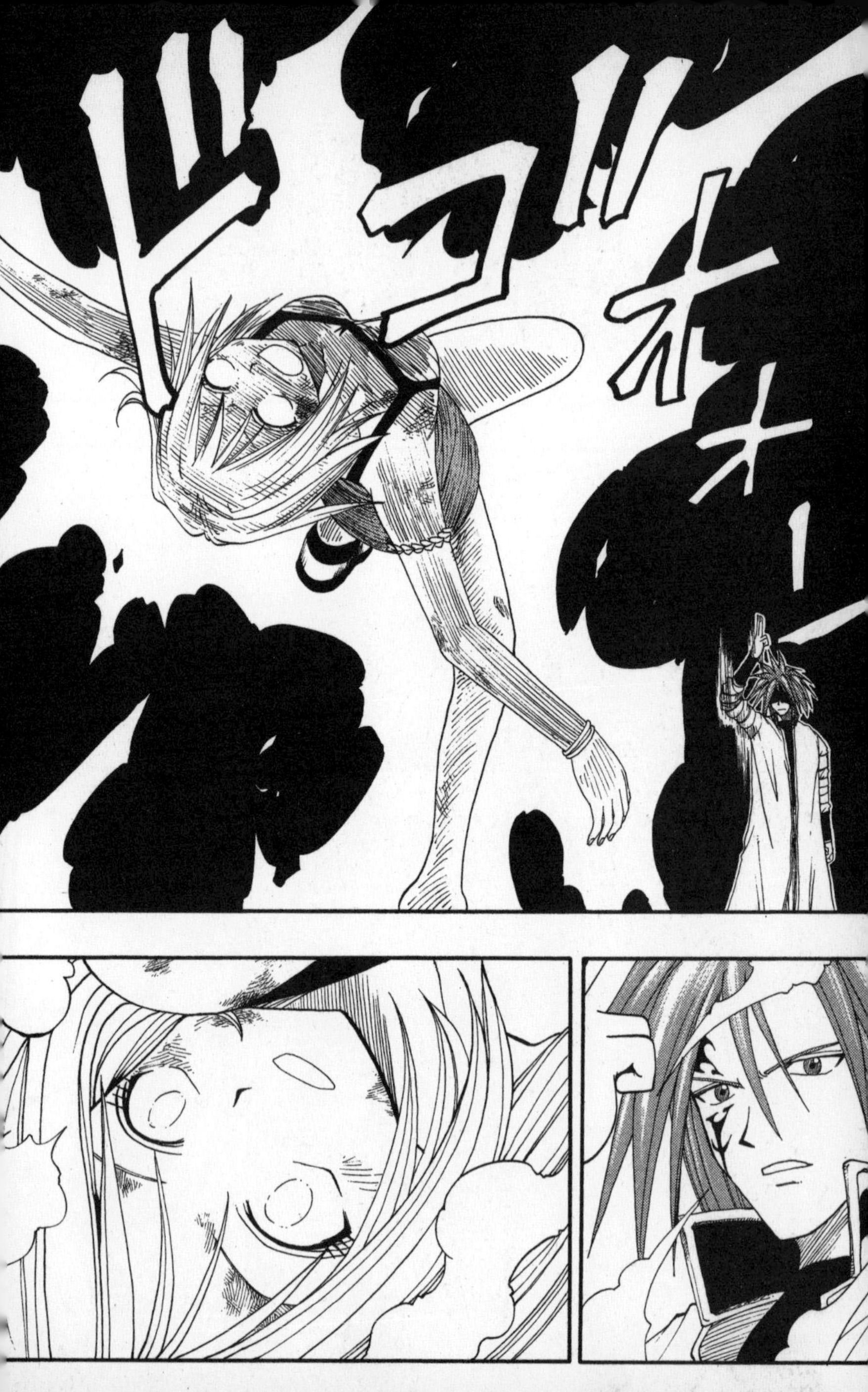

RAVE MASTER

RAVE: 41 ✠ THE SUN IN MY HEART

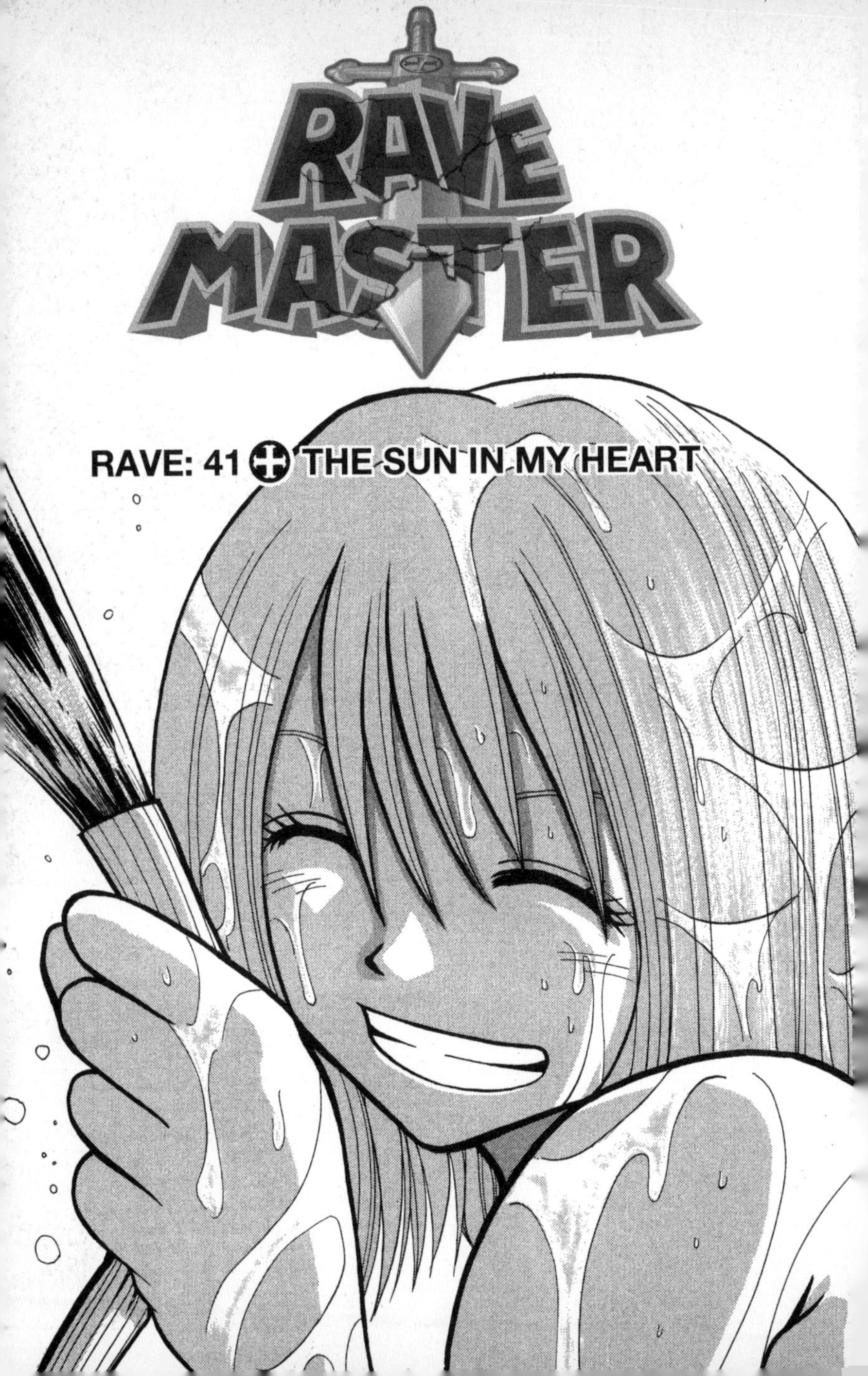

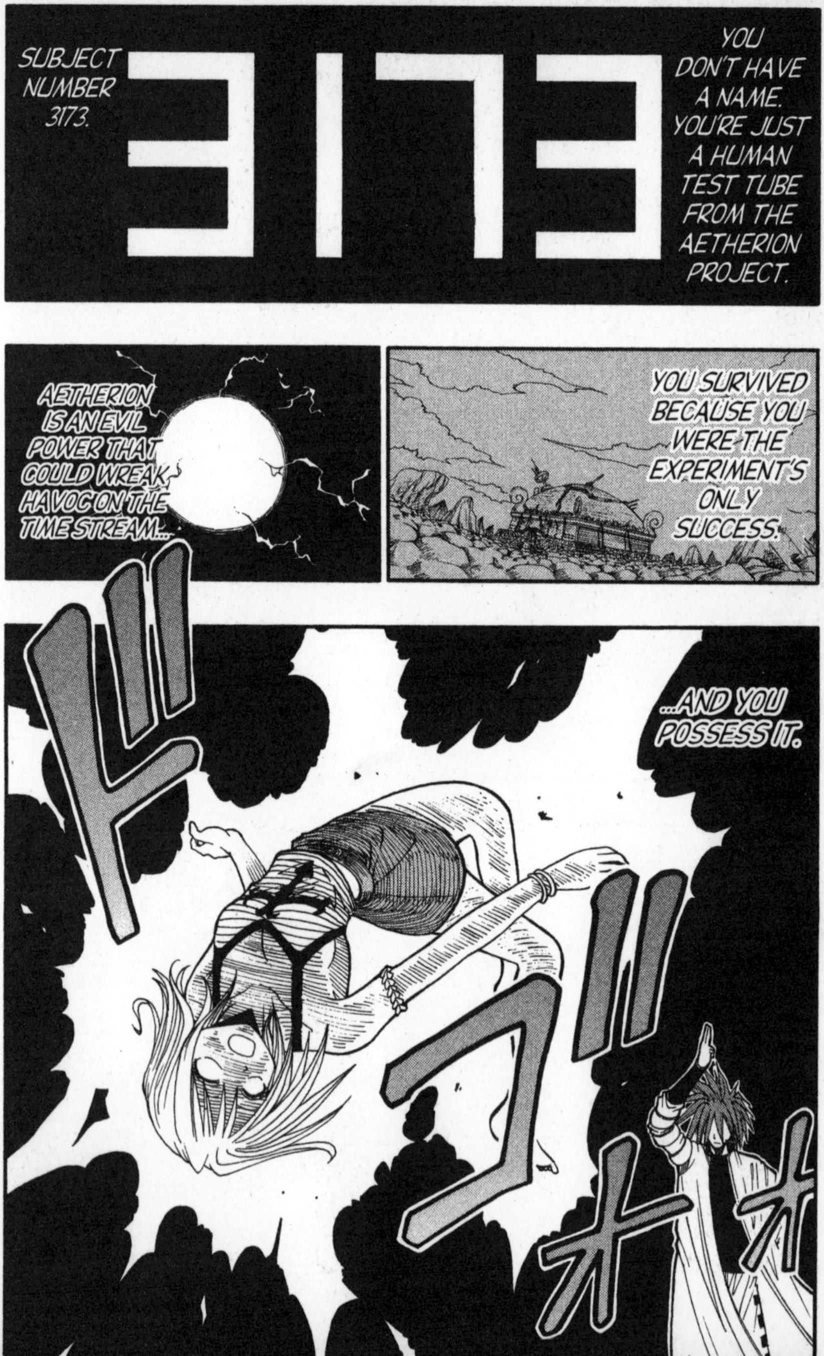
YOU DON'T HAVE A NAME. YOU'RE JUST A HUMAN TEST TUBE FROM THE AETHERION PROJECT.
3173
SUBJECT NUMBER 3173.
YOU SURVIVED BECAUSE YOU WERE THE EXPERIMENT'S ONLY SUCCESS.
AETHERION IS AN EVIL POWER THAT COULD WREAK HAVOC ON THE TIME STREAM...
...AND YOU POSSESS IT.
ドゴオオ

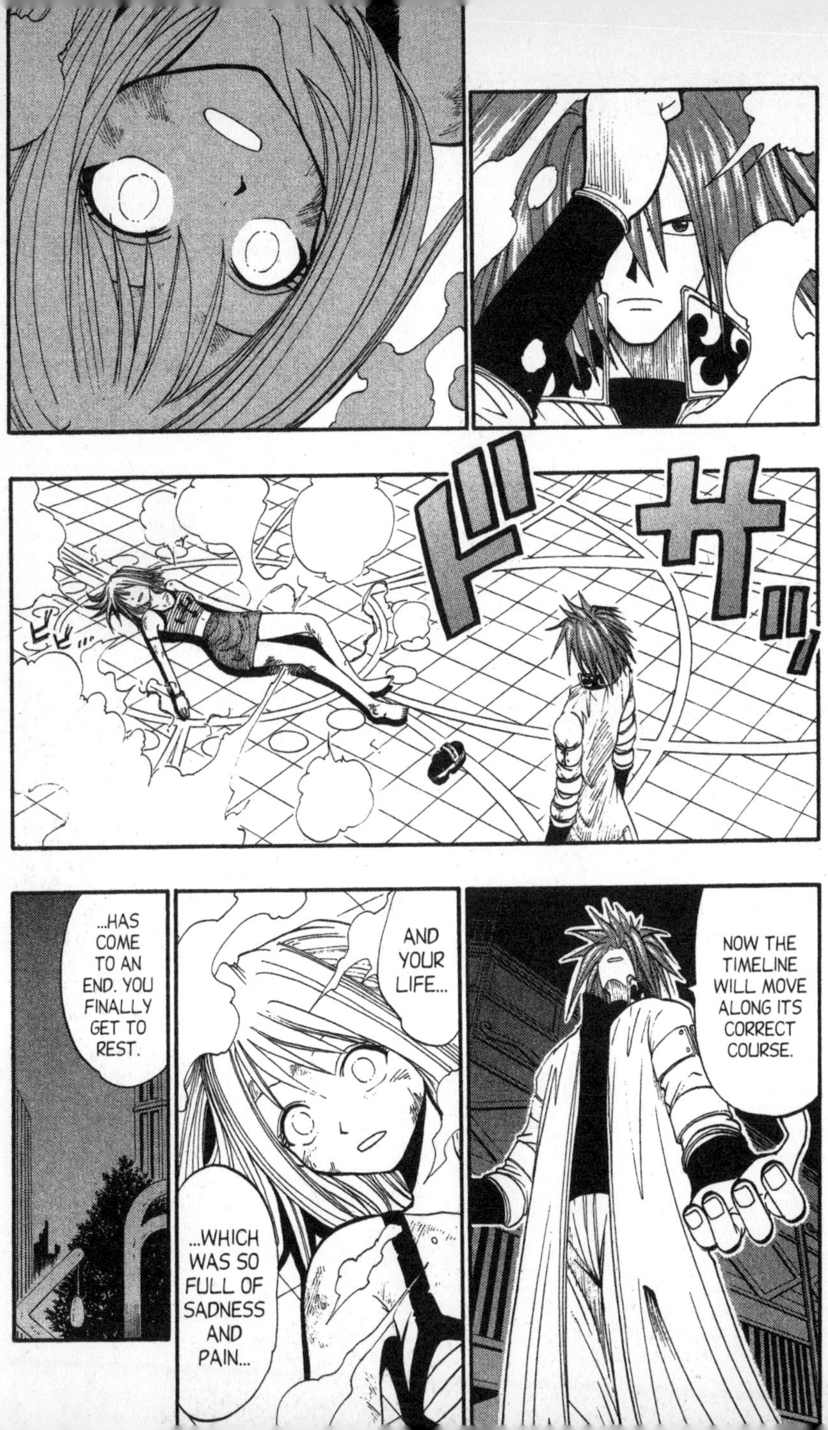
ドサッ
NOW THE TIMELINE WILL MOVE ALONG ITS CORRECT COURSE.
AND YOUR LIFE...
...WHICH WAS SO FULL OF SADNESS AND PAIN...
...HAS COME TO AN END. YOU FINALLY GET TO REST.

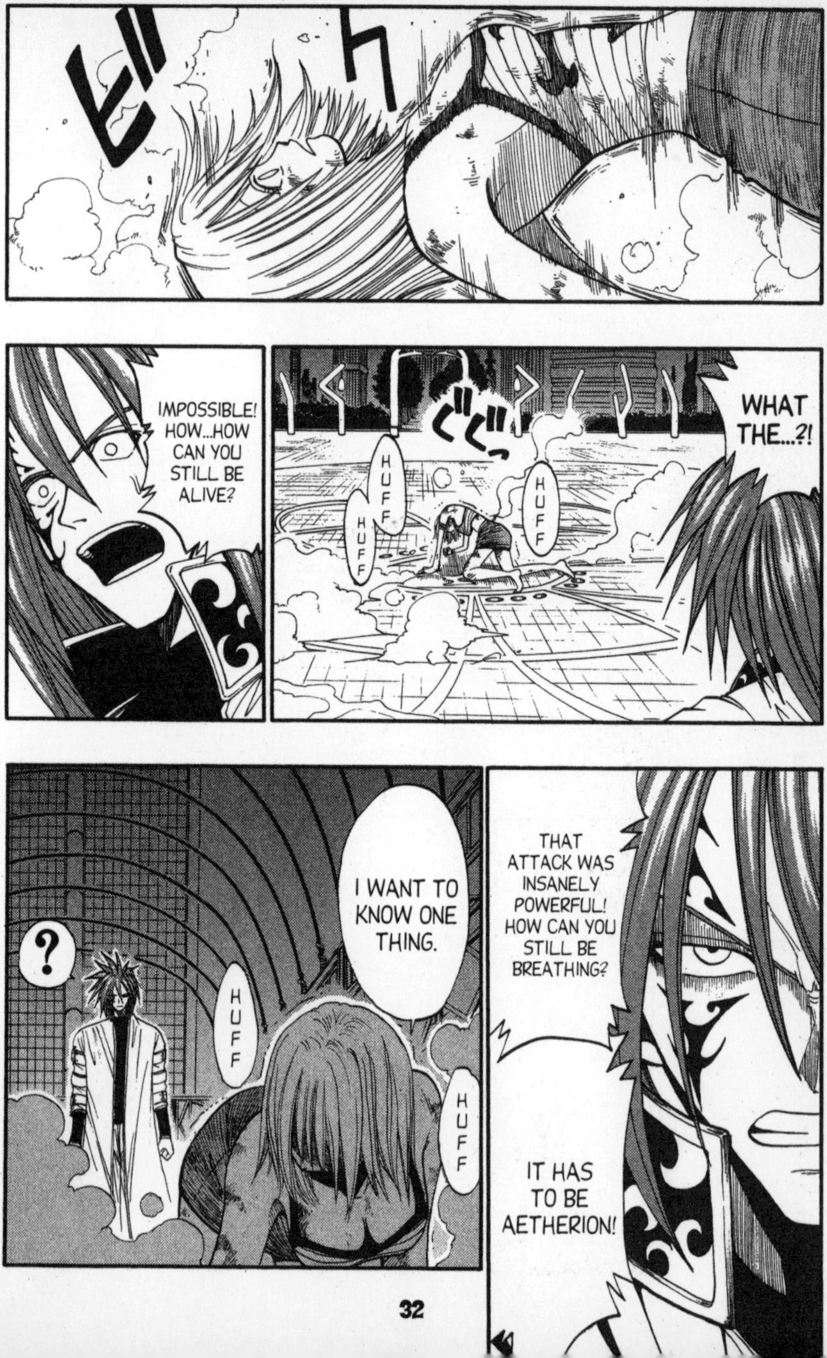
WHAT THE...?!
HUFF
HUFF
HUFF
IMPOSSIBLE! HOW...HOW CAN YOU STILL BE ALIVE?
THAT ATTACK WAS INSANELY POWERFUL! HOW CAN YOU STILL BE BREATHING?
IT HAS TO BE AETHERION!
I WANT TO KNOW ONE THING.
HUFF
HUFF
?

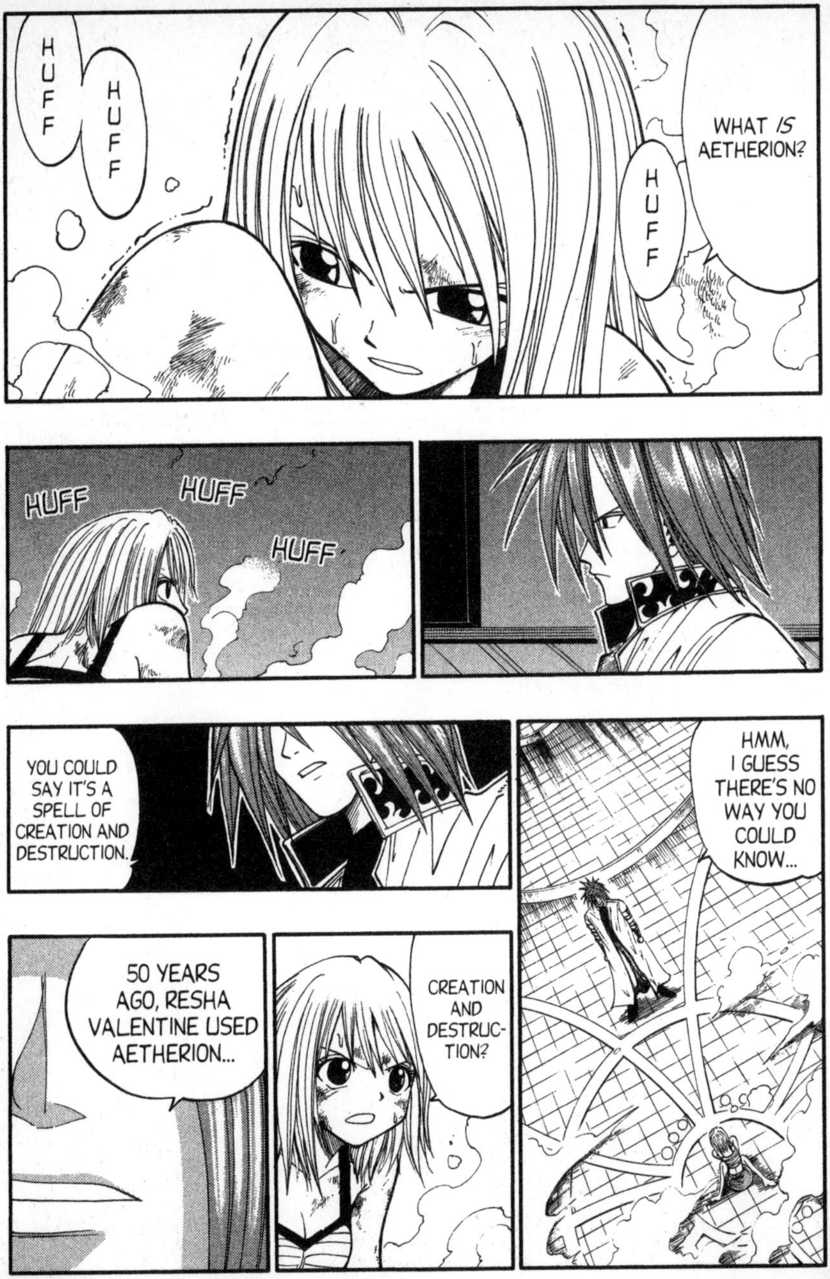

WHAT *IS* AETHERION?
HUFF
HUFF
HUFF
HUFF
HUFF
HUFF
HMM, I GUESS THERE'S NO WAY YOU COULD KNOW...
YOU COULD SAY IT'S A SPELL OF CREATION AND DESTRUCTION.
CREATION AND DESTRUC-TION?
50 YEARS AGO, RESHA VALENTINE USED AETHERION...

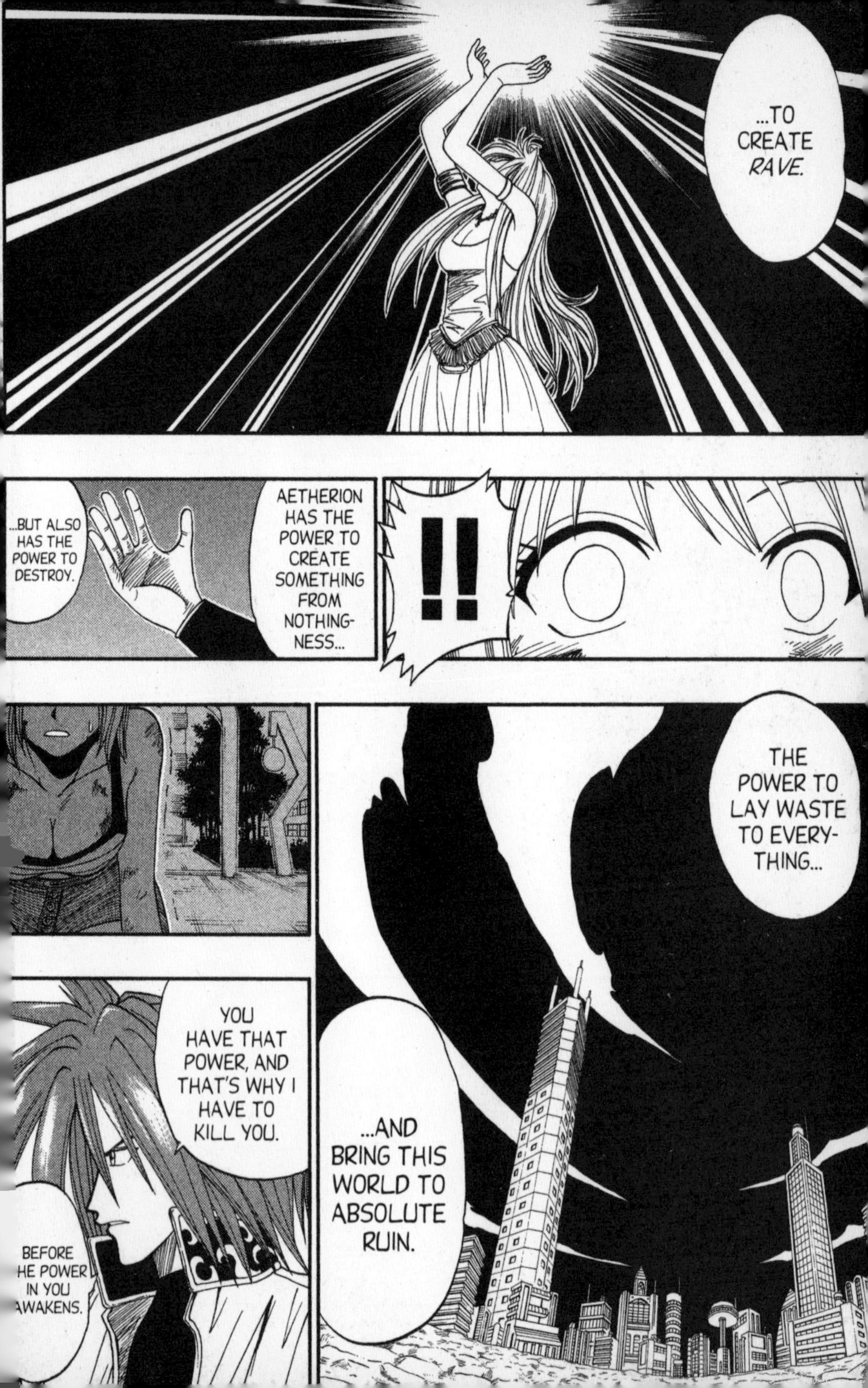
...TO CREATE *RAVE.*
!!
AETHERION HAS THE POWER TO CREATE SOMETHING FROM NOTHING-NESS...
...BUT ALSO HAS THE POWER TO DESTROY.
THE POWER TO LAY WASTE TO EVERY-THING...
...AND BRING THIS WORLD TO ABSOLUTE RUIN.
YOU HAVE THAT POWER, AND THAT'S WHY I HAVE TO KILL YOU.
BEFORE HE POWER IN YOU AWAKENS.

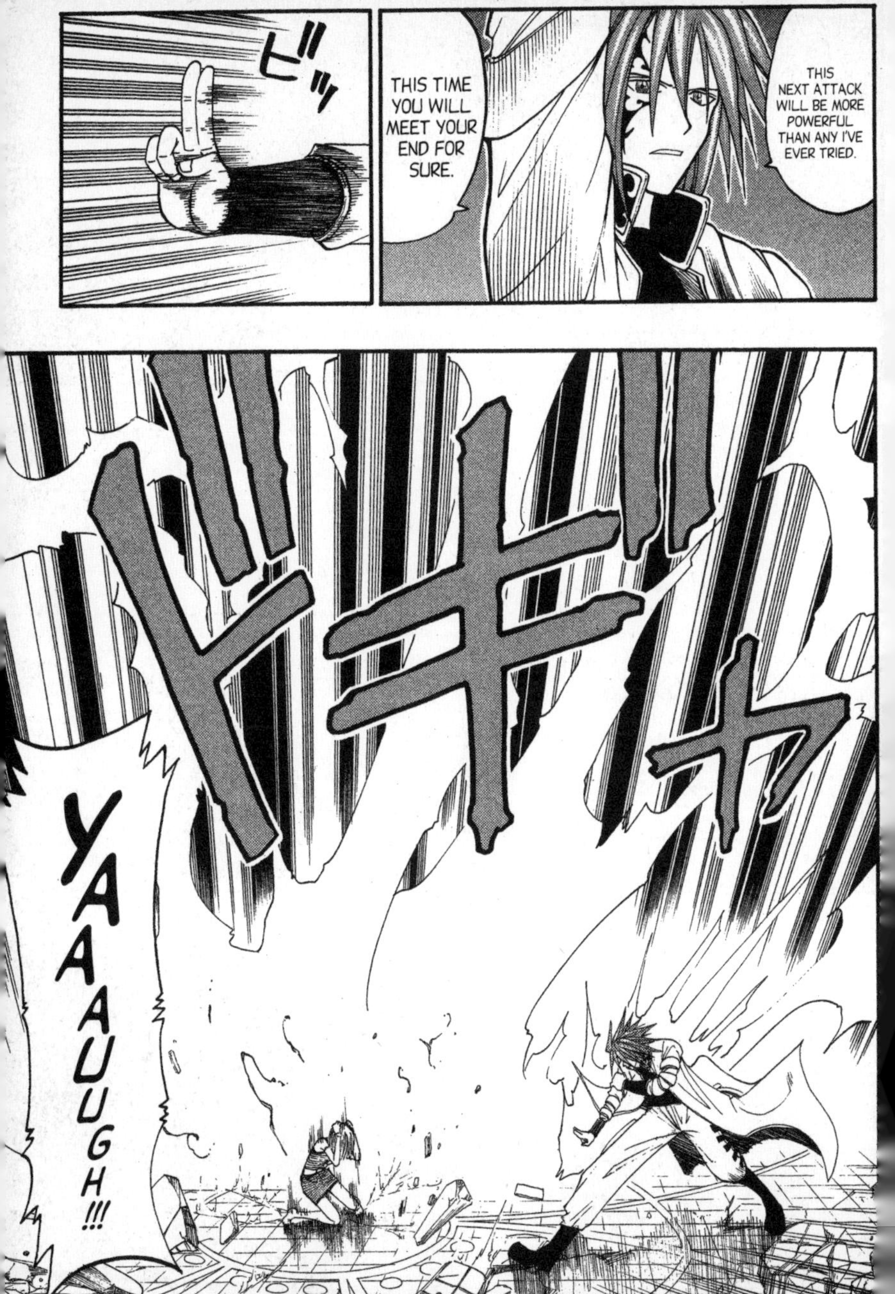
THIS NEXT ATTACK WILL BE MORE POWERFUL THAN ANY I'VE EVER TRIED.
THIS TIME YOU WILL MEET YOUR END FOR SURE.
ビッ
ドギャ
YAAAAUUGH!!!

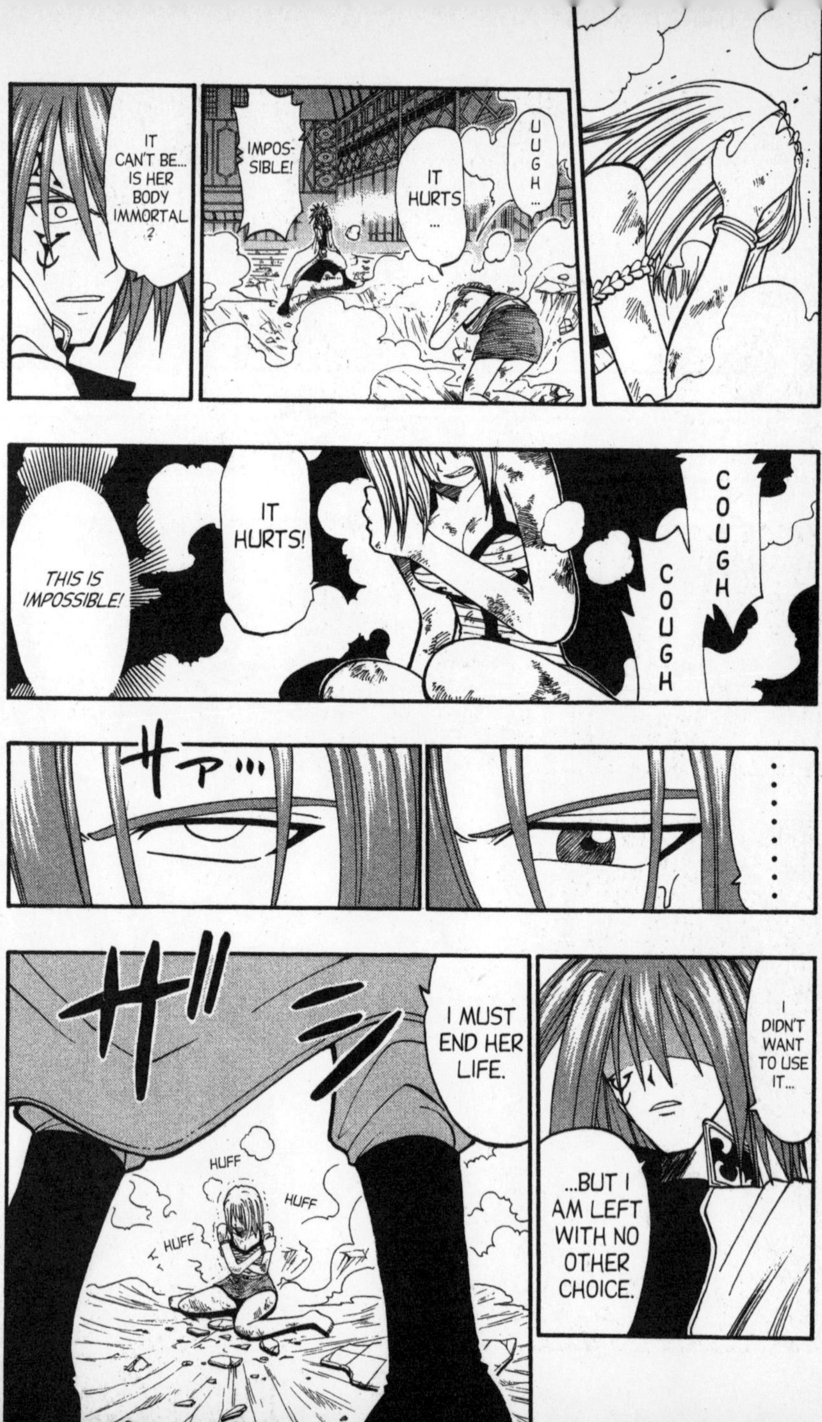
UUGH...
IT HURTS...
IMPOSSIBLE!
IT CAN'T BE... IS HER BODY IMMORTAL?
COUGH
COUGH
IT HURTS!
THIS IS IMPOSSIBLE!
......
サァ
I DIDN'T WANT TO USE IT...
...BUT I AM LEFT WITH NO OTHER CHOICE.
I MUST END HER LIFE.
HUFF
HUFF
HUFF

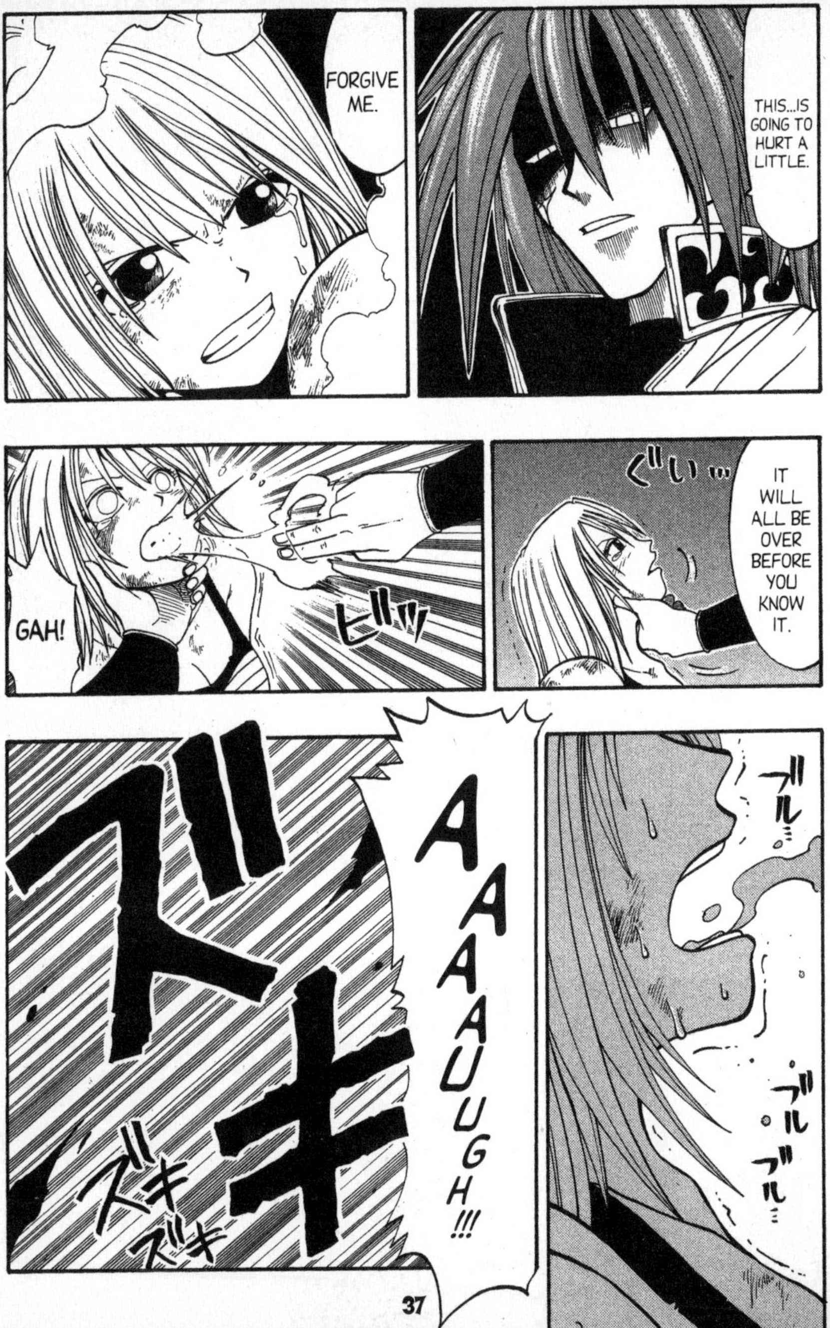
THIS...IS GOING TO HURT A LITTLE.
FORGIVE ME.
ぐいっ
IT WILL ALL BE OVER BEFORE YOU KNOW IT.
ビリッ
GAH!
ブル
ブルブル
AAAAUGH!!!
ズキ
ズキズキ

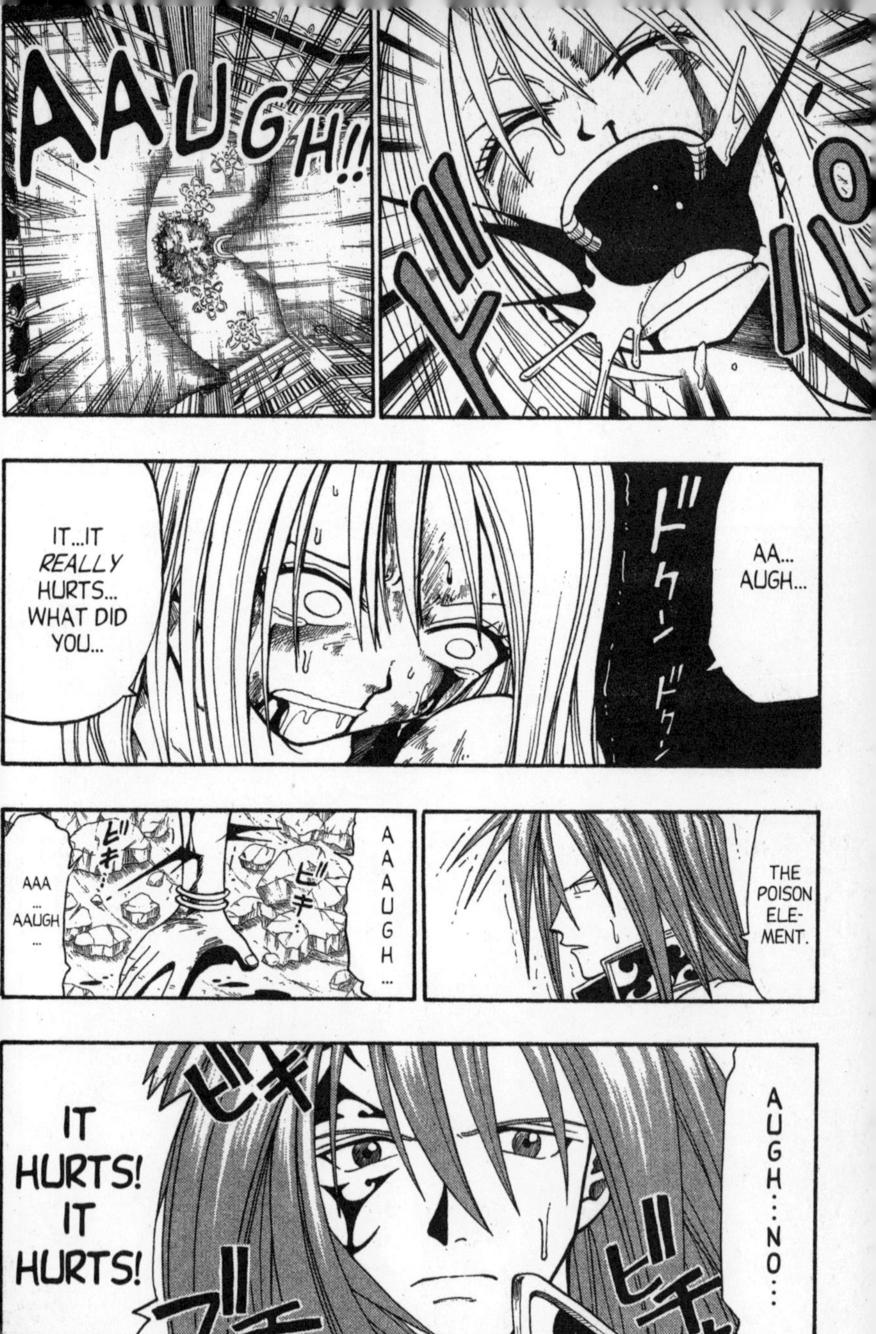
AAUGH!!
AA... AUGH...
IT...IT *REALLY* HURTS... WHAT DID YOU...
THE POISON ELEMENT.
AAAAUGH...
AAA... AAUGH...
AUGH...NO...
IT HURTS! IT HURTS!

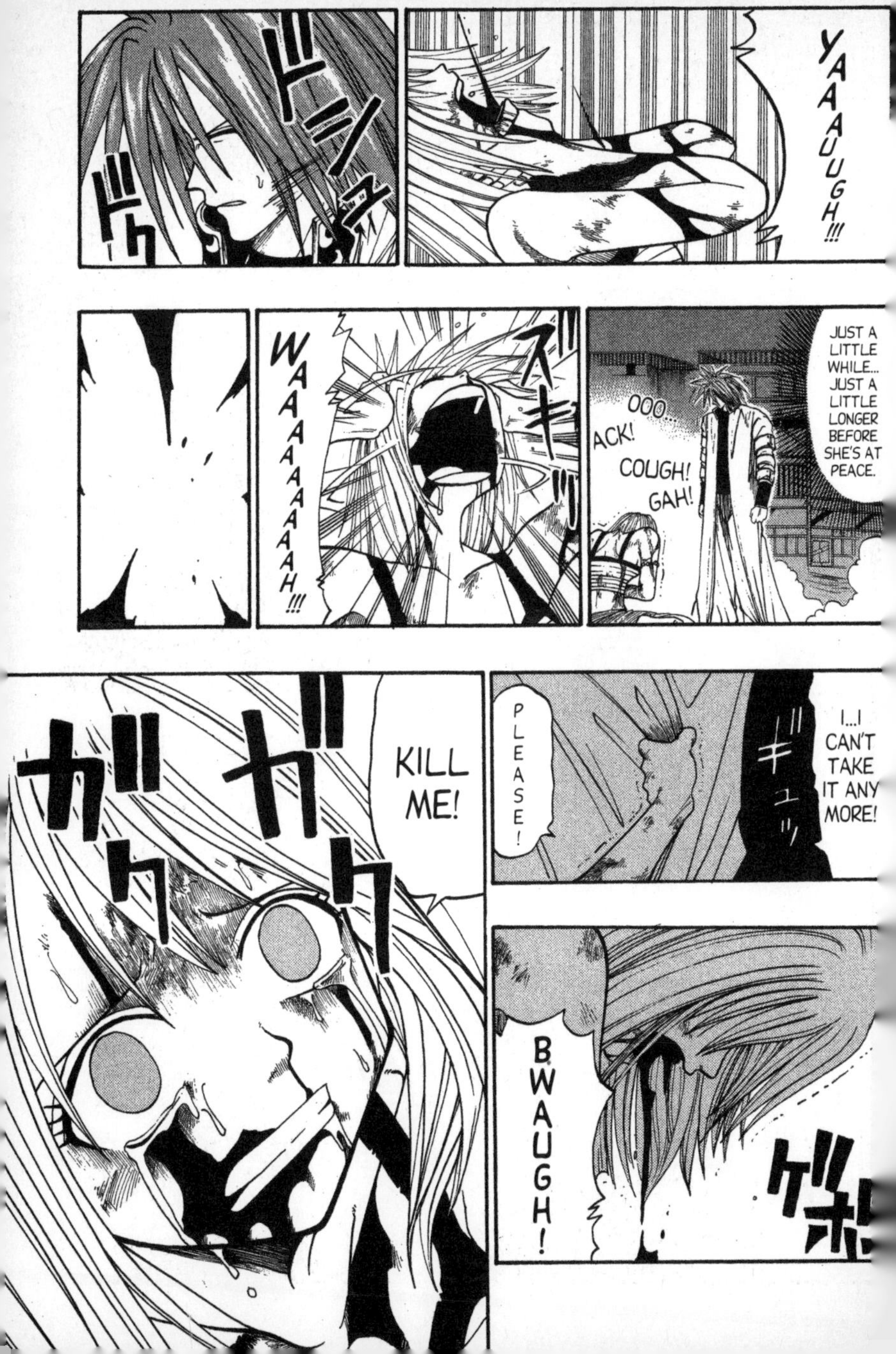
YAAAAUGH!!!
JUST A LITTLE WHILE... JUST A LITTLE LONGER BEFORE SHE'S AT PEACE.
OOO... ACK! COUGH! GAH!
WAAAAAAAAAAH!!!
I...I CAN'T TAKE IT ANY MORE!
PLEASE!
BWAUGH!
KILL ME!

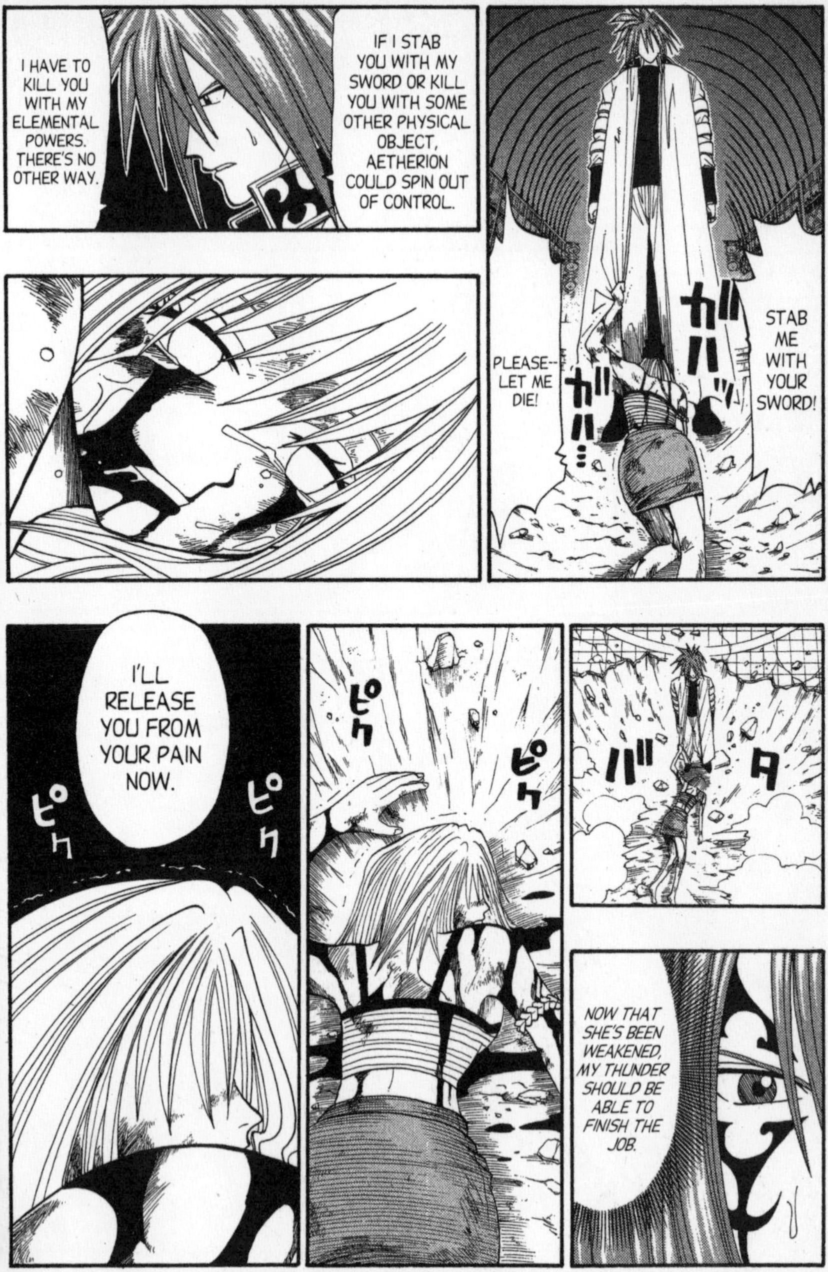
STAB ME WITH YOUR SWORD!
PLEASE-- LET ME DIE!
IF I STAB YOU WITH MY SWORD OR KILL YOU WITH SOME OTHER PHYSICAL OBJECT, AETHERION COULD SPIN OUT OF CONTROL.
I HAVE TO KILL YOU WITH MY ELEMENTAL POWERS. THERE'S NO OTHER WAY.
バタ
NOW THAT SHE'S BEEN WEAKENED, MY THUNDER SHOULD BE ABLE TO FINISH THE JOB.
ピク
ピク
ピク
I'LL RELEASE YOU FROM YOUR PAIN NOW.
ピク

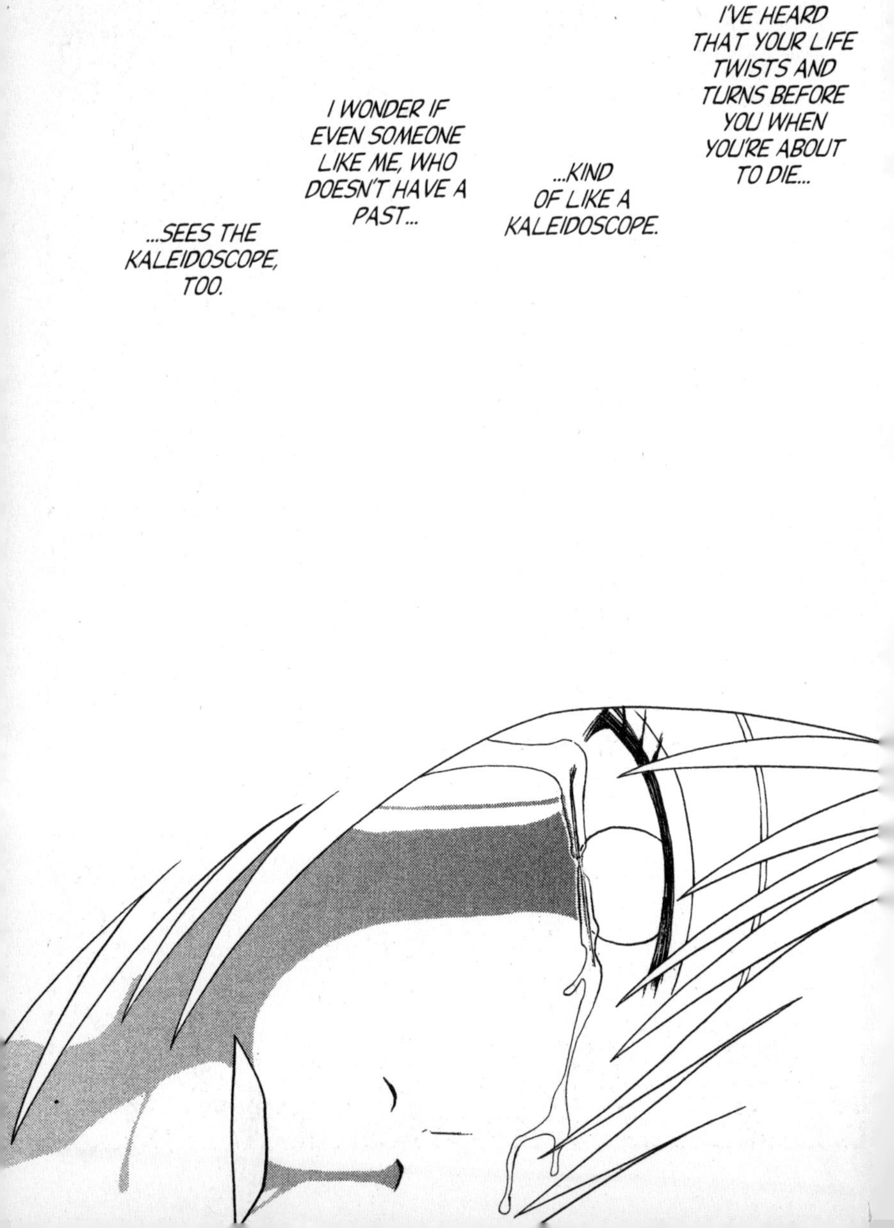
I'VE HEARD THAT YOUR LIFE TWISTS AND TURNS BEFORE YOU WHEN YOU'RE ABOUT TO DIE...
...KIND OF LIKE A KALEIDOSCOPE.
I WONDER IF EVEN SOMEONE LIKE ME, WHO DOESN'T HAVE A PAST...
...SEES THE KALEIDOSCOPE, TOO.

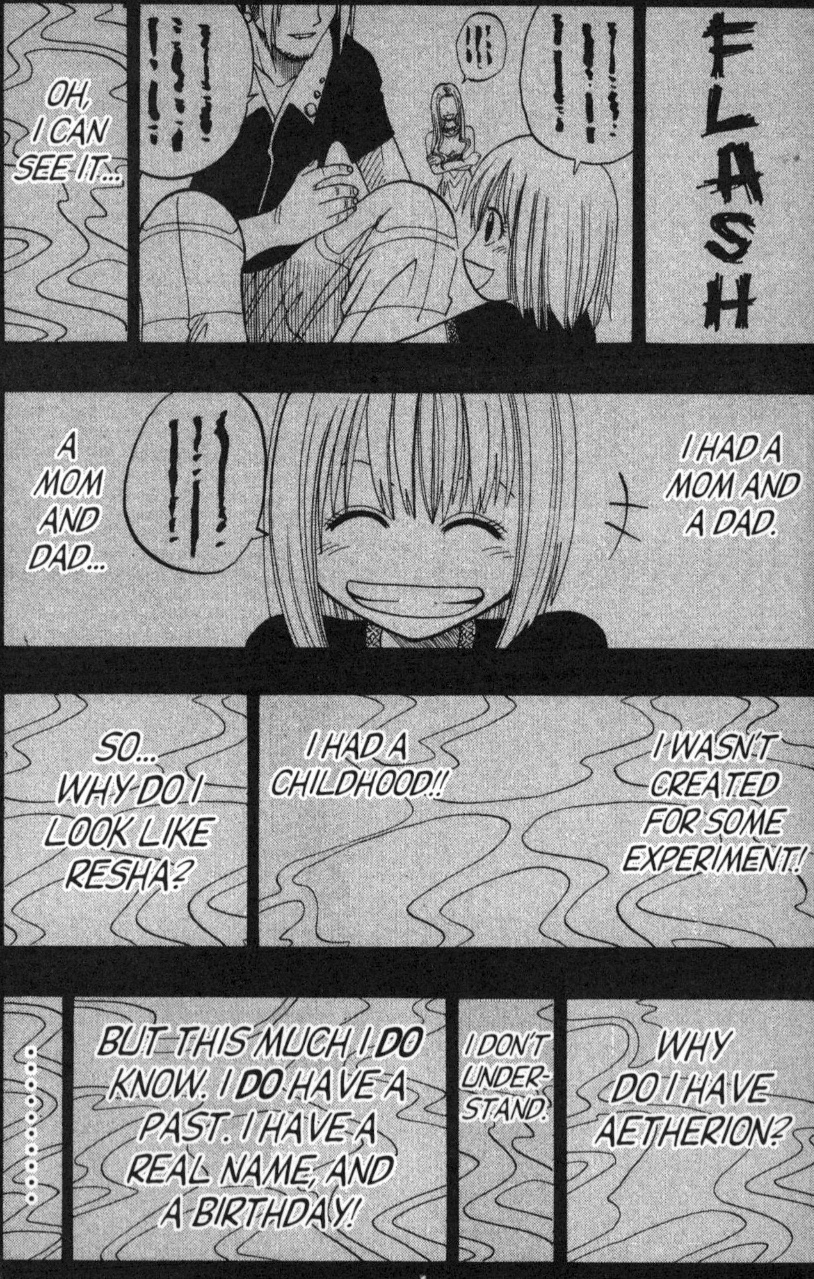
FLASH
OH, I CAN SEE IT...
I HAD A MOM AND A DAD.
A MOM AND DAD...
I WASN'T CREATED FOR SOME EXPERIMENT!
I HAD A CHILDHOOD!!
SO... WHY DO I LOOK LIKE RESHA?
WHY DO I HAVE AETHERION?
I DON'T UNDER-STAND.
BUT THIS MUCH I DO KNOW. I DO HAVE A PAST. I HAVE A REAL NAME, AND A BIRTHDAY!

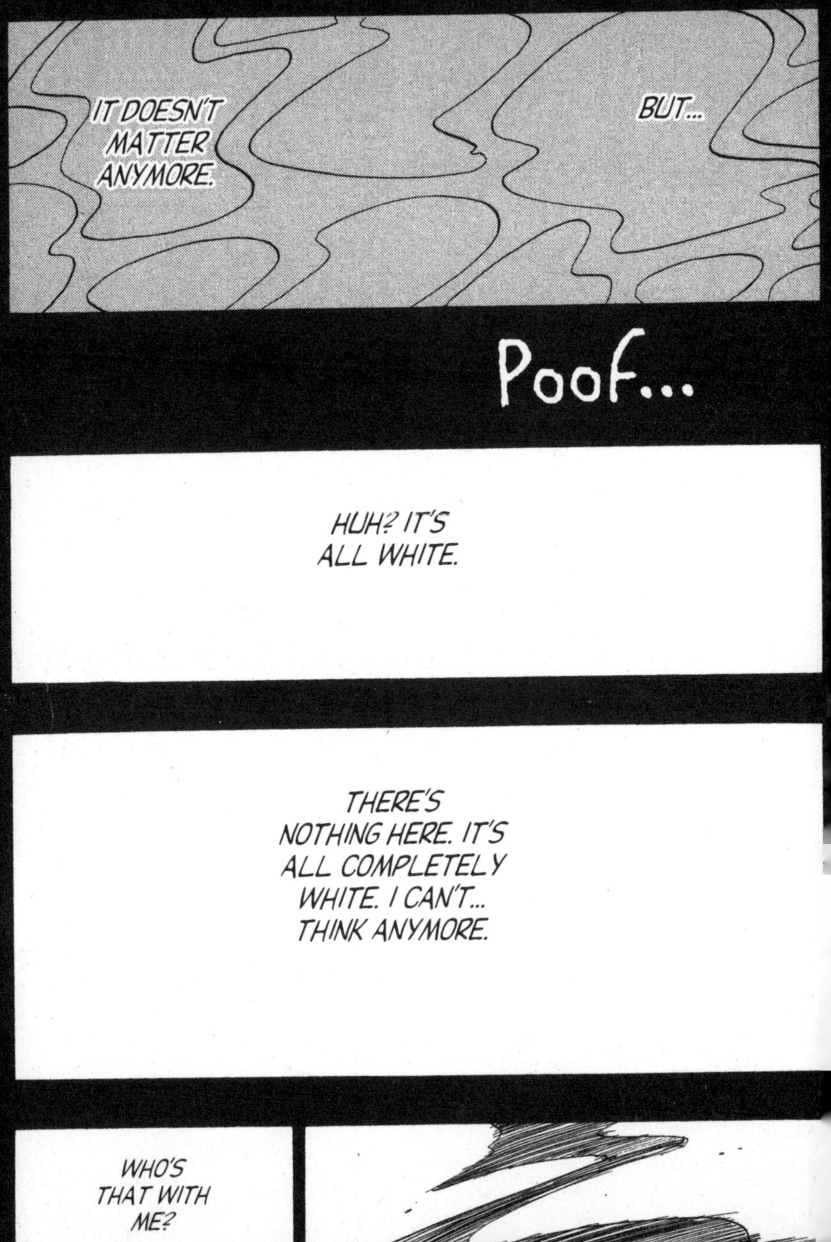
BUT...
IT DOESN'T MATTER ANYMORE.
Poof...
HUH? IT'S ALL WHITE.
THERE'S NOTHING HERE. IT'S ALL COMPLETELY WHITE. I CAN'T... THINK ANYMORE.
WHO'S THAT WITH ME?

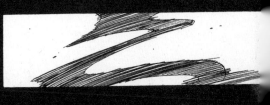

HARU?

HARU?

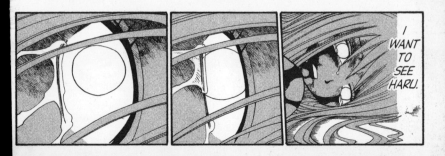

I WANT TO SEE HARU.

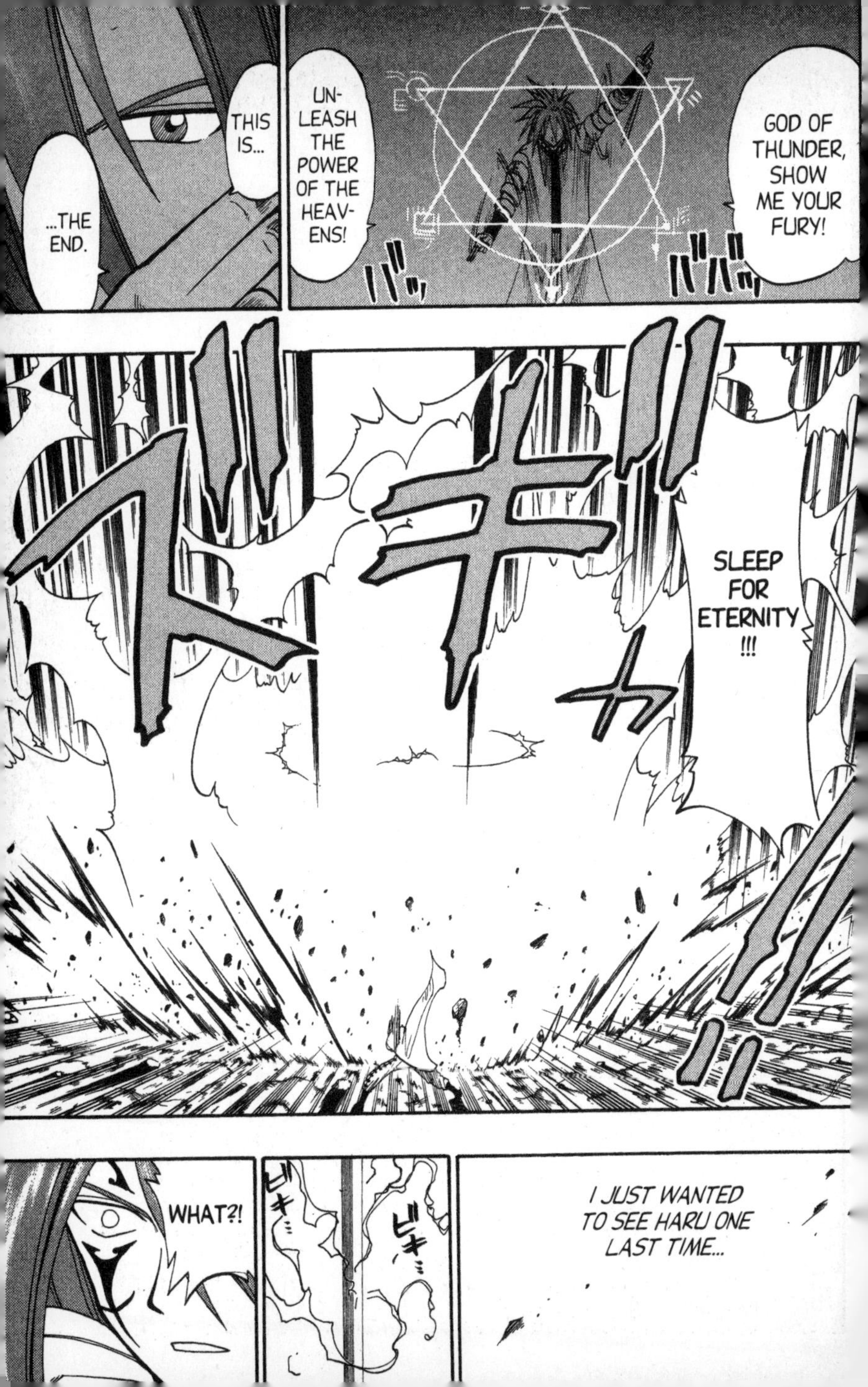
GOD OF THUNDER, SHOW ME YOUR FURY!
UN-LEASH THE POWER OF THE HEAV-ENS!
THIS IS...
...THE END.
SLEEP FOR ETERNITY !!!
I JUST WANTED TO SEE HARU ONE LAST TIME...
WHAT?!

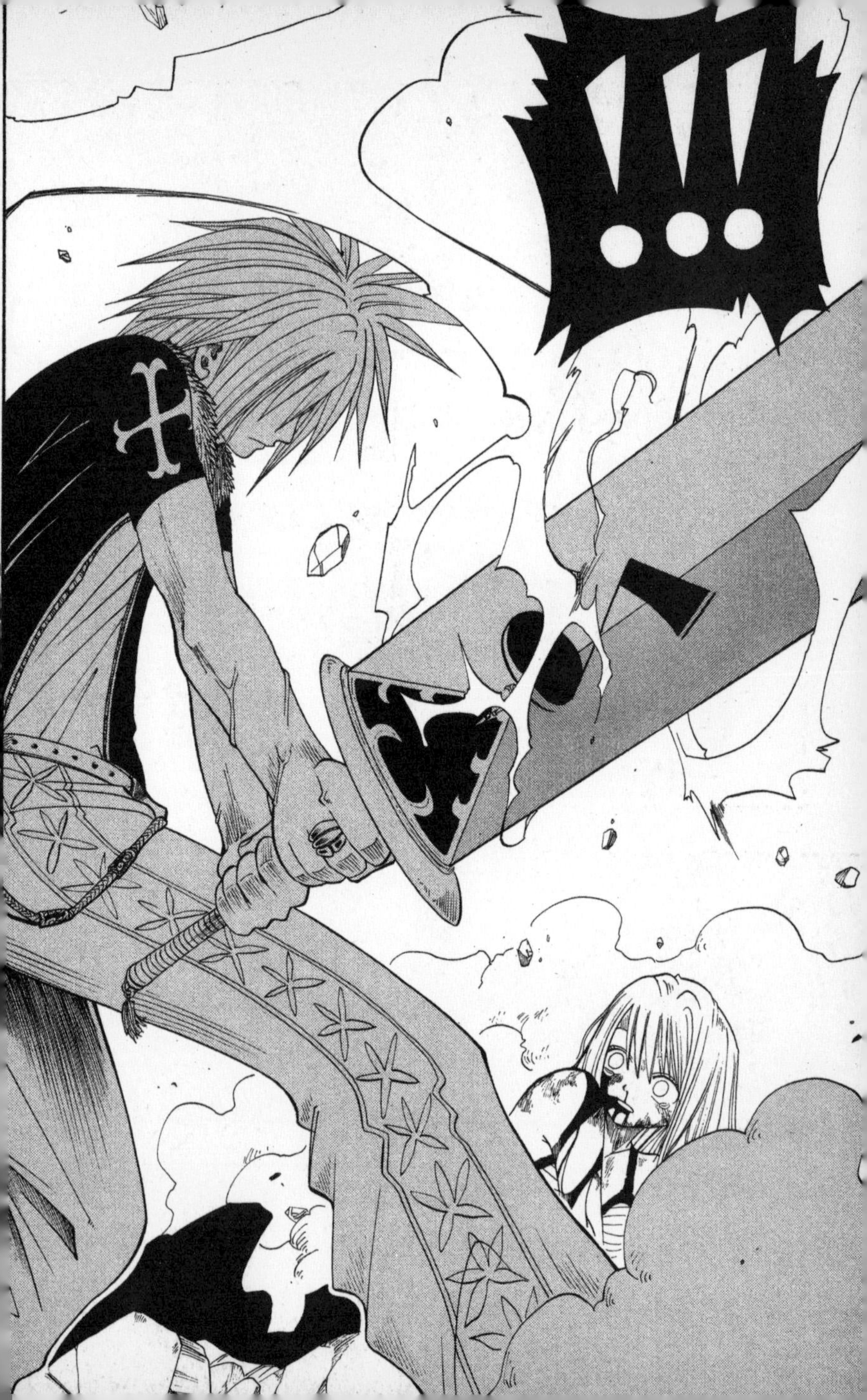
!!!

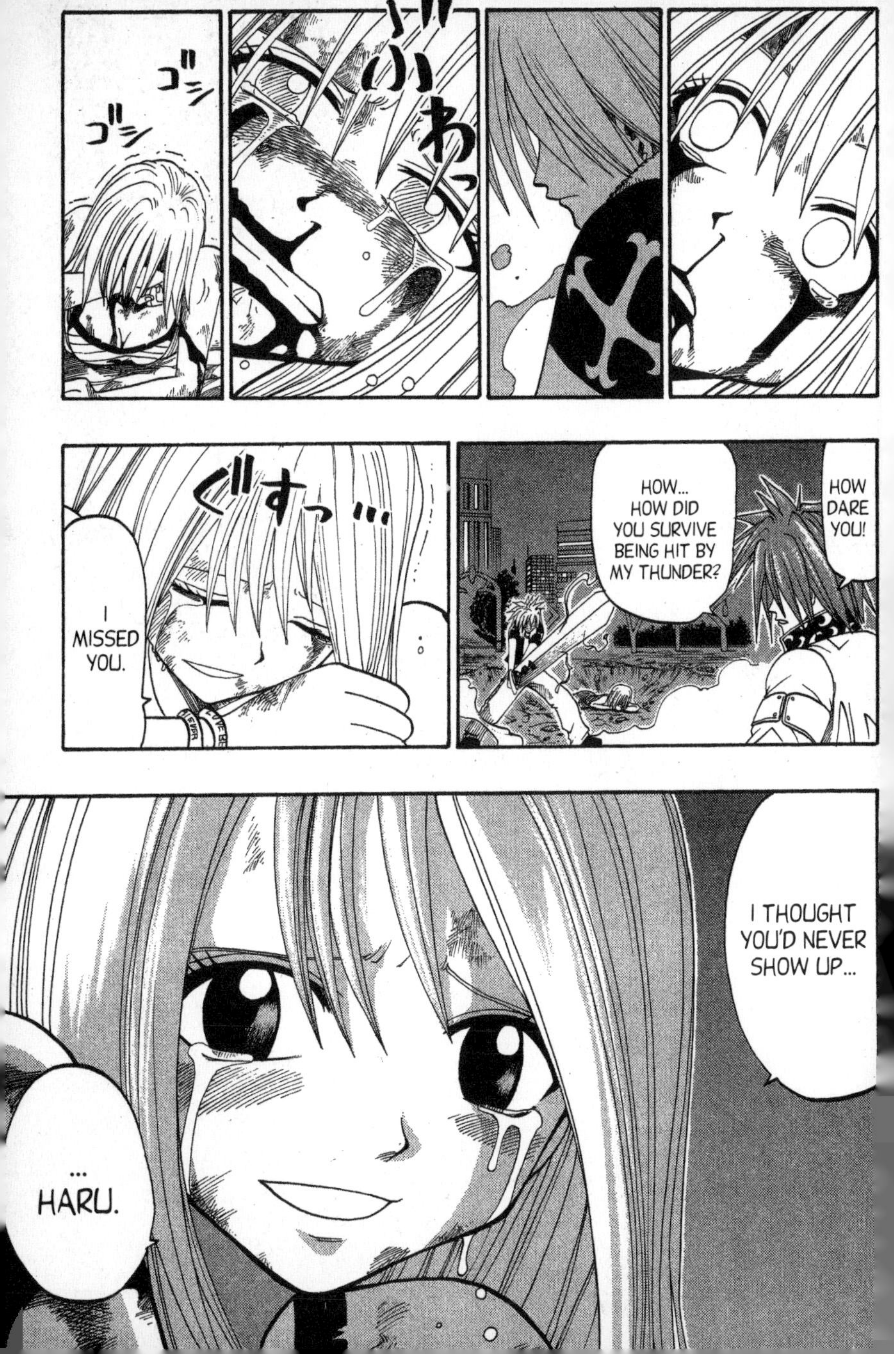
ぶわっ
ゴシ
ゴシ
HOW DARE YOU!
HOW... HOW DID YOU SURVIVE BEING HIT BY MY THUNDER?
ぐすっ…
I MISSED YOU.
I THOUGHT YOU'D NEVER SHOW UP...
... HARU.

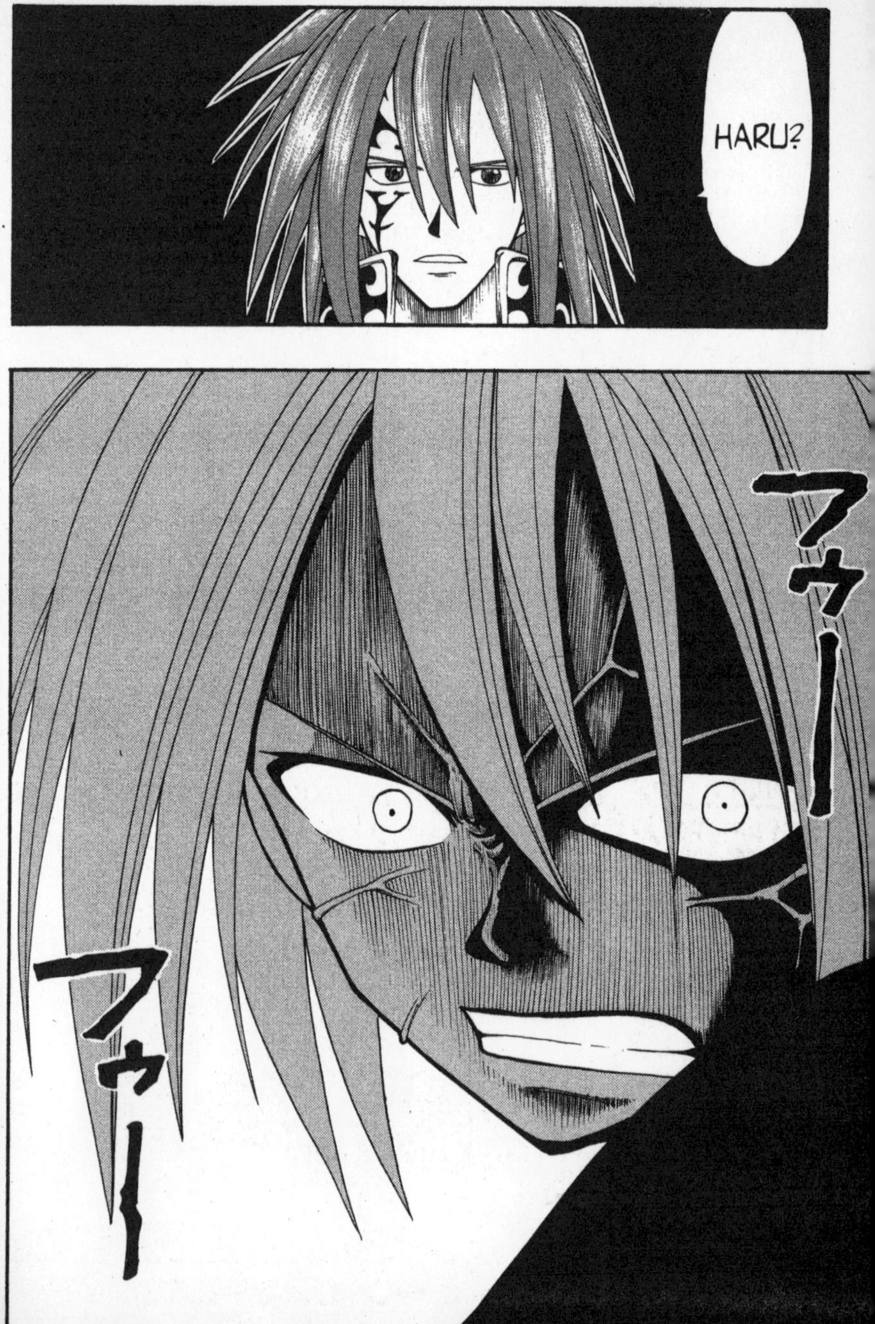
HARU?
フウー
フウー

RAVE MASTER

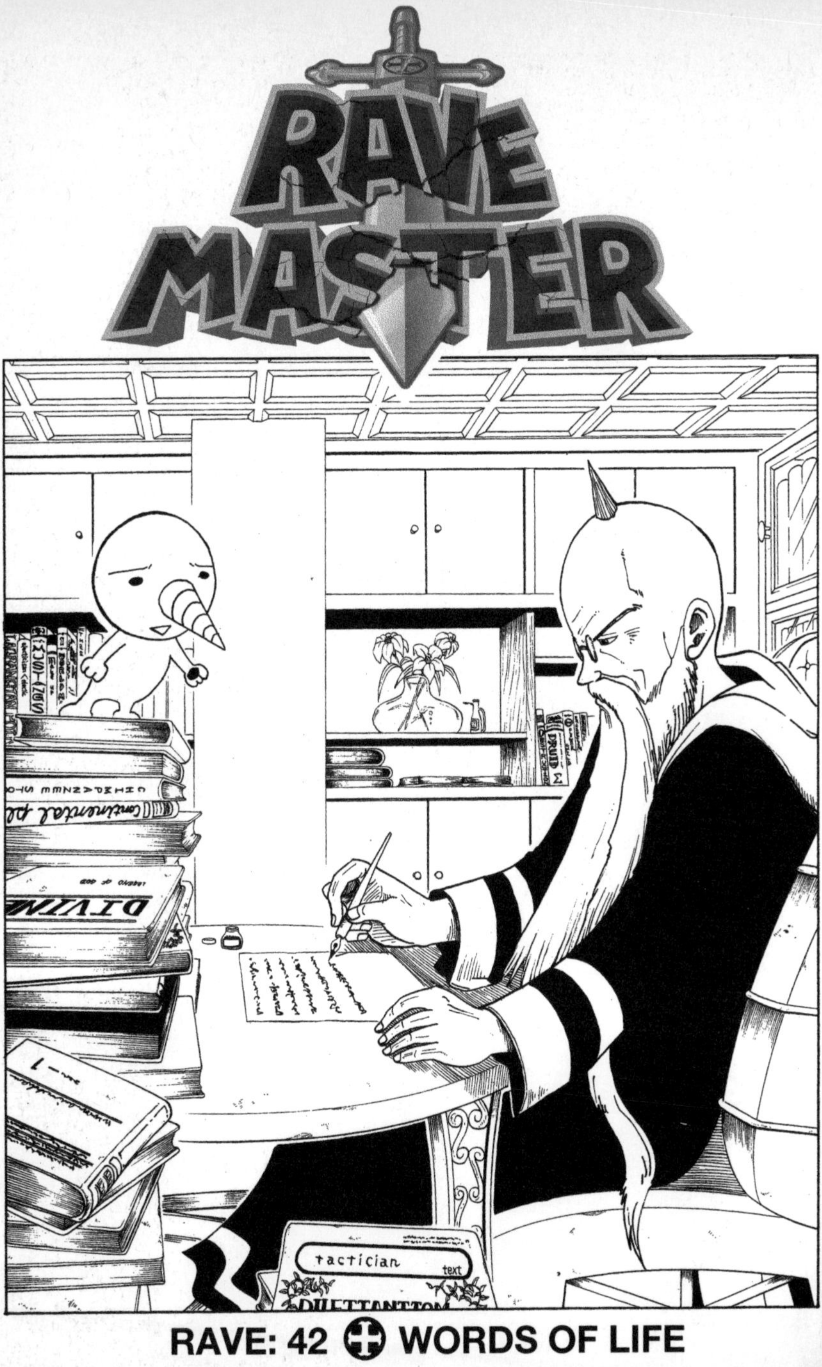
tactician
text
DRUID

RAVE: 42 ✚ WORDS OF LIFE

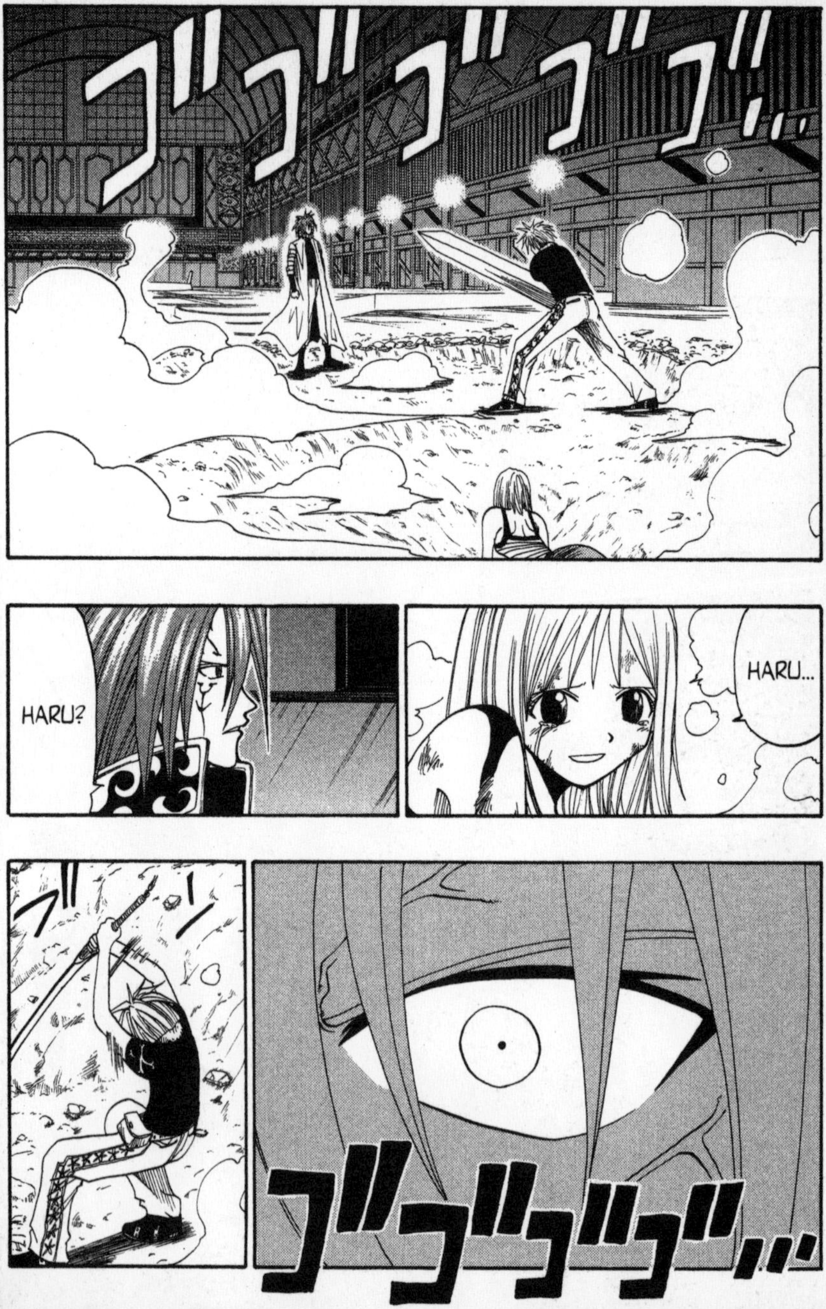
ゴゴゴゴ!!..
HARU...
HARU?
ゴゴゴゴ...

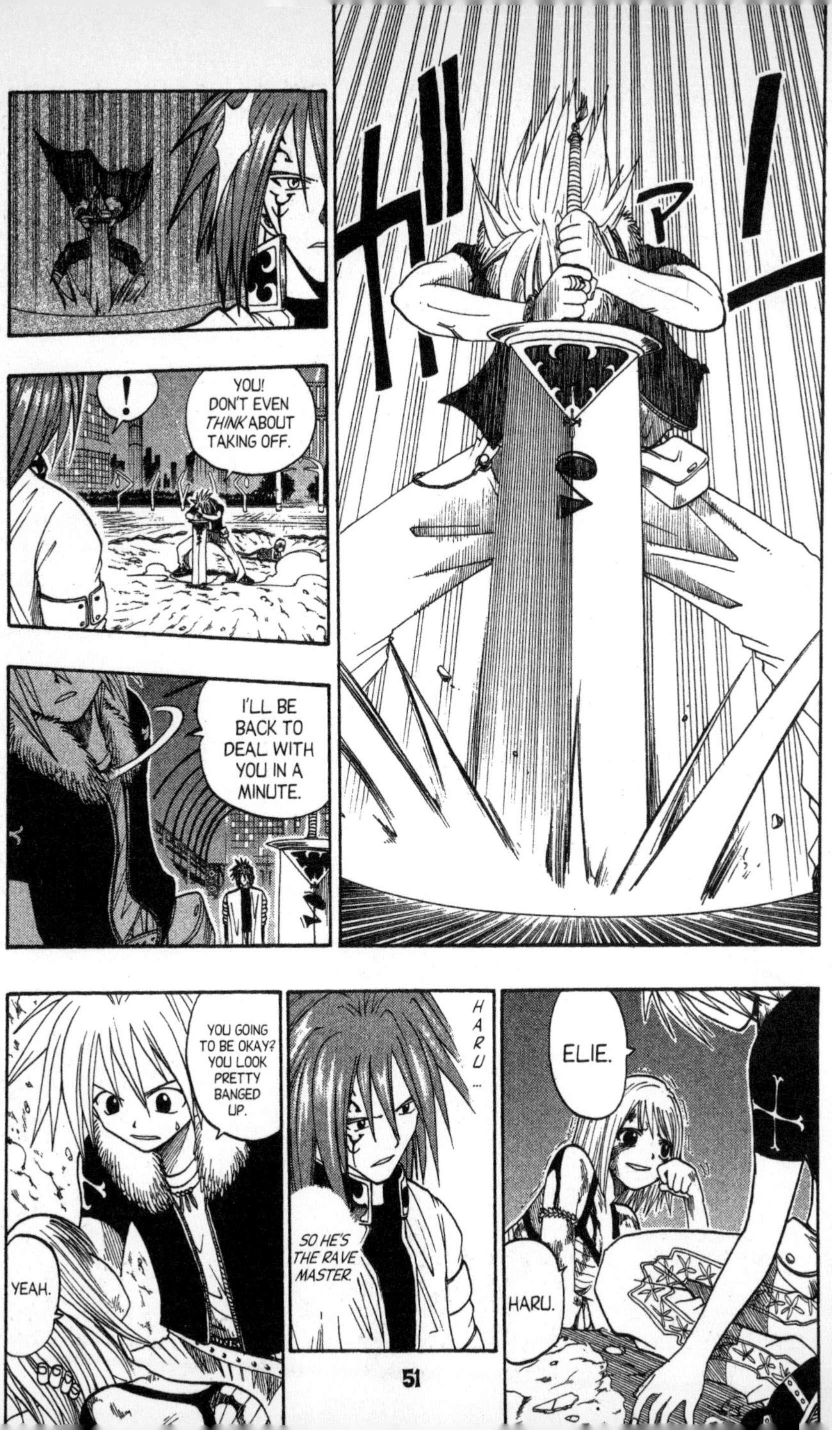
!
YOU! DON'T EVEN THINK ABOUT TAKING OFF.
I'LL BE BACK TO DEAL WITH YOU IN A MINUTE.
ELIE.
HARU.
HARU...
SO HE'S THE RAVE MASTER.
YOU GOING TO BE OKAY? YOU LOOK PRETTY BANGED UP.
YEAH.

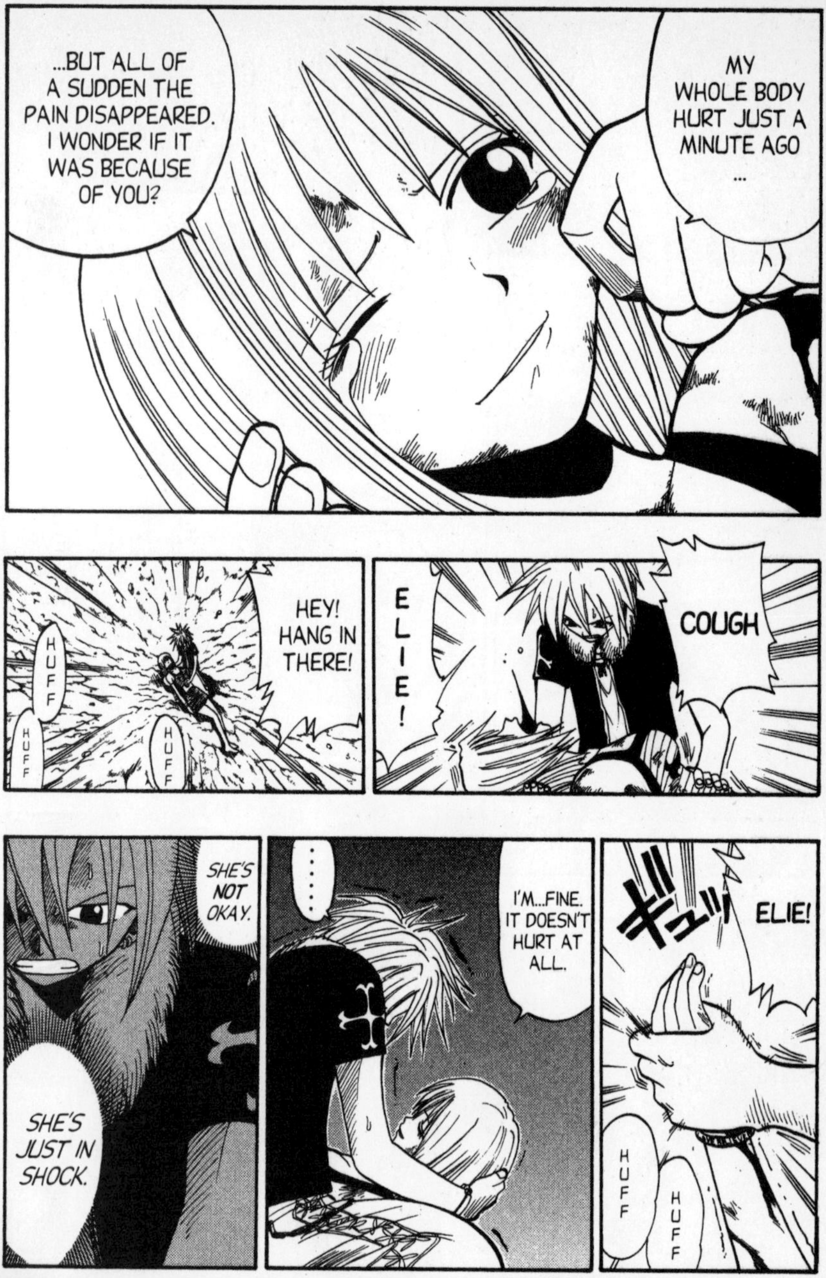
MY WHOLE BODY HURT JUST A MINUTE AGO ...
...BUT ALL OF A SUDDEN THE PAIN DISAPPEARED. I WONDER IF IT WAS BECAUSE OF YOU?
COUGH
ELIE!
HEY! HANG IN THERE!
HUFF
HUFF
HUFF
ギュッ
ELIE!
HUFF
HUFF
I'M...FINE. IT DOESN'T HURT AT ALL.
......
SHE'S NOT OKAY.
SHE'S JUST IN SHOCK.

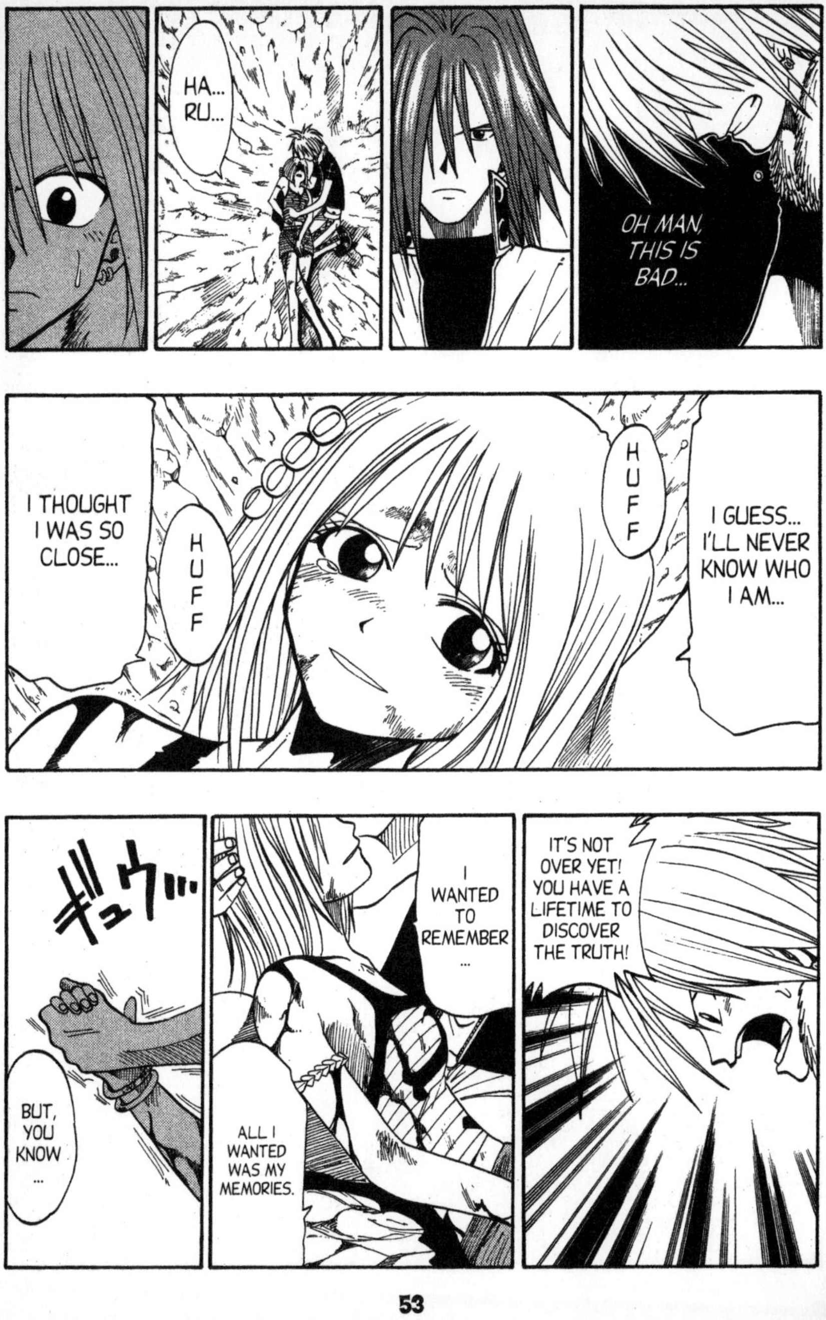
OH MAN, THIS IS BAD...
HA... RU...
HUFF
I GUESS... I'LL NEVER KNOW WHO I AM...
I THOUGHT I WAS SO CLOSE...
HUFF
IT'S NOT OVER YET! YOU HAVE A LIFETIME TO DISCOVER THE TRUTH!
I WANTED TO REMEMBER ...
ALL I WANTED WAS MY MEMORIES.
ギュウッ
BUT, YOU KNOW ...

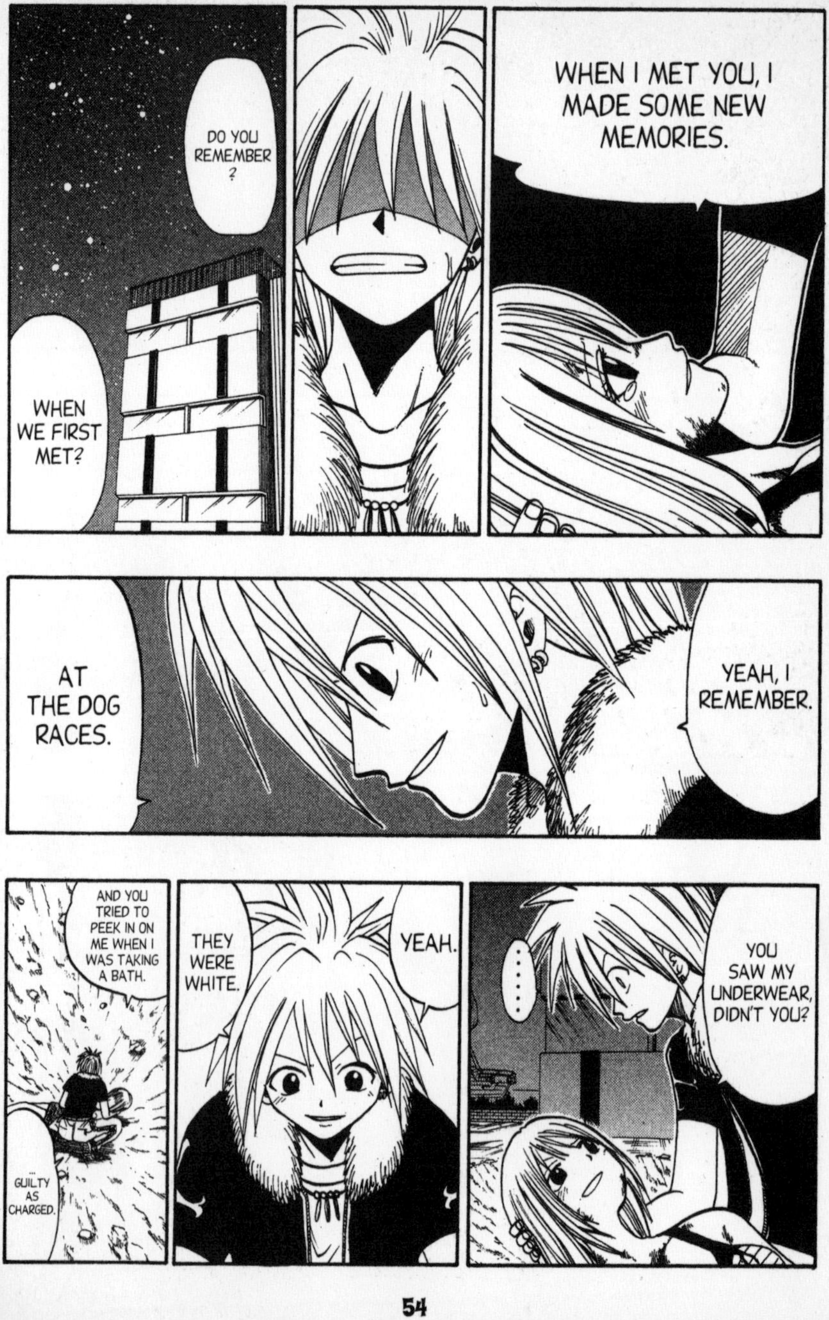
WHEN I MET YOU, I MADE SOME NEW MEMORIES.
DO YOU REMEMBER?
WHEN WE FIRST MET?
YEAH, I REMEMBER.
AT THE DOG RACES.
YOU SAW MY UNDERWEAR, DIDN'T YOU?
......
YEAH.
THEY WERE WHITE.
AND YOU TRIED TO PEEK IN ON ME WHEN I WAS TAKING A BATH.
... GUILTY AS CHARGED.

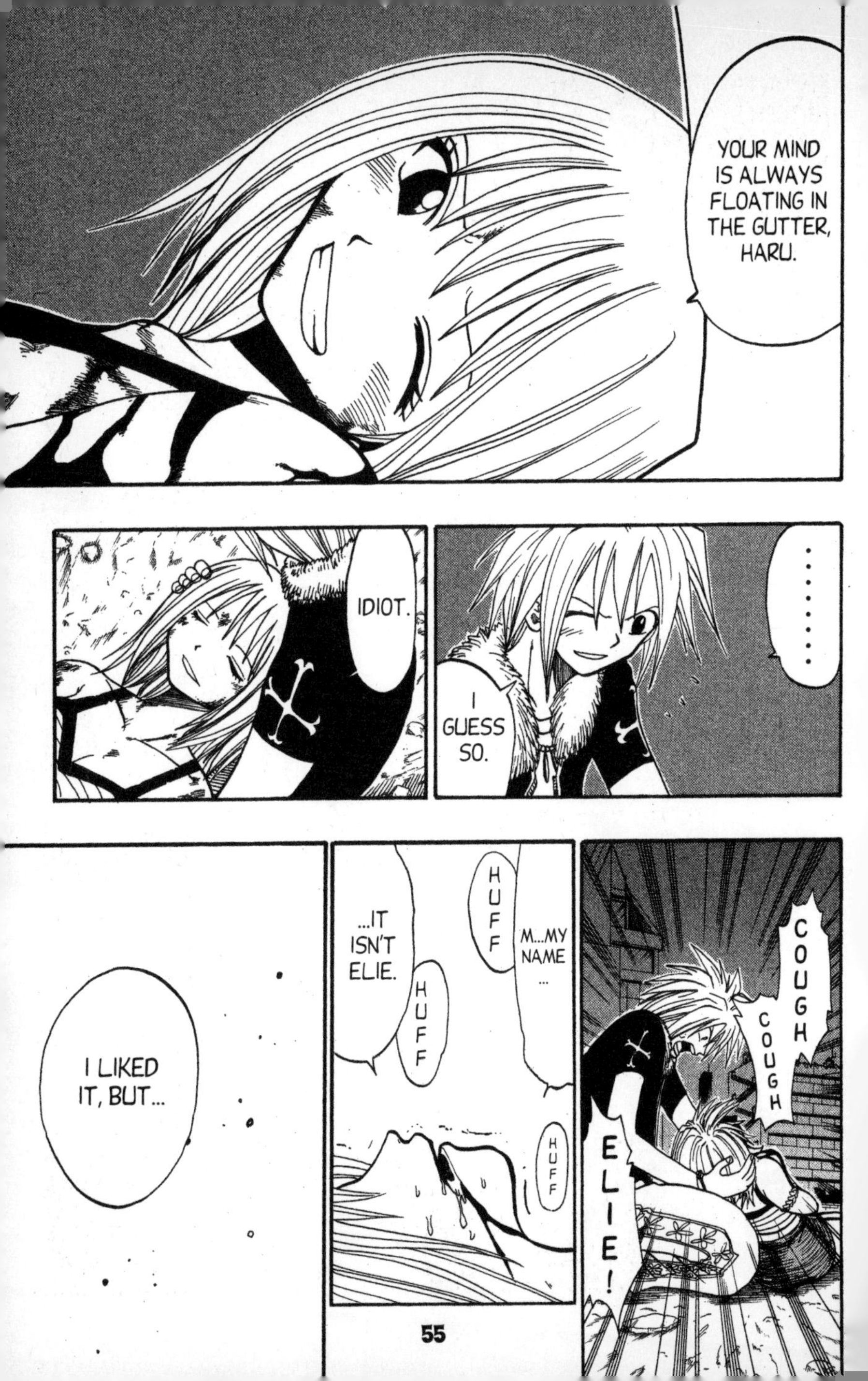
YOUR MIND IS ALWAYS FLOATING IN THE GUTTER, HARU.
....
I GUESS SO.
IDIOT.
COUGH
COUGH COUGH
ELIE!
M...MY NAME ...
HUFF HUFF
...IT ISN'T ELIE.
HUFF HUFF
HUFF HUFF
I LIKED IT, BUT...

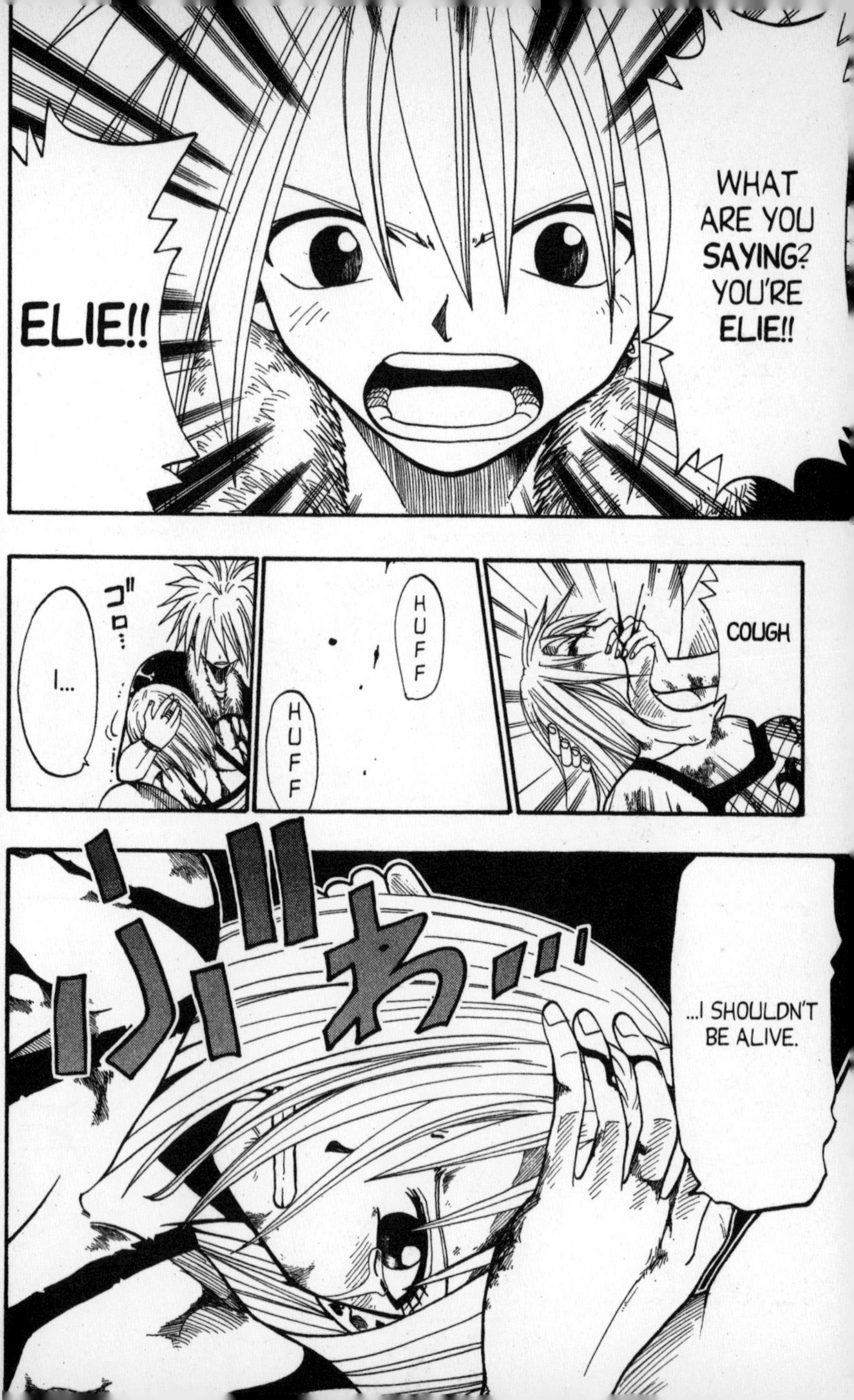
WHAT ARE YOU SAYING? YOU'RE ELIE!!
ELIE!!
COUGH
HUFF
HUFF
ゴロ…
I...
...I SHOULDN'T BE ALIVE.
ぶわ

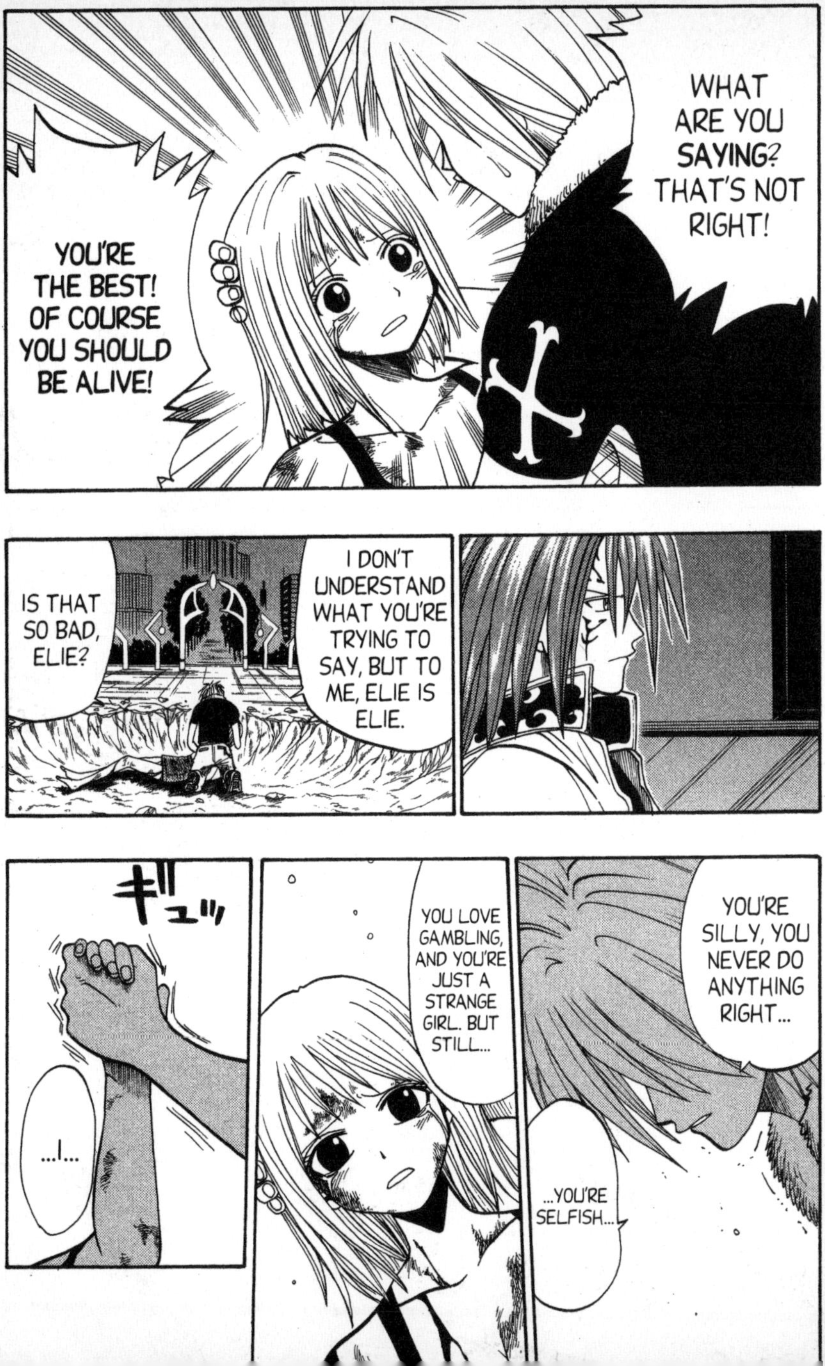
WHAT ARE YOU SAYING? THAT'S NOT RIGHT!
YOU'RE THE BEST! OF COURSE YOU SHOULD BE ALIVE!
I DON'T UNDERSTAND WHAT YOU'RE TRYING TO SAY, BUT TO ME, ELIE IS ELIE.
IS THAT SO BAD, ELIE?
YOU'RE SILLY, YOU NEVER DO ANYTHING RIGHT...
...YOU'RE SELFISH...
YOU LOVE GAMBLING, AND YOU'RE JUST A STRANGE GIRL. BUT STILL...
ギュッ
...I...

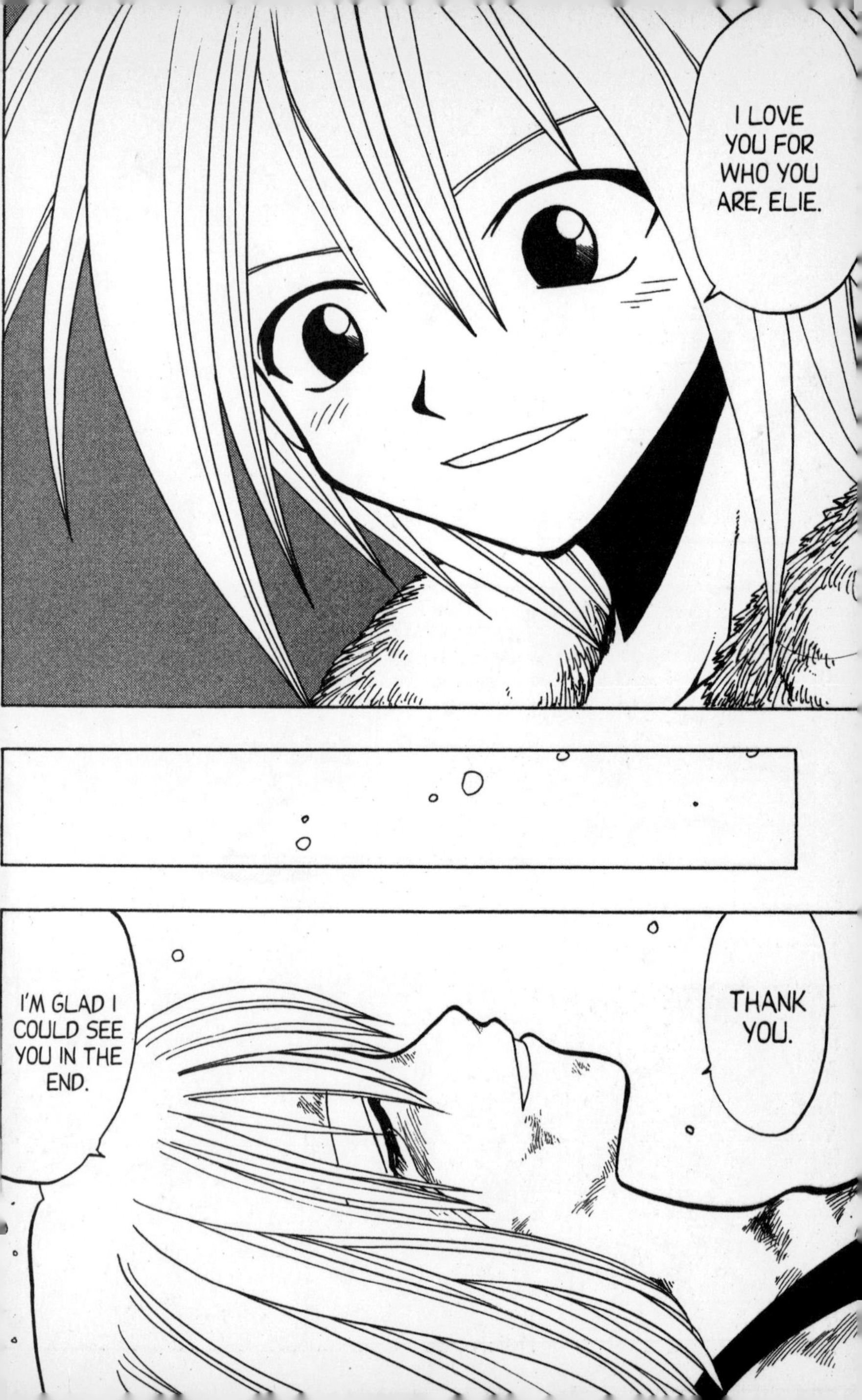
I LOVE YOU FOR WHO YOU ARE, ELIE.
THANK YOU.
I'M GLAD I COULD SEE YOU IN THE END.

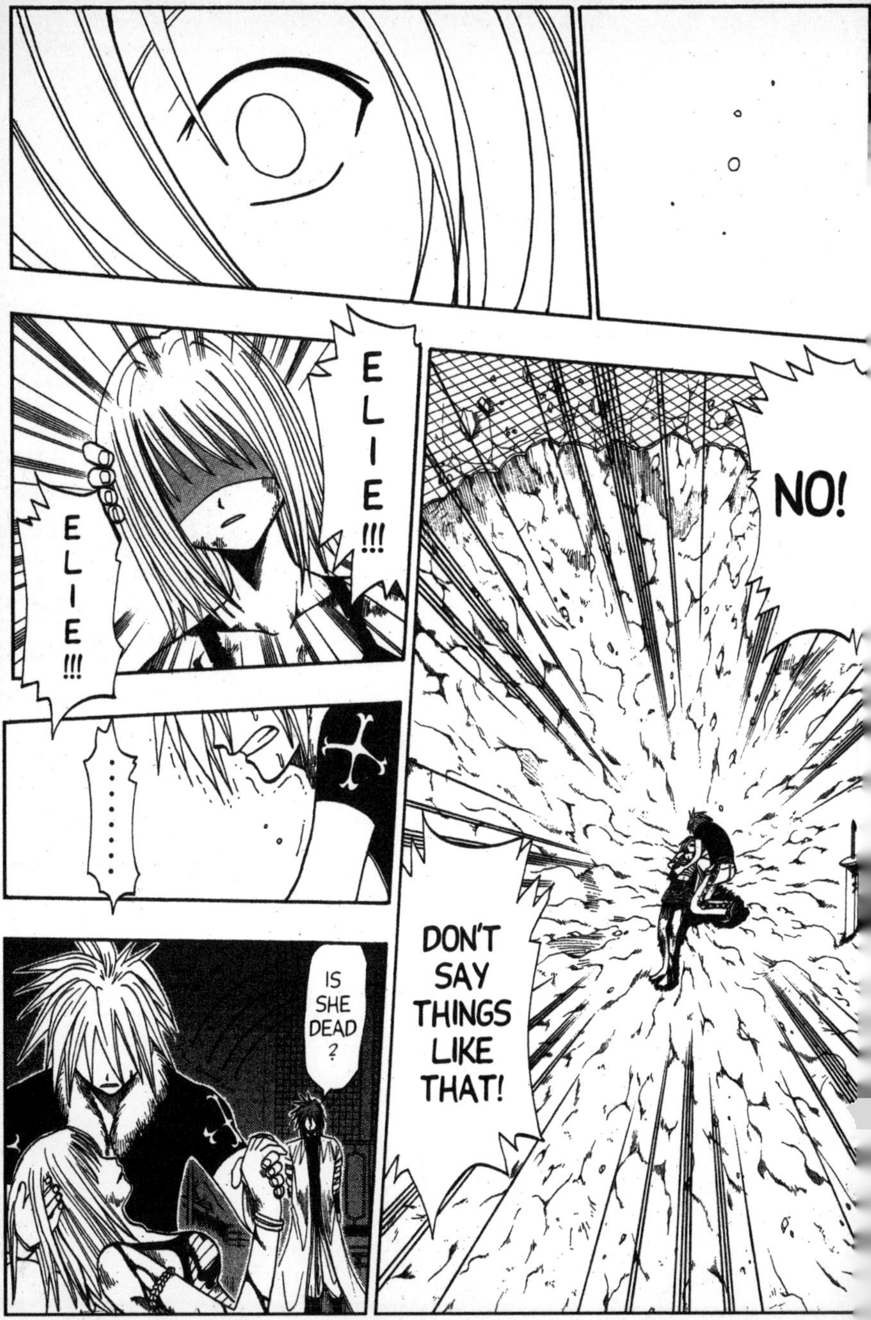

NO!
DON'T SAY THINGS LIKE THAT!
ELIE!!!
ELIE!!!
......
IS SHE DEAD?

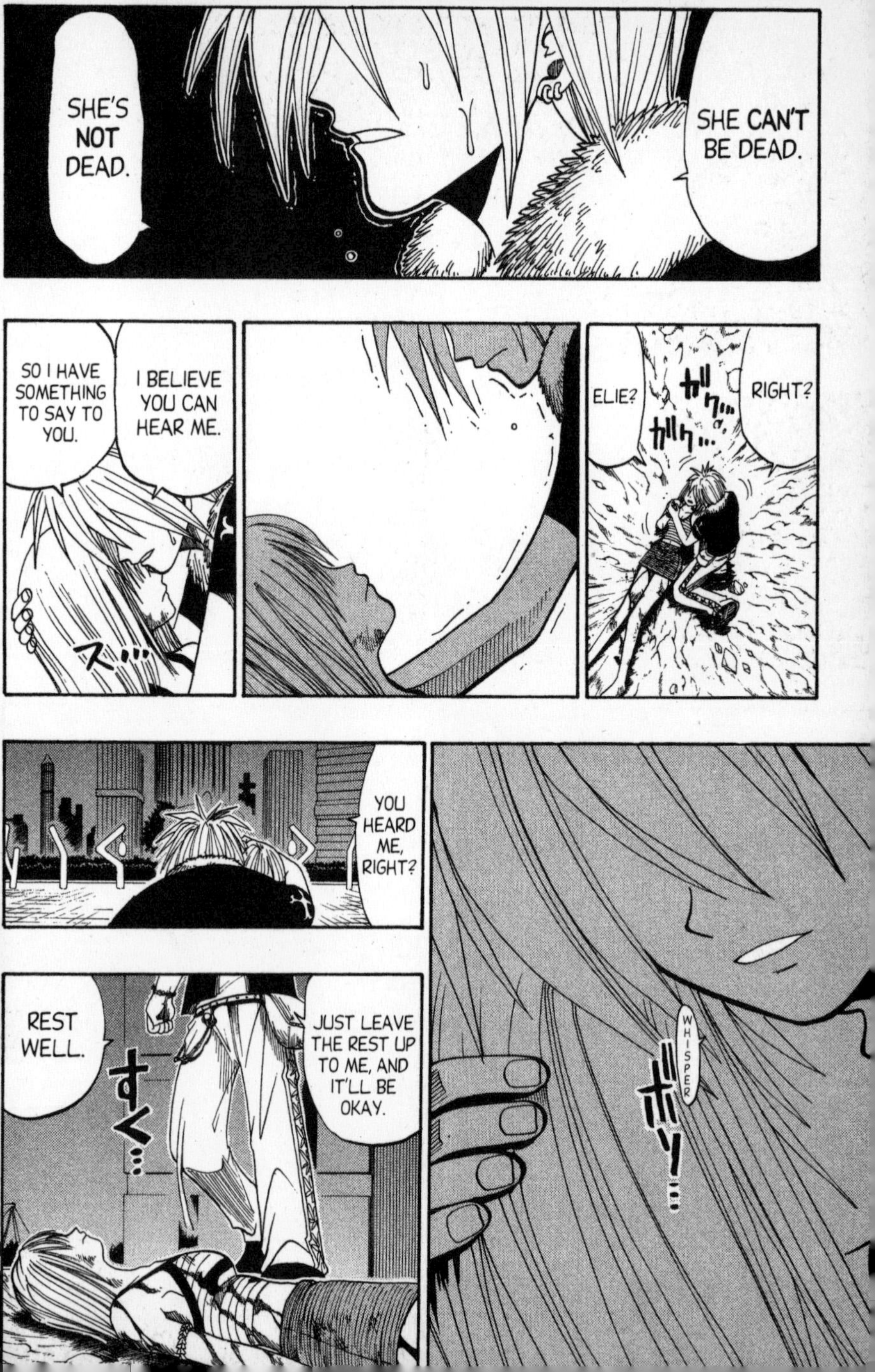
SHE CAN'T BE DEAD.
SHE'S NOT DEAD.
RIGHT?
ガク…
ガク…
ELIE?
I BELIEVE YOU CAN HEAR ME.
SO I HAVE SOMETHING TO SAY TO YOU.
ス…
WHISPER
ボソ…
YOU HEARD ME, RIGHT?
JUST LEAVE THE REST UP TO ME, AND IT'LL BE OKAY.
REST WELL.
すく…

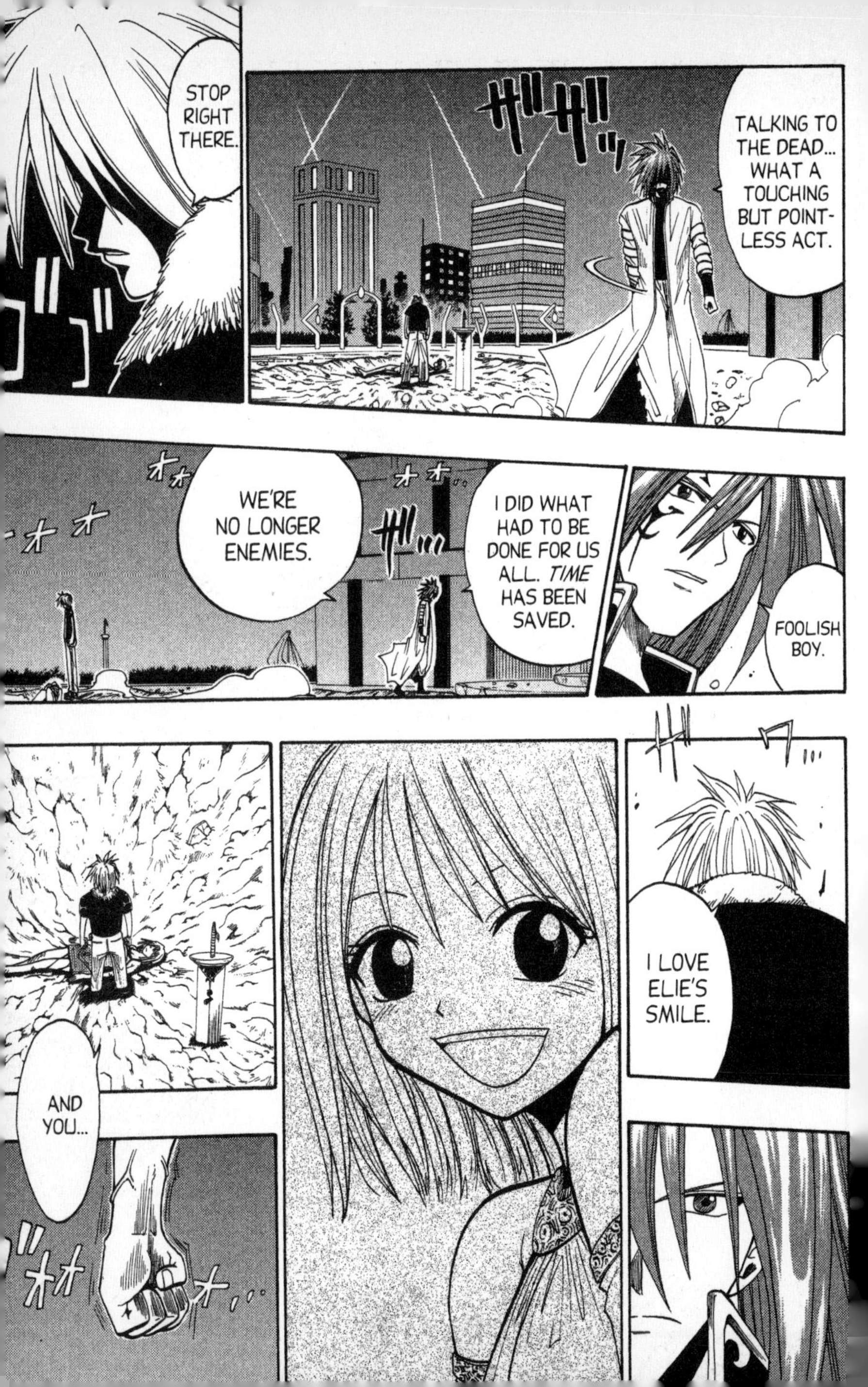

TALKING TO THE DEAD... WHAT A TOUCHING BUT POINTLESS ACT.
STOP RIGHT THERE.
FOOLISH BOY.
I DID WHAT HAD TO BE DONE FOR US ALL. *TIME* HAS BEEN SAVED.
WE'RE NO LONGER ENEMIES.
I LOVE ELIE'S SMILE.
AND YOU...

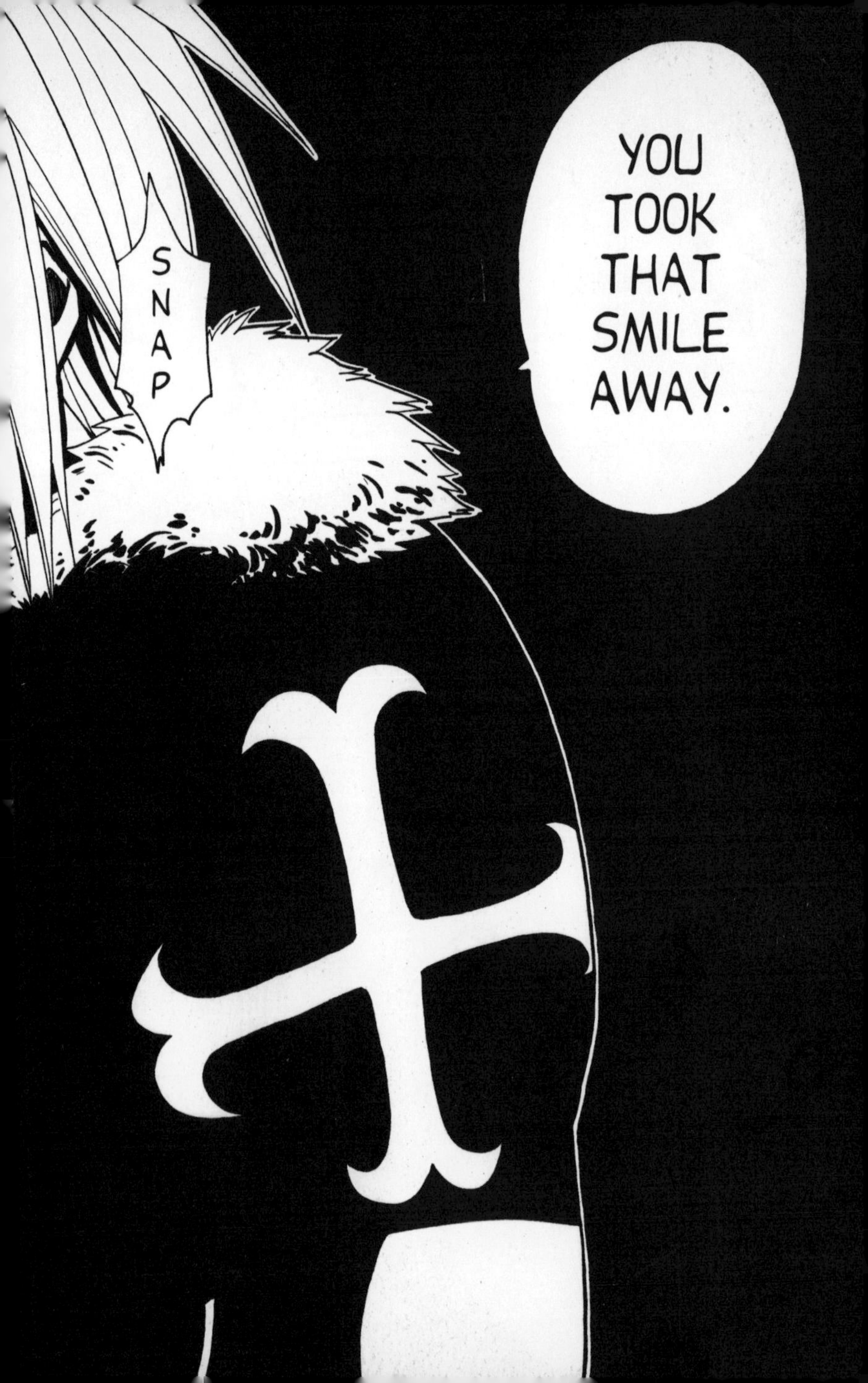
YOU TOOK THAT SMILE AWAY.
SNAP

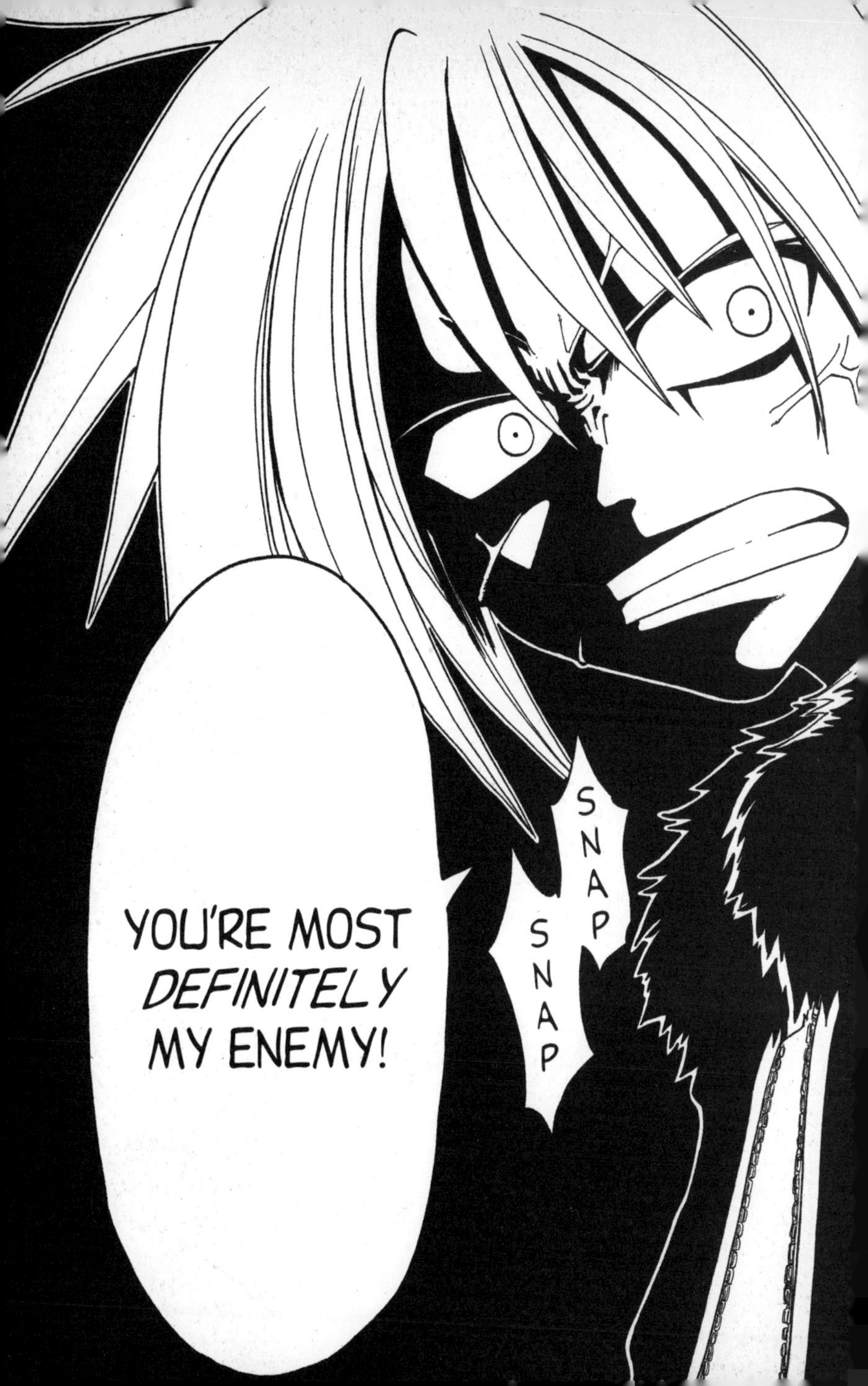
YOU'RE MOST *DEFINITELY* MY ENEMY!
SNAP
SNAP

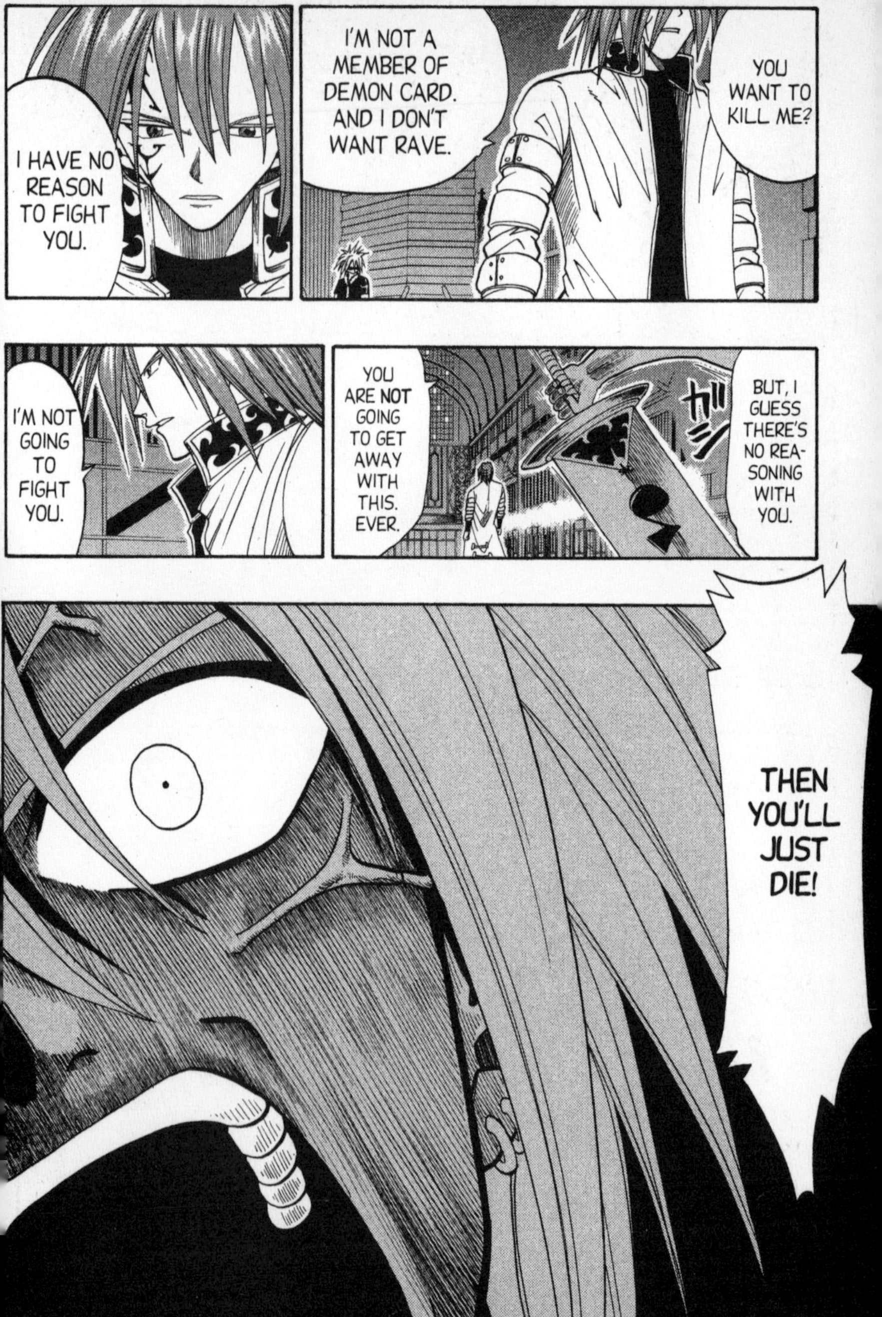
YOU WANT TO KILL ME?
I'M NOT A MEMBER OF DEMON CARD. AND I DON'T WANT RAVE.
I HAVE NO REASON TO FIGHT YOU.
BUT, I GUESS THERE'S NO REA-SONING WITH YOU.
YOU ARE **NOT** GOING TO GET AWAY WITH THIS. EVER.
I'M NOT GOING TO FIGHT YOU.
THEN YOU'LL JUST DIE!

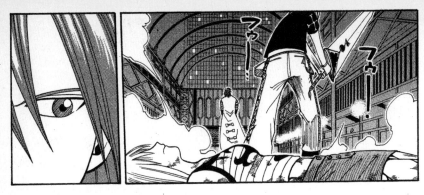

...I HEARD WHAT YOU WHISPERED TO ME...

HARU...

...I WANT TO LIVE !!!

I...

I...

ヒョッ...

IT WAS A PROMISE...

...I CAN'T WAIT...

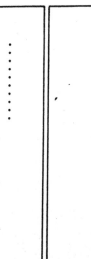

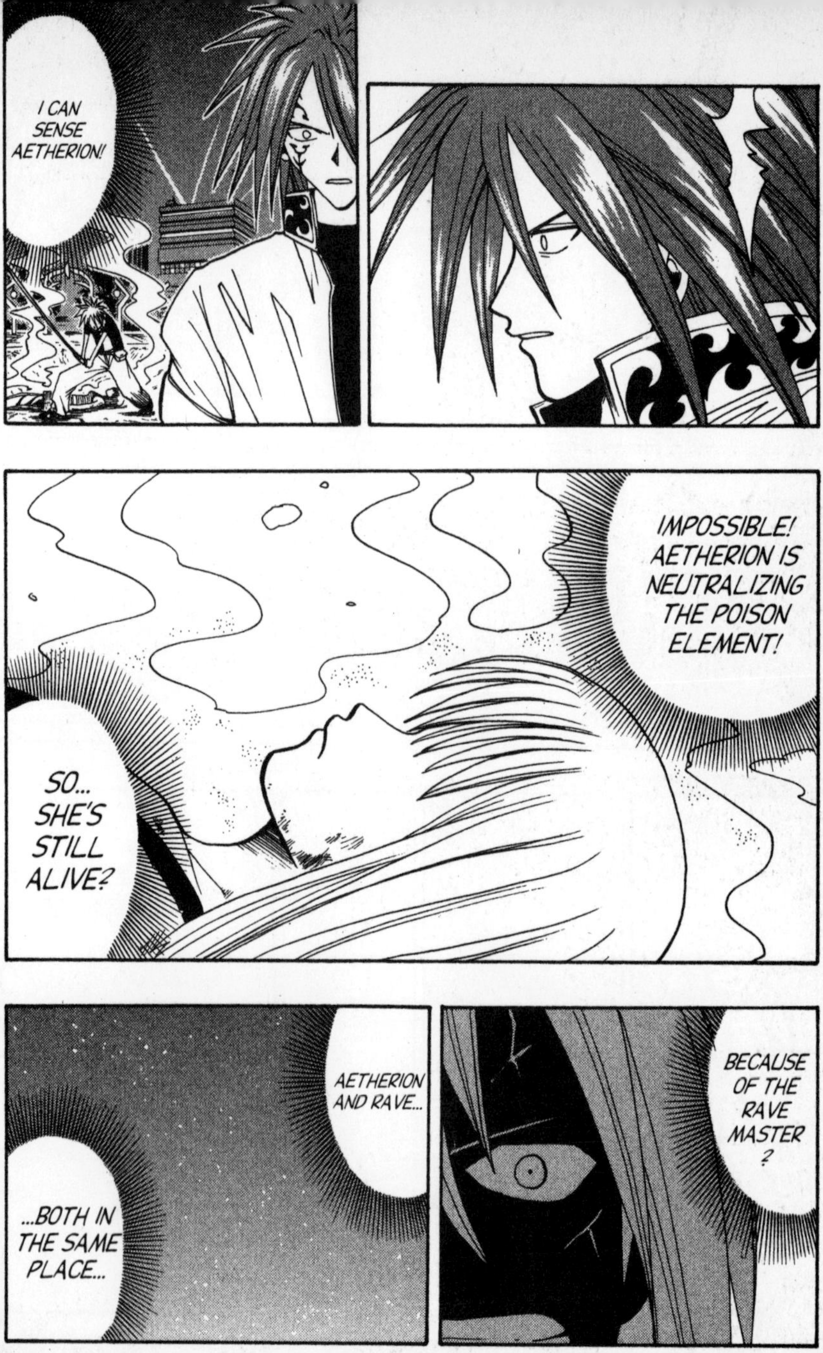
I CAN SENSE AETHERION!
IMPOSSIBLE! AETHERION IS NEUTRALIZING THE POISON ELEMENT!
SO... SHE'S STILL ALIVE?
BECAUSE OF THE RAVE MASTER?
AETHERION AND RAVE...
...BOTH IN THE SAME PLACE...

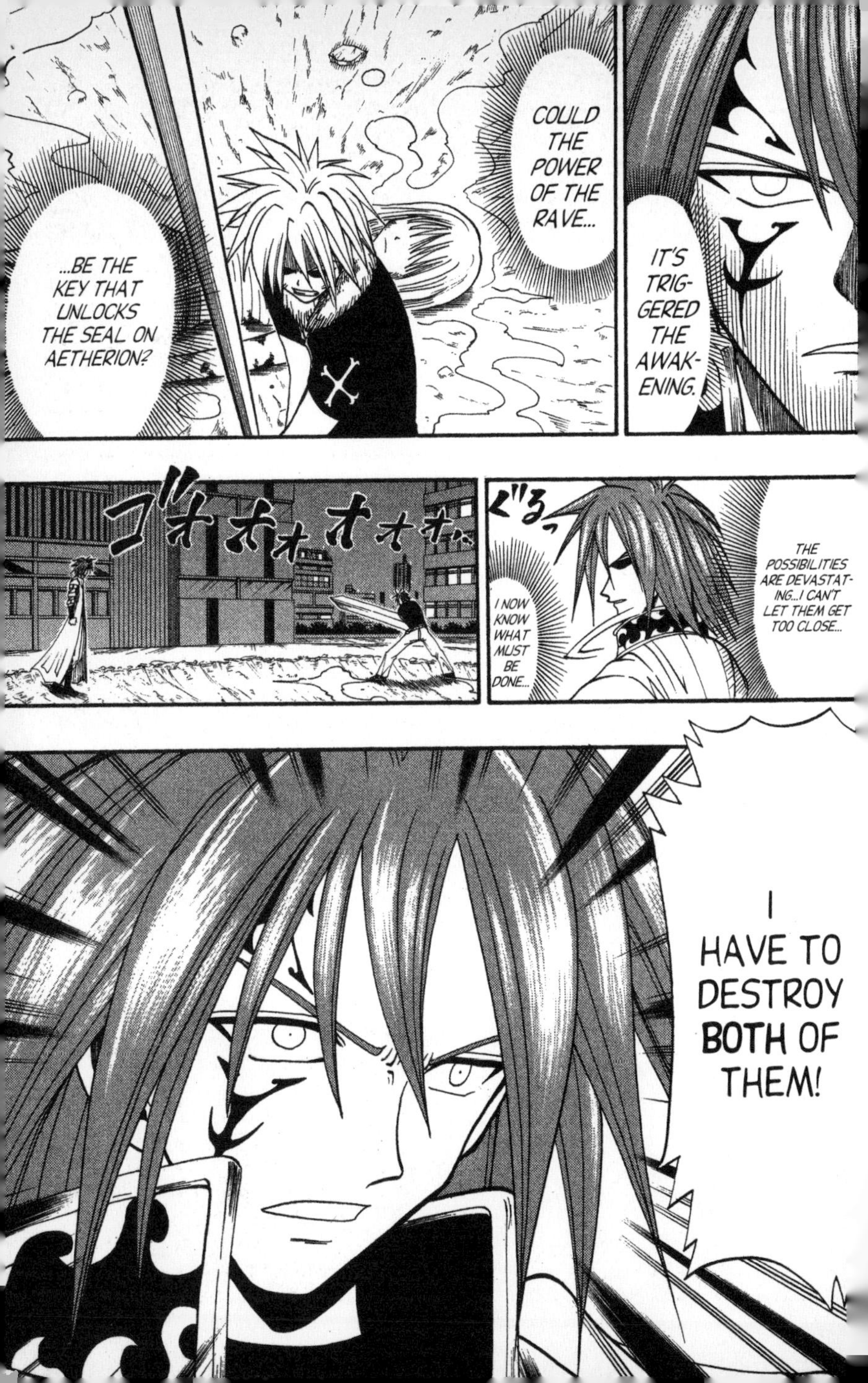
IT'S TRIG-GERED THE AWAK-ENING.
COULD THE POWER OF THE RAVE...
...BE THE KEY THAT UNLOCKS THE SEAL ON AETHERION?
ぐるっ
THE POSSIBILITIES ARE DEVASTATING...I CAN'T LET THEM GET TOO CLOSE...
I NOW KNOW WHAT MUST BE DONE...
ゴオオオオオオ
I HAVE TO DESTROY **BOTH** OF THEM!

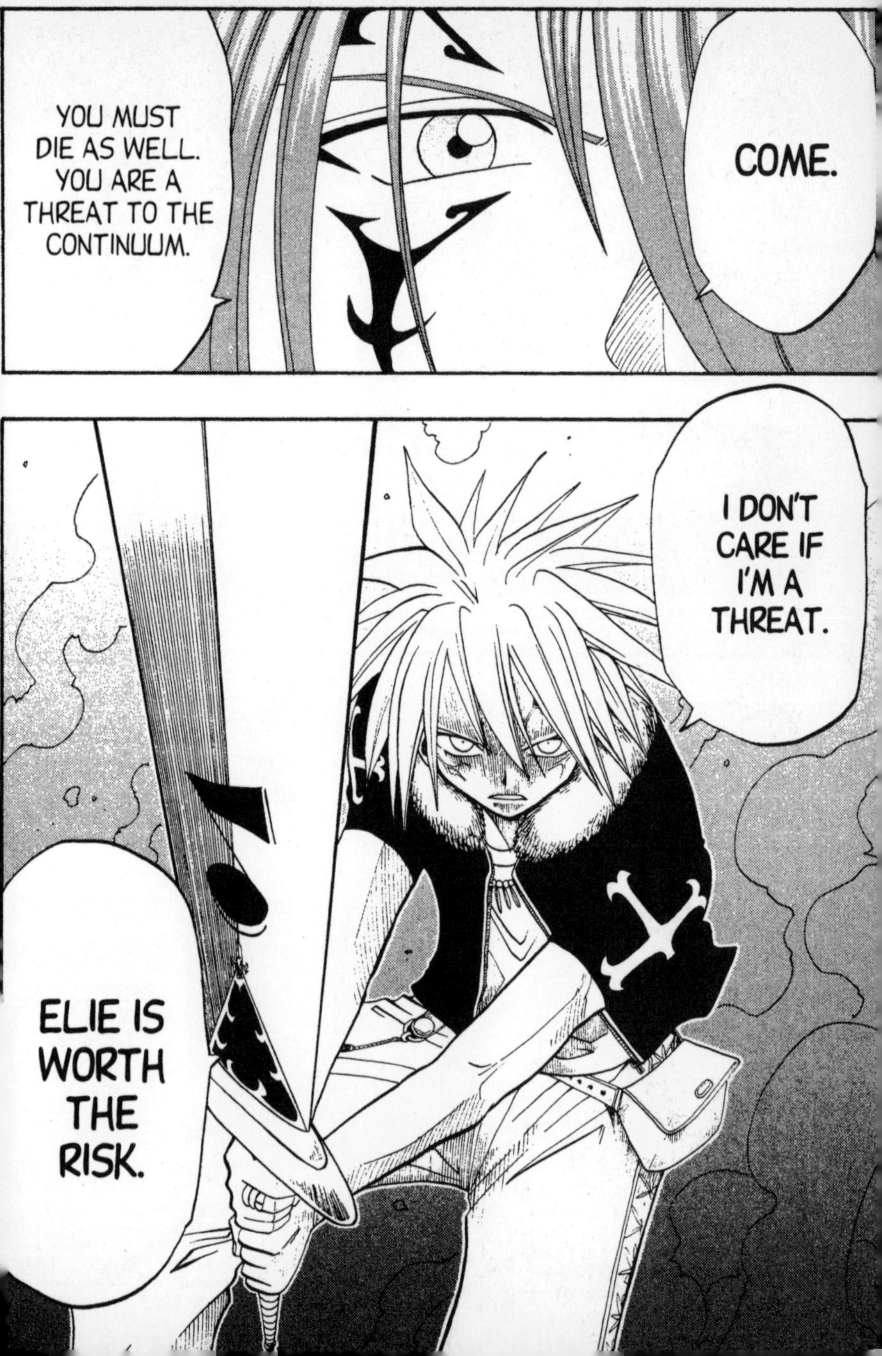
COME.
YOU MUST DIE AS WELL. YOU ARE A THREAT TO THE CONTINUUM.
I DON'T CARE IF I'M A THREAT.
ELIE IS WORTH THE RISK.

RAVE: 43 ✠ THE KNOCK OF DESPAIR!

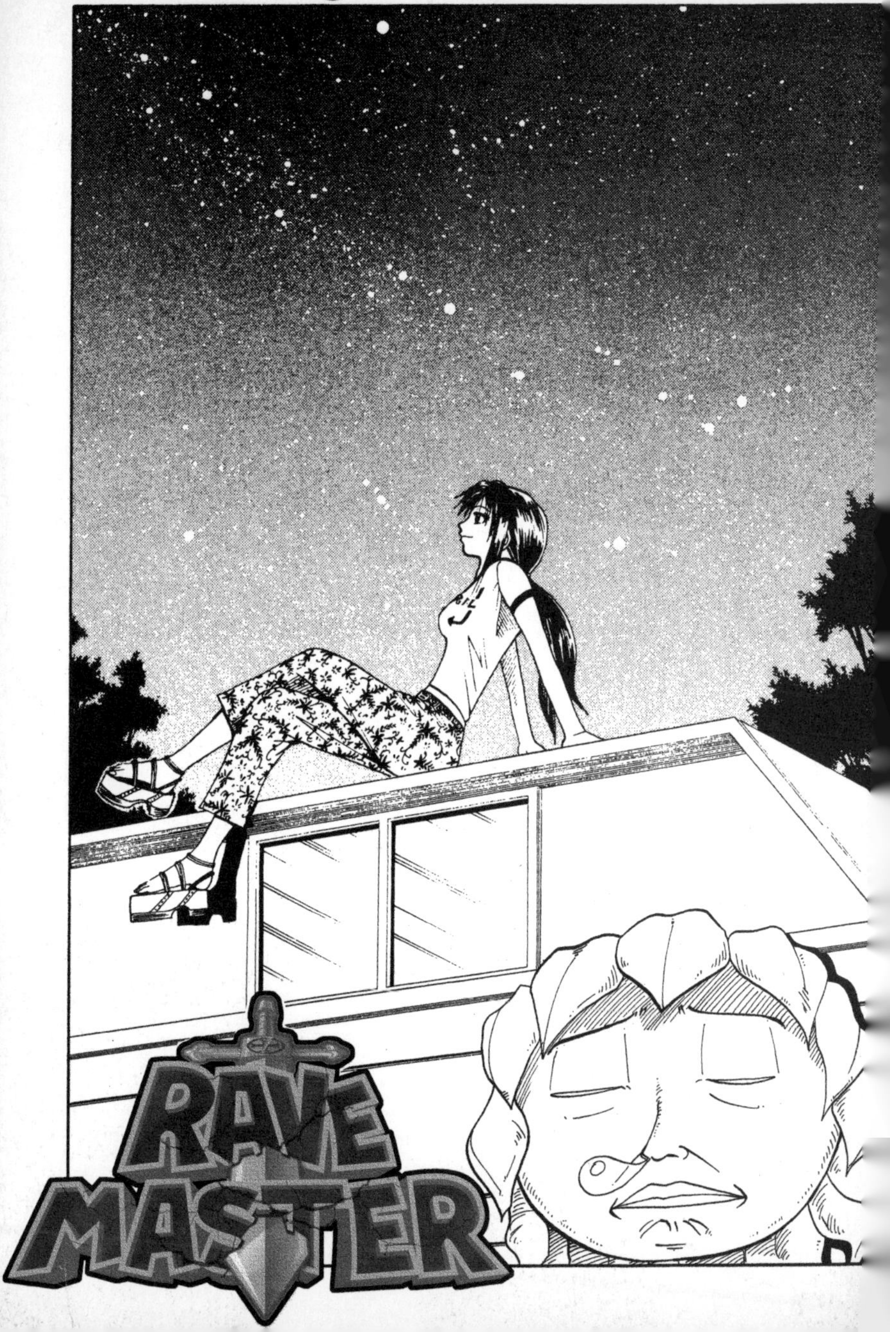
RAVE MASTER

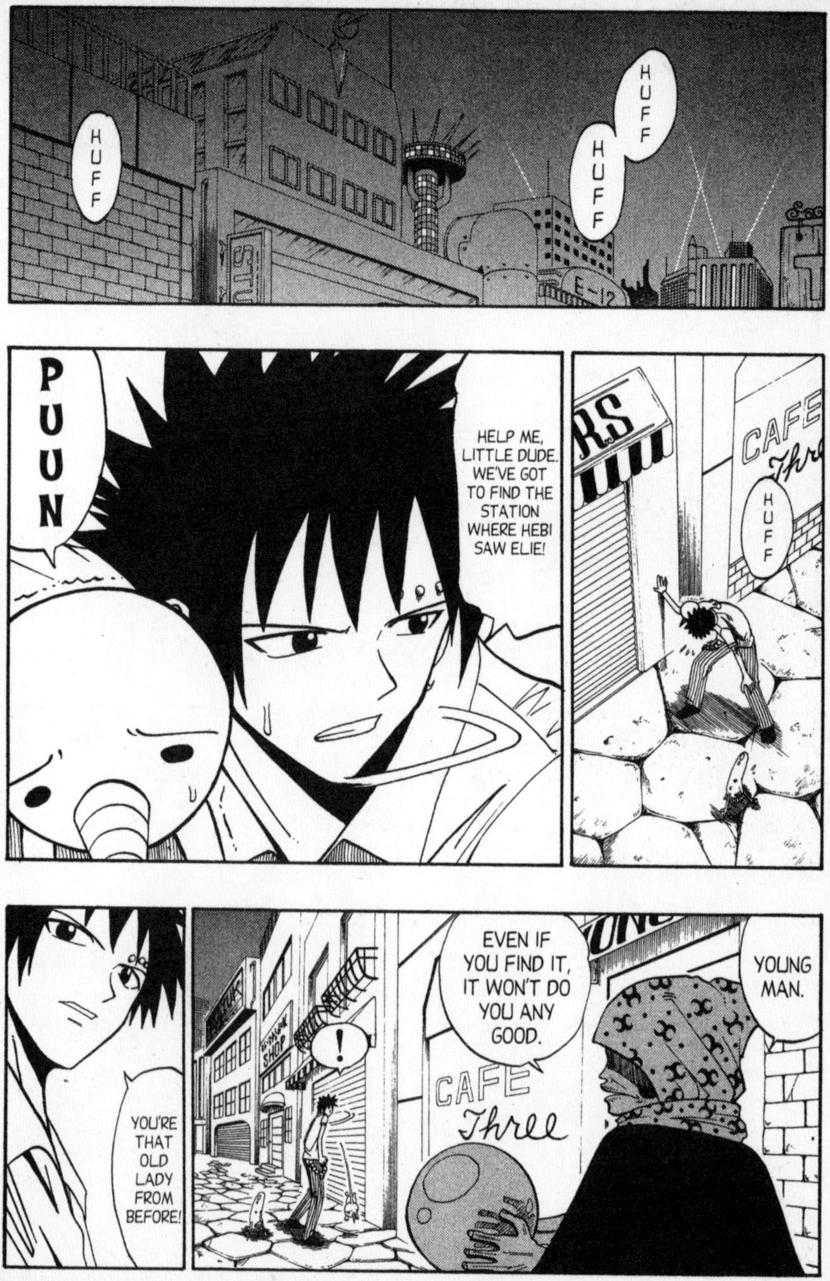
HUFF HUFF
HUFF HUFF
HUFF
HUFF HUFF
HELP ME, LITTLE DUDE. WE'VE GOT TO FIND THE STATION WHERE HEBI SAW ELIE!
PUUN
YOUNG MAN.
EVEN IF YOU FIND IT, IT WON'T DO YOU ANY GOOD.
!
CAFE Three
YOU'RE THAT OLD LADY FROM BEFORE!

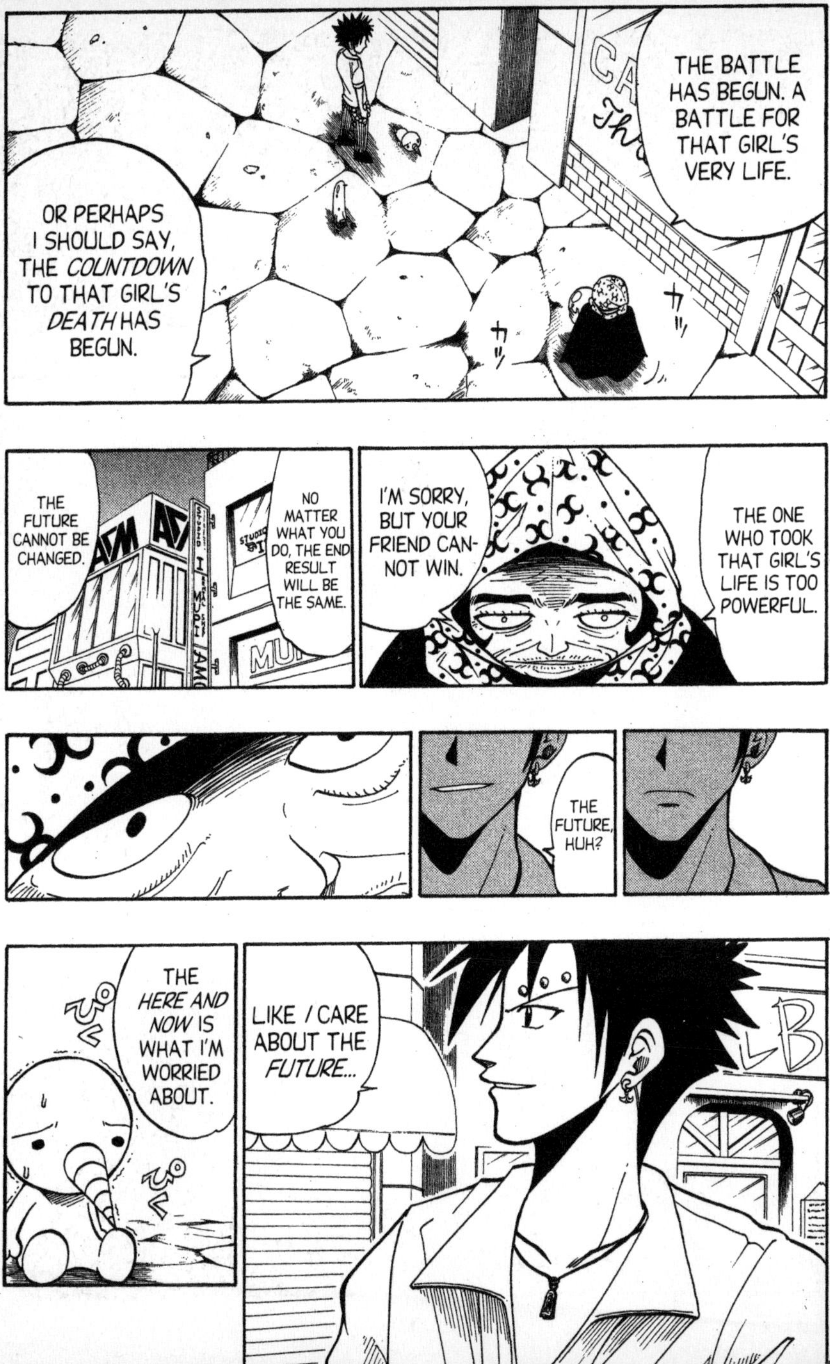
THE BATTLE HAS BEGUN. A BATTLE FOR THAT GIRL'S VERY LIFE.
OR PERHAPS I SHOULD SAY, THE *COUNTDOWN* TO THAT GIRL'S *DEATH* HAS BEGUN.
THE ONE WHO TOOK THAT GIRL'S LIFE IS TOO POWERFUL.
I'M SORRY, BUT YOUR FRIEND CAN-NOT WIN.
NO MATTER WHAT YOU DO, THE END RESULT WILL BE THE SAME.
THE FUTURE CANNOT BE CHANGED.
THE FUTURE, HUH?
LIKE *I* CARE ABOUT THE *FUTURE*...
THE *HERE AND NOW* IS WHAT I'M WORRIED ABOUT.

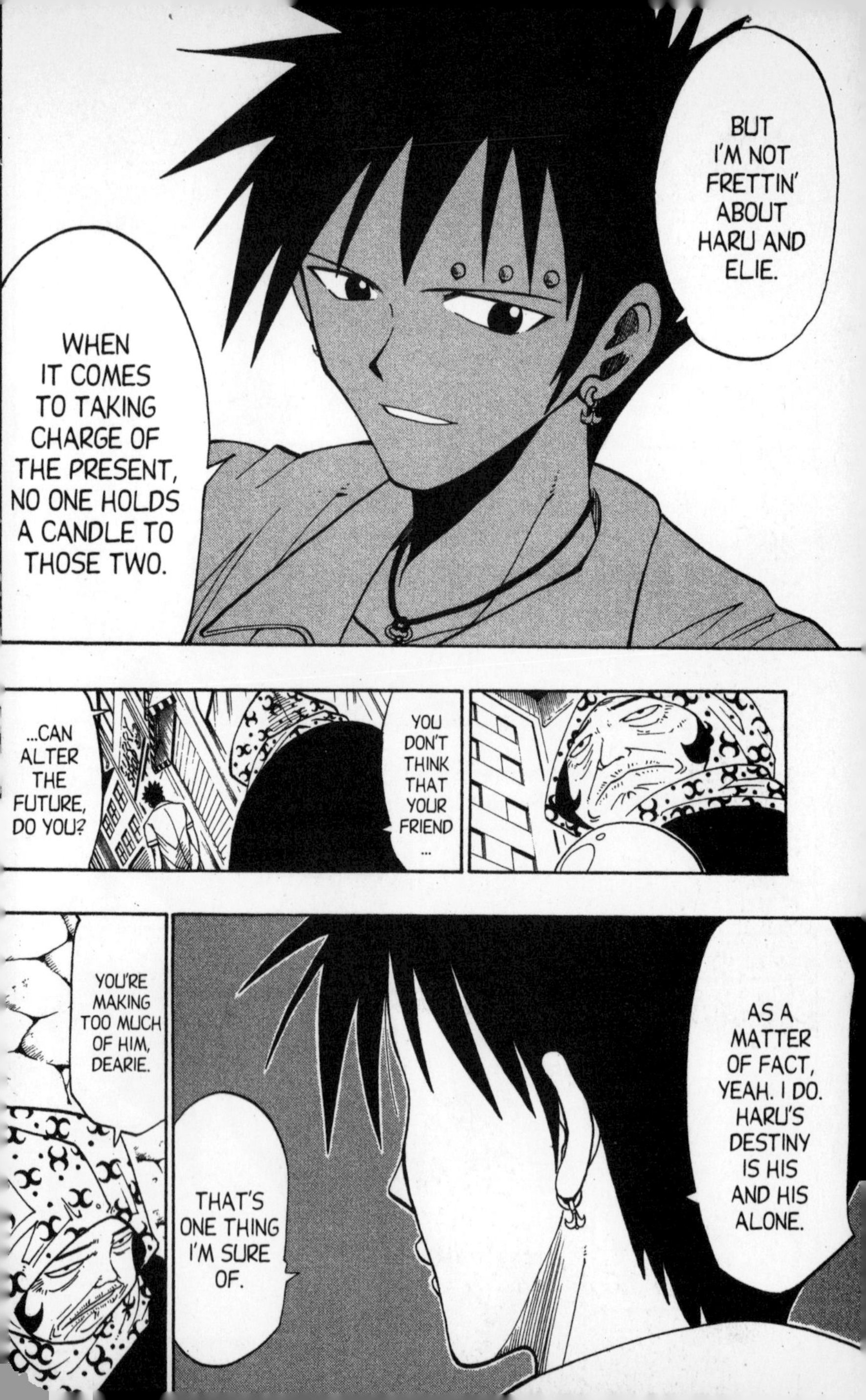
BUT I'M NOT FRETTIN' ABOUT HARU AND ELIE.
WHEN IT COMES TO TAKING CHARGE OF THE PRESENT, NO ONE HOLDS A CANDLE TO THOSE TWO.
YOU DON'T THINK THAT YOUR FRIEND ...
...CAN ALTER THE FUTURE, DO YOU?
AS A MATTER OF FACT, YEAH. I DO. HARU'S DESTINY IS HIS AND HIS ALONE.
THAT'S ONE THING I'M SURE OF.
YOU'RE MAKING TOO MUCH OF HIM, DEARIE.

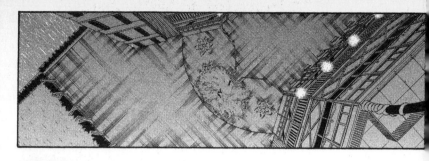

A MAN WHO CAN CHANGE THE FUTURE, HUH?

ELIE.

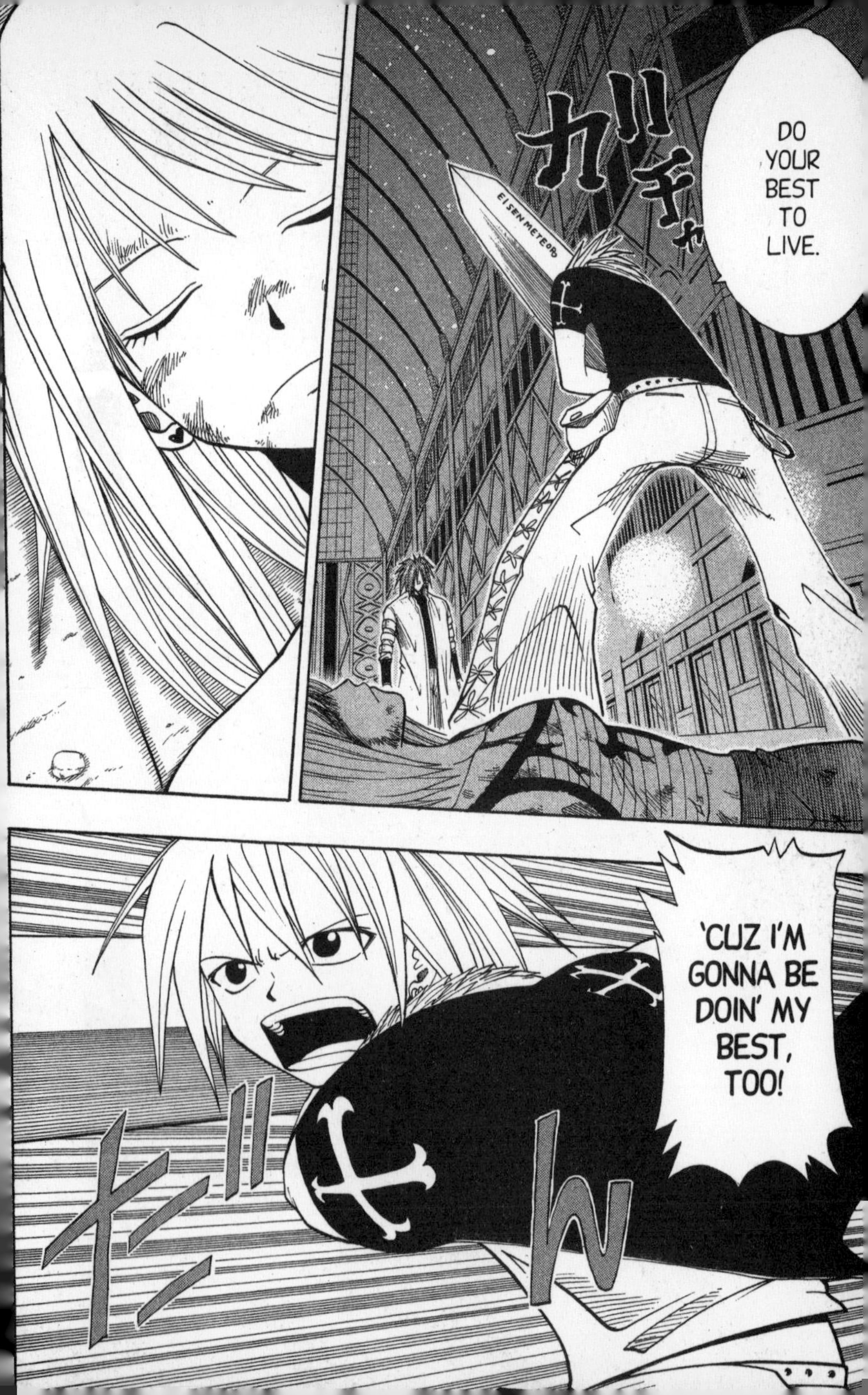
DO YOUR BEST TO LIVE.
EISENMETEOR
'CUZ I'M GONNA BE DOIN' MY BEST, TOO!

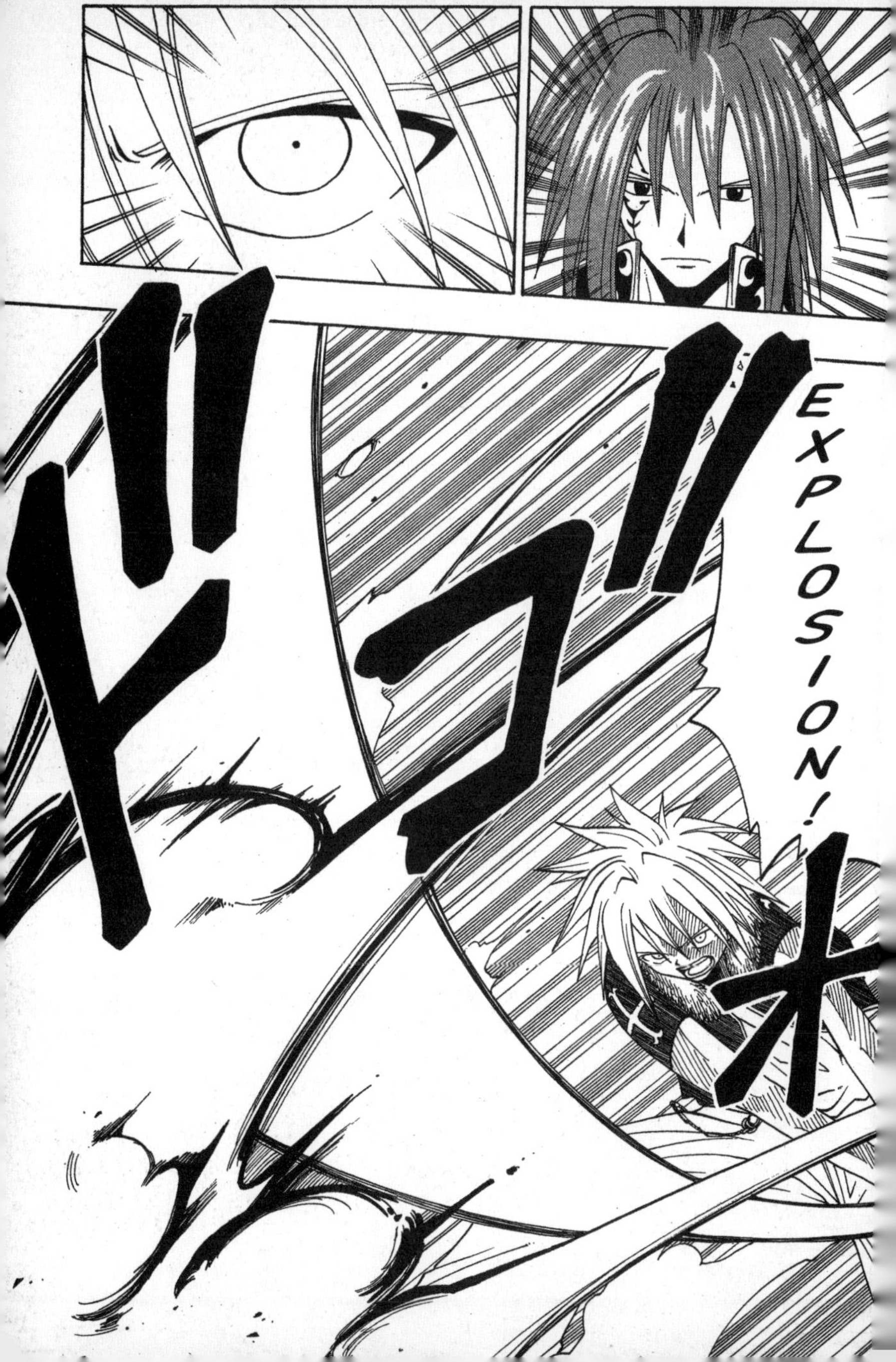
ドゴォ
EXPLOSION!

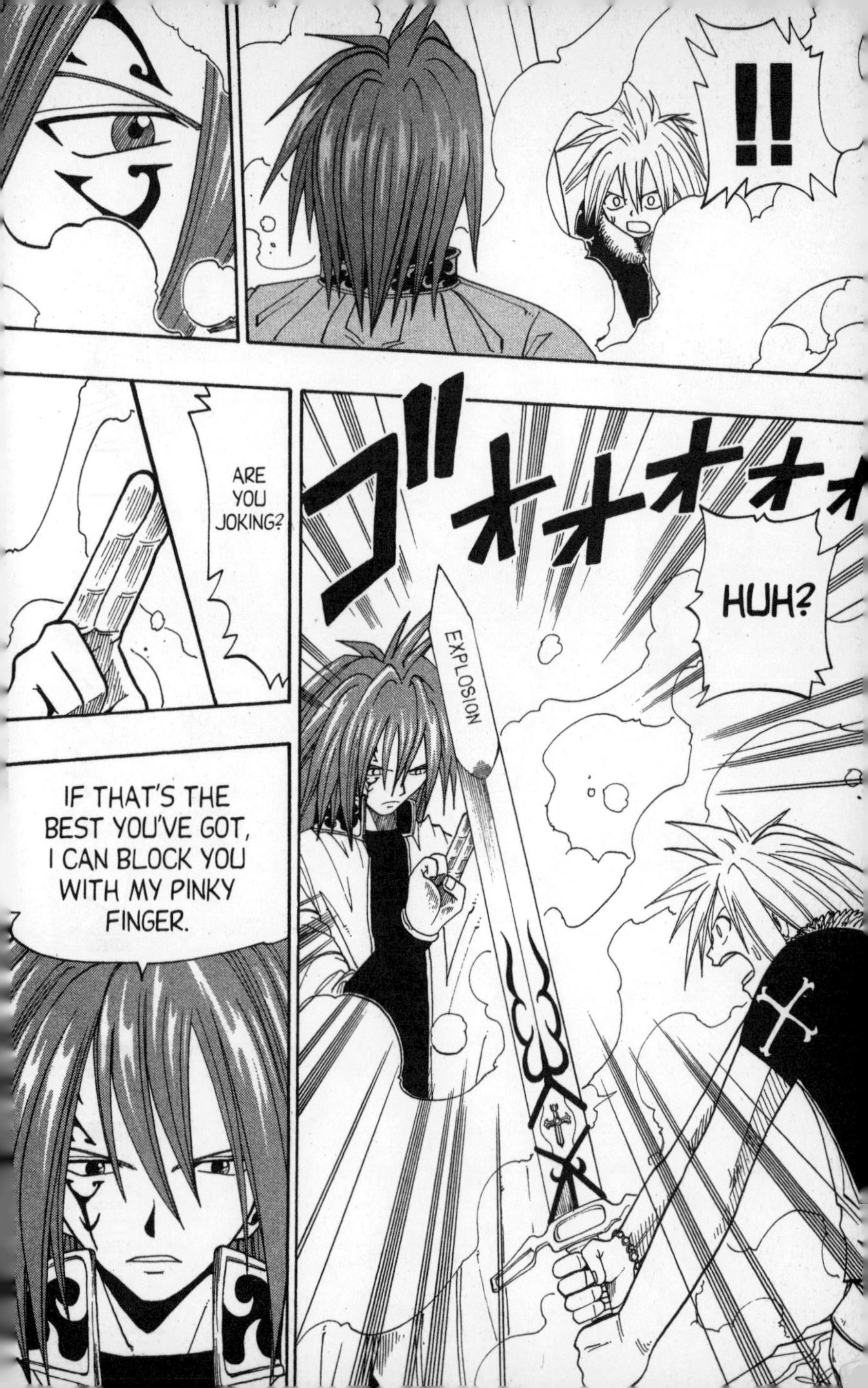
!!
ゴオオオオオ
HUH?
EXPLOSION
ARE YOU JOKING?
IF THAT'S THE BEST YOU'VE GOT, I CAN BLOCK YOU WITH MY PINKY FINGER.

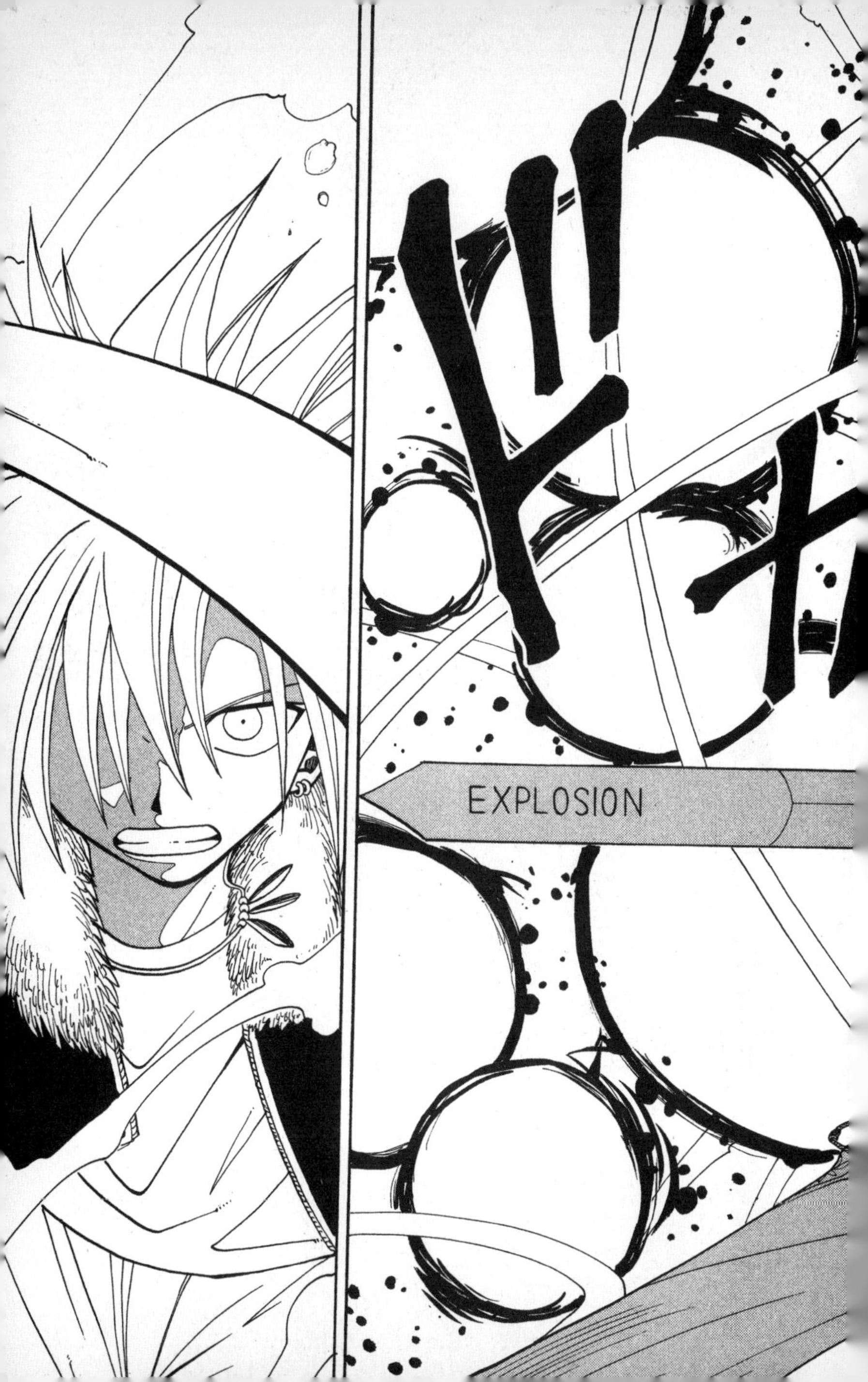
EXPLOSION

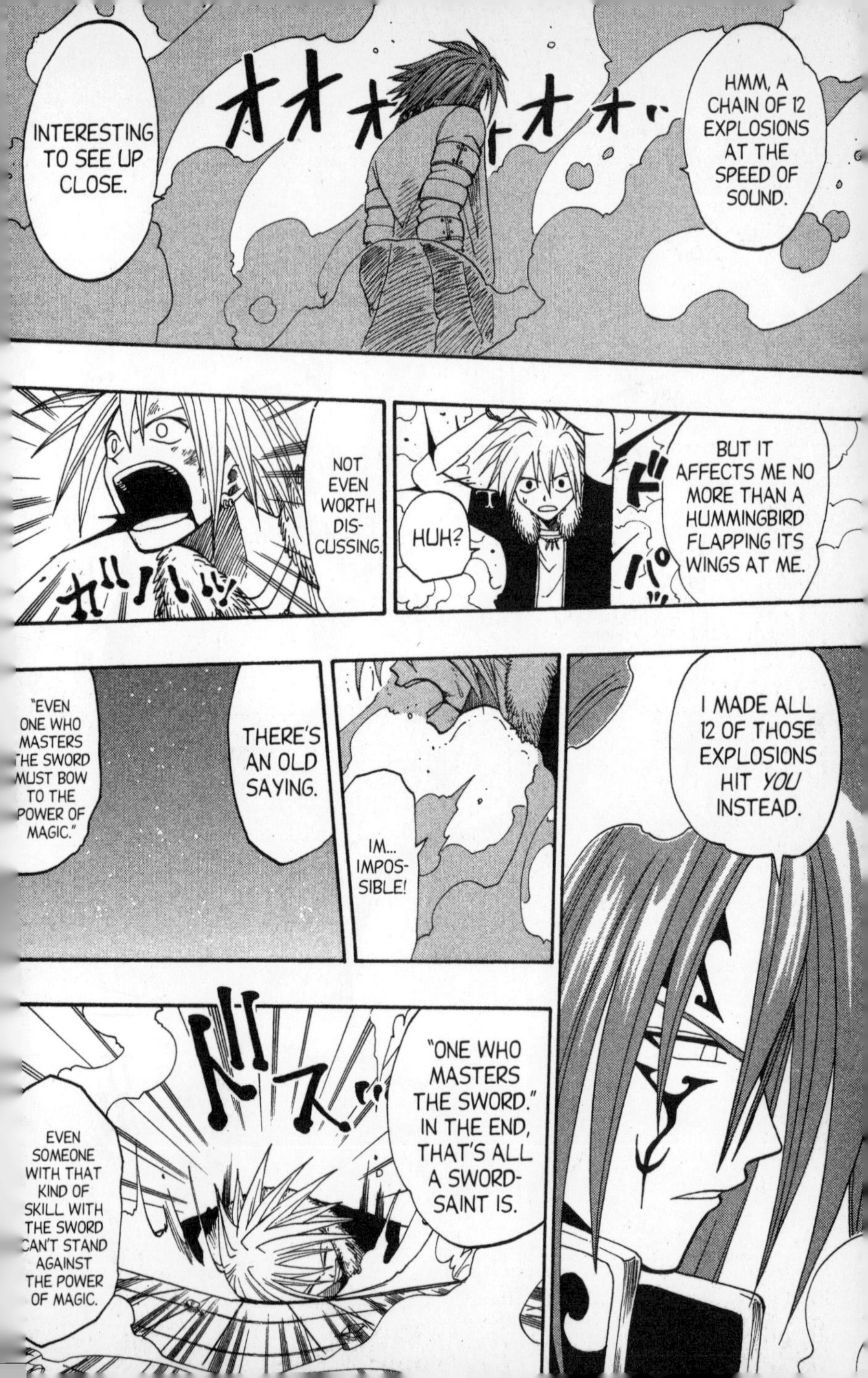
HMM, A CHAIN OF 12 EXPLOSIONS AT THE SPEED OF SOUND.
INTERESTING TO SEE UP CLOSE.
BUT IT AFFECTS ME NO MORE THAN A HUMMINGBIRD FLAPPING ITS WINGS AT ME.
HUH?
NOT EVEN WORTH DIS- CUSSING.
I MADE ALL 12 OF THOSE EXPLOSIONS HIT *YOU* INSTEAD.
IM... IMPOSSIBLE!
THERE'S AN OLD SAYING.
"EVEN ONE WHO MASTERS THE SWORD MUST BOW TO THE POWER OF MAGIC."
"ONE WHO MASTERS THE SWORD." IN THE END, THAT'S ALL A SWORD-SAINT IS.
EVEN SOMEONE WITH THAT KIND OF SKILL WITH THE SWORD CAN'T STAND AGAINST THE POWER OF MAGIC.

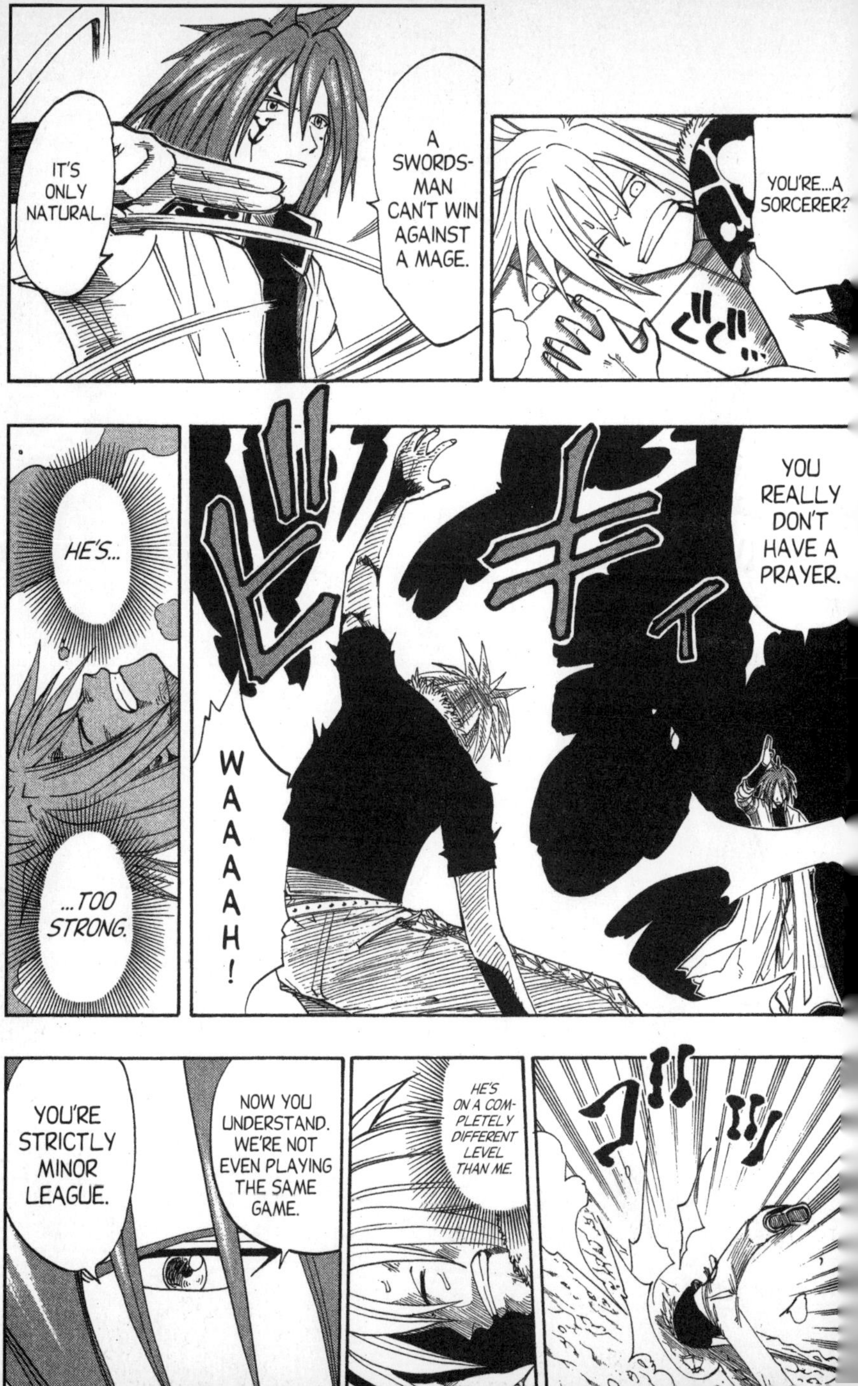
YOU'RE...A SORCERER?
ぐぐ...
A SWORDS-MAN CAN'T WIN AGAINST A MAGE.
IT'S ONLY NATURAL.
YOU REALLY DON'T HAVE A PRAYER.
ビキィ
WAAAAAAH!
HE'S...
...TOO STRONG.
HE'S ON A COM-PLETELY DIFFERENT LEVEL THAN ME.
NOW YOU UNDERSTAND. WE'RE NOT EVEN PLAYING THE SAME GAME.
YOU'RE STRICTLY MINOR LEAGUE.

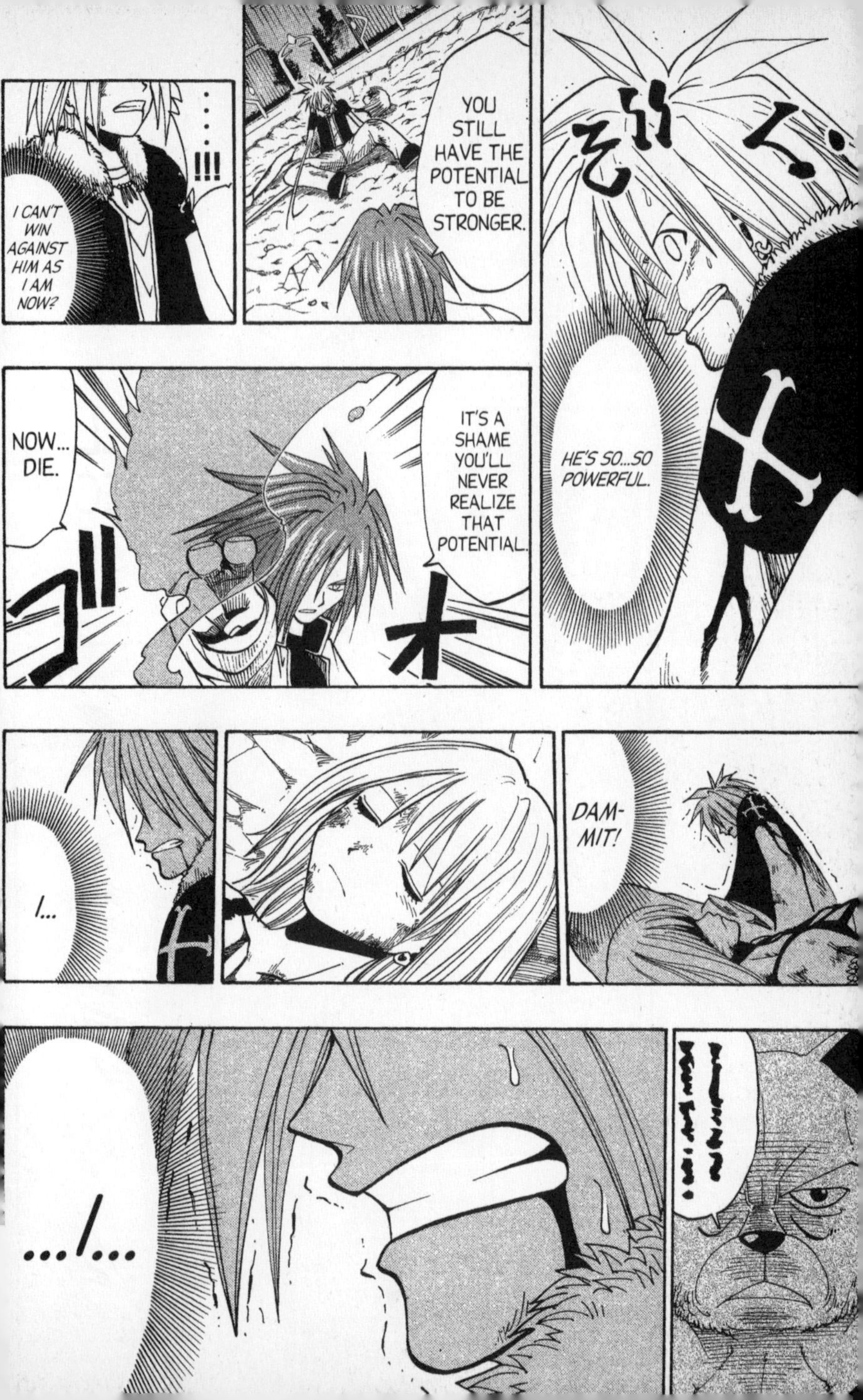
HE'S SO...SO POWERFUL.
YOU STILL HAVE THE POTENTIAL TO BE STRONGER.
......
!!!
I CAN'T WIN AGAINST HIM AS I AM NOW?
IT'S A SHAME YOU'LL NEVER REALIZE THAT POTENTIAL.
NOW... DIE.
DAM-MIT!
I...
...I...

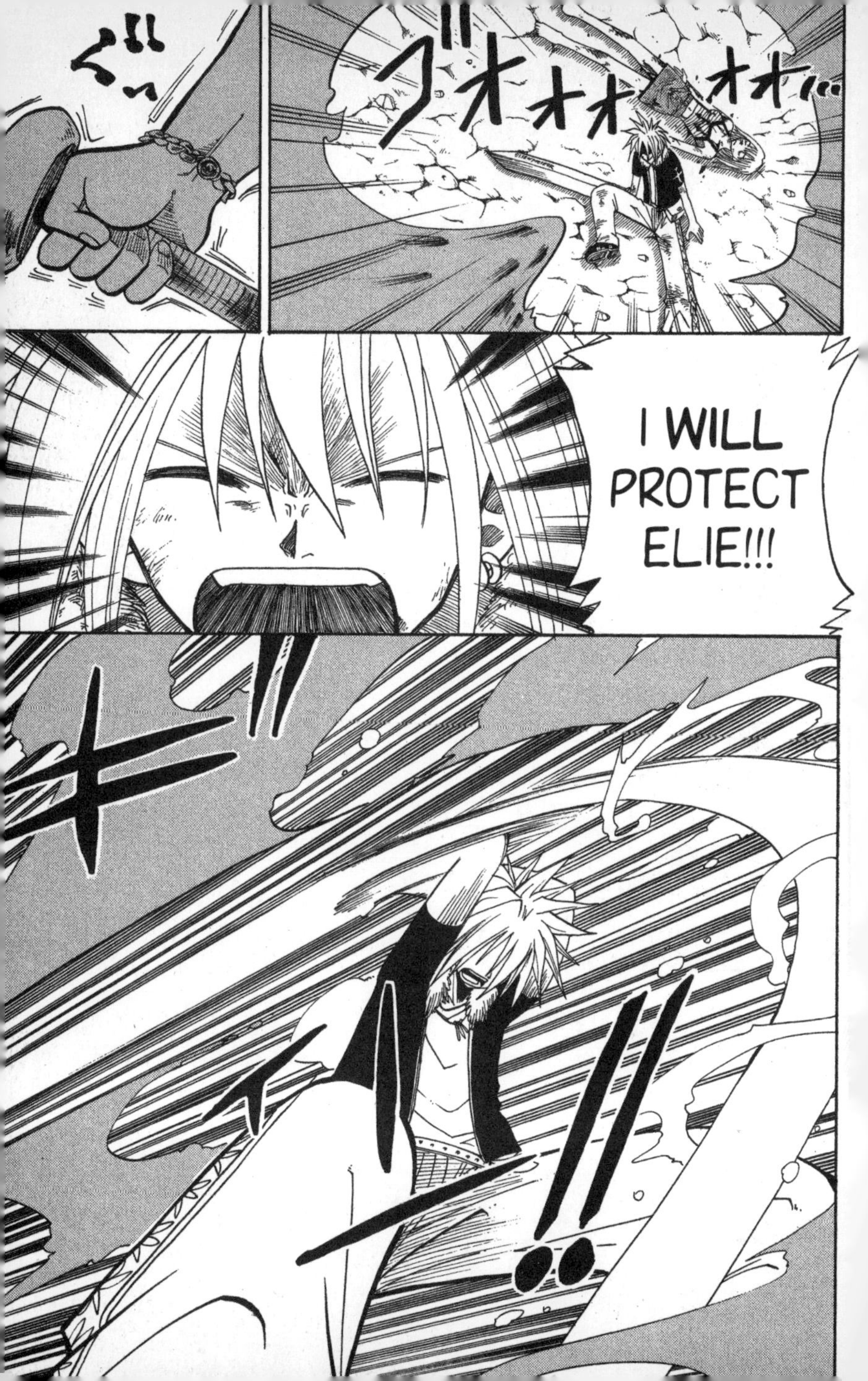
I WILL PROTECT ELIE!!!

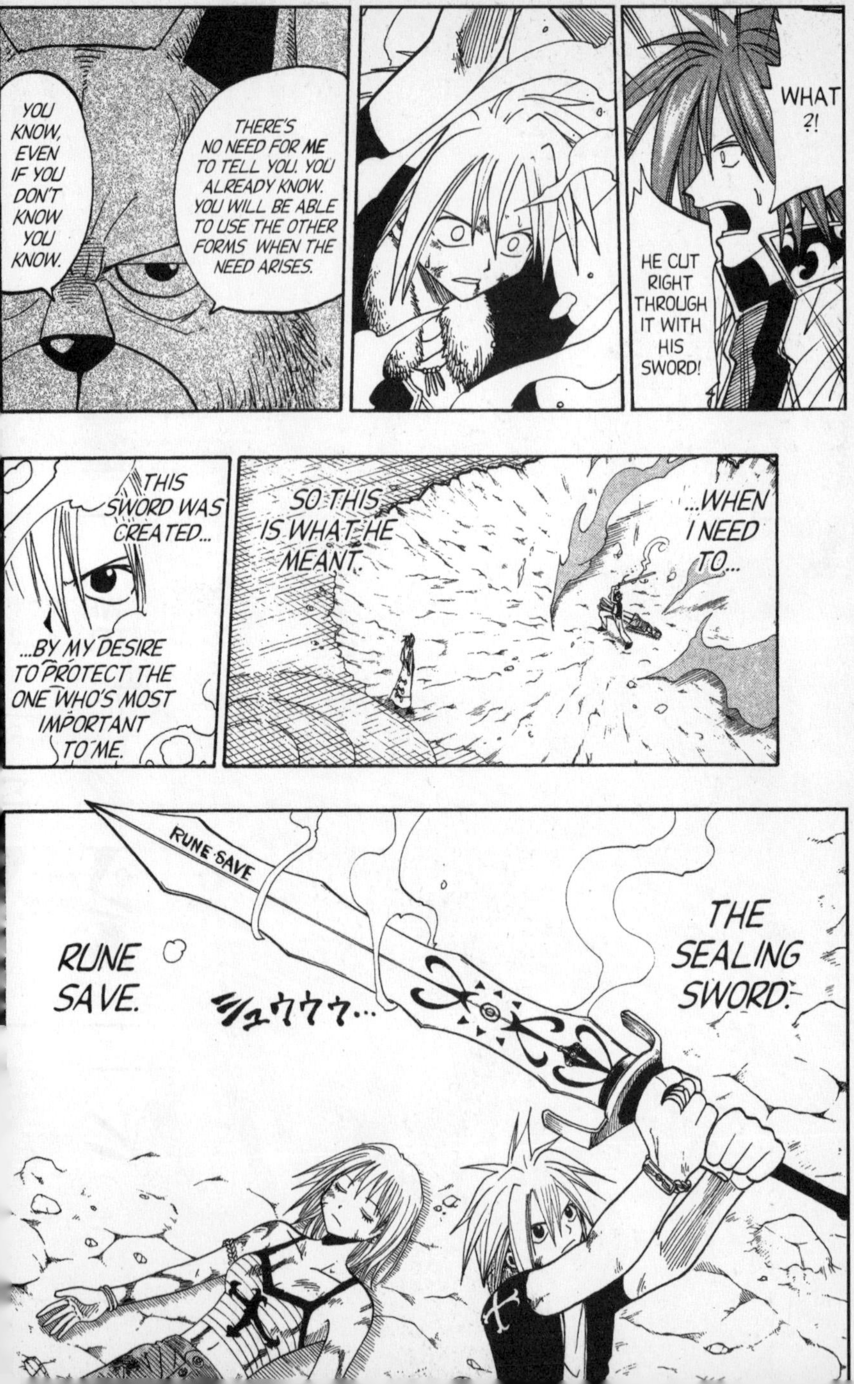
WHAT?!
HE CUT RIGHT THROUGH IT WITH HIS SWORD!
THERE'S NO NEED FOR ME TO TELL YOU. YOU ALREADY KNOW. YOU WILL BE ABLE TO USE THE OTHER FORMS WHEN THE NEED ARISES.
YOU KNOW, EVEN IF YOU DON'T KNOW YOU KNOW.
...WHEN I NEED TO...
SO THIS IS WHAT HE MEANT.
THIS SWORD WAS CREATED...
...BY MY DESIRE TO PROTECT THE ONE WHO'S MOST IMPORTANT TO ME.
THE SEALING SWORD.
RUNE SAVE
シュウウウ…
RUNE SAVE.

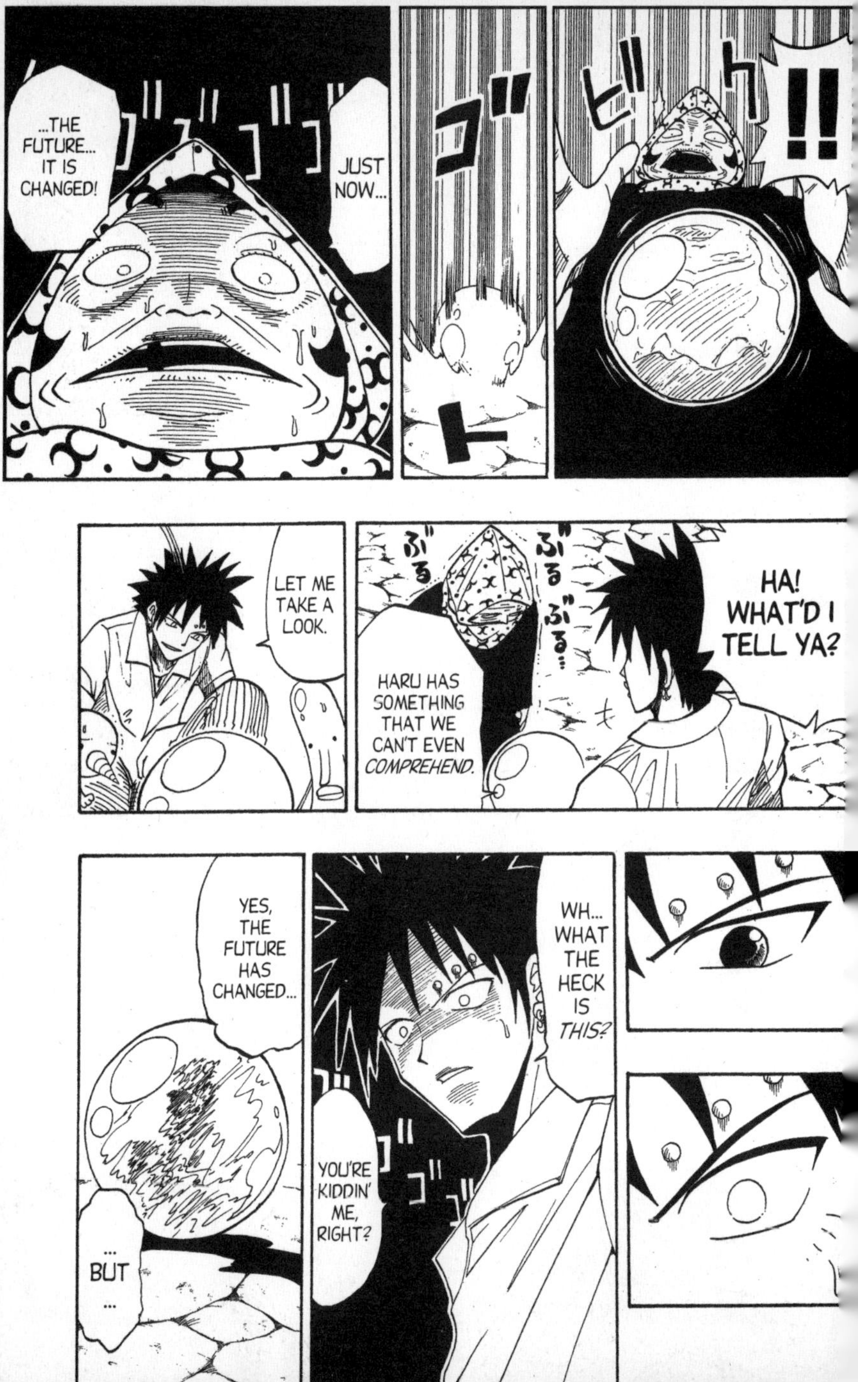
ビン!!
ゴト
ゴゴゴゴ
JUST NOW...
...THE FUTURE... IT IS CHANGED!
HA! WHAT'D I TELL YA?
ぶるぶるぶる...
HARU HAS SOMETHING THAT WE CAN'T EVEN *COMPREHEND.*
LET ME TAKE A LOOK.
WH... WHAT THE HECK IS *THIS?*
YOU'RE KIDDIN' ME, RIGHT?
YES, THE FUTURE HAS CHANGED...
... BUT ...

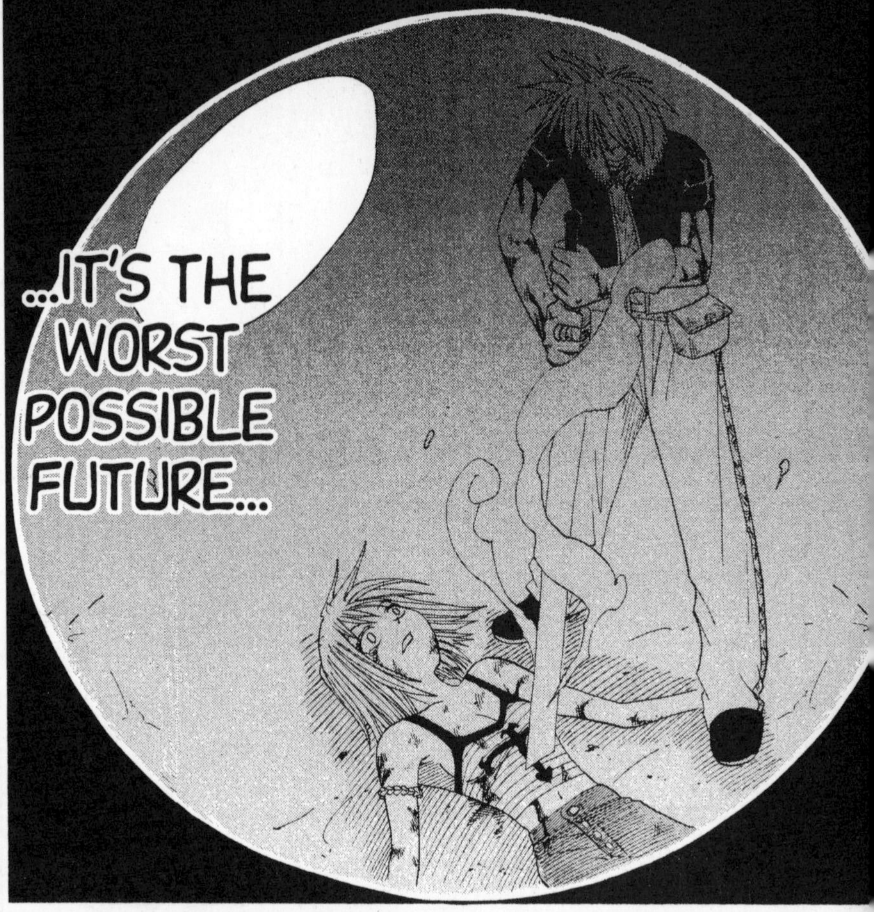
...IT'S THE WORST POSSIBLE FUTURE...

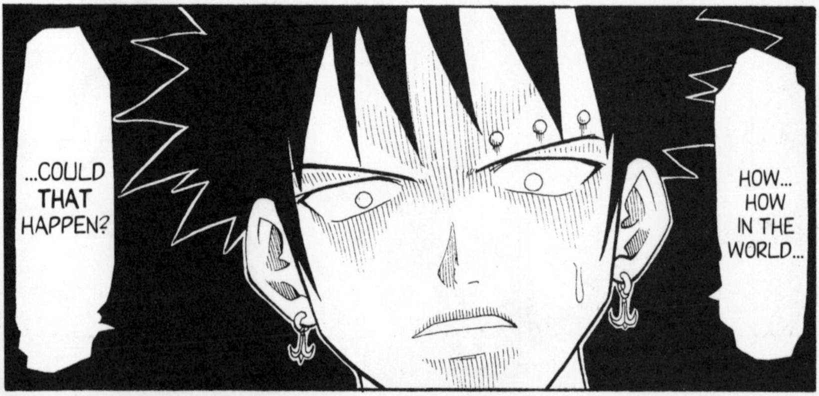
HOW... HOW IN THE WORLD...
...COULD THAT HAPPEN?

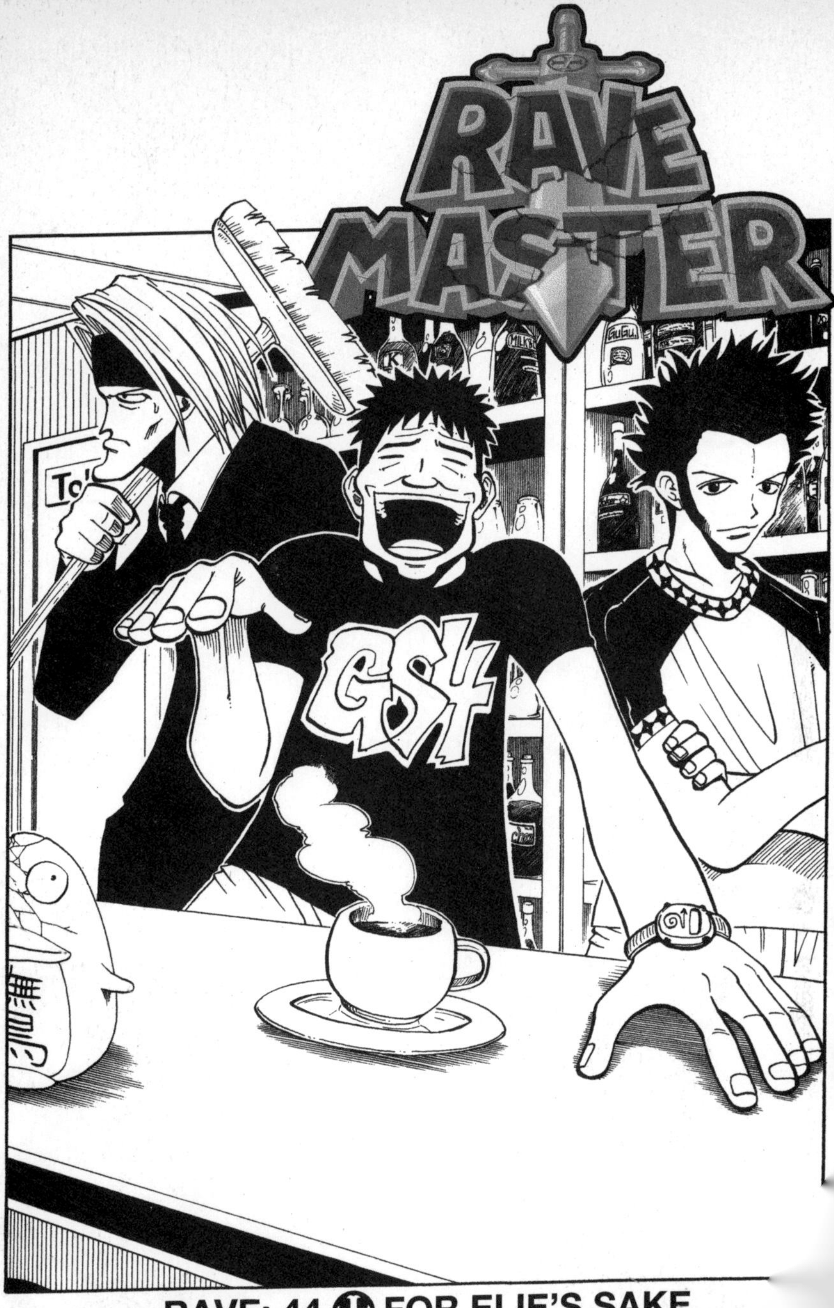
RAVE MASTER

RAVE: 44 ✠ FOR ELIE'S SAKE

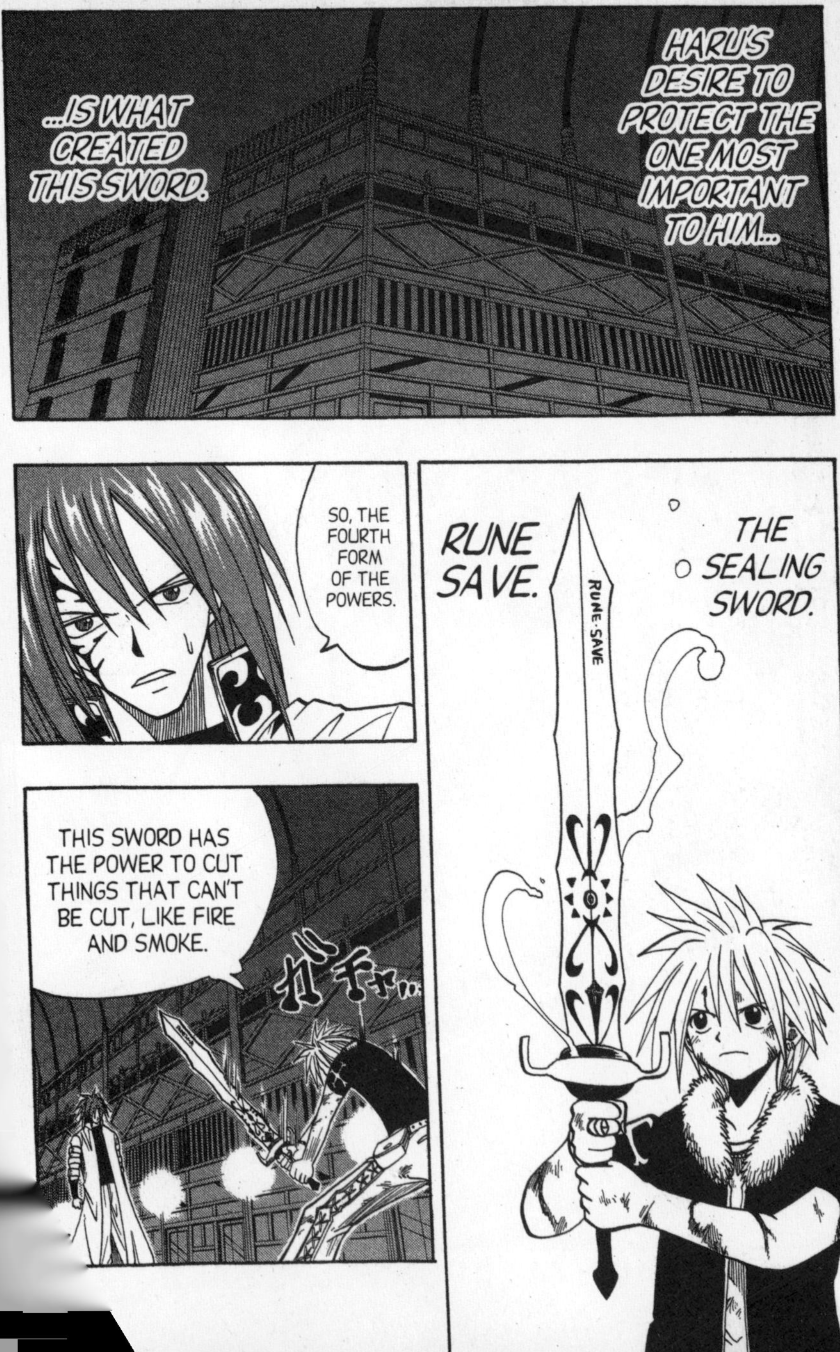
HARU'S DESIRE TO PROTECT THE ONE MOST IMPORTANT TO HIM...
...IS WHAT CREATED THIS SWORD.
THE SEALING SWORD.
RUNE SAVE.
RUNE·SAVE
SO, THE FOURTH FORM OF THE POWERS.
THIS SWORD HAS THE POWER TO CUT THINGS THAT CAN'T BE CUT, LIKE FIRE AND SMOKE.
ガチャ…

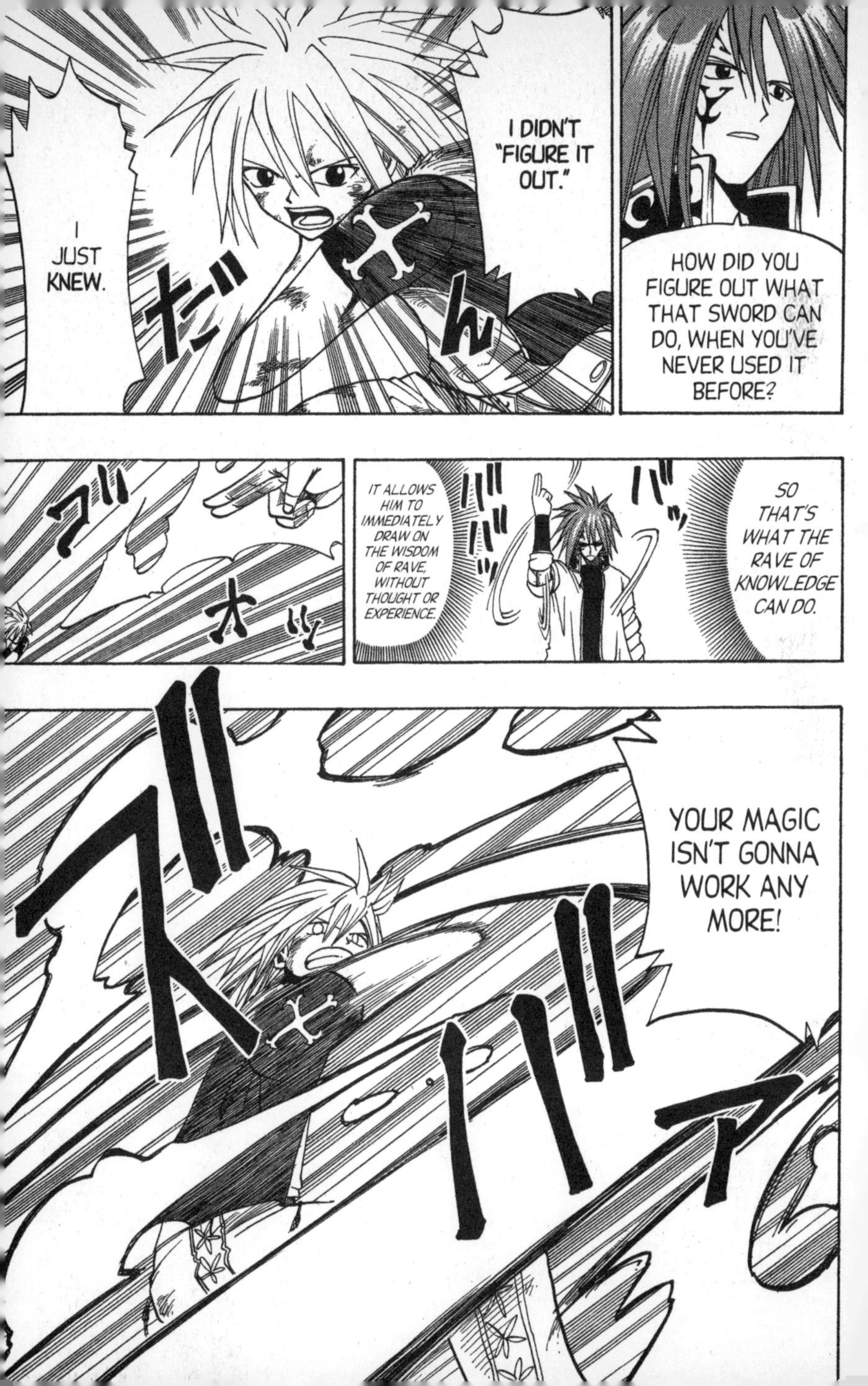
HOW DID YOU FIGURE OUT WHAT THAT SWORD CAN DO, WHEN YOU'VE NEVER USED IT BEFORE?
I DIDN'T "FIGURE IT OUT."
I JUST KNEW.
SO THAT'S WHAT THE RAVE OF KNOWLEDGE CAN DO.
IT ALLOWS HIM TO IMMEDIATELY DRAW ON THE WISDOM OF RAVE, WITHOUT THOUGHT OR EXPERIENCE.
YOUR MAGIC ISN'T GONNA WORK ANY MORE!

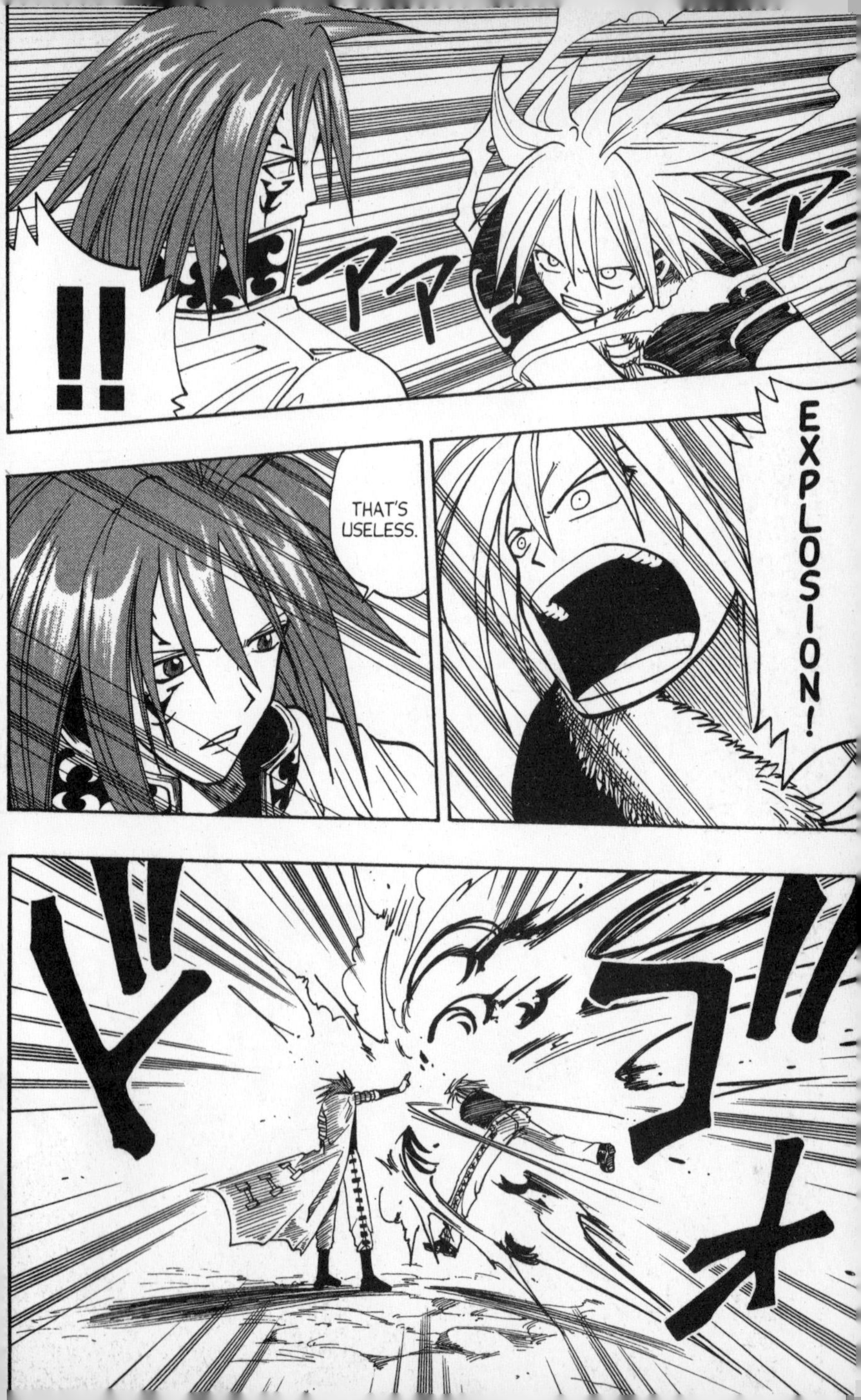
アア
アー
!!
EXPLOSION!
THAT'S USELESS.
ドゴオ

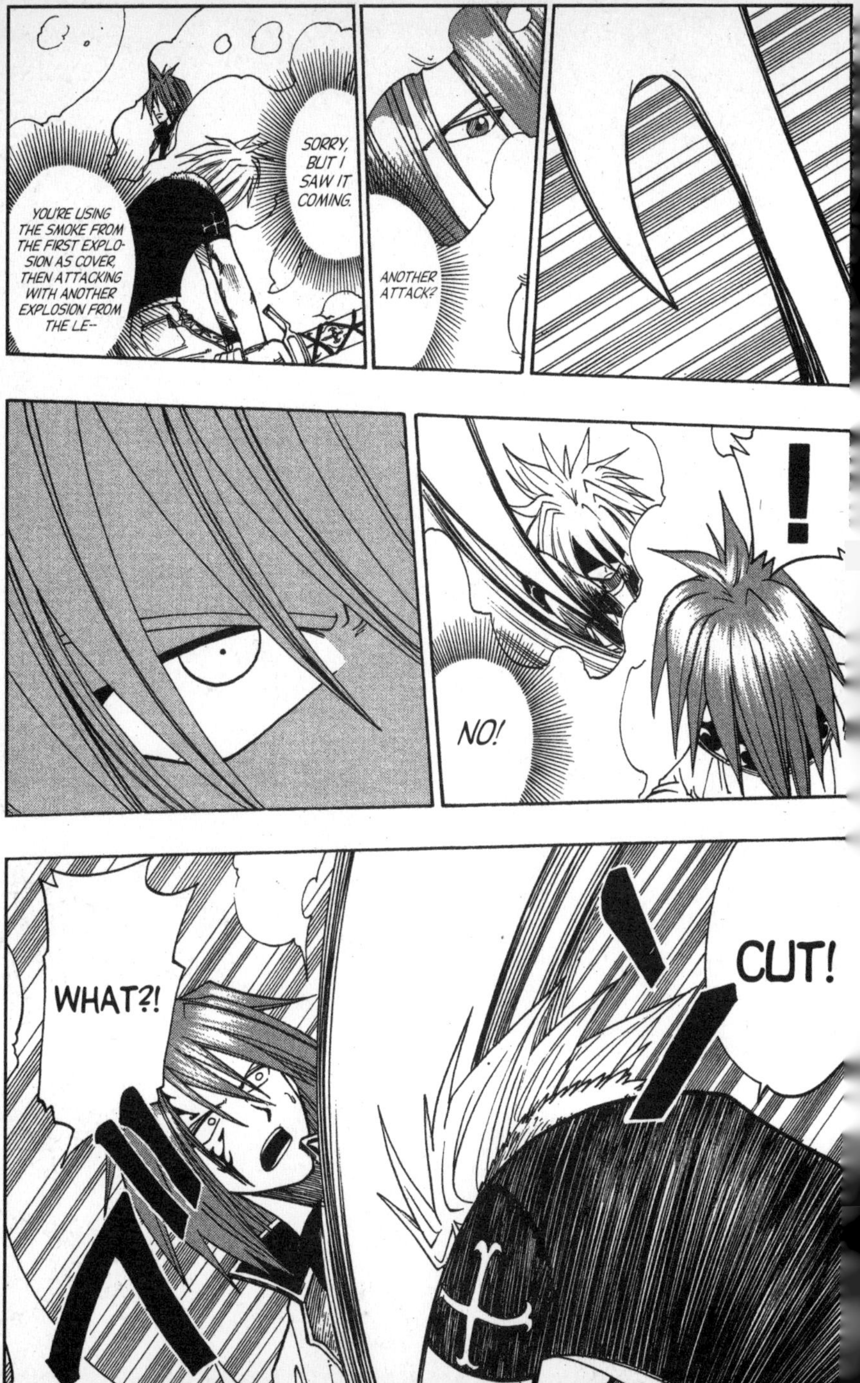
ANOTHER ATTACK?
SORRY, BUT I SAW IT COMING.
YOU'RE USING THE SMOKE FROM THE FIRST EXPLOSION AS COVER, THEN ATTACKING WITH ANOTHER EXPLOSION FROM THE LE--
!
NO!
CUT!
WHAT?!

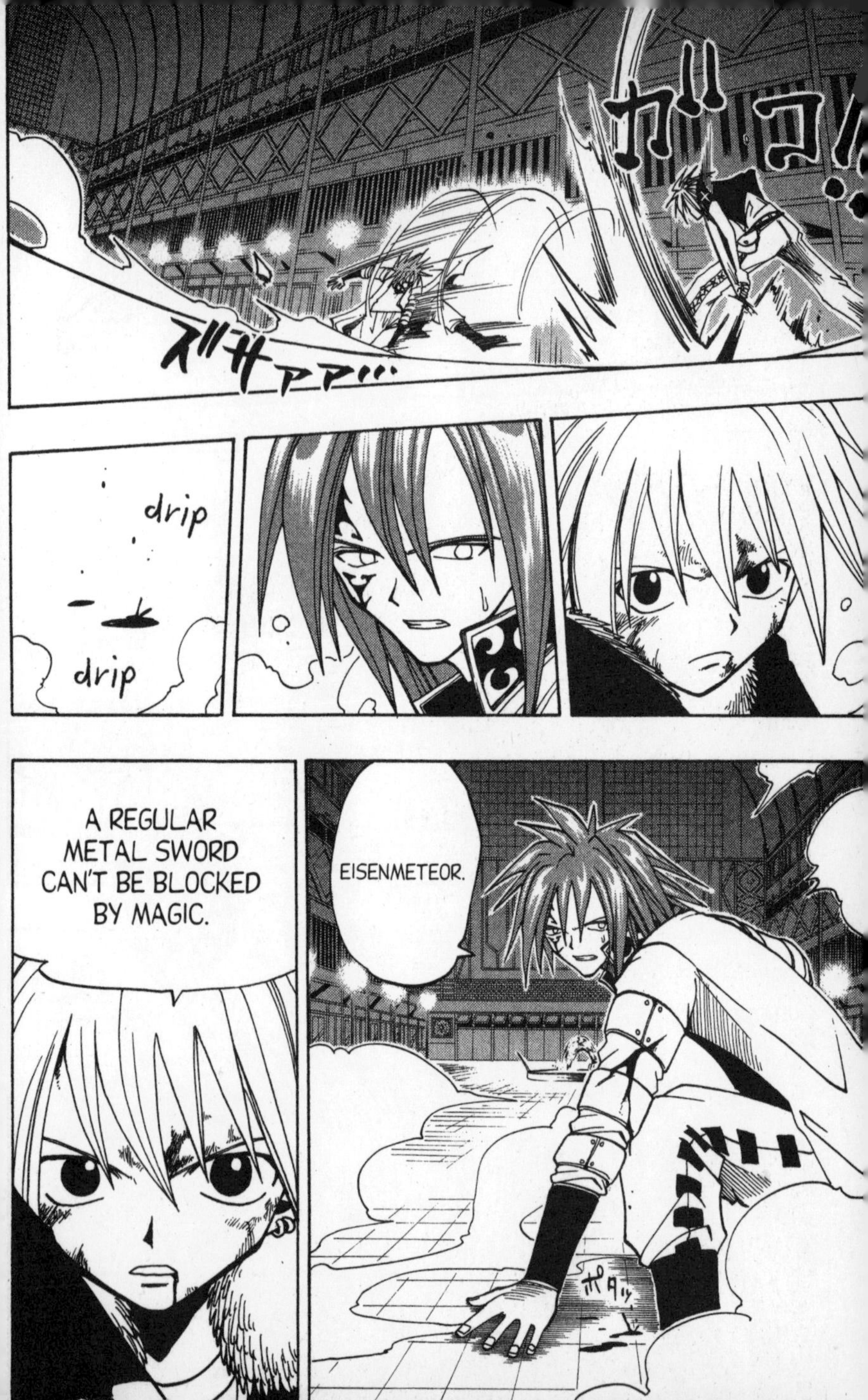
ズザァァ…
drip
drip
EISENMETEOR.
ポタッ
A REGULAR METAL SWORD CAN'T BE BLOCKED BY MAGIC.

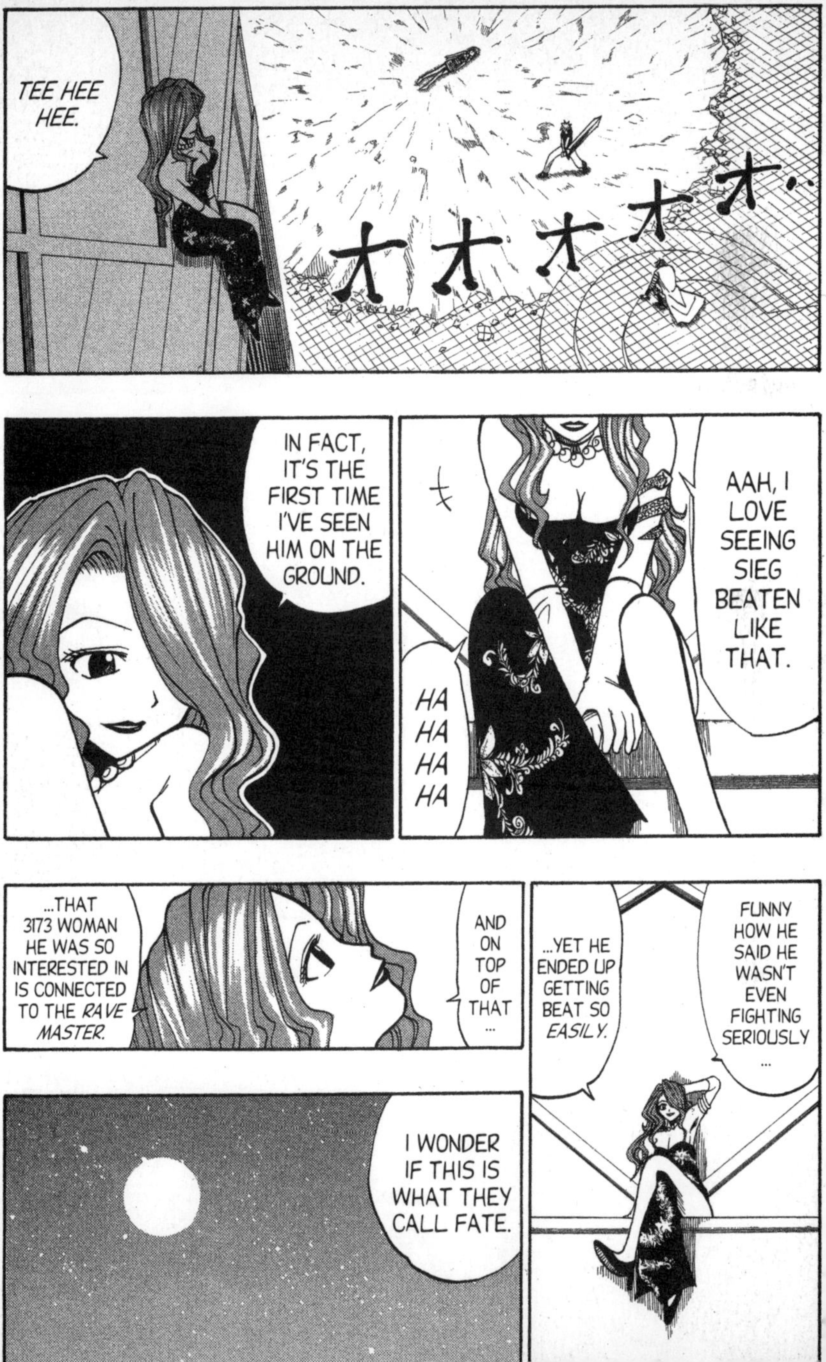
オオオオオ…
TEE HEE HEE.
AAH, I LOVE SEEING SIEG BEATEN LIKE THAT.
HA HA HA HA
IN FACT, IT'S THE FIRST TIME I'VE SEEN HIM ON THE GROUND.
FUNNY HOW HE SAID HE WASN'T EVEN FIGHTING SERIOUSLY ...
...YET HE ENDED UP GETTING BEAT SO *EASILY.*
AND ON TOP OF THAT ...
...THAT 3173 WOMAN HE WAS SO INTERESTED IN IS CONNECTED TO THE *RAVE MASTER.*
I WONDER IF THIS IS WHAT THEY CALL FATE.

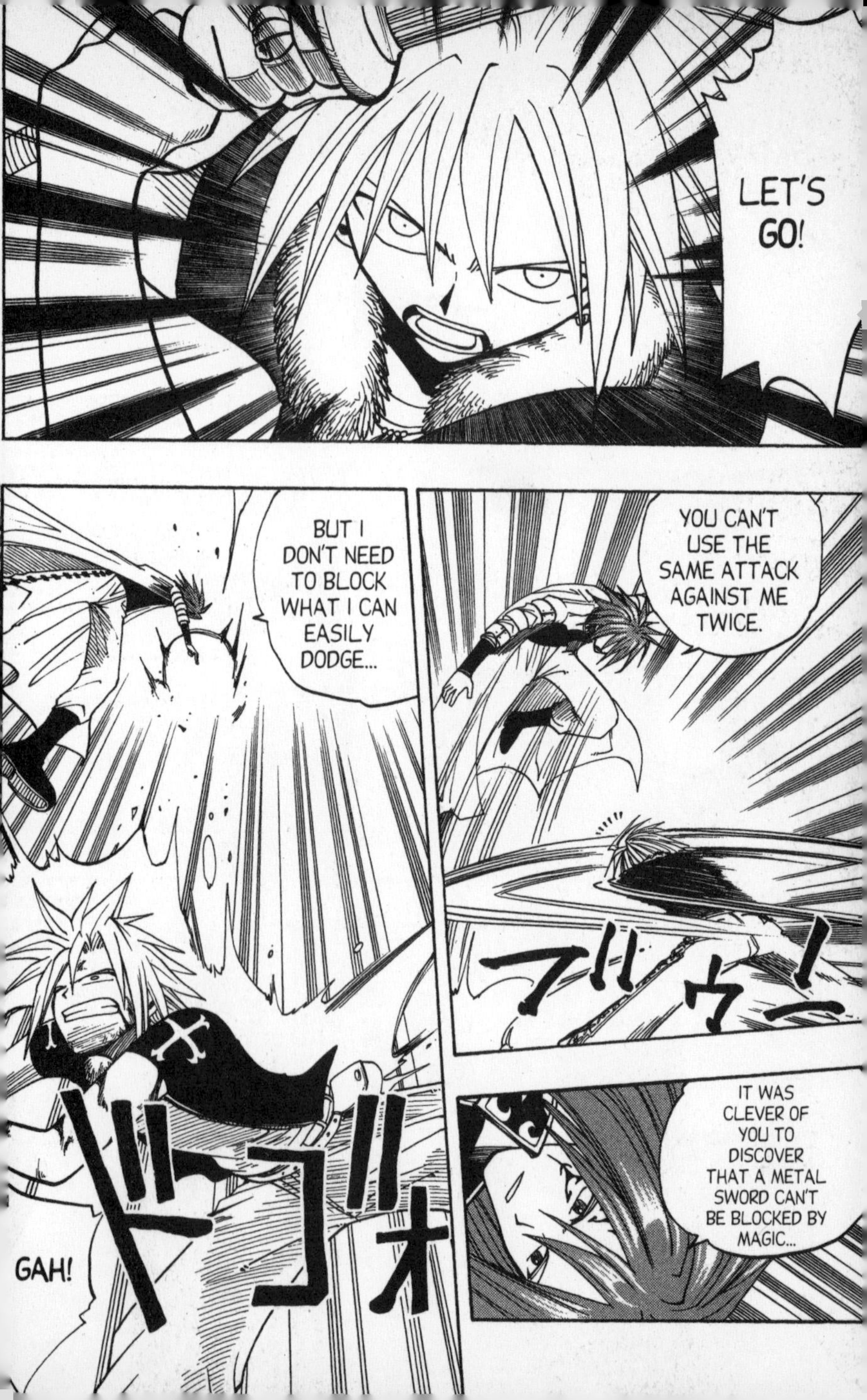
LET'S GO!
YOU CAN'T USE THE SAME ATTACK AGAINST ME TWICE.
フルゥ〜
IT WAS CLEVER OF YOU TO DISCOVER THAT A METAL SWORD CAN'T BE BLOCKED BY MAGIC...
BUT I DON'T NEED TO BLOCK WHAT I CAN EASILY DODGE...
ドゴォ
GAH!

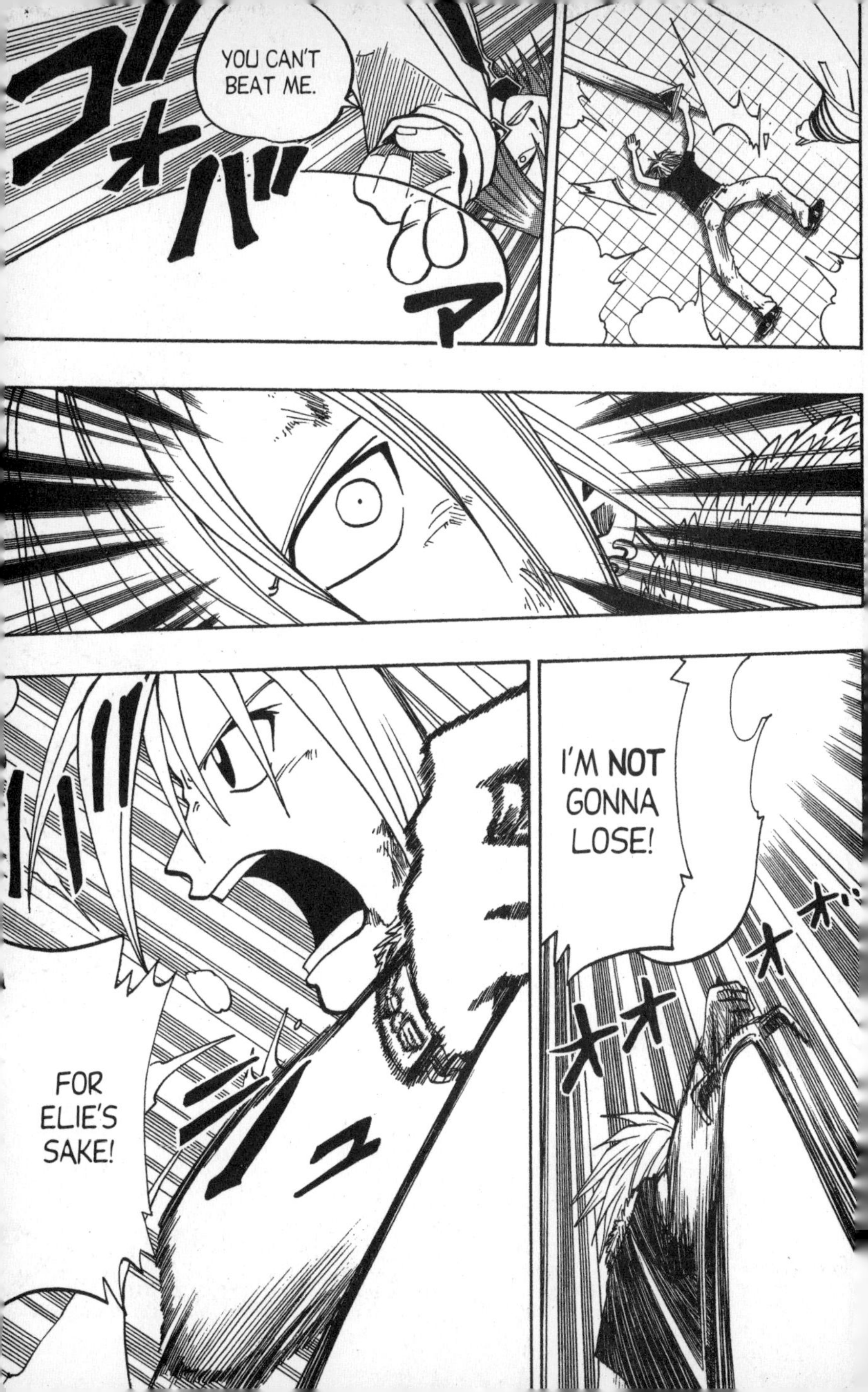
YOU CAN'T BEAT ME.
I'M NOT GONNA LOSE!
FOR ELIE'S SAKE!

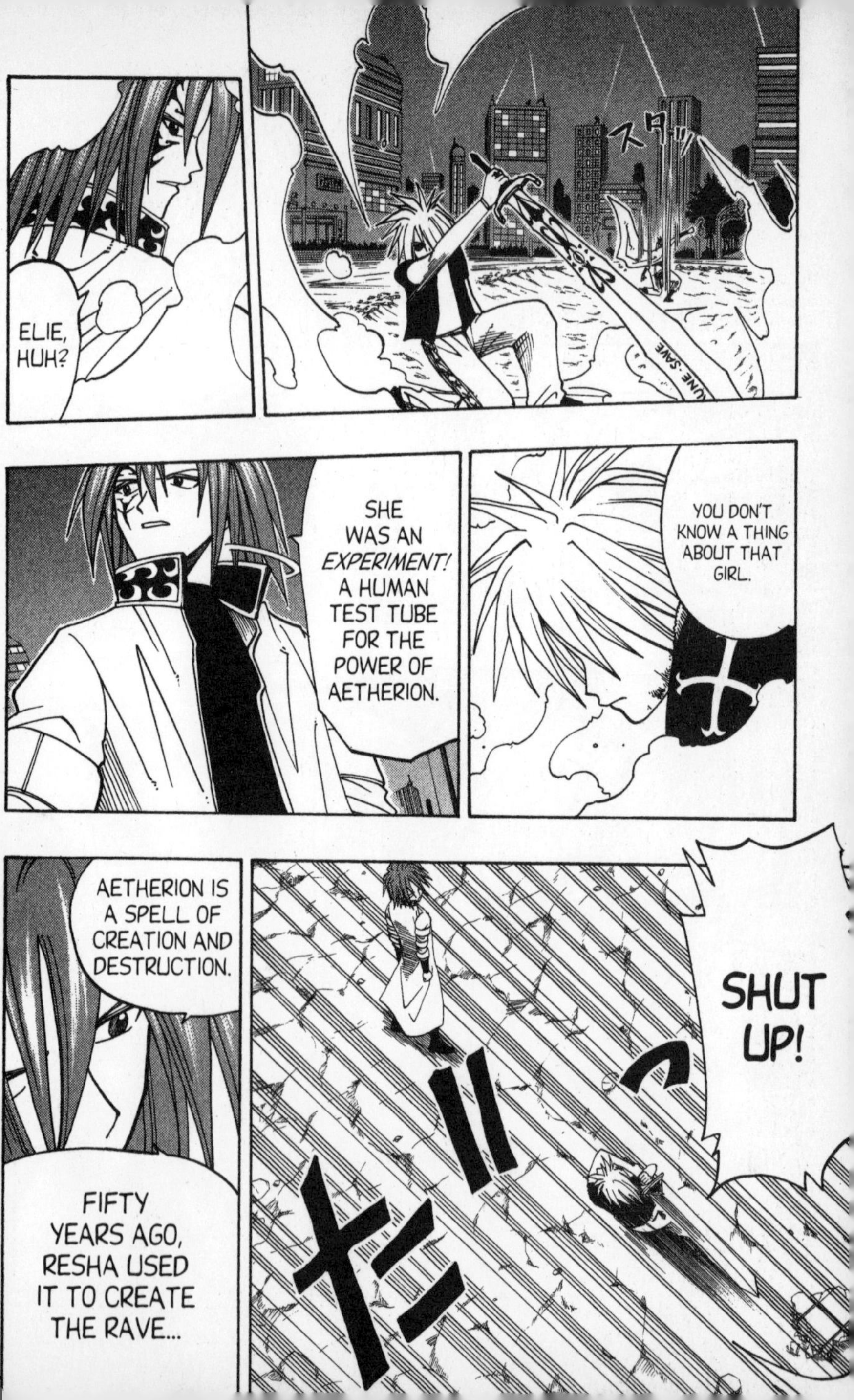
ELIE, HUH?
YOU DON'T KNOW A THING ABOUT THAT GIRL.
SHE WAS AN *EXPERIMENT!* A HUMAN TEST TUBE FOR THE POWER OF AETHERION.
SHUT UP!
AETHERION IS A SPELL OF CREATION AND DESTRUCTION.
FIFTY YEARS AGO, RESHA USED IT TO CREATE THE RAVE...

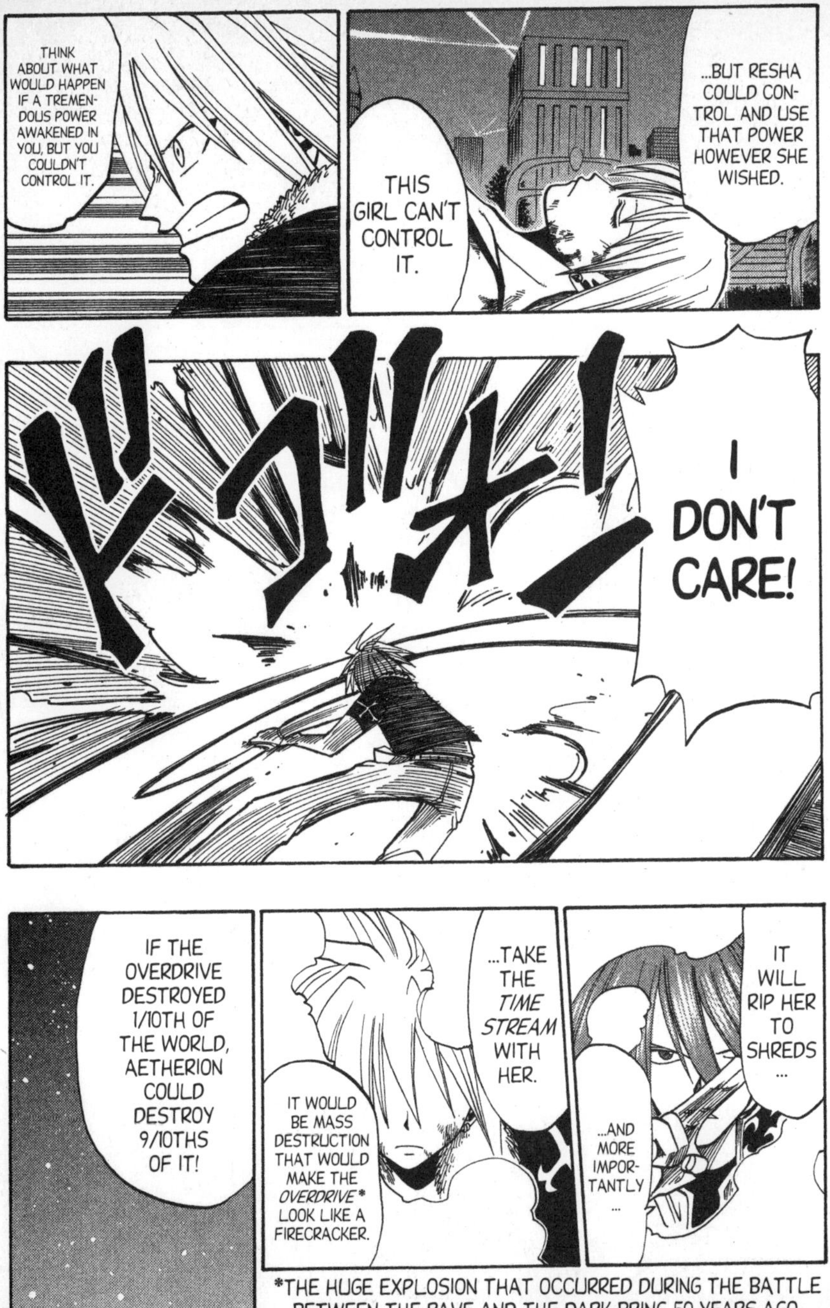
...BUT RESHA COULD CONTROL AND USE THAT POWER HOWEVER SHE WISHED.
THIS GIRL CAN'T CONTROL IT.
THINK ABOUT WHAT WOULD HAPPEN IF A TREMENDOUS POWER AWAKENED IN YOU, BUT YOU COULDN'T CONTROL IT.
I DON'T CARE!
IT WILL RIP HER TO SHREDS...
...AND MORE IMPORTANTLY...
...TAKE THE *TIME STREAM* WITH HER.
IT WOULD BE MASS DESTRUCTION THAT WOULD MAKE THE *OVERDRIVE** LOOK LIKE A FIRECRACKER.
IF THE OVERDRIVE DESTROYED 1/10TH OF THE WORLD, AETHERION COULD DESTROY 9/10THS OF IT!

*THE HUGE EXPLOSION THAT OCCURRED DURING THE BATTLE BETWEEN THE RAVE AND THE DARK BRING 50 YEARS AGO.

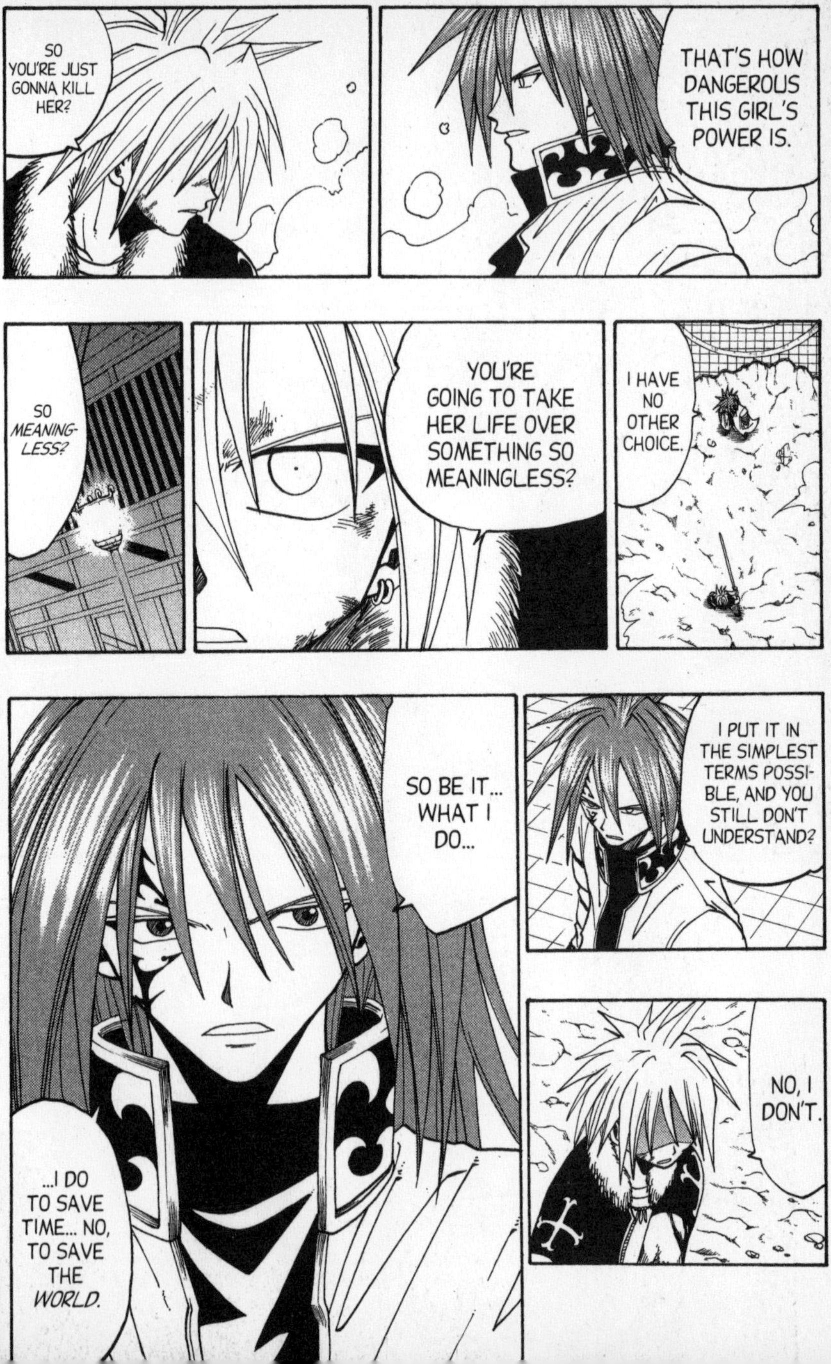
THAT'S HOW DANGEROUS THIS GIRL'S POWER IS.
SO YOU'RE JUST GONNA KILL HER?
I HAVE NO OTHER CHOICE.
YOU'RE GOING TO TAKE HER LIFE OVER SOMETHING SO MEANINGLESS?
SO *MEANING-LESS?*
I PUT IT IN THE SIMPLEST TERMS POSSI-BLE, AND YOU STILL DON'T UNDERSTAND?
NO, I DON'T.
SO BE IT... WHAT I DO...
...I DO TO SAVE TIME... NO, TO SAVE THE *WORLD.*

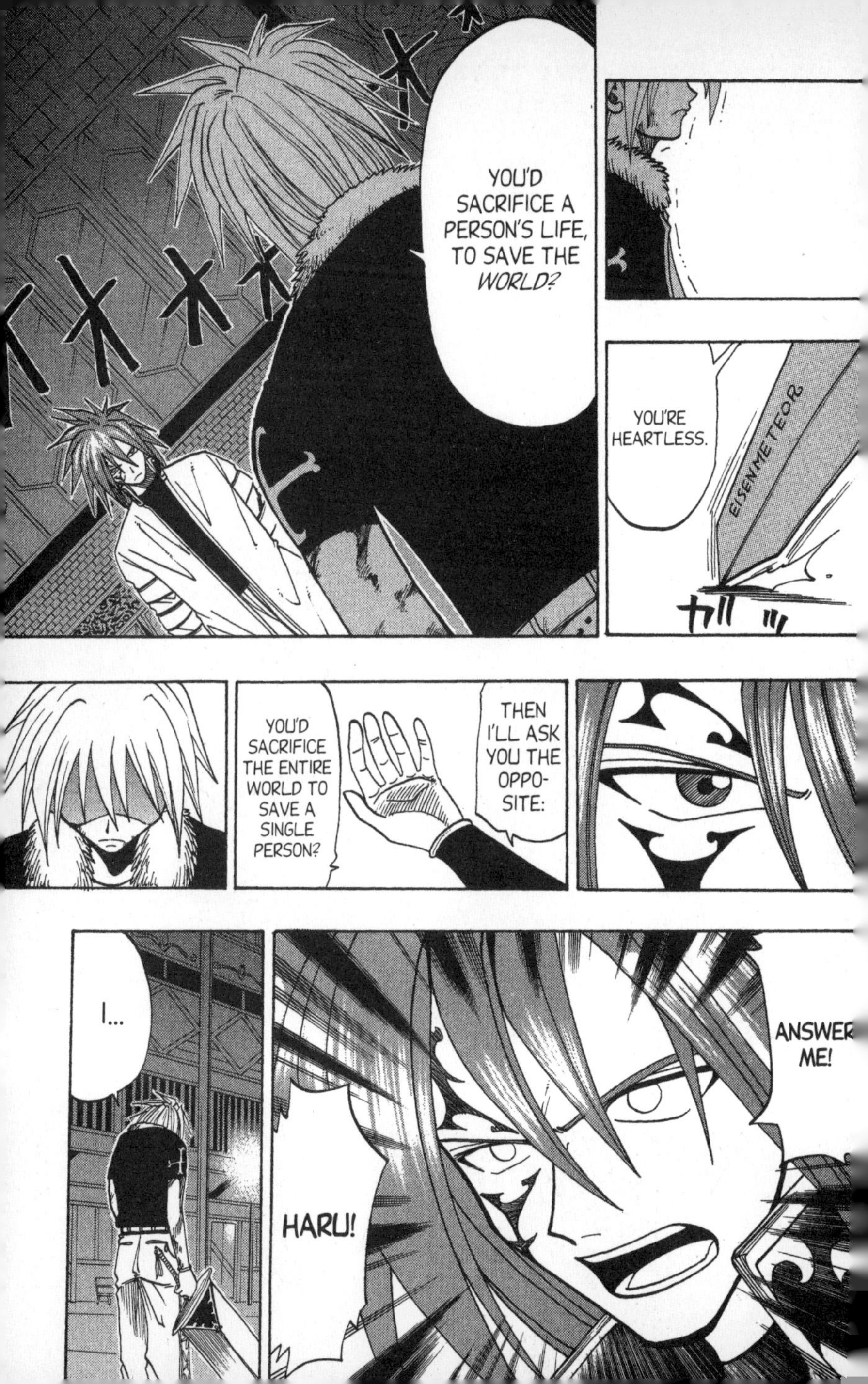

YOU'RE HEARTLESS.
EISENMETEOR
YOU'D SACRIFICE A PERSON'S LIFE, TO SAVE THE *WORLD*?
THEN I'LL ASK YOU THE OPPO-SITE:
YOU'D SACRIFICE THE ENTIRE WORLD TO SAVE A SINGLE PERSON?
ANSWER ME!
HARU!
I...

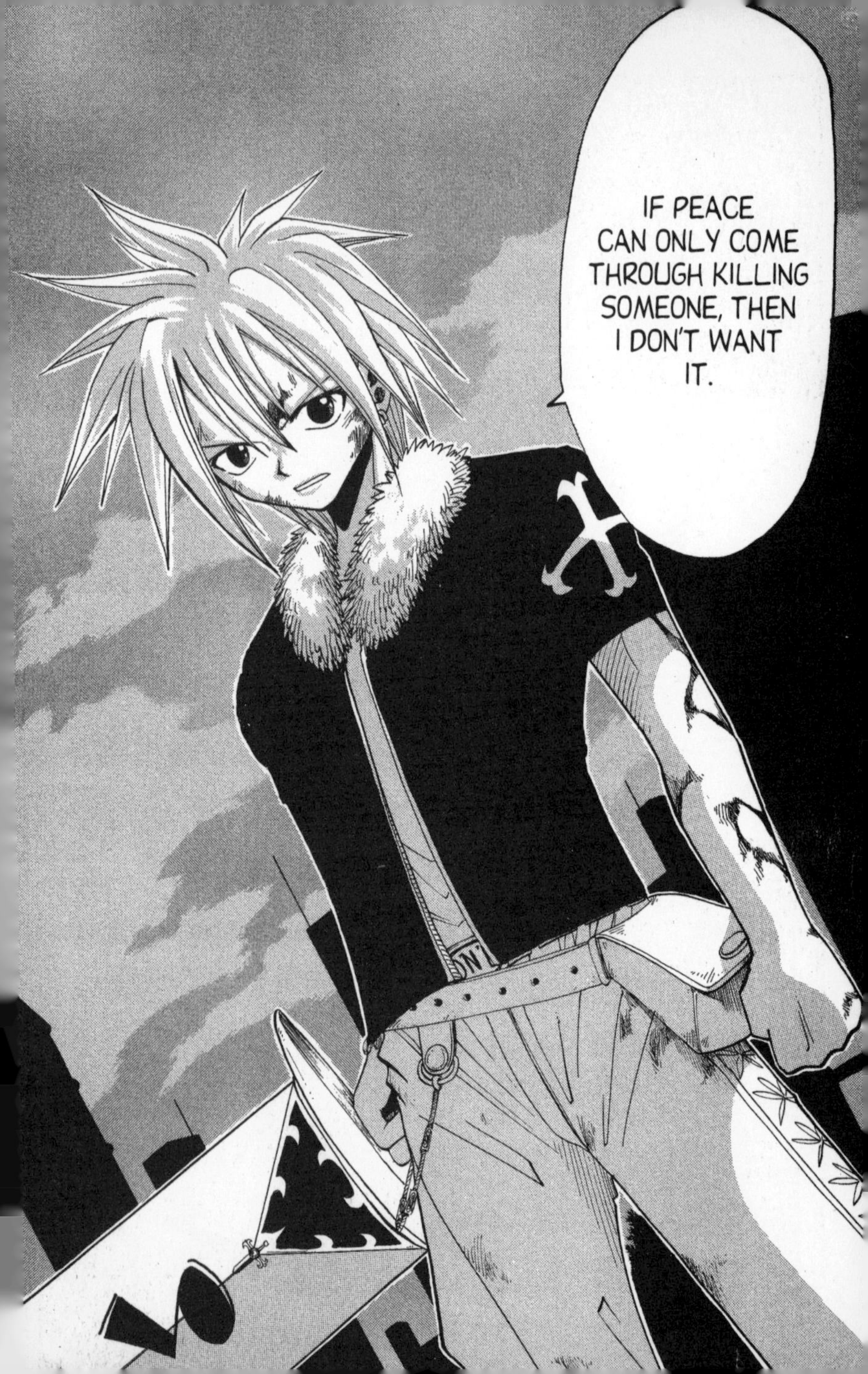
IF PEACE CAN ONLY COME THROUGH KILLING SOMEONE, THEN I DON'T WANT IT.

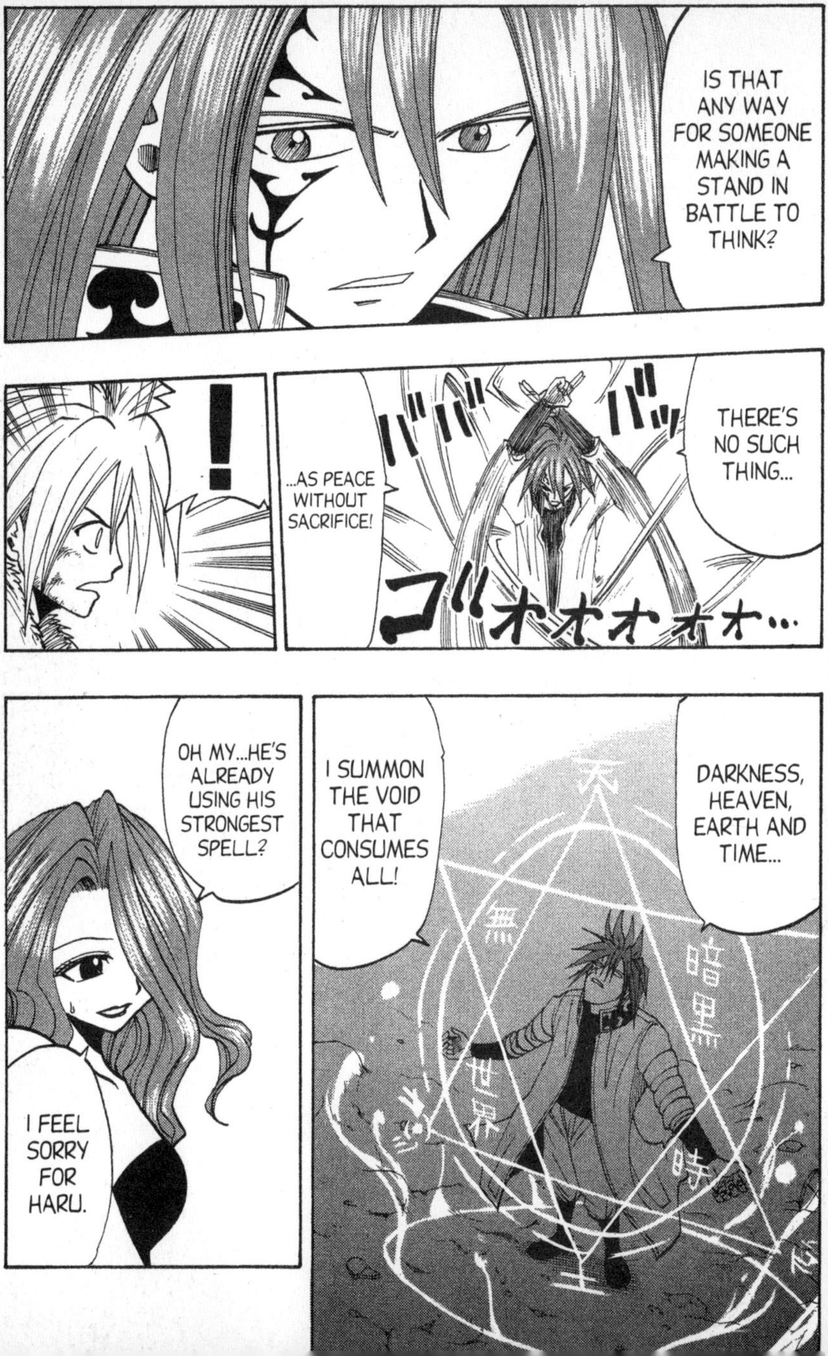
IS THAT ANY WAY FOR SOMEONE MAKING A STAND IN BATTLE TO THINK?
THERE'S NO SUCH THING...
バッ
ババ
...AS PEACE WITHOUT SACRIFICE!
ゴオオオオオ…
!
DARKNESS, HEAVEN, EARTH AND TIME...
I SUMMON THE VOID THAT CONSUMES ALL!
暗黒
無
世界
時
OH MY...HE'S ALREADY USING HIS STRONGEST SPELL?
I FEEL SORRY FOR HARU.

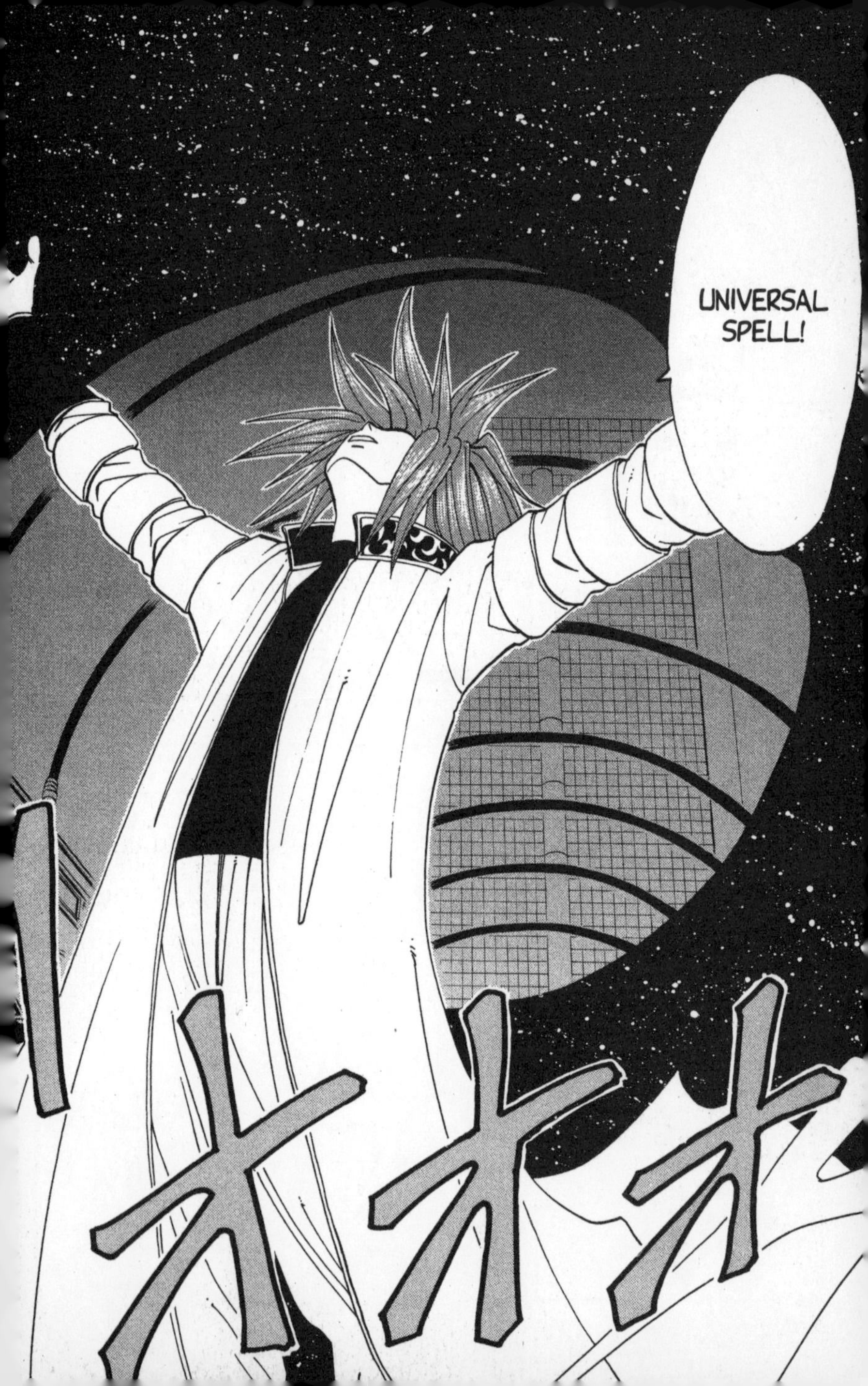
UNIVERSAL SPELL!

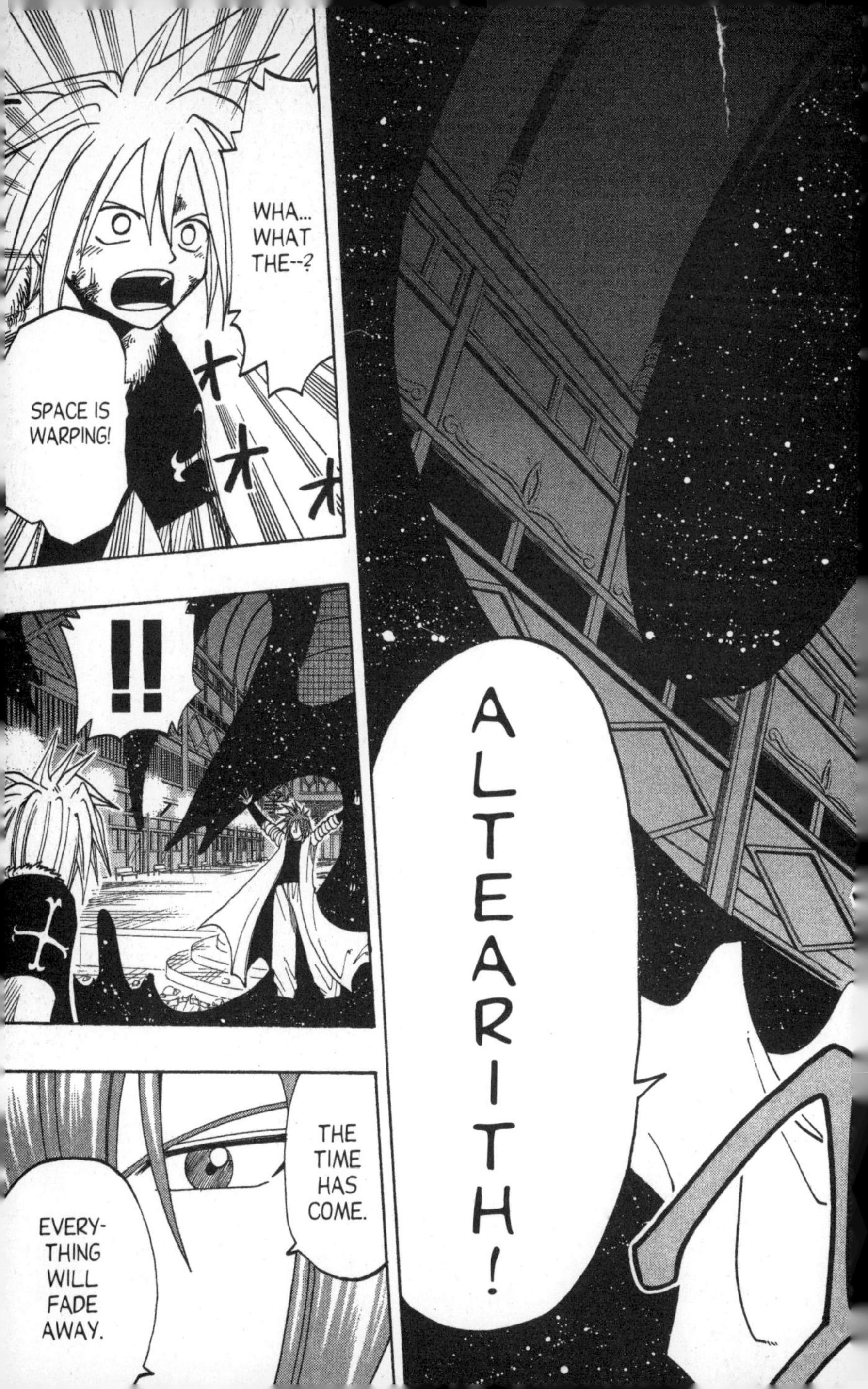
ALTEARITH!
WHA... WHAT THE--?
SPACE IS WARPING!
!!
THE TIME HAS COME.
EVERY-THING WILL FADE AWAY.

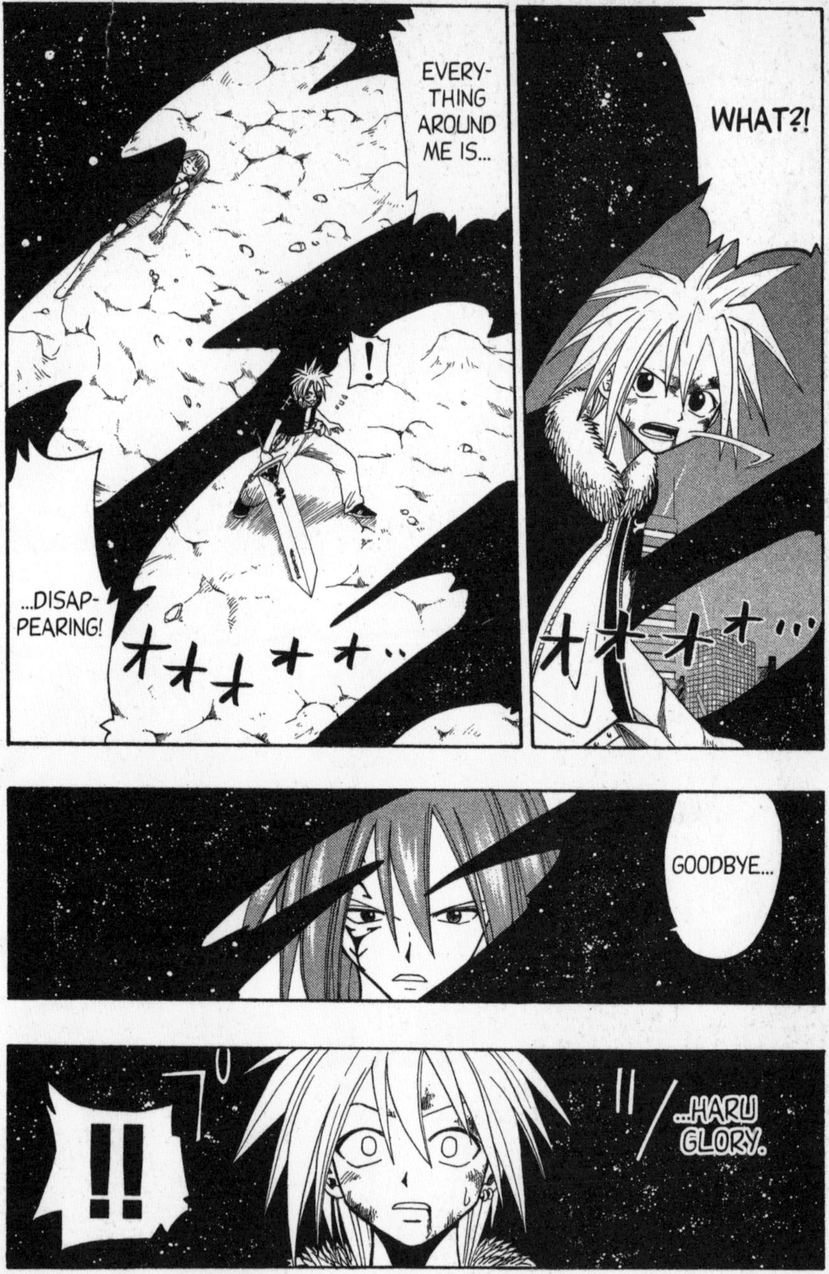
WHAT?!
EVERY-THING AROUND ME IS...
!
...DISAP-PEARING!
GOODBYE...
...HARU GLORY.
!!

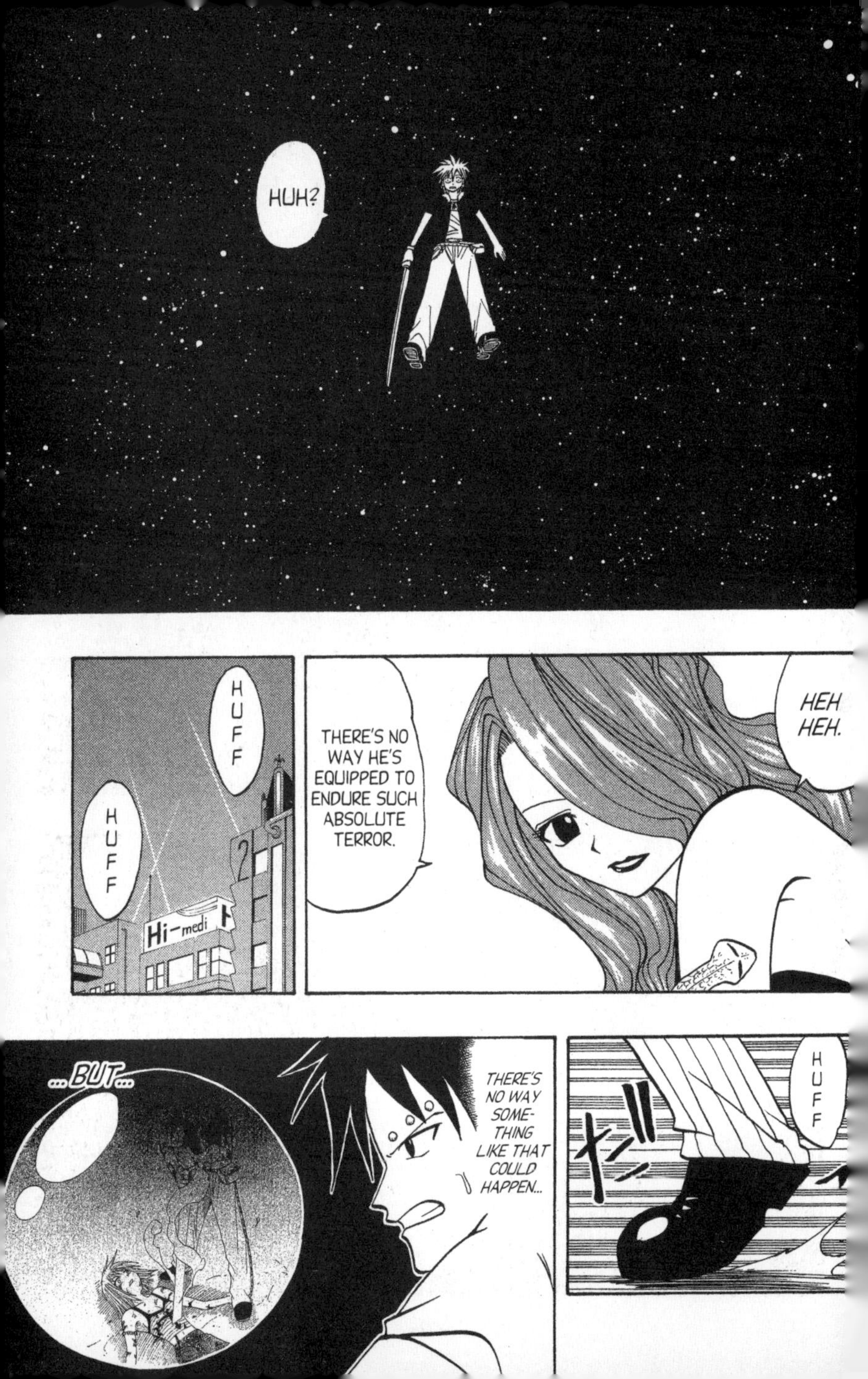
HUH?
HEH HEH.
THERE'S NO WAY HE'S EQUIPPED TO ENDURE SUCH ABSOLUTE TERROR.
HUFF
HUFF
Hi-medi
HUFF
THERE'S NO WAY SOME-THING LIKE THAT COULD HAPPEN...
...BUT...

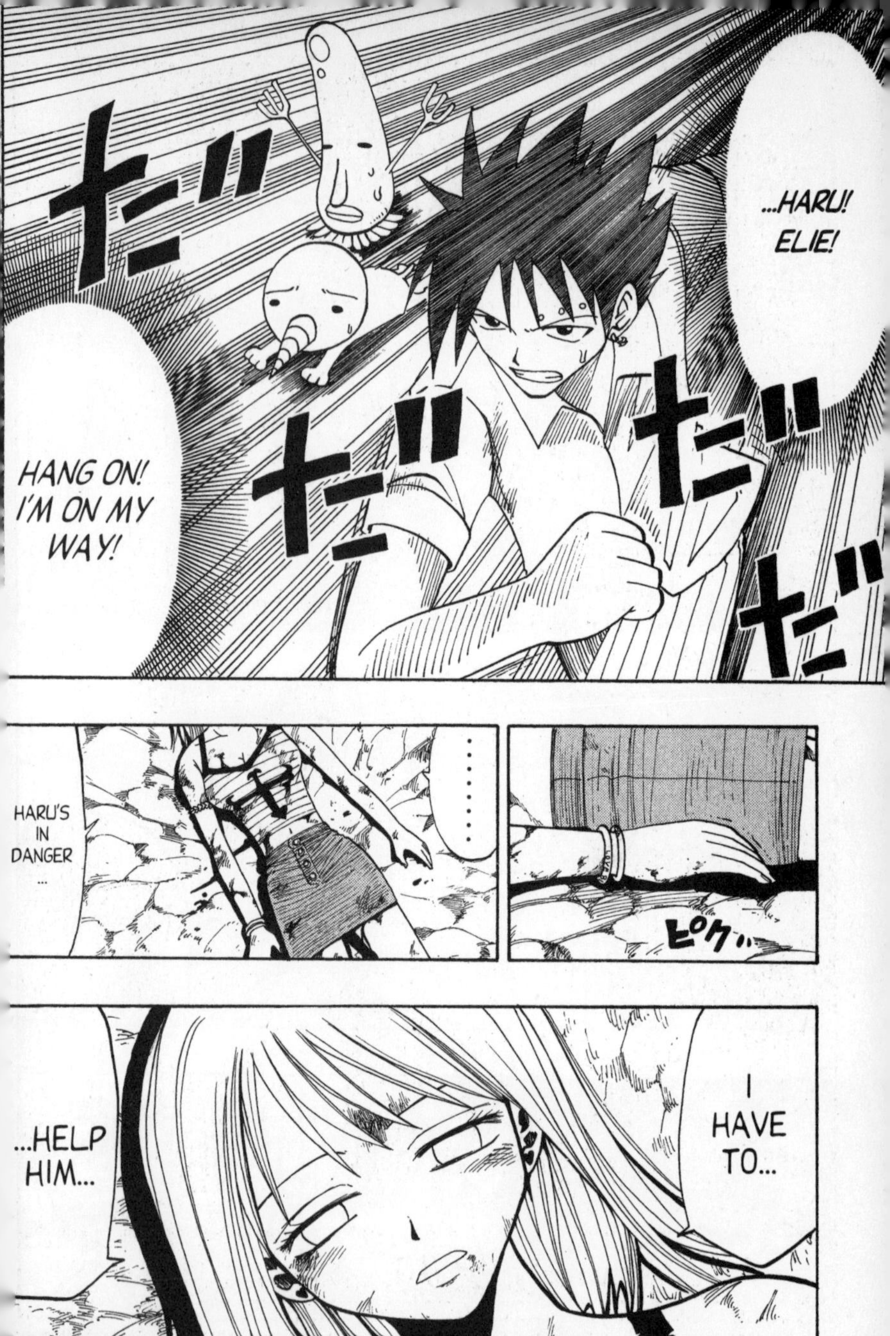

...HARU! ELIE!
HANG ON! I'M ON MY WAY!
......
HARU'S IN DANGER ...
I HAVE TO...
...HELP HIM...

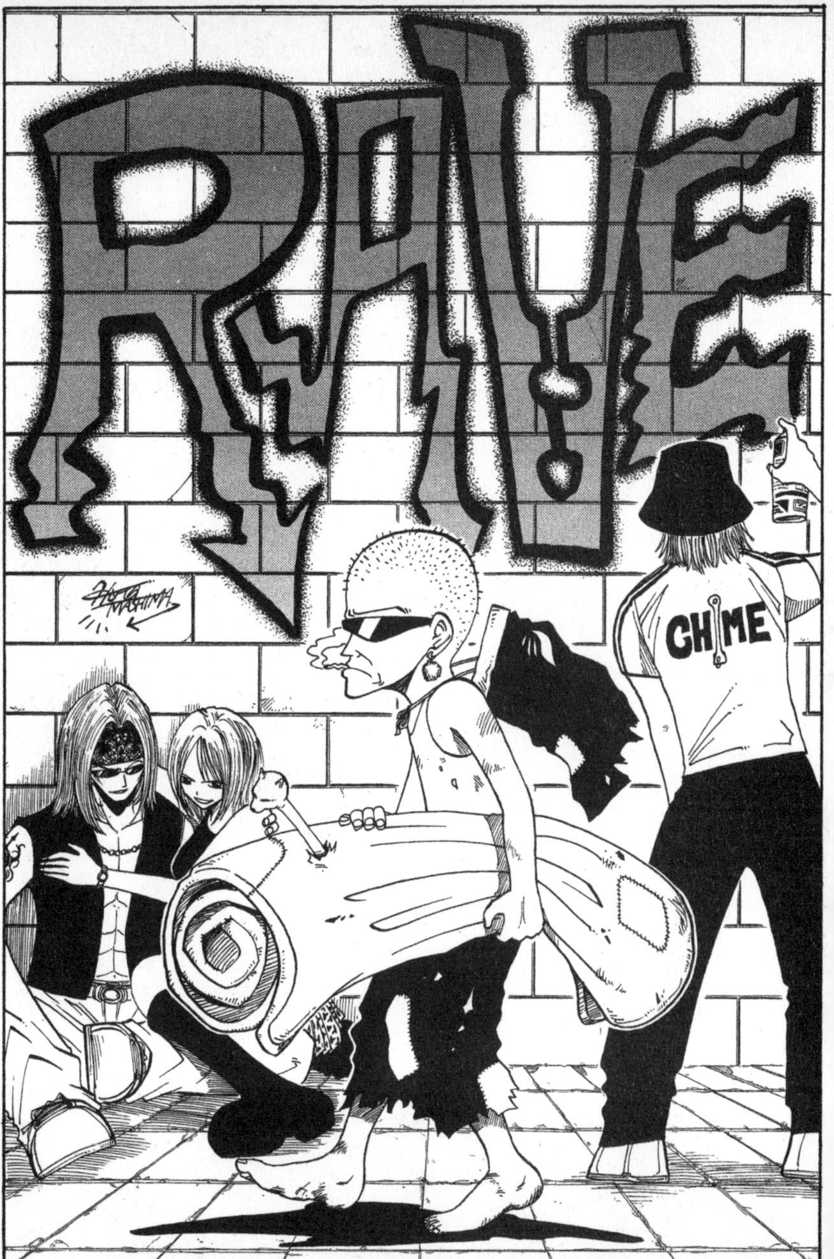
RAVE
CHIME

RAVE: 45 ✠ THE TRIGGER OF DESTRUCTION

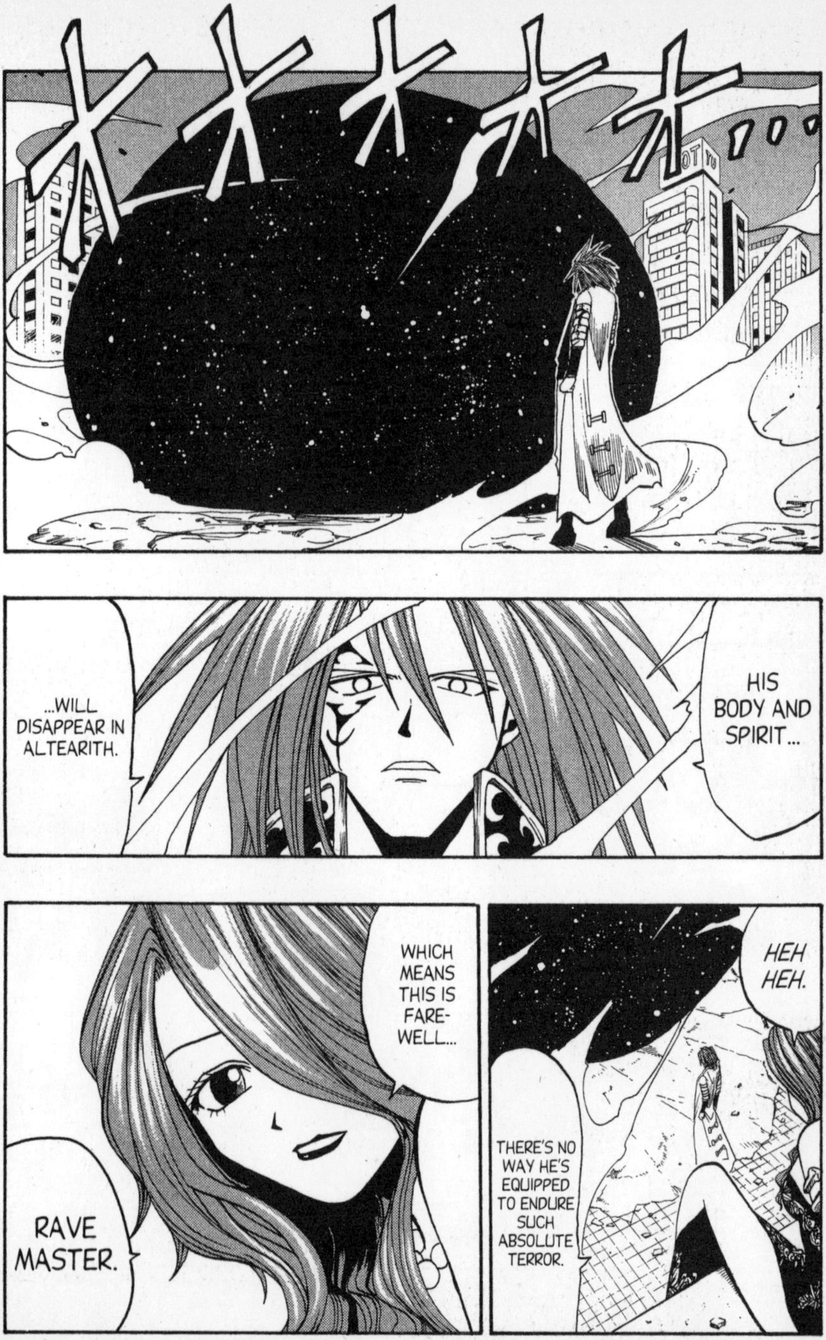
オオオオオ…
HIS BODY AND SPIRIT...
...WILL DISAPPEAR IN ALTEARITH.
HEH HEH.
THERE'S NO WAY HE'S EQUIPPED TO ENDURE SUCH ABSOLUTE TERROR.
WHICH MEANS THIS IS FARE-WELL...
RAVE MASTER.

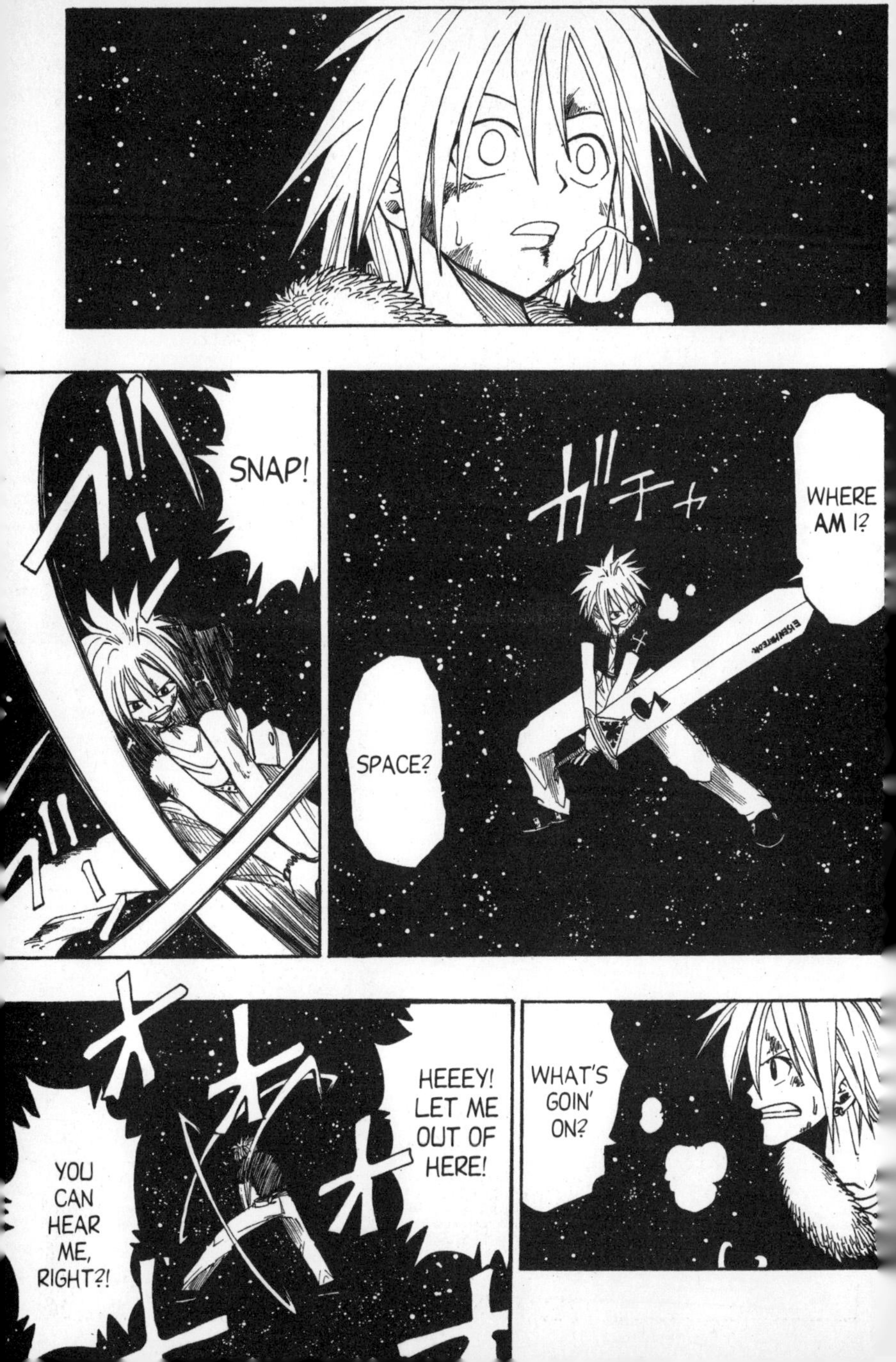
ガチャ
WHERE AM I?
SPACE?
SNAP!
WHAT'S GOIN' ON?
HEEEY! LET ME OUT OF HERE!
YOU CAN HEAR ME, RIGHT?!

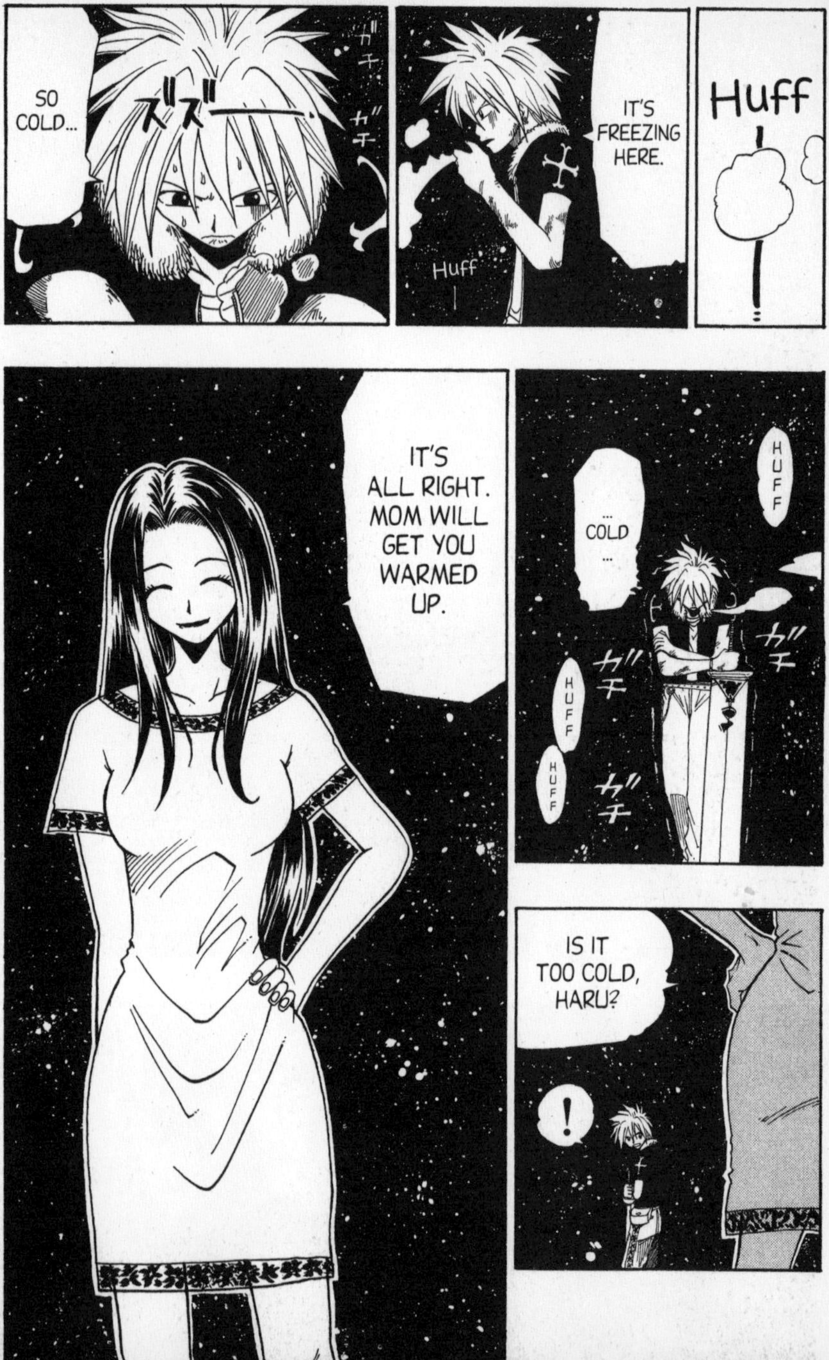
Huff
!
IT'S FREEZING HERE.
Huff
SO COLD...
ズズー
ガチ ガチ
HUFF
... COLD ...
ガチ
HUFF
HUFF
ガチ
ガチ
IS IT TOO COLD, HARU?
!
IT'S ALL RIGHT. MOM WILL GET YOU WARMED UP.

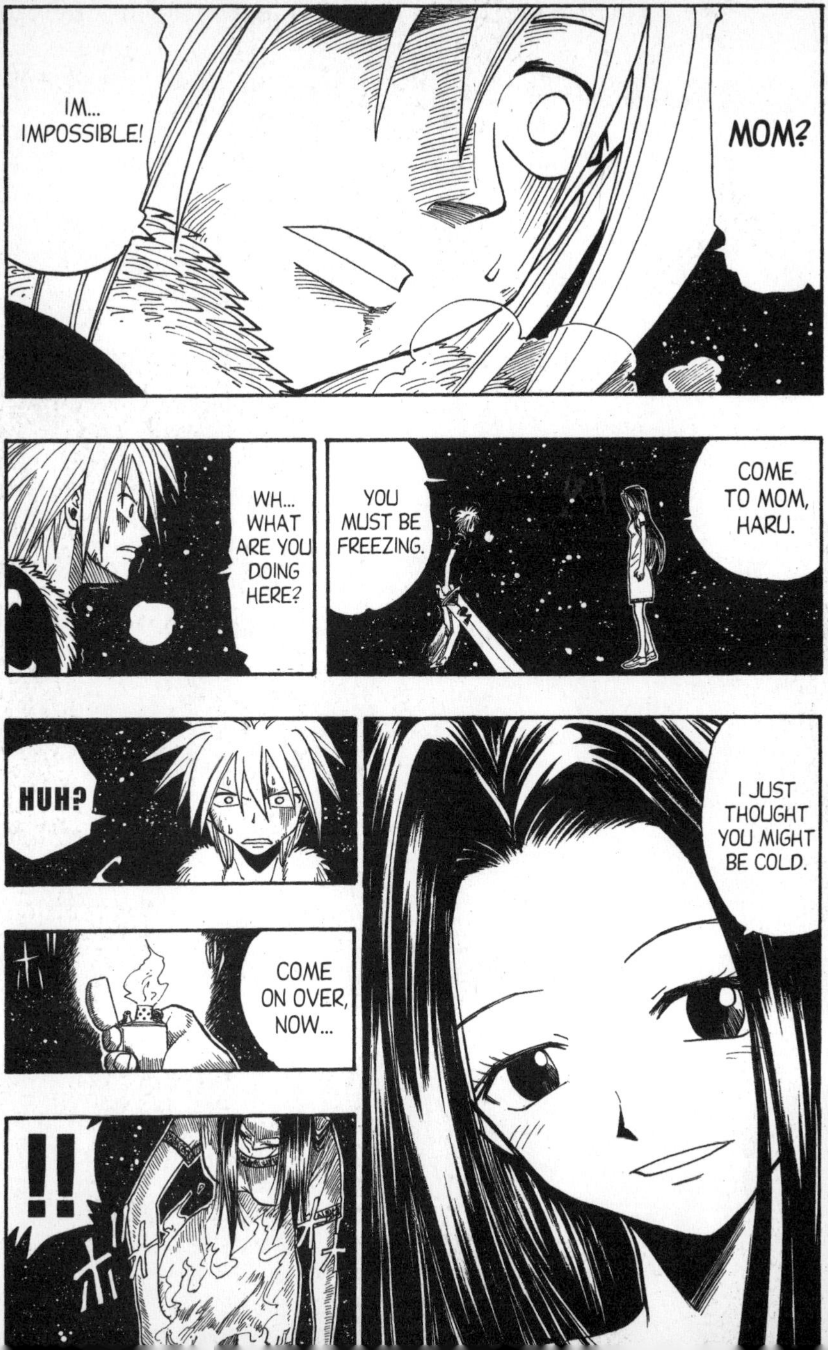
MOM?
IM... IMPOSSIBLE!
COME TO MOM, HARU.
YOU MUST BE FREEZING.
WH... WHAT ARE YOU DOING HERE?
I JUST THOUGHT YOU MIGHT BE COLD.
HUH?
COME ON OVER, NOW...
!!

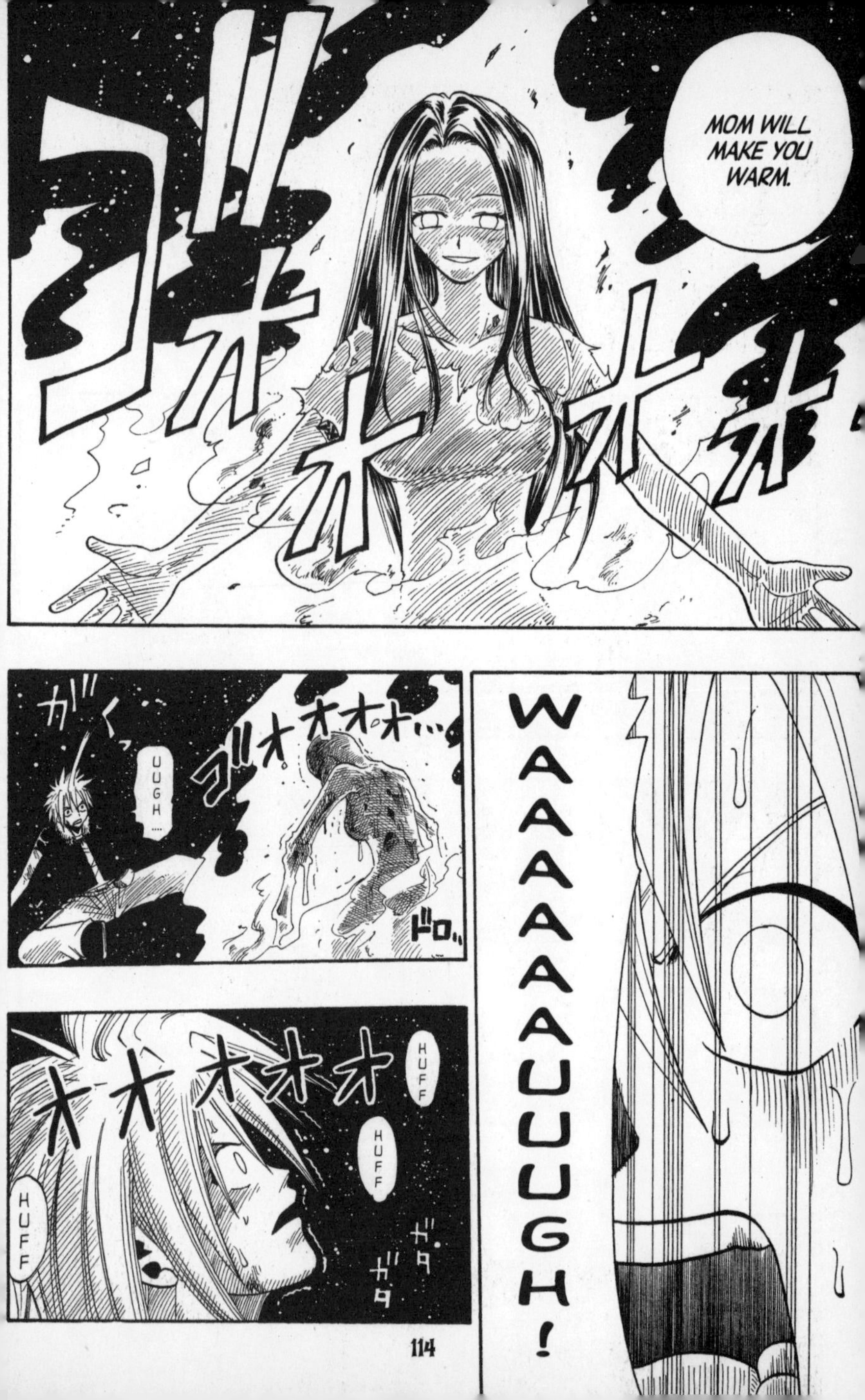
MOM WILL MAKE YOU WARM.
ゴオオオオ
WAAAAAAAUUUGH!
ガくっ
UUGH....
ゴオオオオ…
ドロッ
オオオオオ
HUFF
HUFF
HUFF
ガタガタ

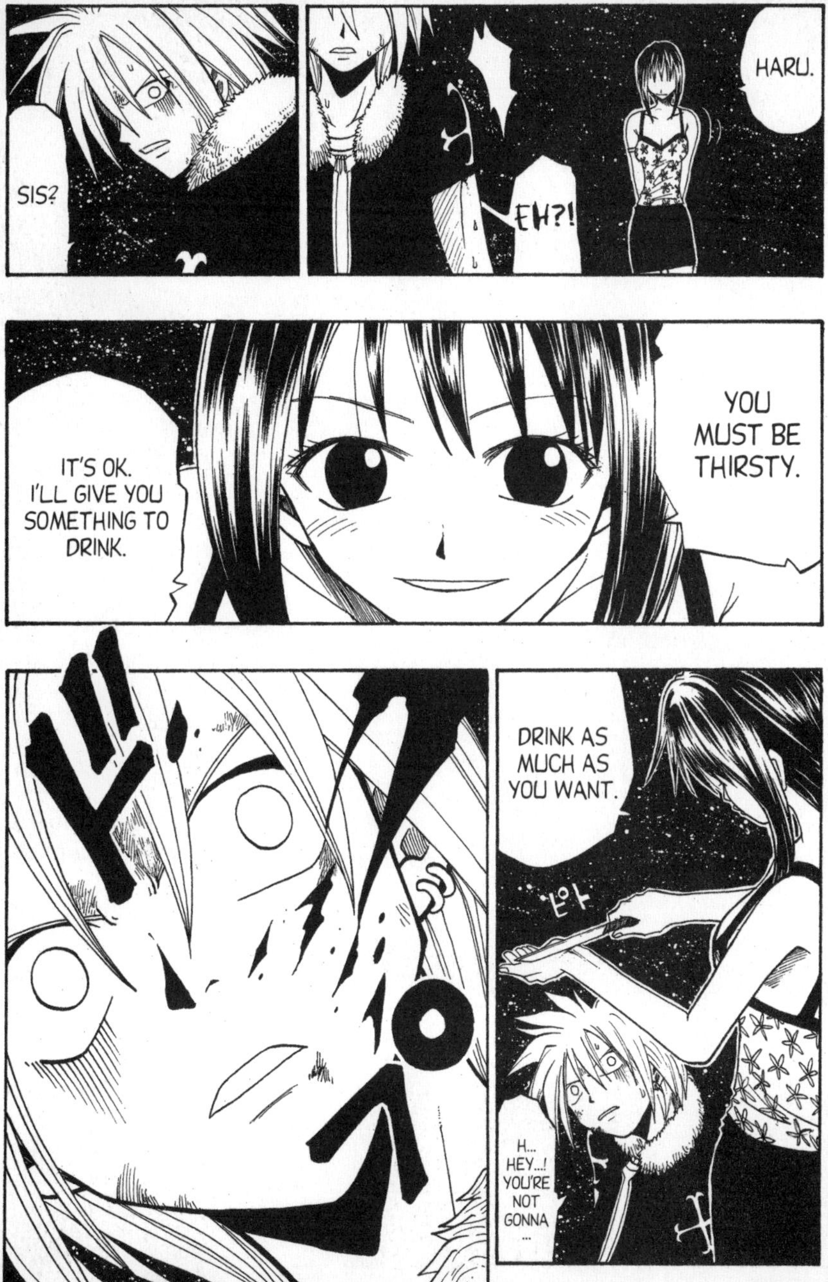
HARU.
EH?!
SIS?
YOU MUST BE THIRSTY.
IT'S OK. I'LL GIVE YOU SOMETHING TO DRINK.
DRINK AS MUCH AS YOU WANT.
H... HEY...! YOU'RE NOT GONNA ...

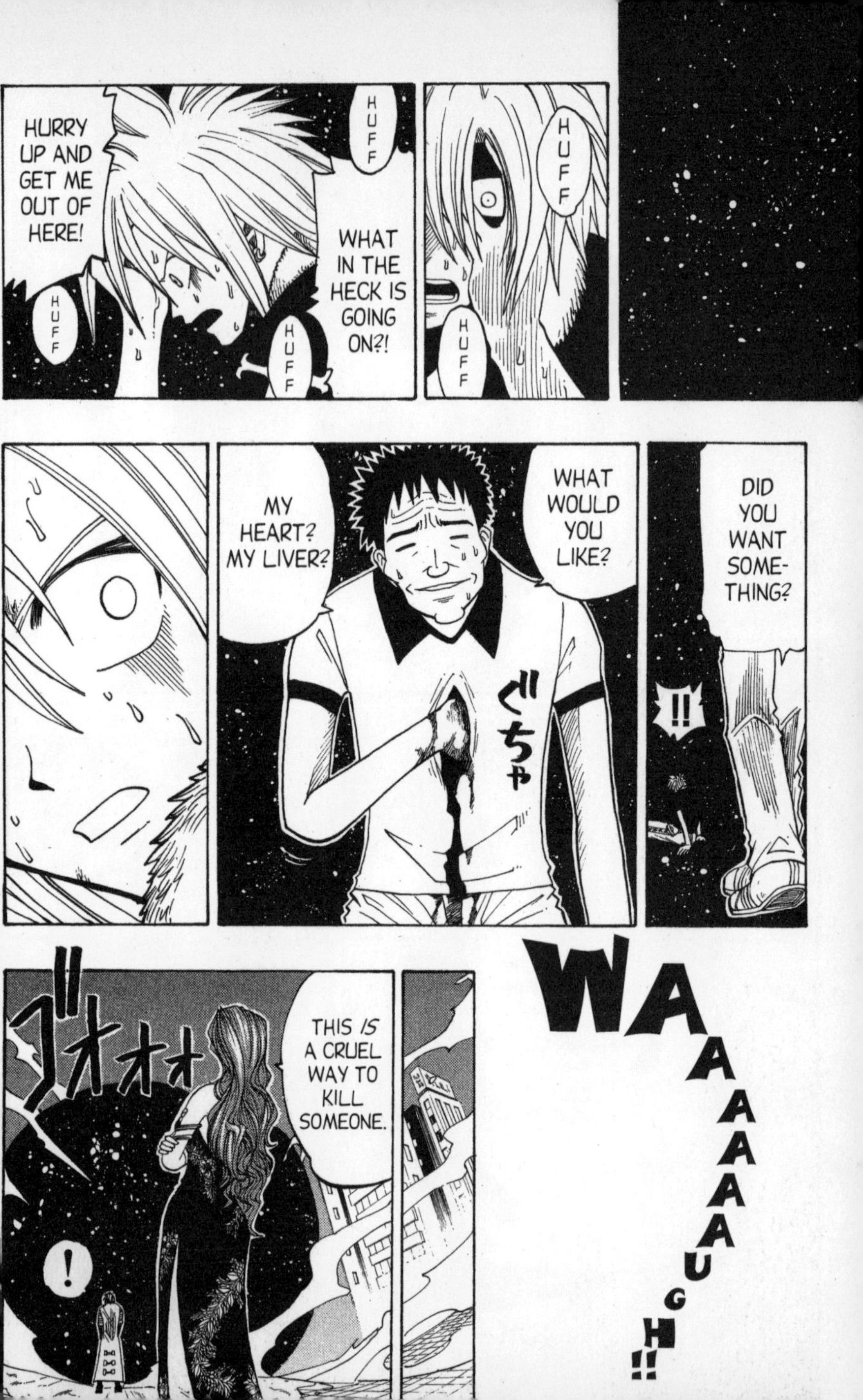
HUFF
HUFF
HUFF
HURRY UP AND GET ME OUT OF HERE!
WHAT IN THE HECK IS GOING ON?!
HUFF
HUFF
DID YOU WANT SOMETHING?
!!
WHAT WOULD YOU LIKE?
MY HEART? MY LIVER?
ぐちゃ
WAAAAAAAUGH!!
ゴオオオ
THIS *IS* A CRUEL WAY TO KILL SOMEONE.
!

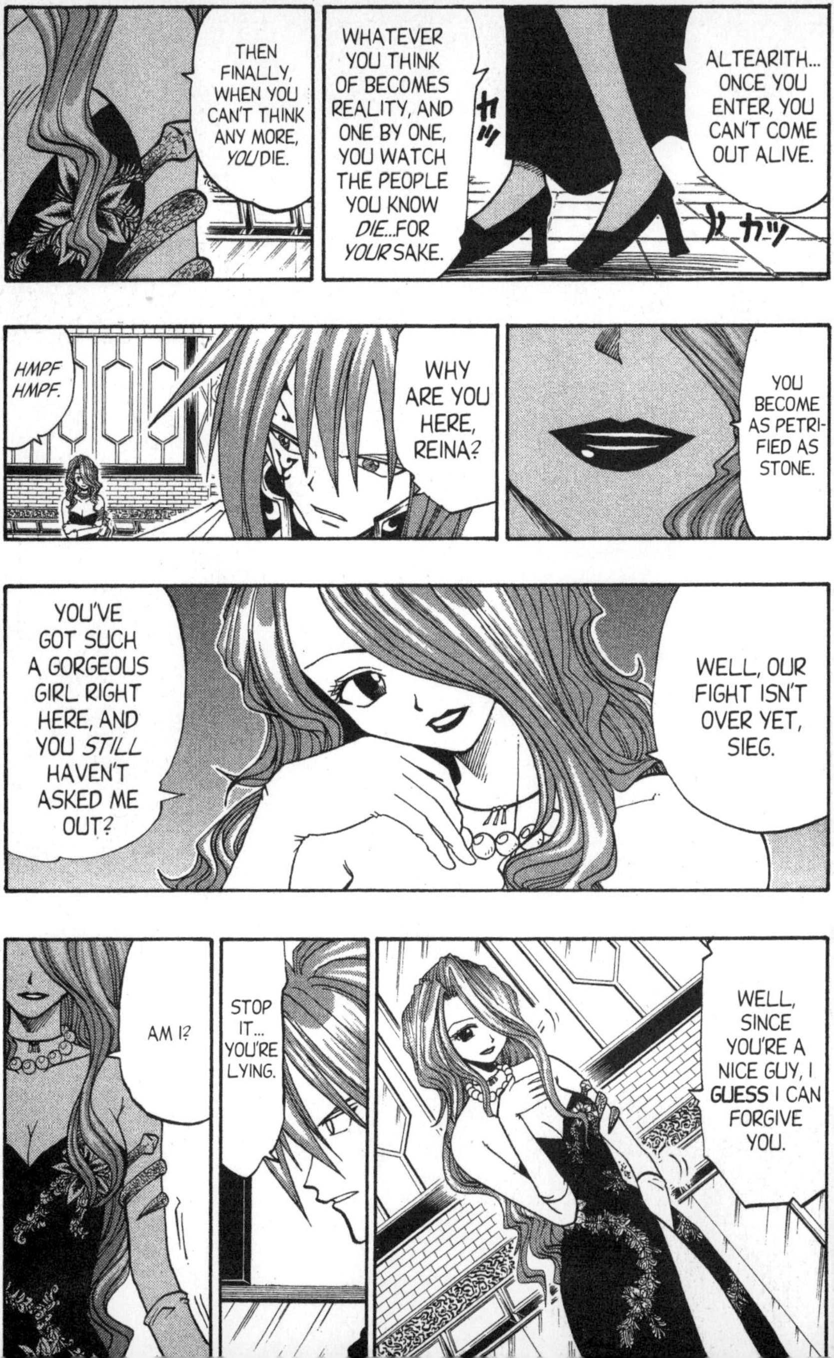
ALTEARITH... ONCE YOU ENTER, YOU CAN'T COME OUT ALIVE.
カッ
カッ
WHATEVER YOU THINK OF BECOMES REALITY, AND ONE BY ONE, YOU WATCH THE PEOPLE YOU KNOW *DIE*...FOR *YOUR* SAKE.
THEN FINALLY, WHEN YOU CAN'T THINK ANY MORE, *YOU* DIE.
YOU BECOME AS PETRIFIED AS STONE.
WHY ARE YOU HERE, REINA?
HMPF HMPF.
WELL, OUR FIGHT ISN'T OVER YET, SIEG.
YOU'VE GOT SUCH A GORGEOUS GIRL RIGHT HERE, AND YOU *STILL* HAVEN'T ASKED ME OUT?
WELL, SINCE YOU'RE A NICE GUY, I **GUESS** I CAN FORGIVE YOU.
STOP IT... YOU'RE LYING.
AM I?

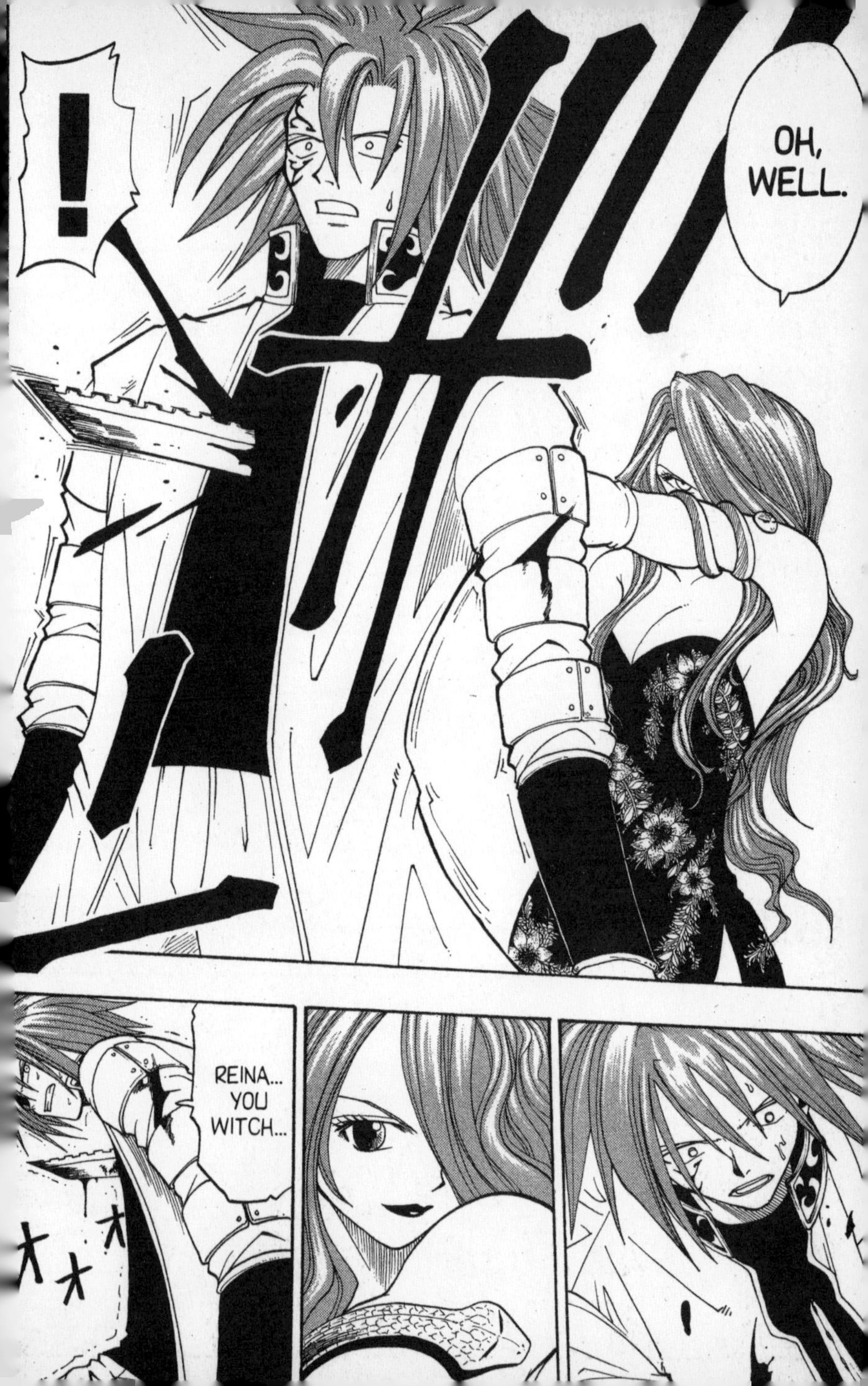
OH, WELL.
!
REINA... YOU WITCH...

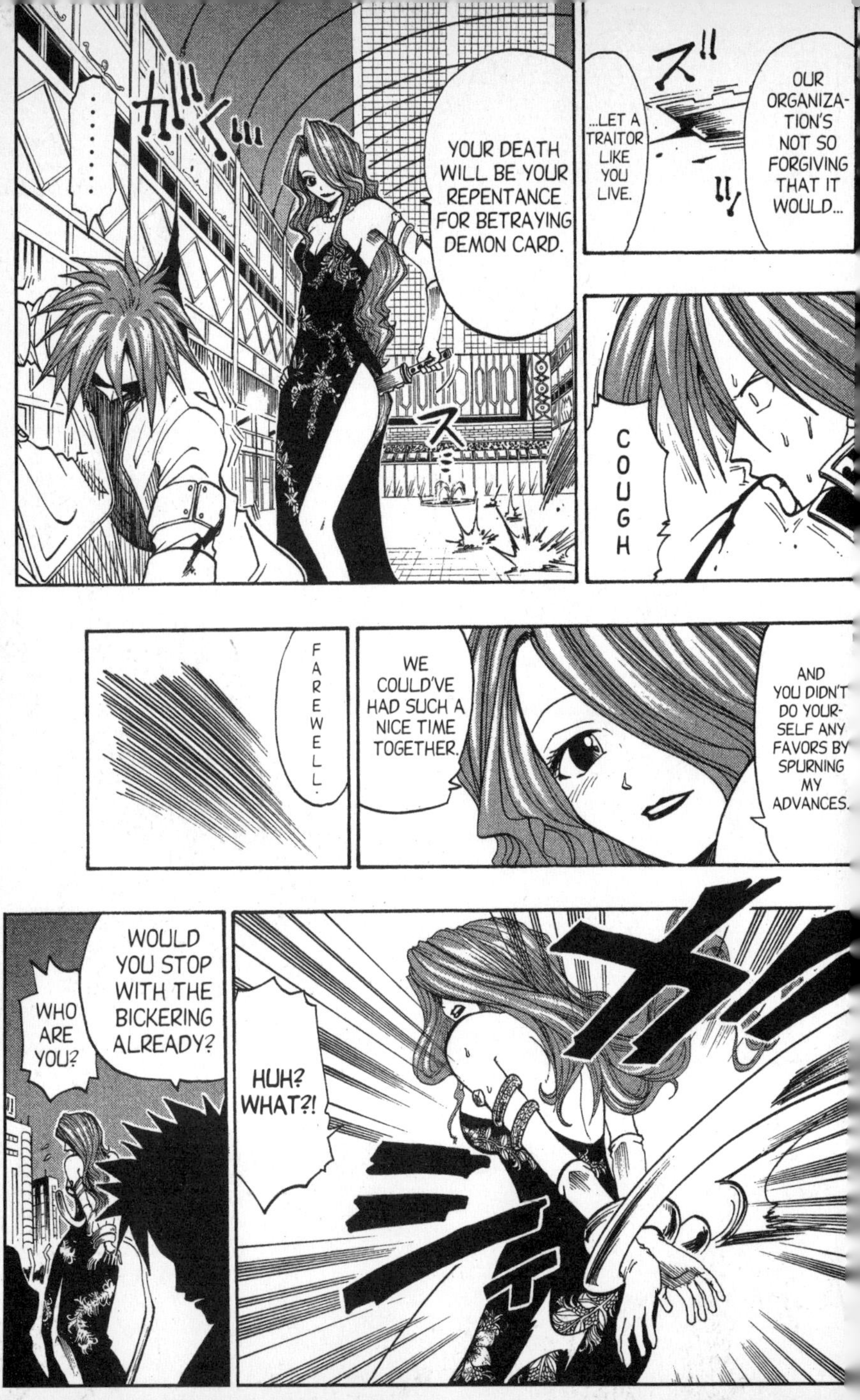
OUR ORGANIZATION'S NOT SO FORGIVING THAT IT WOULD...
ズ!!
...LET A TRAITOR LIKE YOU LIVE.
COUGH
YOUR DEATH WILL BE YOUR REPENTANCE FOR BETRAYING DEMON CARD.
......
AND YOU DIDN'T DO YOURSELF ANY FAVORS BY SPURNING MY ADVANCES.
WE COULD'VE HAD SUCH A NICE TIME TOGETHER.
FAREWELL.
HUH? WHAT?!
WOULD YOU STOP WITH THE BICKERING ALREADY?
WHO ARE YOU?

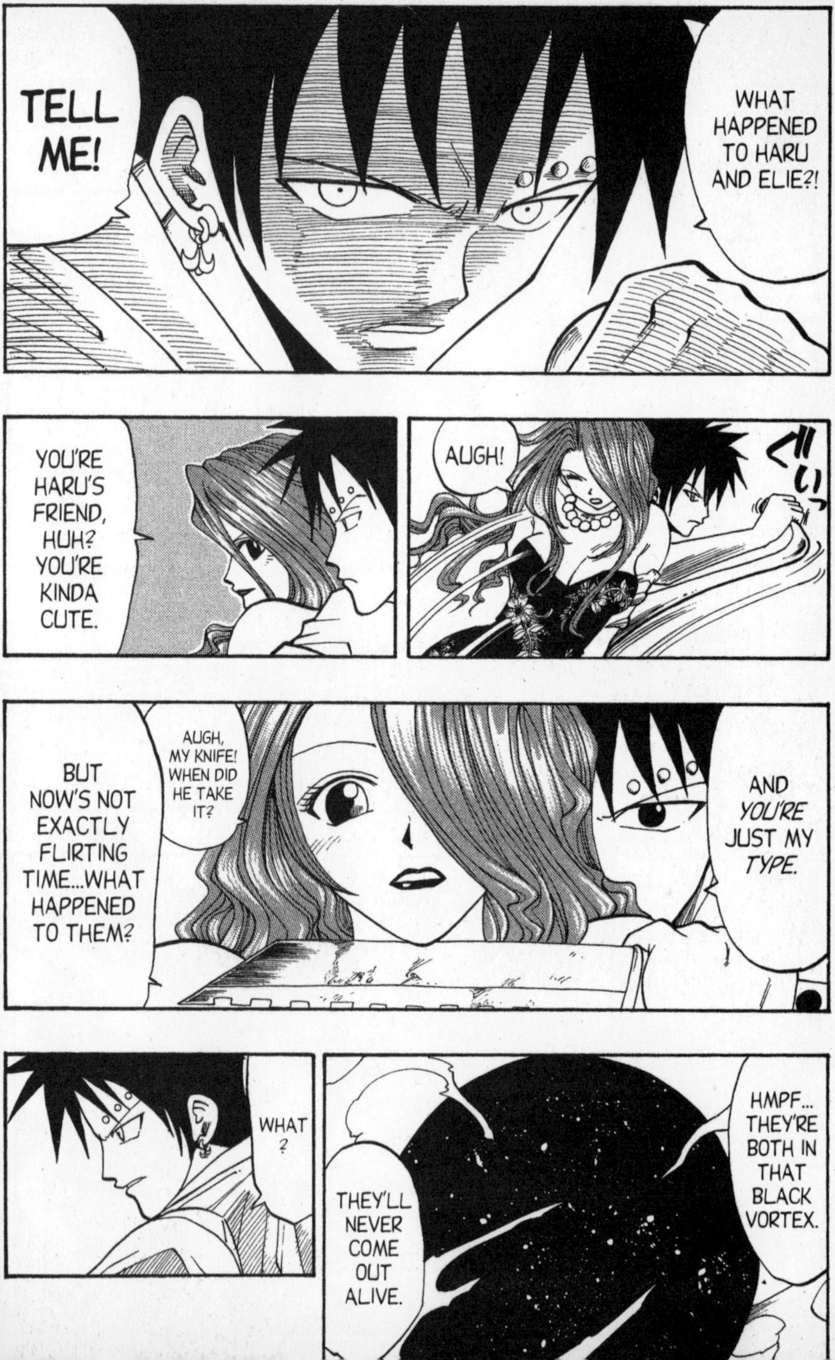
WHAT HAPPENED TO HARU AND ELIE?!
TELL ME!
AUGH!
ぐいっ
YOU'RE HARU'S FRIEND, HUH? YOU'RE KINDA CUTE.
AND *YOU'RE* JUST MY *TYPE.*
AUGH, MY KNIFE! WHEN DID HE TAKE IT?
BUT NOW'S NOT EXACTLY FLIRTING TIME...WHAT HAPPENED TO THEM?
HMPF... THEY'RE BOTH IN THAT BLACK VORTEX.
THEY'LL NEVER COME OUT ALIVE.
WHAT?

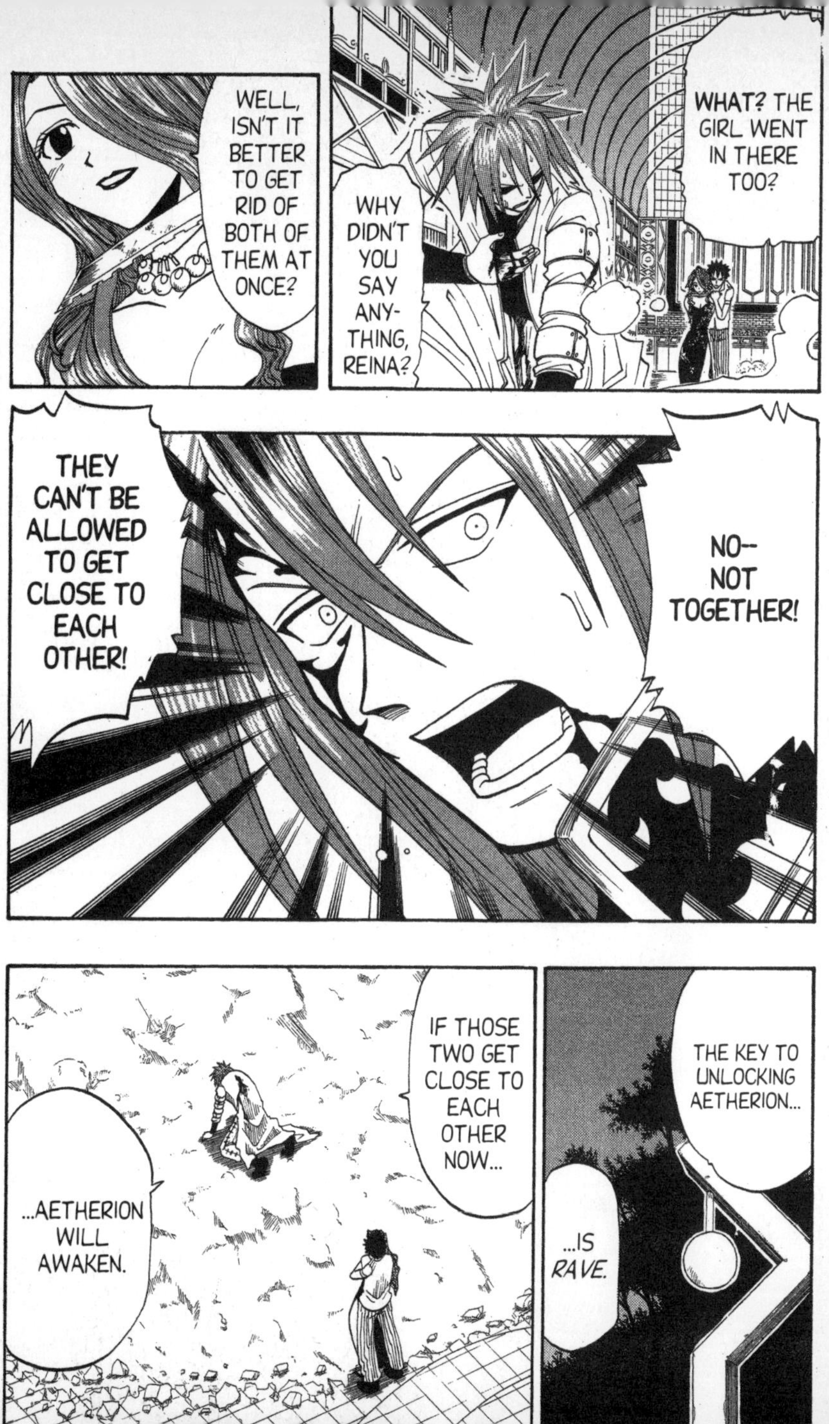
WHAT? THE GIRL WENT IN THERE TOO?
WHY DIDN'T YOU SAY ANY-THING, REINA?
WELL, ISN'T IT BETTER TO GET RID OF BOTH OF THEM AT ONCE?
NO-- NOT TOGETHER!
THEY CAN'T BE ALLOWED TO GET CLOSE TO EACH OTHER!
THE KEY TO UNLOCKING AETHERION...
...IS *RAVE*.
IF THOSE TWO GET CLOSE TO EACH OTHER NOW...
...AETHERION WILL AWAKEN.

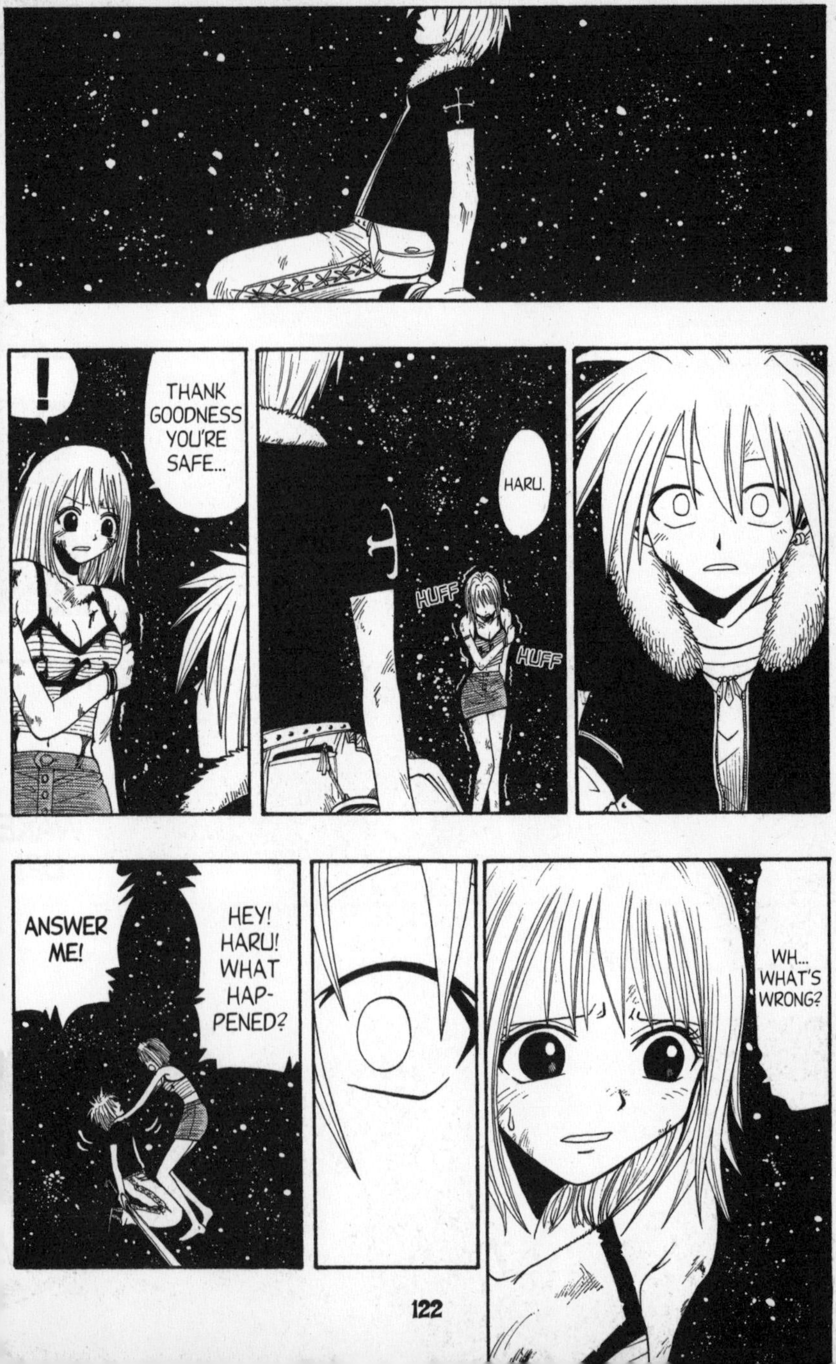
HARU.
HUFF
HUFF
!
THANK GOODNESS YOU'RE SAFE...
WH... WHAT'S WRONG?
HEY! HARU! WHAT HAP-PENED?
ANSWER ME!

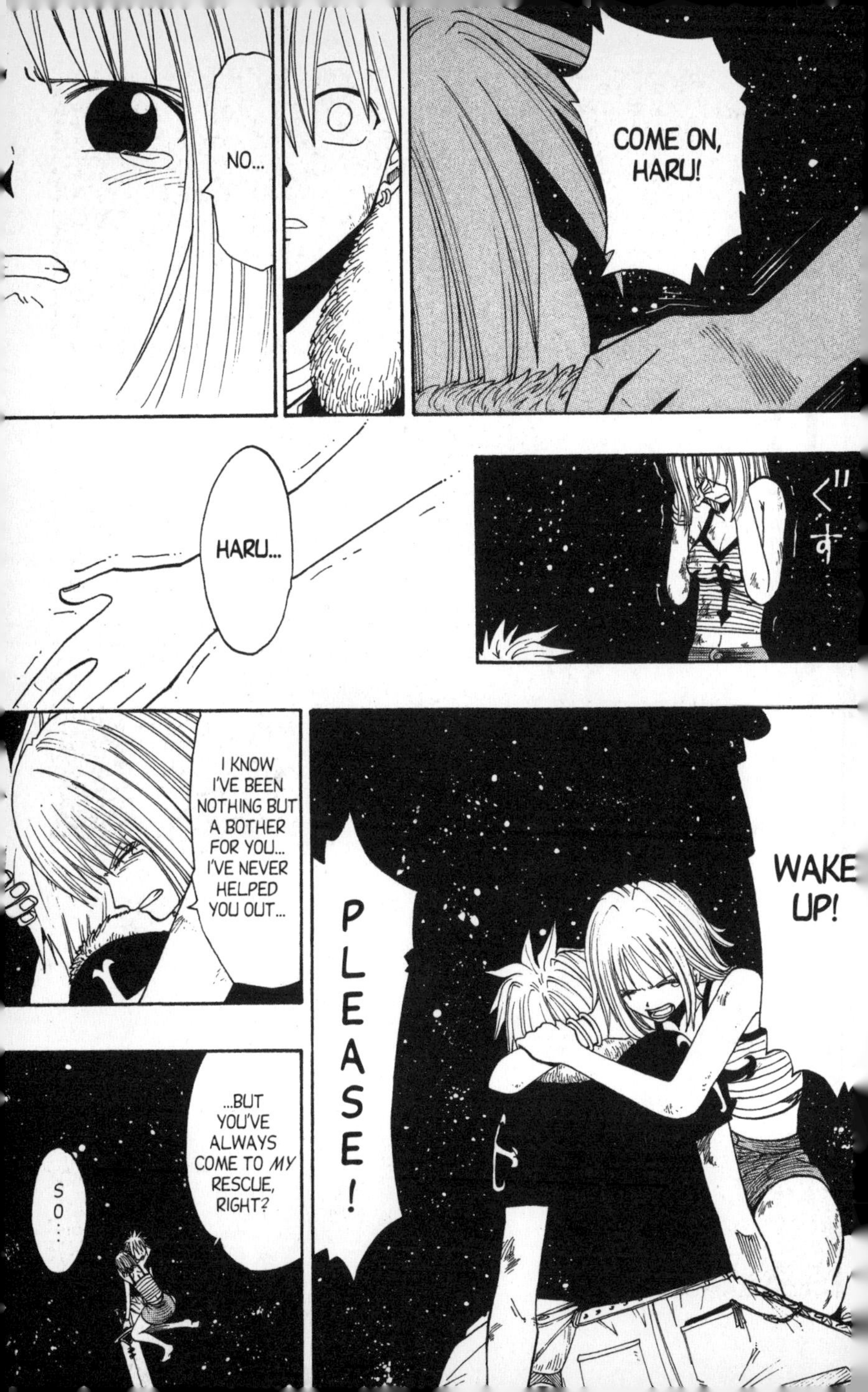
COME ON, HARU!
NO...
ぐす
HARU...
WAKE UP!
PLEASE!
I KNOW I'VE BEEN NOTHING BUT A BOTHER FOR YOU... I'VE NEVER HELPED YOU OUT...
...BUT YOU'VE ALWAYS COME TO *MY* RESCUE, RIGHT?
SO...

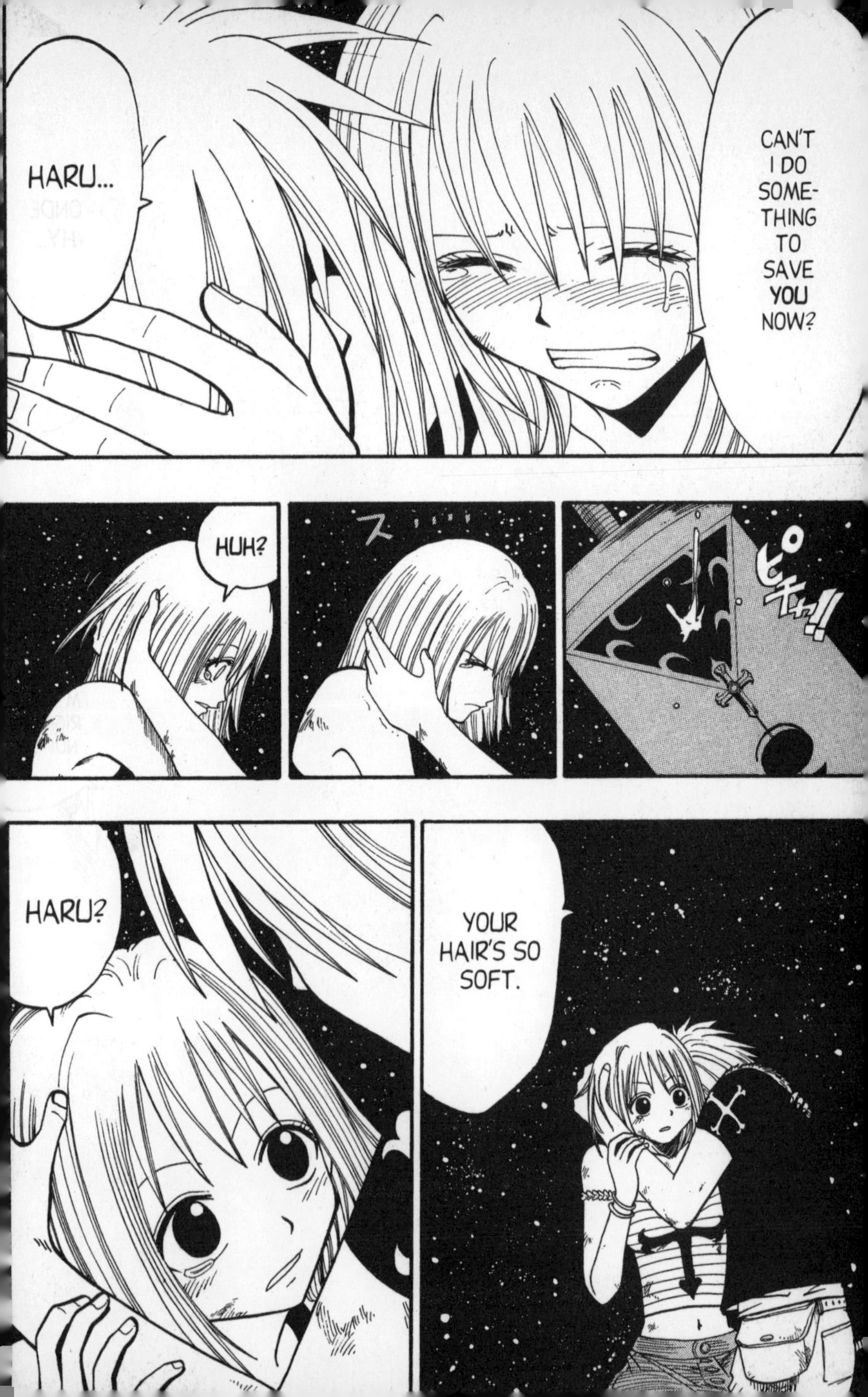
CAN'T I DO SOMETHING TO SAVE YOU NOW?
HARU...
ピチャ!!
ス
HUH?
YOUR HAIR'S SO SOFT.
HARU?

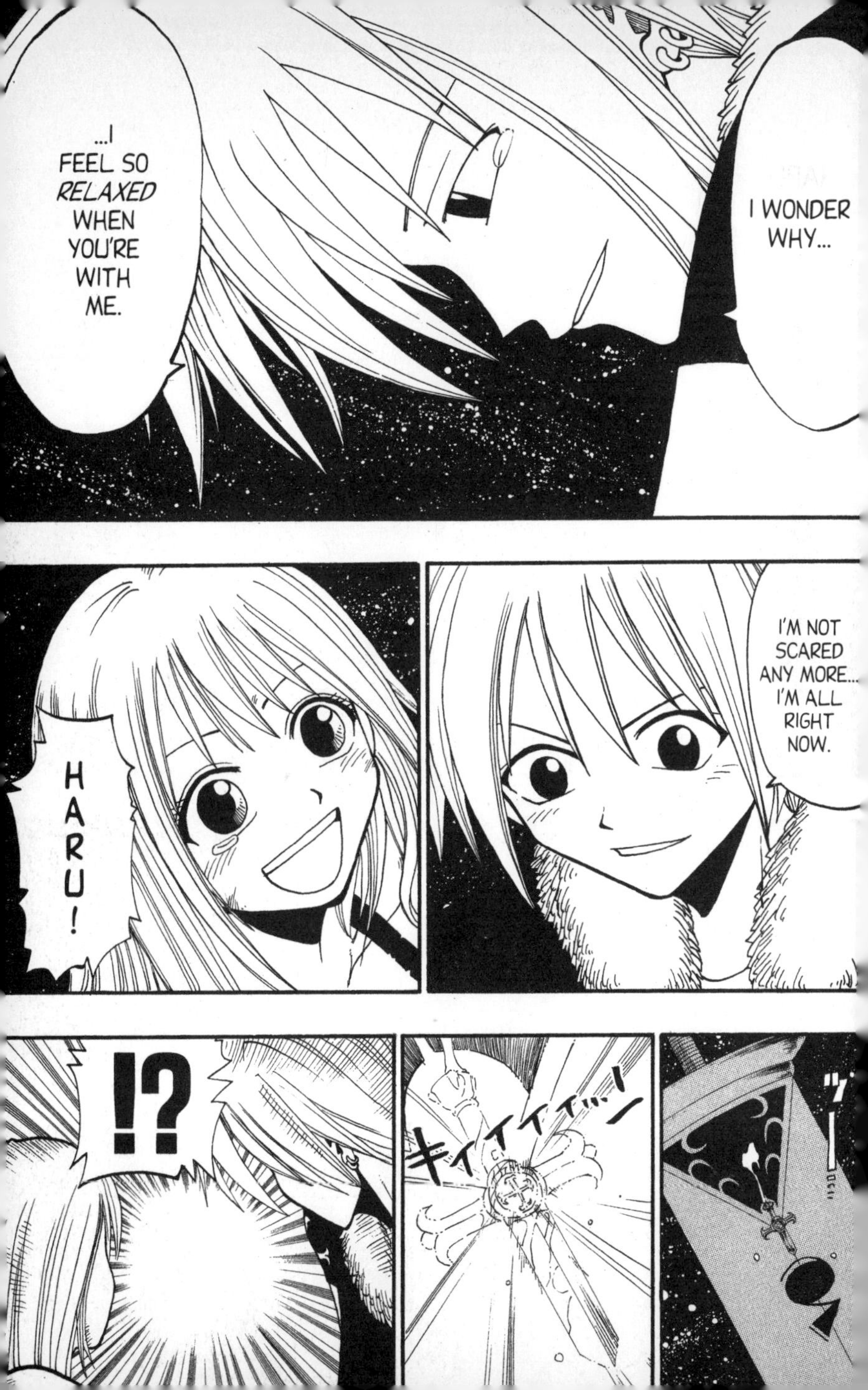
...I FEEL SO *RELAXED* WHEN YOU'RE WITH ME.
I WONDER WHY...
I'M NOT SCARED ANY MORE... I'M ALL RIGHT NOW.
HARU!
キイイイイ…ン
!?

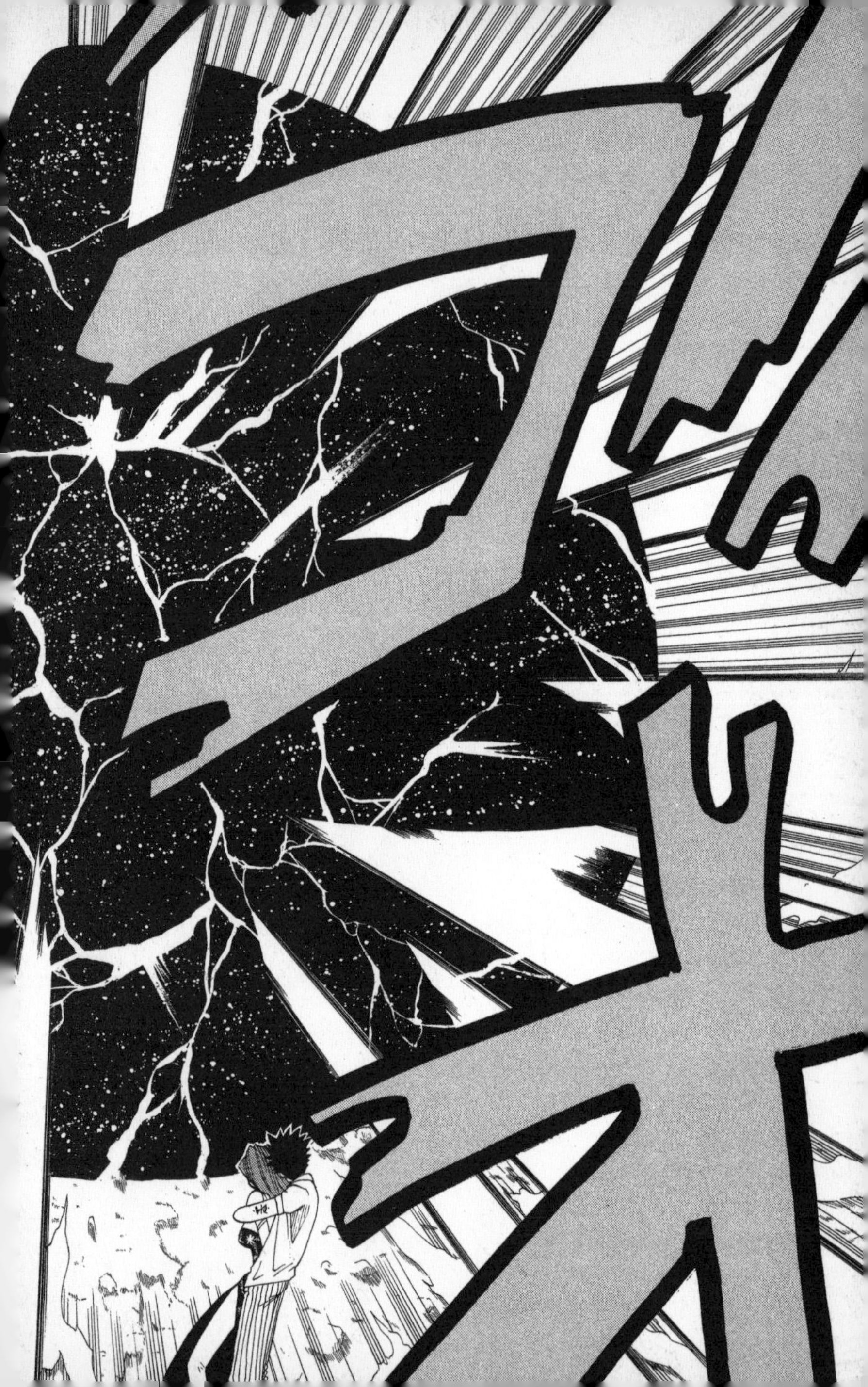

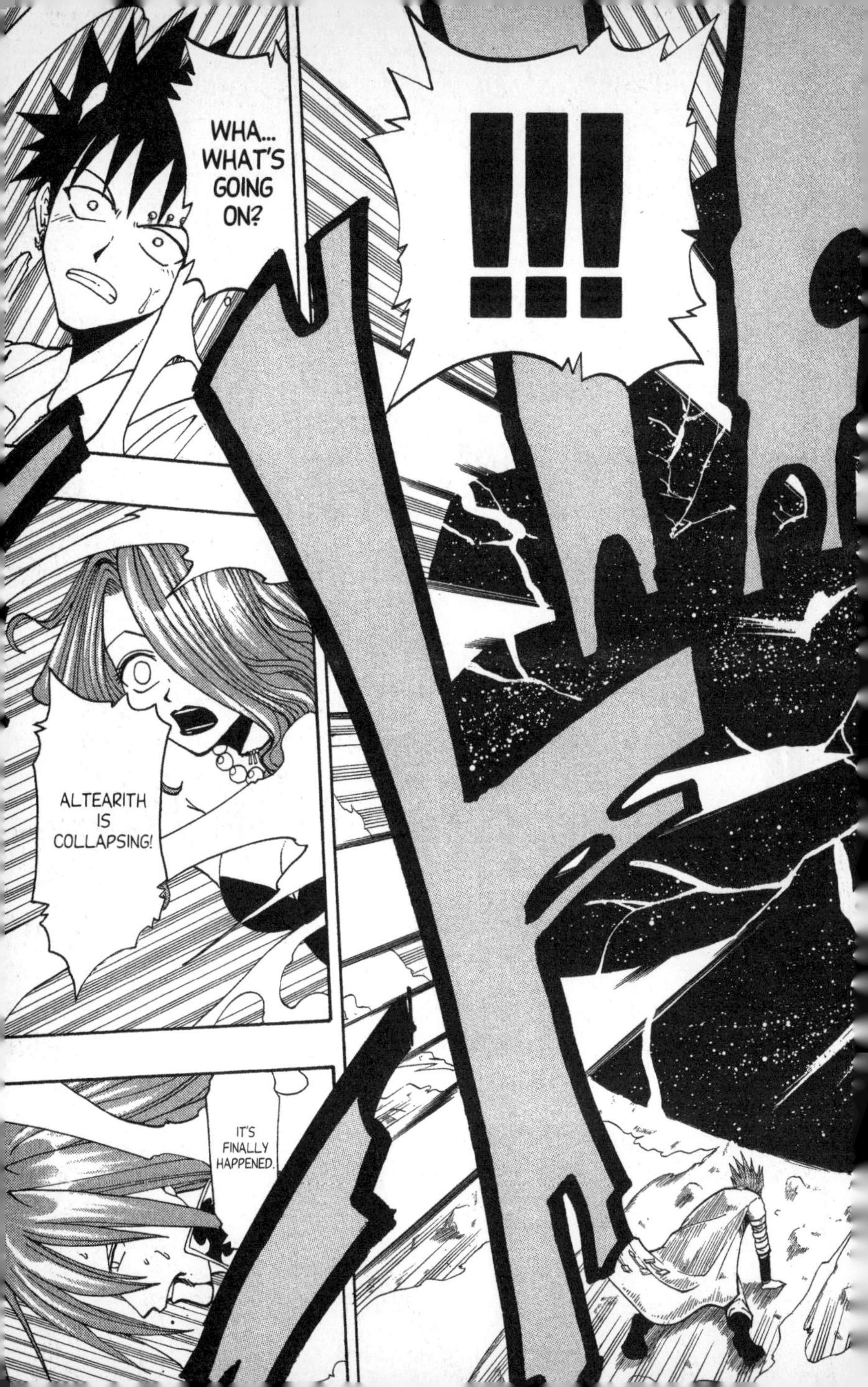
!!!
WHA... WHAT'S GOING ON?
ALTEARITH IS COLLAPSING!
IT'S FINALLY HAPPENED.

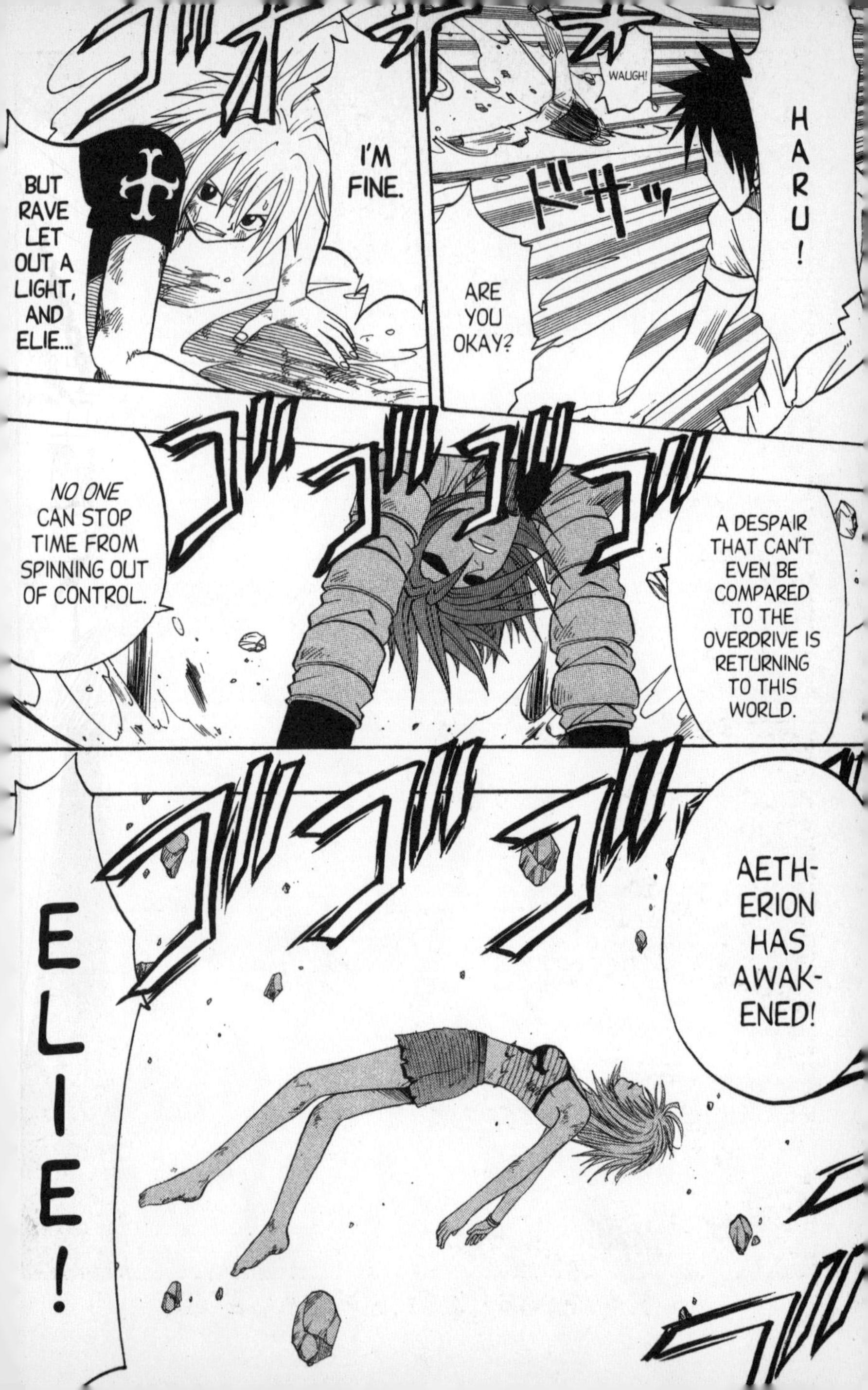
HARU!
WAUGH!
ARE YOU OKAY?
I'M FINE.
BUT RAVE LET OUT A LIGHT, AND ELIE...
A DESPAIR THAT CAN'T EVEN BE COMPARED TO THE OVERDRIVE IS RETURNING TO THIS WORLD.
NO ONE CAN STOP TIME FROM SPINNING OUT OF CONTROL.
AETH-ERION HAS AWAK-ENED!
ELIE!

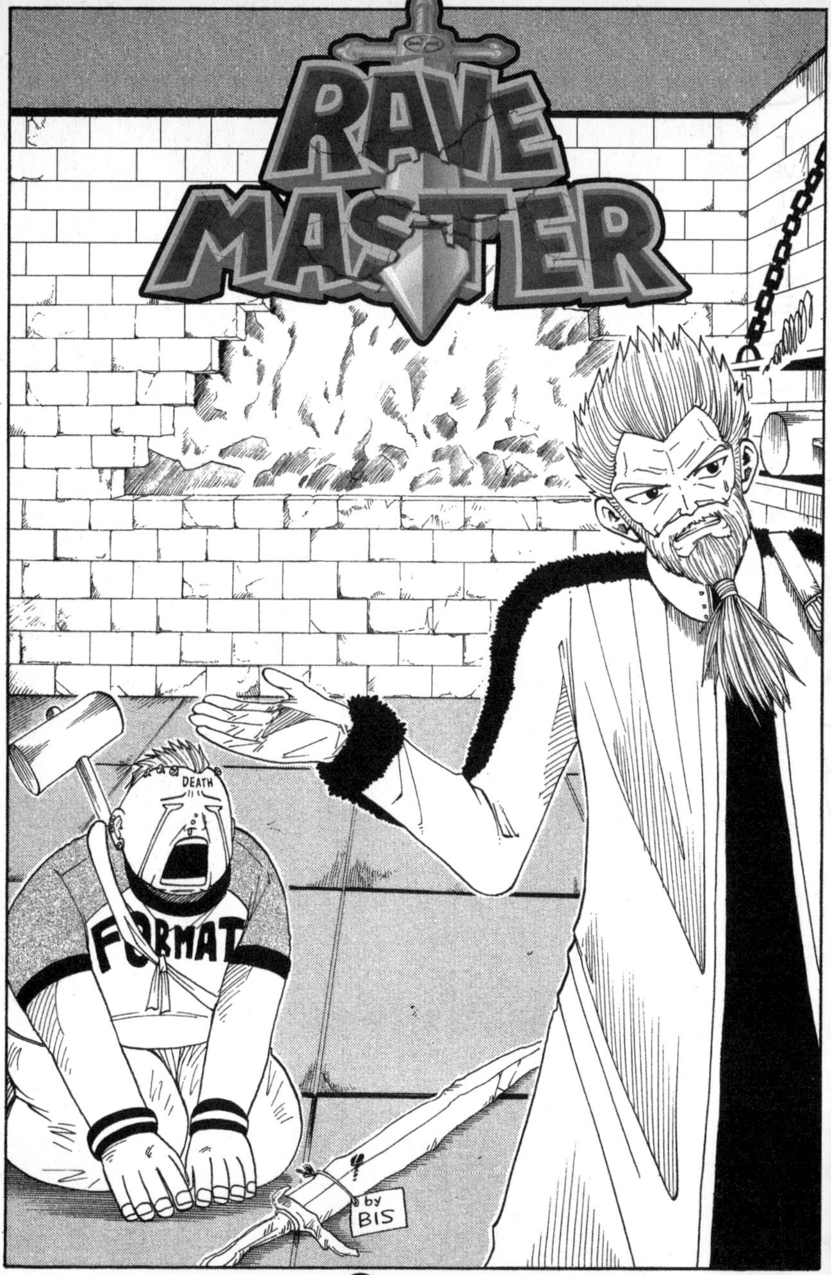
RAVE MASTER
DEATH
FORMAT
by BIS

RAVE: 46 THE FINAL RISK

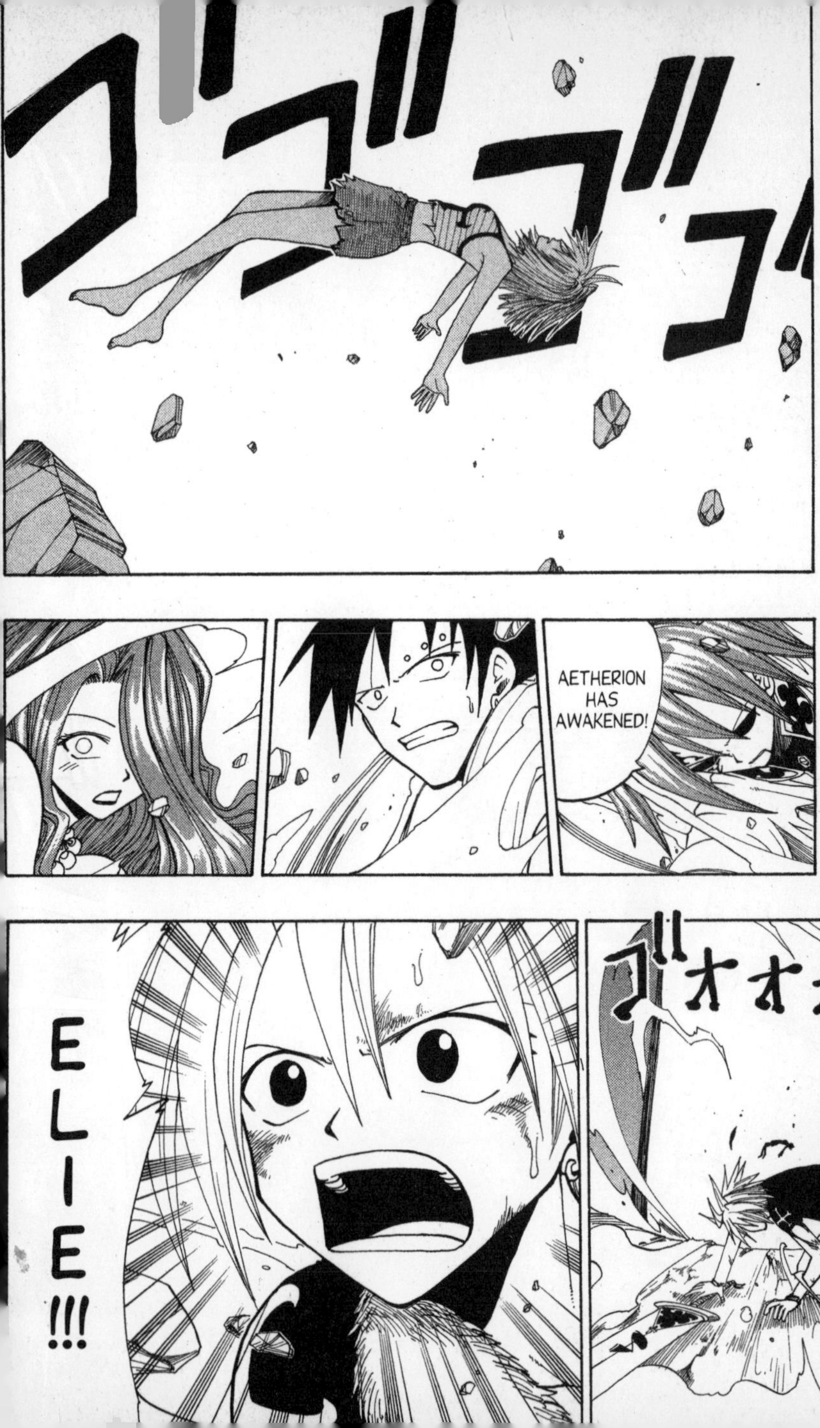
ゴゴゴ
AETHERION HAS AWAKENED!
ゴオオオ
ELIE!!!

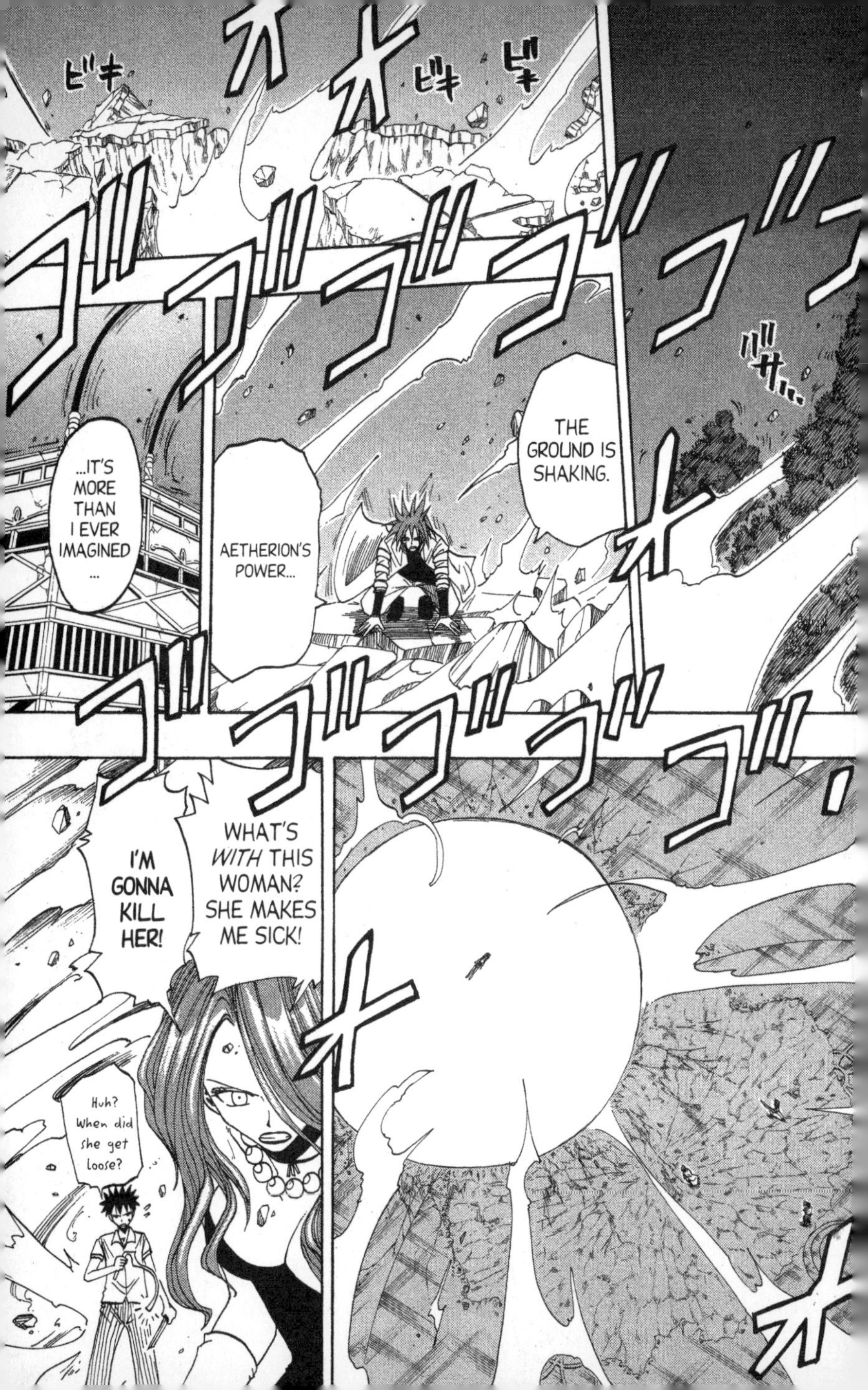
THE GROUND IS SHAKING.
AETHERION'S POWER...
...IT'S MORE THAN I EVER IMAGINED ...
WHAT'S *WITH* THIS WOMAN? SHE MAKES ME SICK!
I'M GONNA KILL HER!
Huh? When did she get loose?

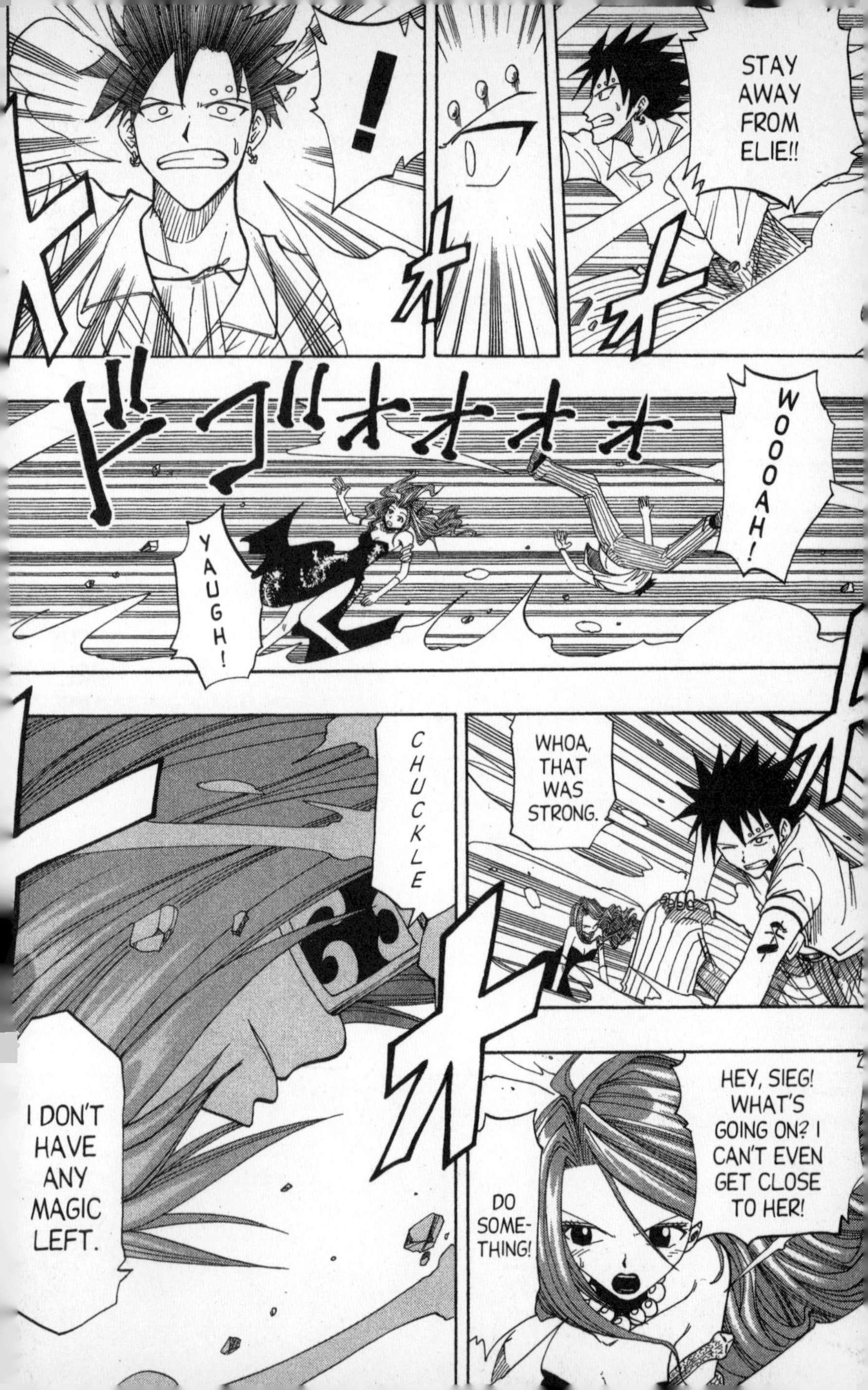
STAY AWAY FROM ELIE!!
!
ドゴオオオオ
WOOOOAH!
YAUGH!
WHOA, THAT WAS STRONG.
CHUCKLE
HEY, SIEG! WHAT'S GOING ON? I CAN'T EVEN GET CLOSE TO HER!
DO SOME-THING!
I DON'T HAVE ANY MAGIC LEFT.

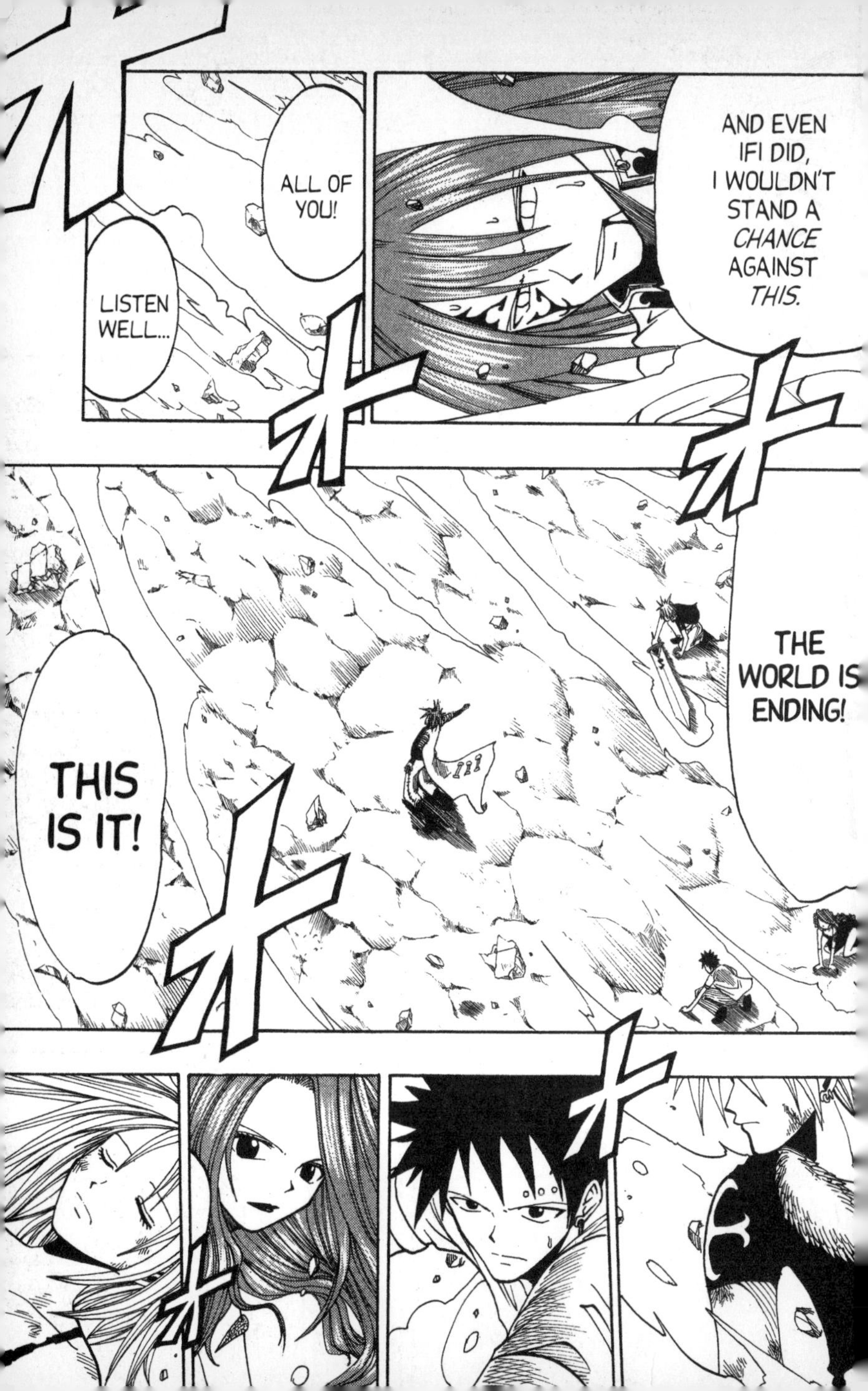
AND EVEN IFI DID, I WOULDN'T STAND A *CHANCE* AGAINST *THIS.*
ALL OF YOU!
LISTEN WELL...
THE WORLD IS ENDING!
THIS IS IT!

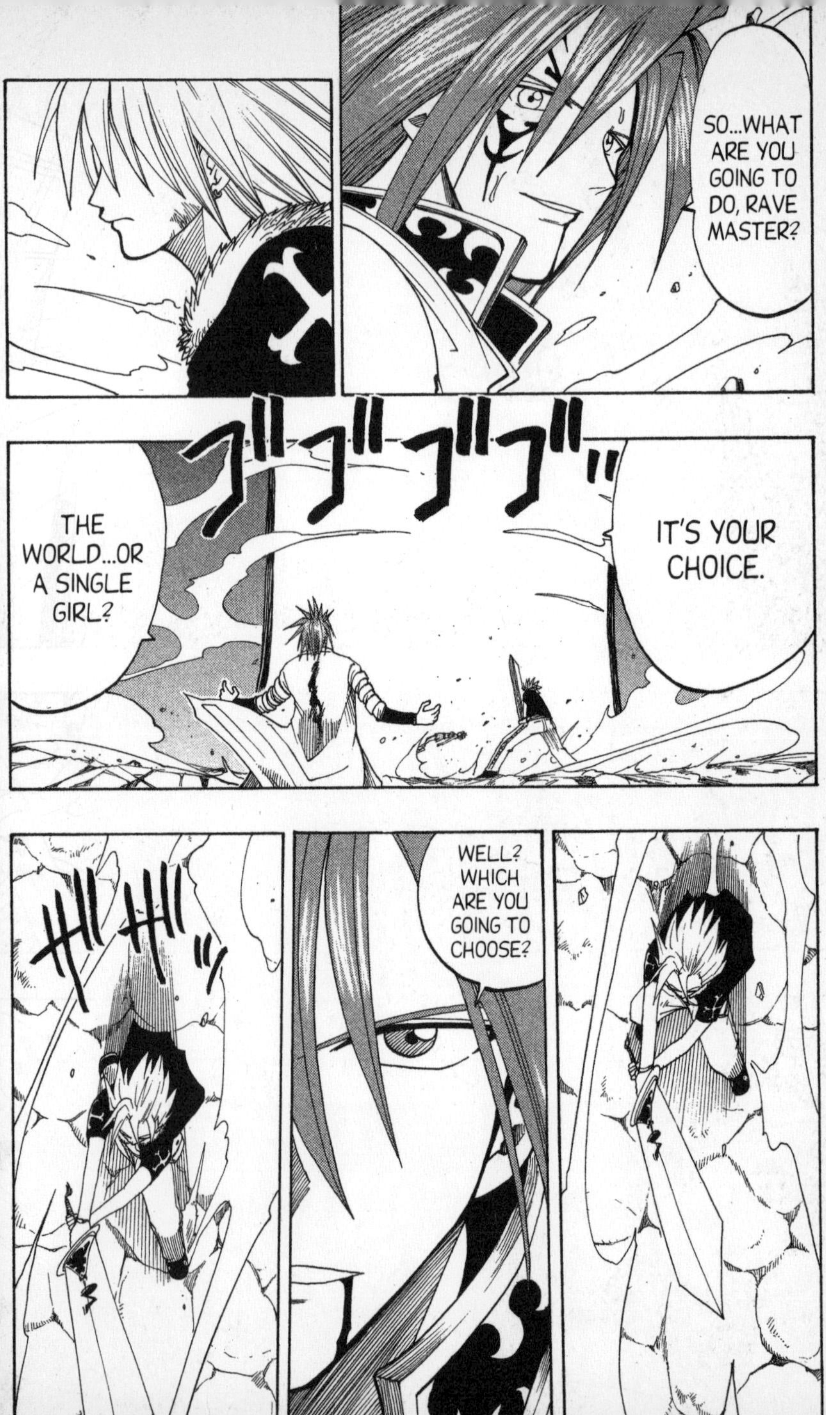
SO...WHAT ARE YOU GOING TO DO, RAVE MASTER?
ゴゴゴゴ
IT'S YOUR CHOICE.
THE WORLD...OR A SINGLE GIRL?
WELL? WHICH ARE YOU GOING TO CHOOSE?
ザザッ

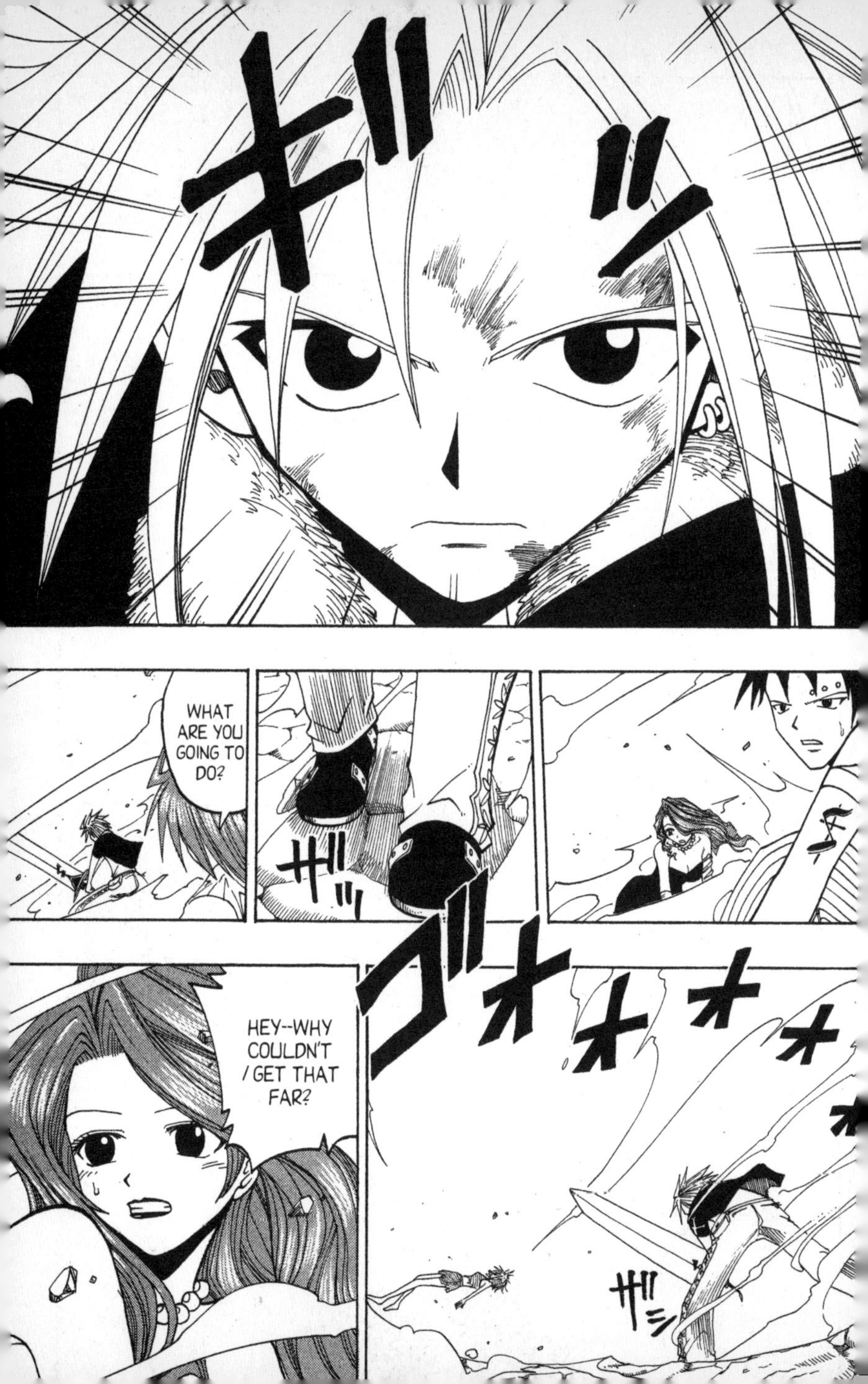
WHAT ARE YOU GOING TO DO?
HEY--WHY COULDN'T I GET THAT FAR?

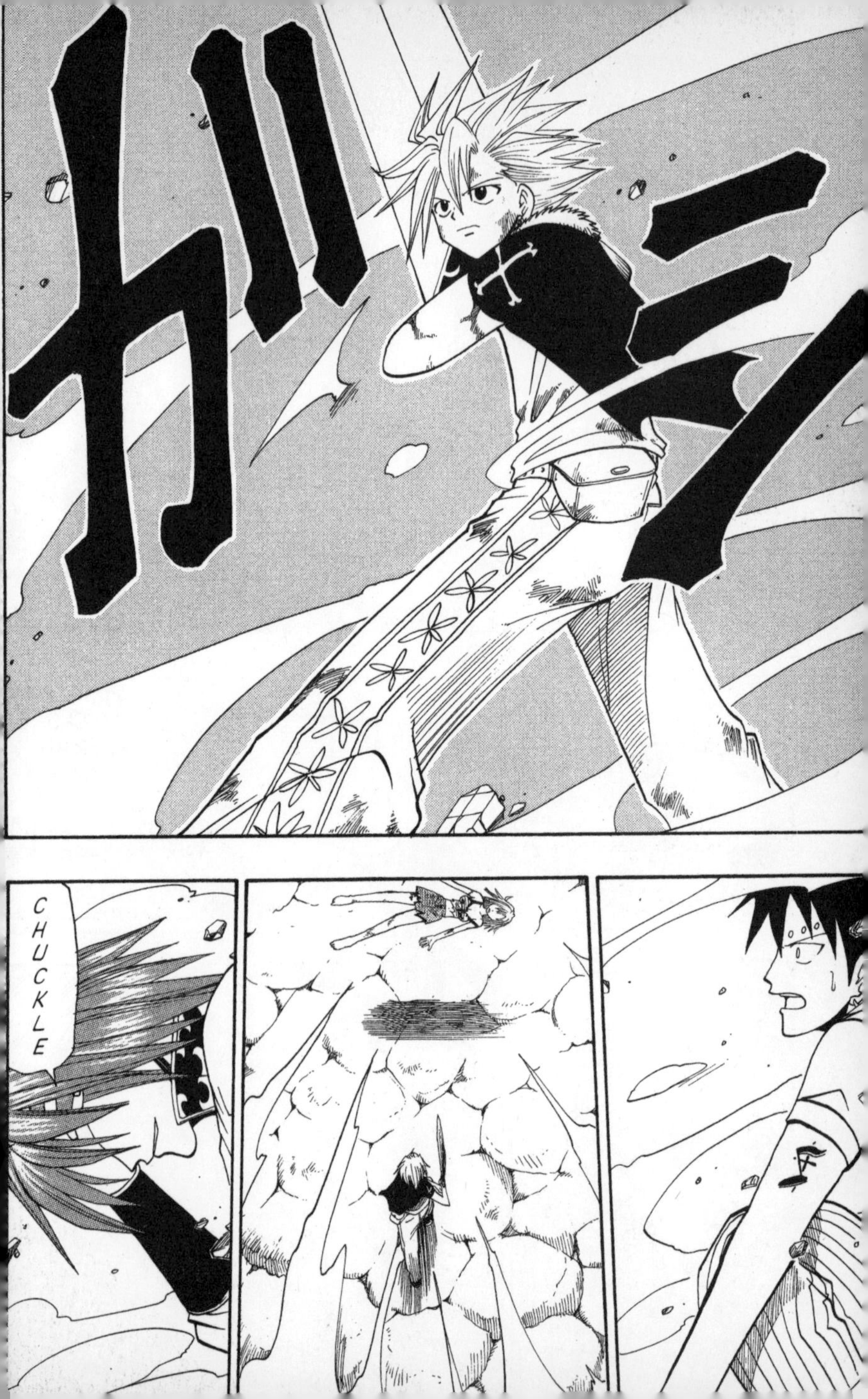
CHUCKLE

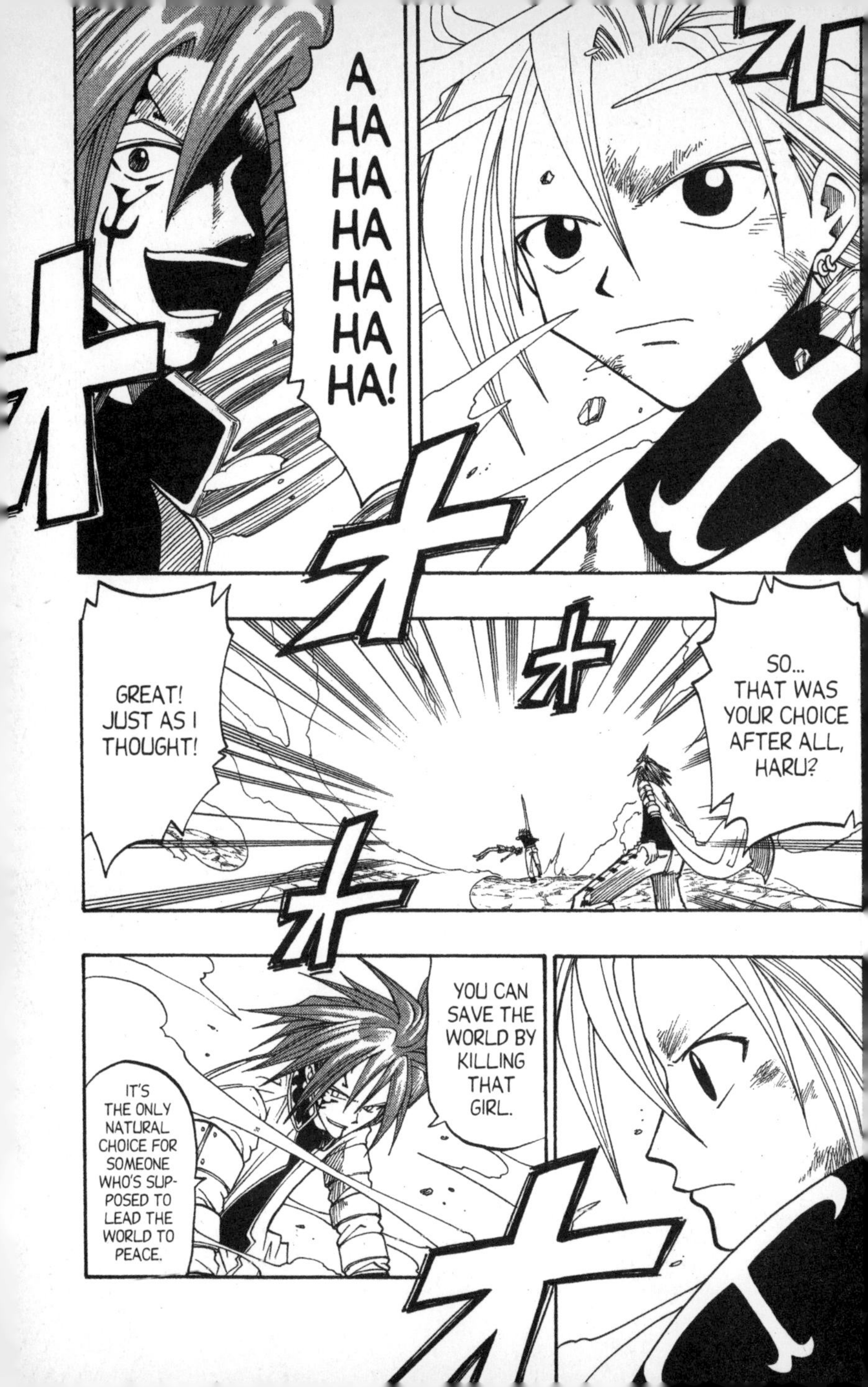
A HA HA HA HA HA HA HA!
SO... THAT WAS YOUR CHOICE AFTER ALL, HARU?
GREAT! JUST AS I THOUGHT!
YOU CAN SAVE THE WORLD BY KILLING THAT GIRL.
IT'S THE ONLY NATURAL CHOICE FOR SOMEONE WHO'S SUP-POSED TO LEAD THE WORLD TO PEACE.

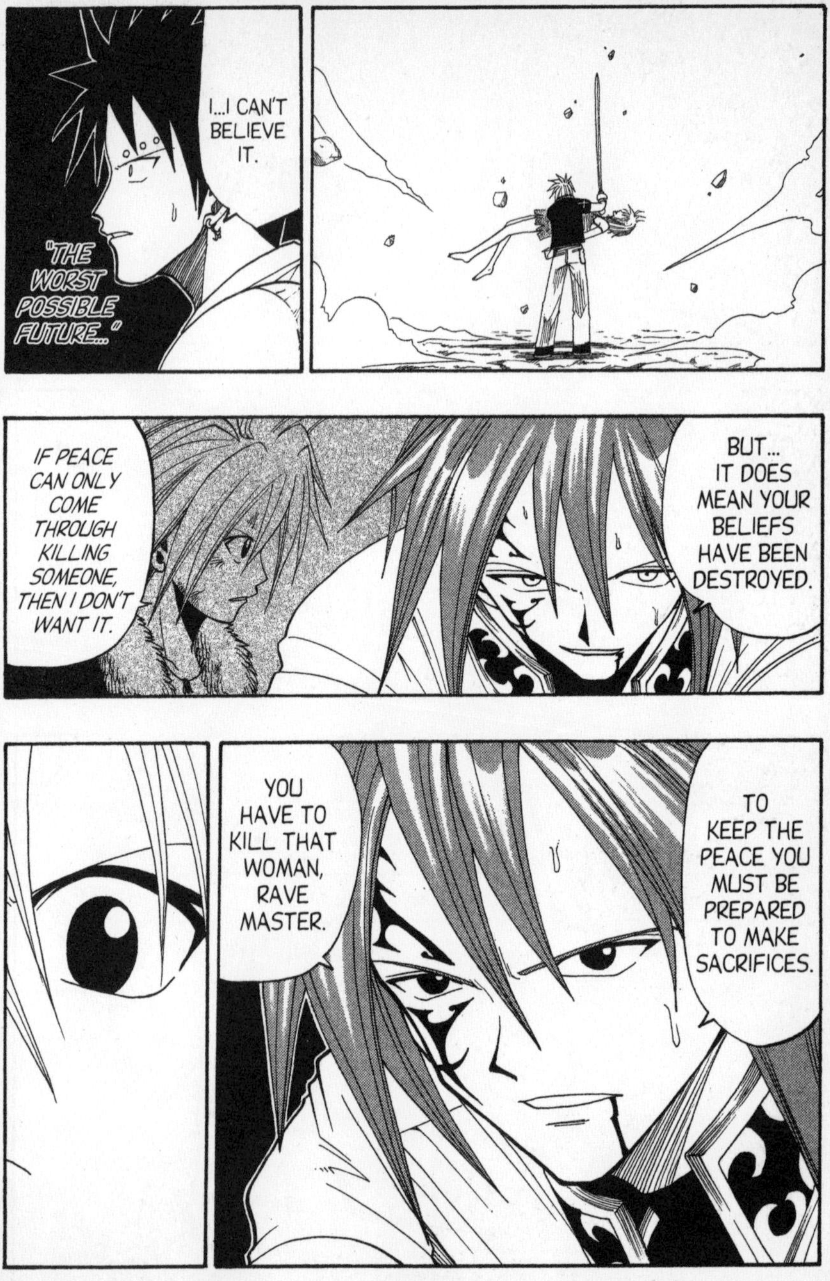
I...I CAN'T BELIEVE IT.
"THE WORST POSSIBLE FUTURE..."
BUT... IT DOES MEAN YOUR BELIEFS HAVE BEEN DESTROYED.
IF PEACE CAN ONLY COME THROUGH KILLING SOMEONE, THEN I DON'T WANT IT.
TO KEEP THE PEACE YOU MUST BE PREPARED TO MAKE SACRIFICES.
YOU HAVE TO KILL THAT WOMAN, RAVE MASTER.

HARU!

THIS CAN'T BE HAPPENING!

STOP IT, HARU!

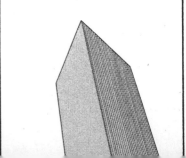

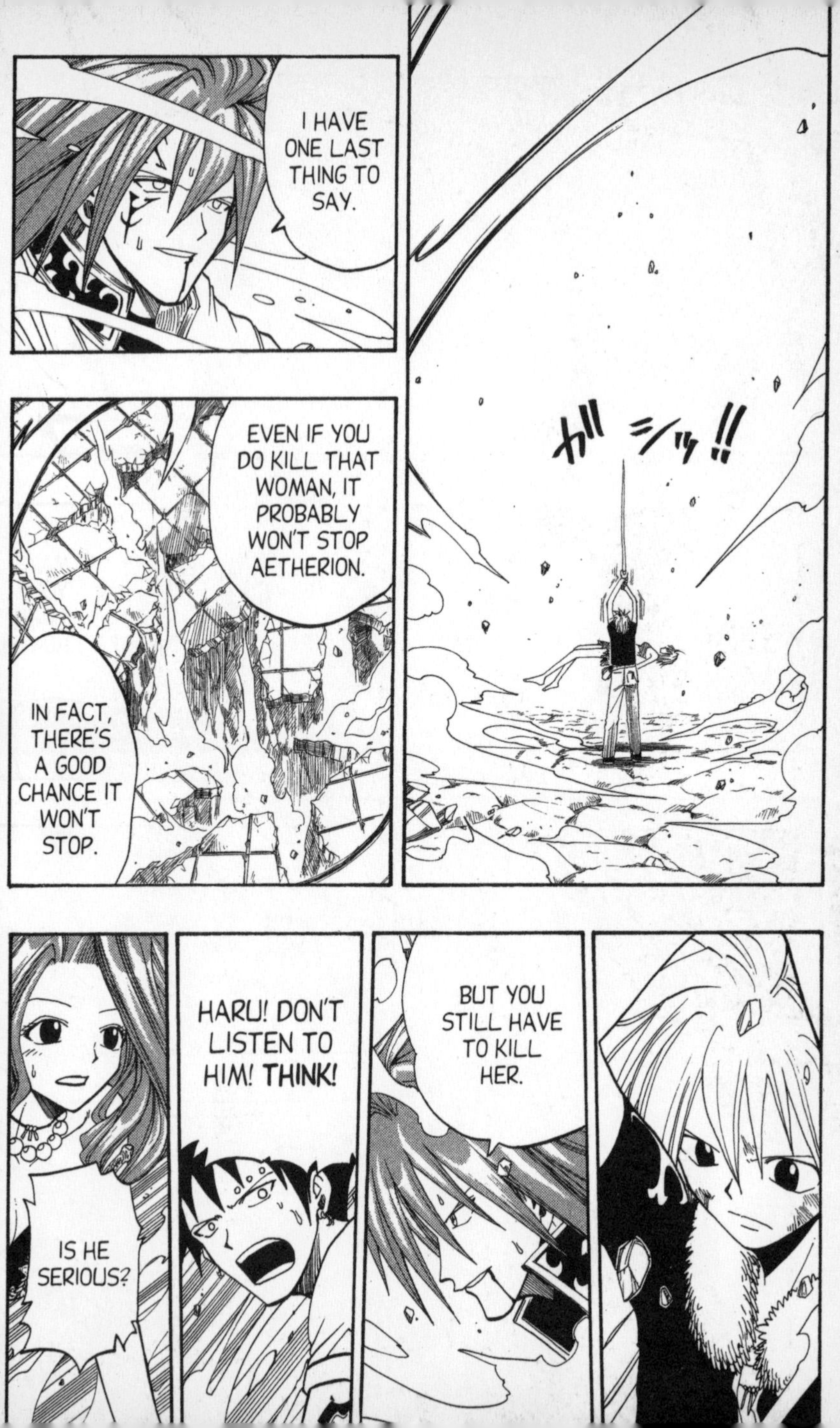
ガシッ!!
I HAVE ONE LAST THING TO SAY.
EVEN IF YOU DO KILL THAT WOMAN, IT PROBABLY WON'T STOP AETHERION.
IN FACT, THERE'S A GOOD CHANCE IT WON'T STOP.
BUT YOU STILL HAVE TO KILL HER.
HARU! DON'T LISTEN TO HIM! THINK!
IS HE SERIOUS?

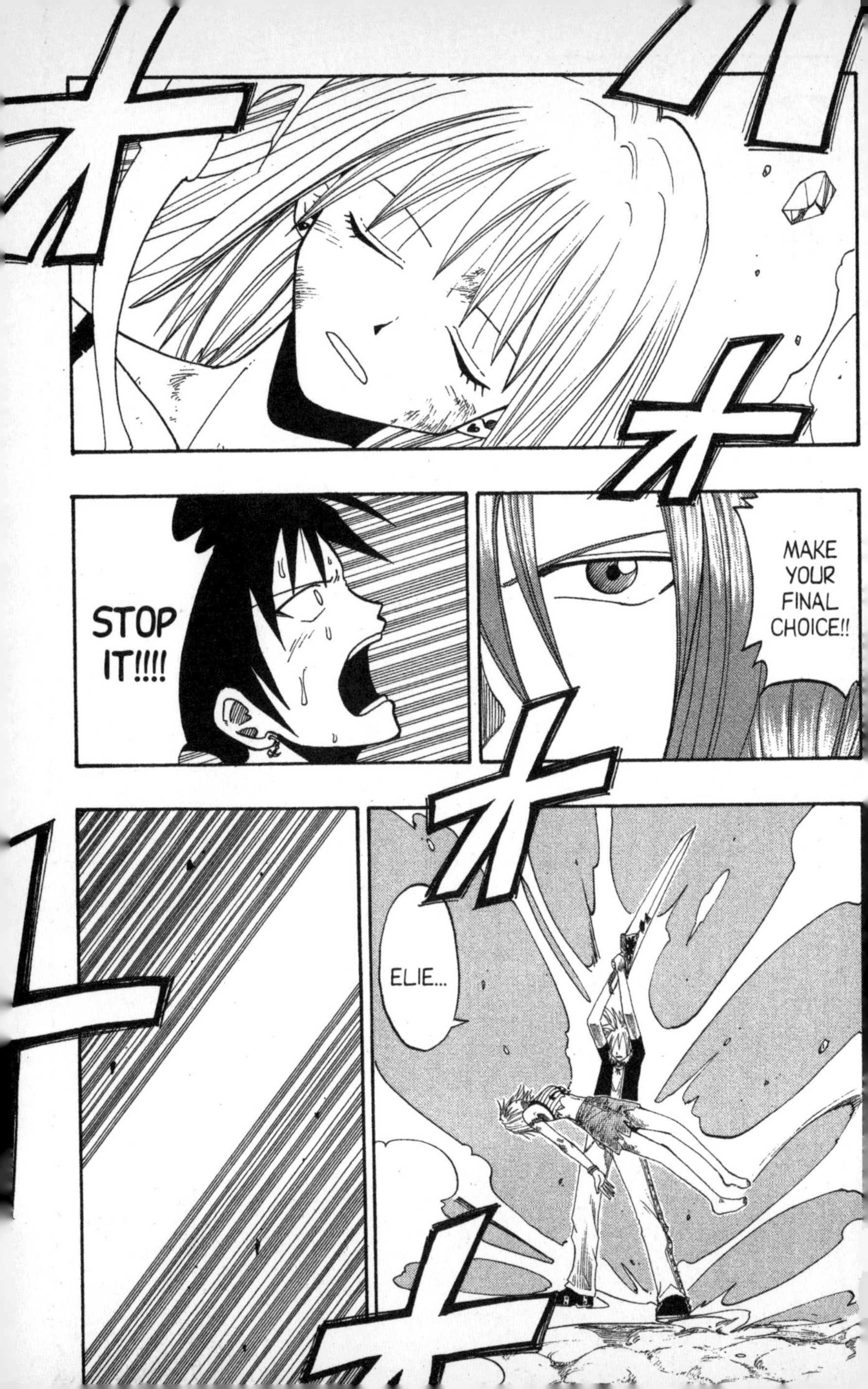
MAKE YOUR FINAL CHOICE!!
STOP IT!!!!!
ELIE...

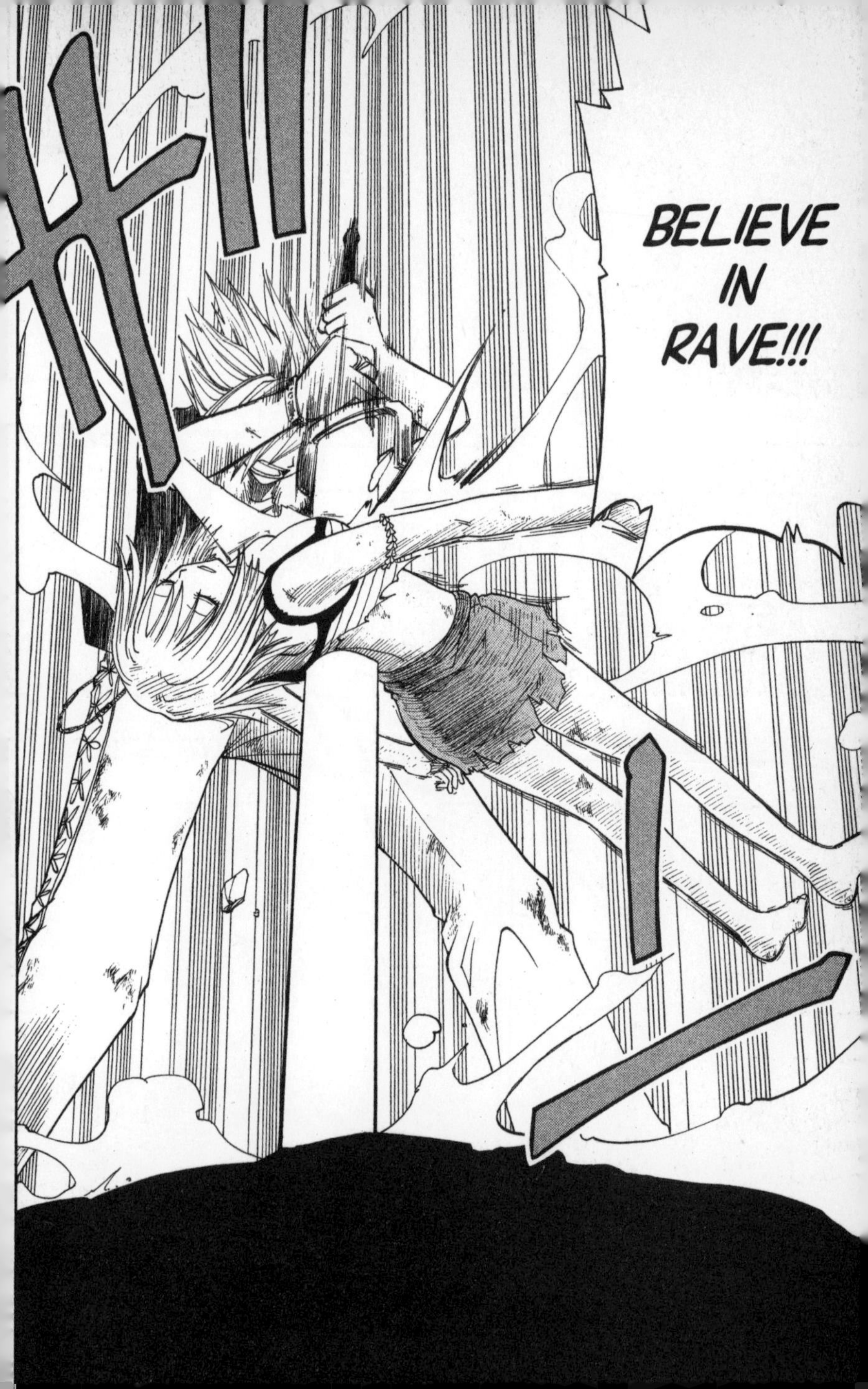
BELIEVE IN RAVE!!!

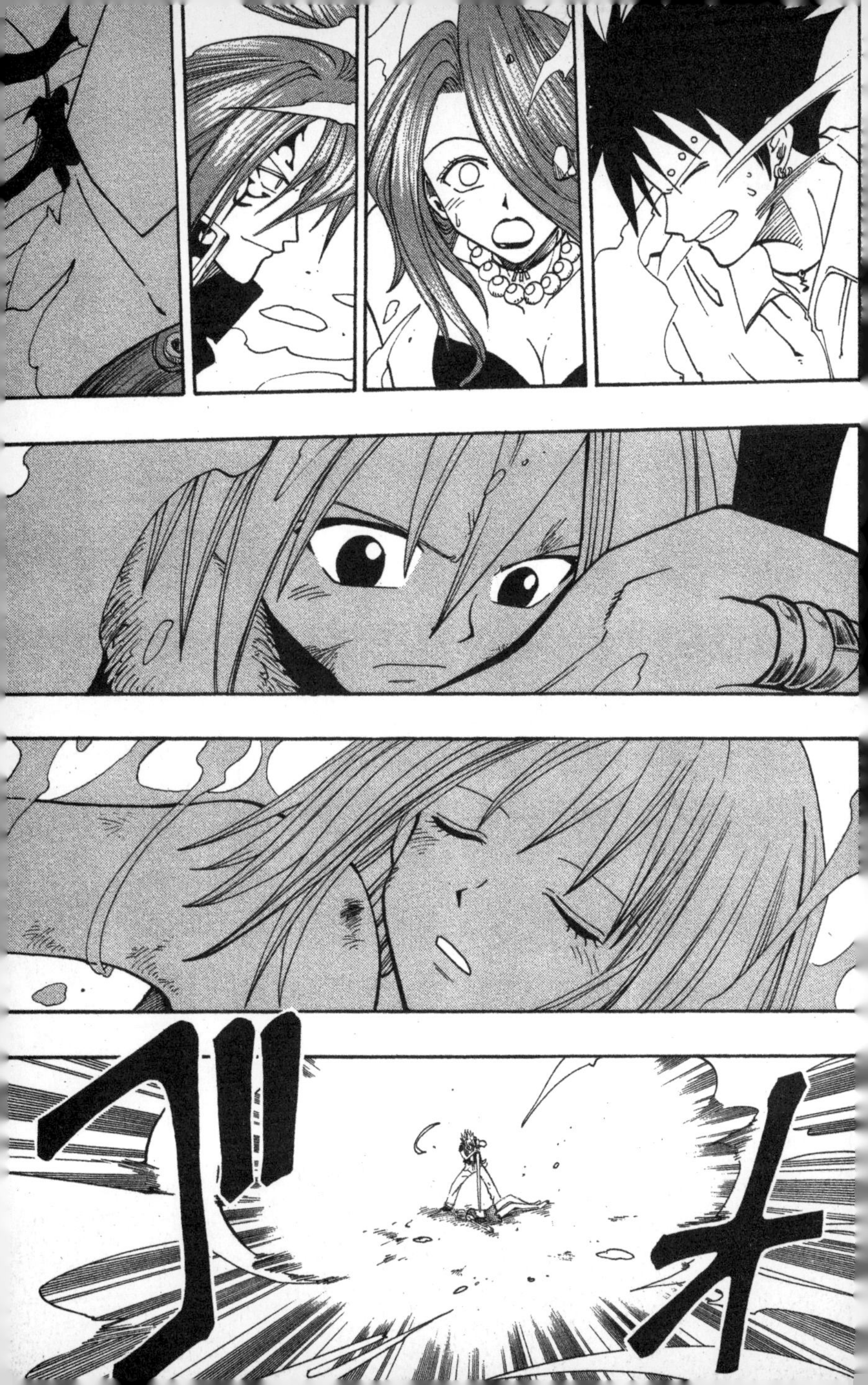

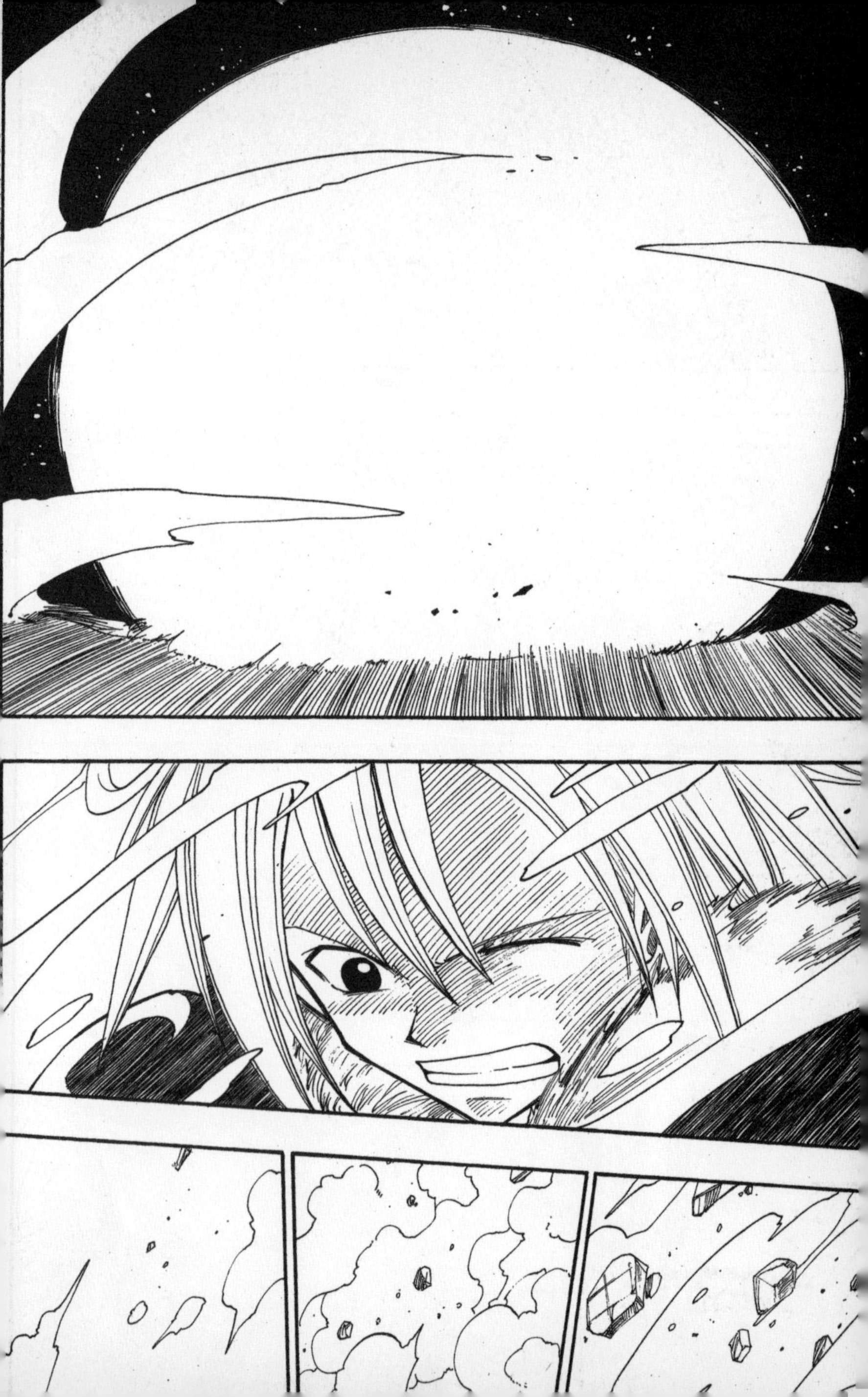

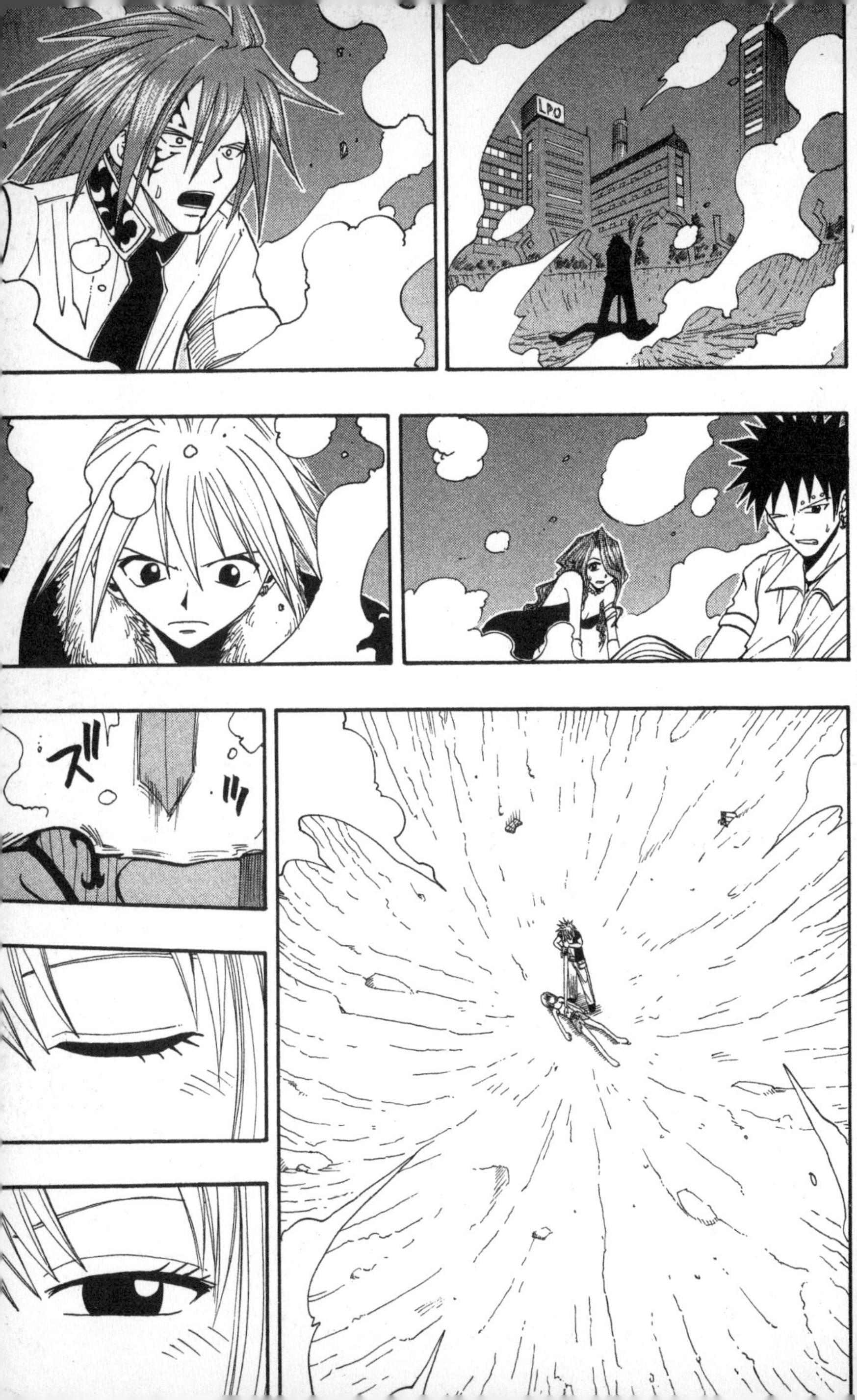

LPO
ズッ

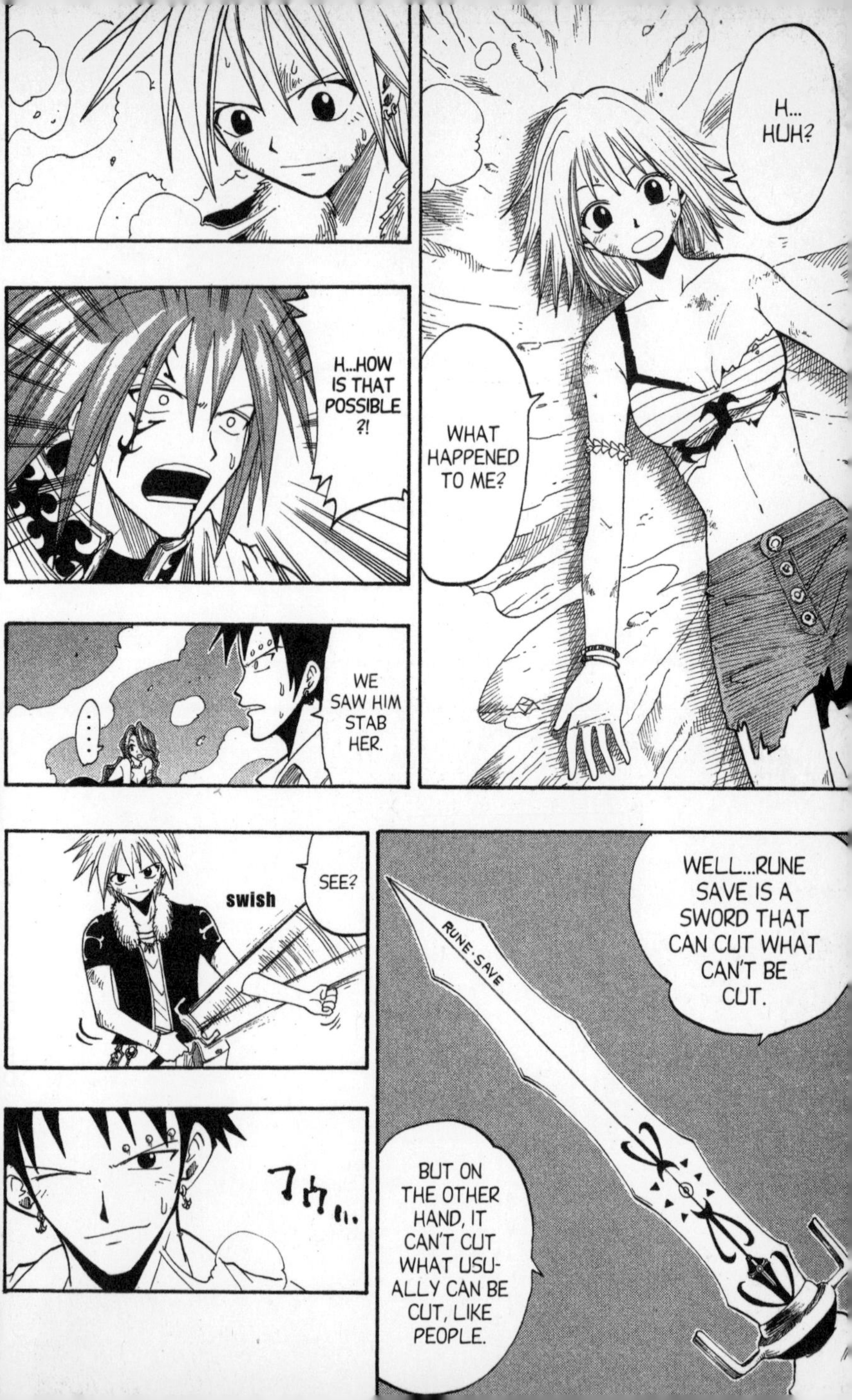
H... HUH?
WHAT HAPPENED TO ME?
H...HOW IS THAT POSSIBLE ?!
...
WE SAW HIM STAB HER.
RUNE・SAVE
WELL...RUNE SAVE IS A SWORD THAT CAN CUT WHAT CAN'T BE CUT.
BUT ON THE OTHER HAND, IT CAN'T CUT WHAT USU-ALLY CAN BE CUT, LIKE PEOPLE.
SEE?
swish

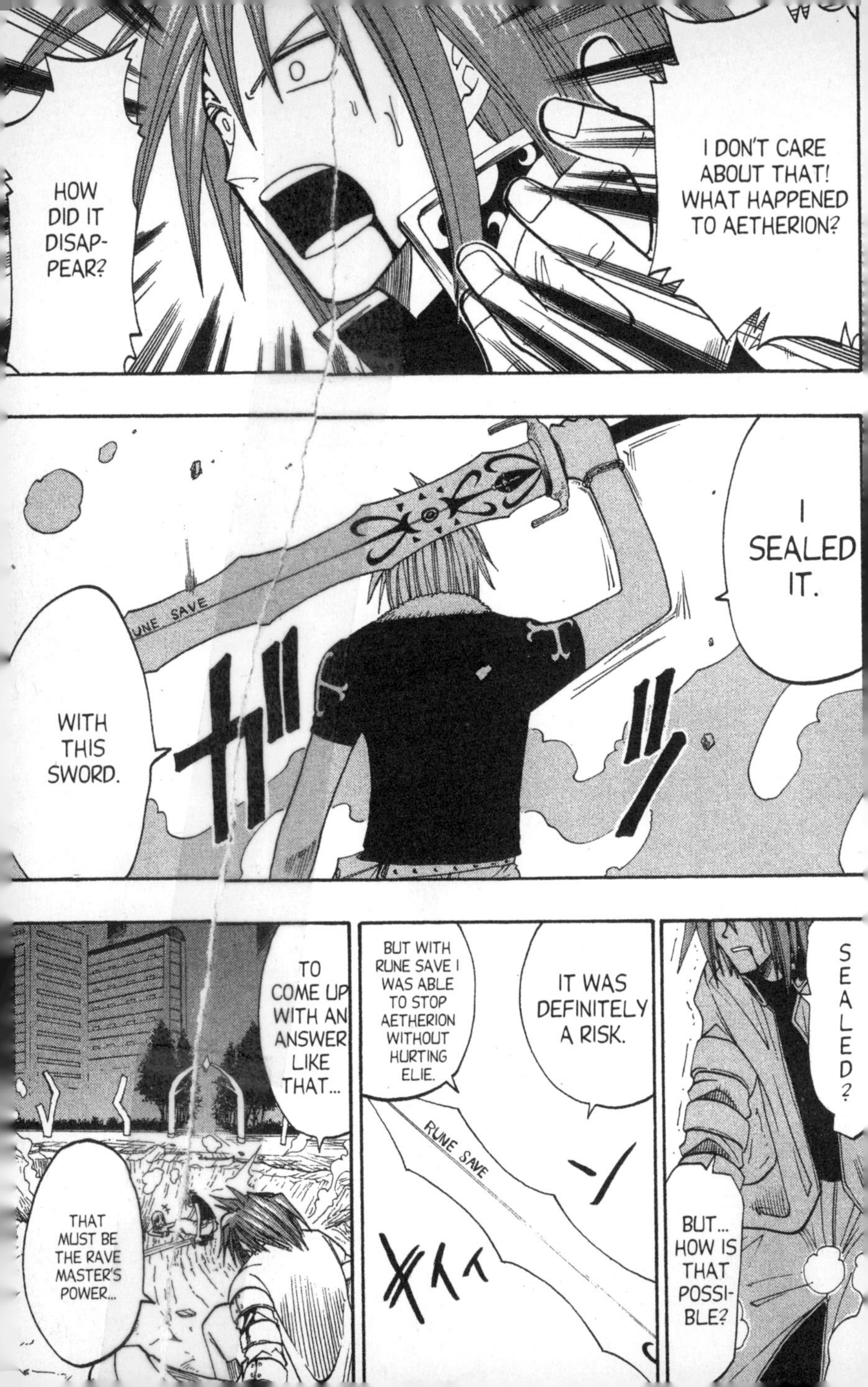
I DON'T CARE ABOUT THAT! WHAT HAPPENED TO AETHERION?
HOW DID IT DISAP-PEAR?
I SEALED IT.
RUNE SAVE
WITH THIS SWORD.
SEALED?
BUT... HOW IS THAT POSSI-BLE?
IT WAS DEFINITELY A RISK.
BUT WITH RUNE SAVE I WAS ABLE TO STOP AETHERION WITHOUT HURTING ELIE.
RUNE SAVE
TO COME UP WITH AN ANSWER LIKE THAT...
THAT MUST BE THE RAVE MASTER'S POWER...

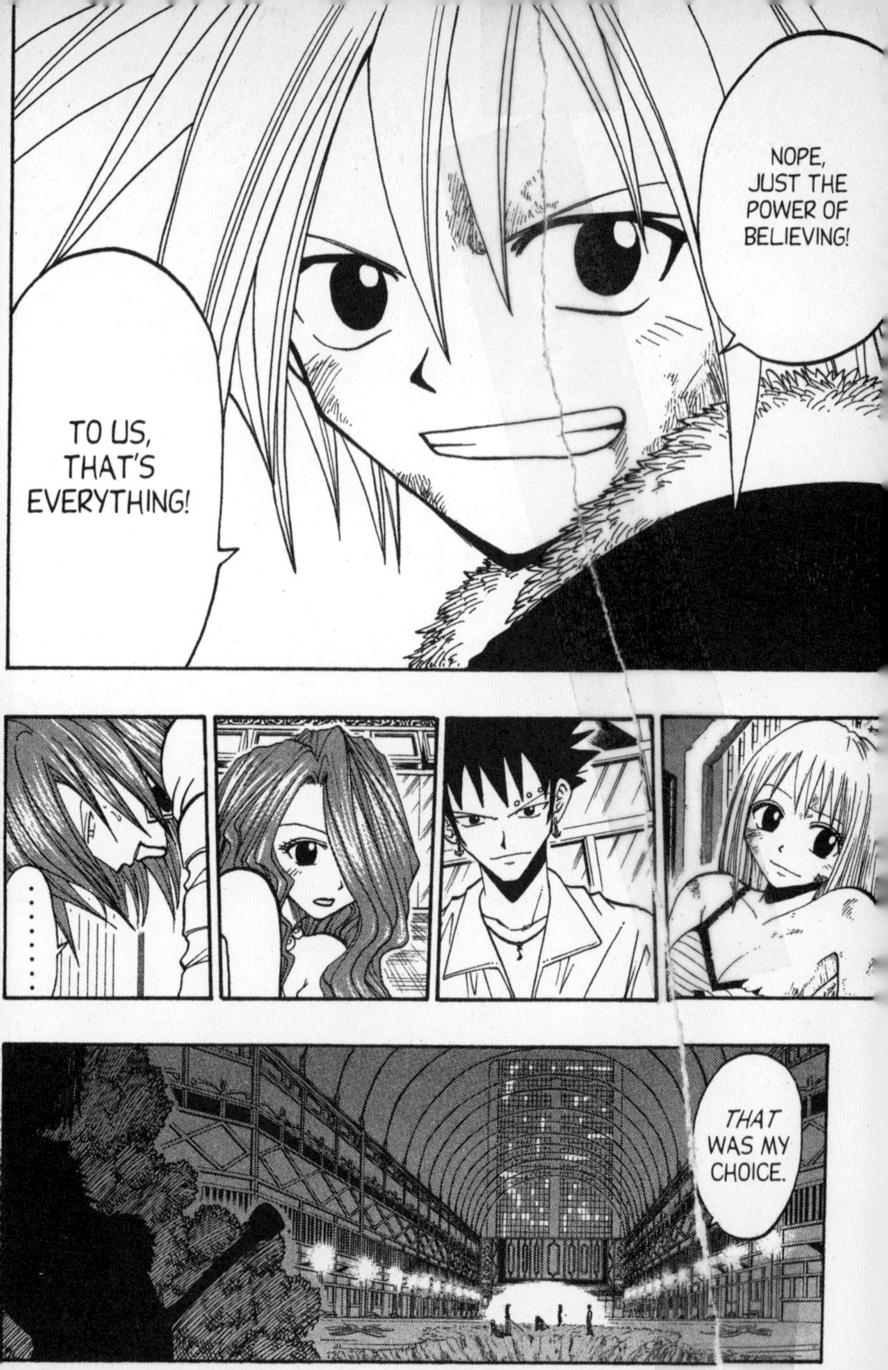
NOPE, JUST THE POWER OF BELIEVING!
TO US, THAT'S EVERYTHING!
......
THAT WAS MY CHOICE.

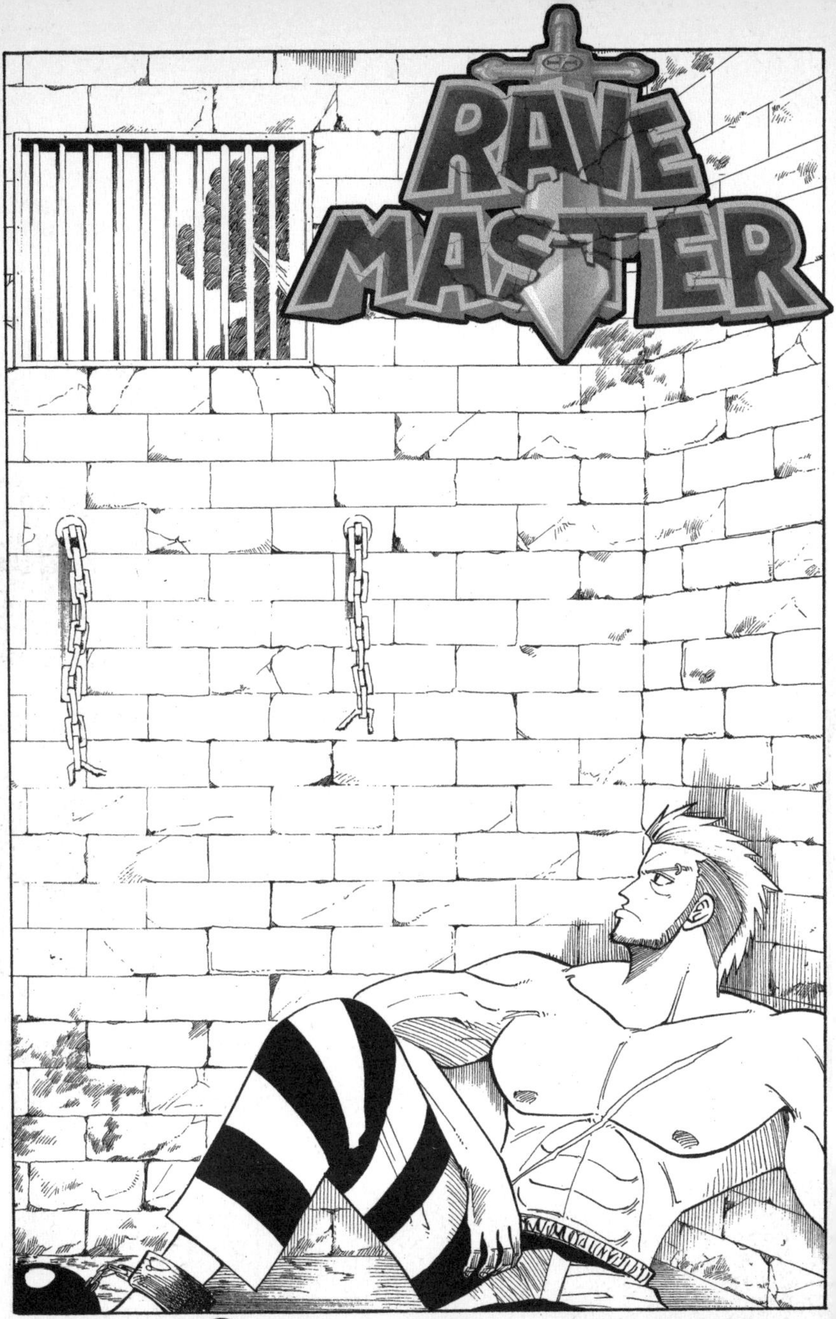
RAVE MASTER

RAVE: 47 HOLD TIGHT TO THE MOMENT

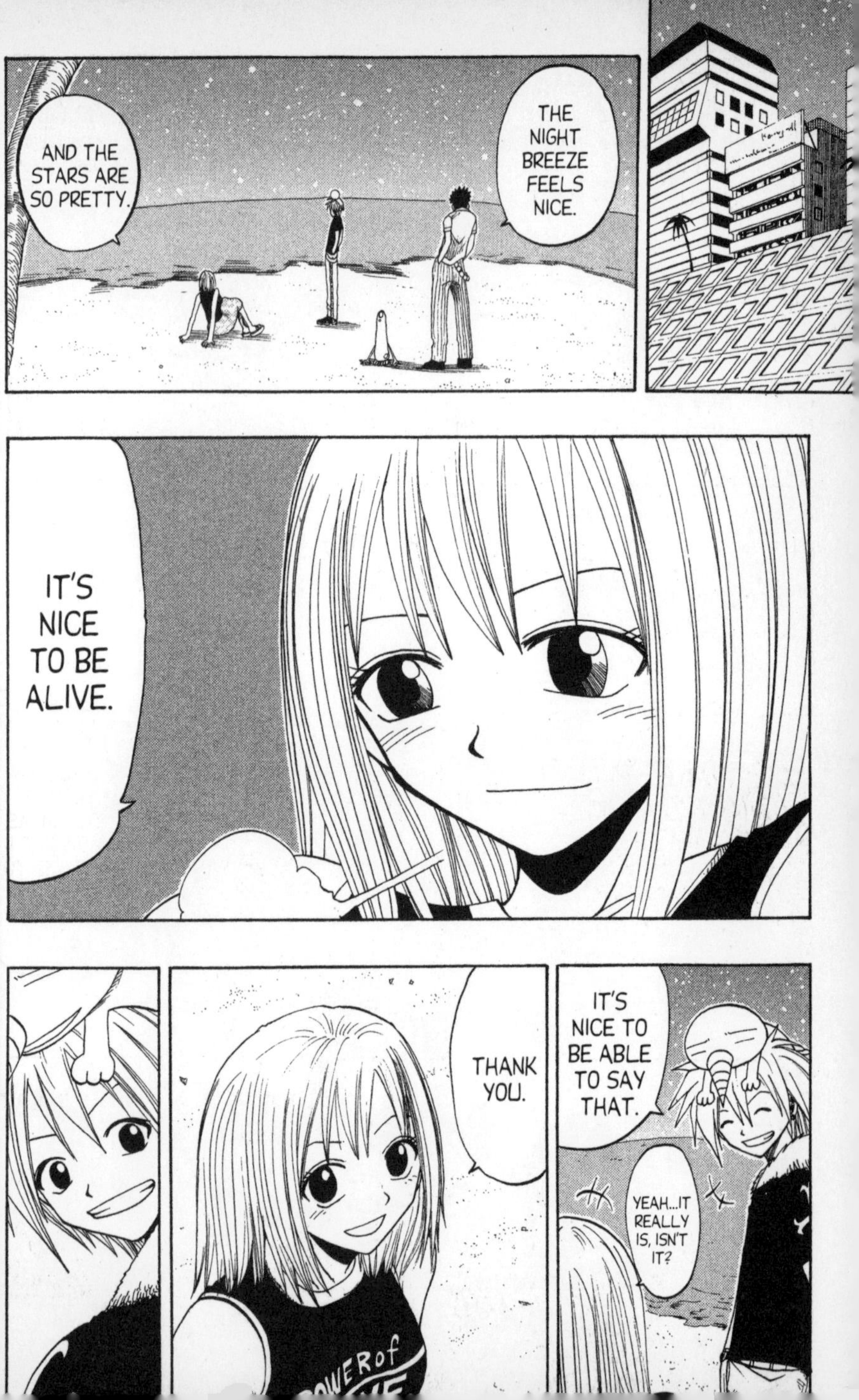
THE NIGHT BREEZE FEELS NICE.
AND THE STARS ARE SO PRETTY.
IT'S NICE TO BE ALIVE.
IT'S NICE TO BE ABLE TO SAY THAT.
YEAH...IT REALLY IS, ISN'T IT?
THANK YOU.

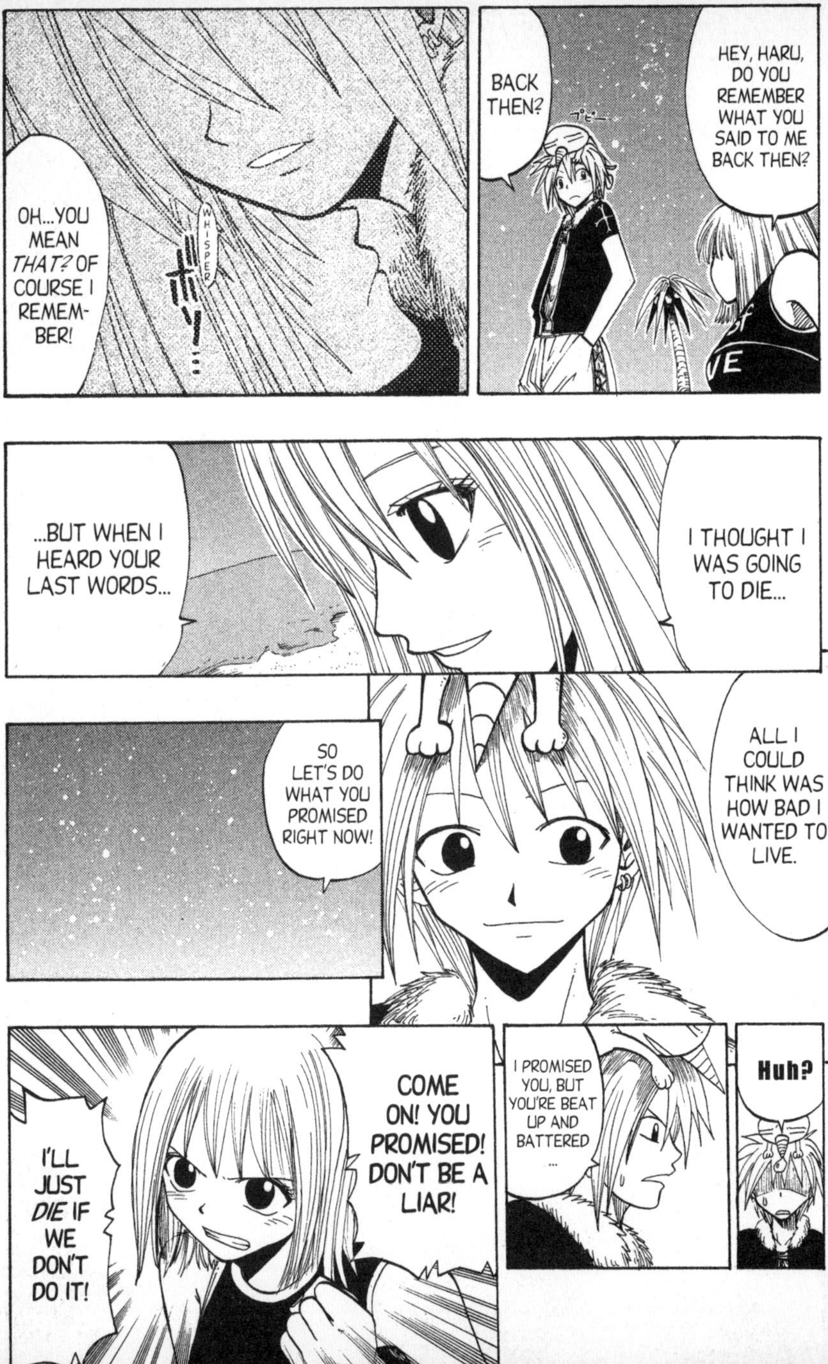

HEY, HARU, DO YOU REMEMBER WHAT YOU SAID TO ME BACK THEN?
BACK THEN?
OH...YOU MEAN *THAT?* OF COURSE I REMEM-BER!
WHISPER
I THOUGHT I WAS GOING TO DIE...
...BUT WHEN I HEARD YOUR LAST WORDS...
ALL I COULD THINK WAS HOW BAD I WANTED TO LIVE.
SO LET'S DO WHAT YOU PROMISED RIGHT NOW!
Huh?
I PROMISED YOU, BUT YOU'RE BEAT UP AND BATTERED ...
COME ON! YOU PROMISED! DON'T BE A LIAR!
I'LL JUST *DIE* IF WE DON'T DO IT!

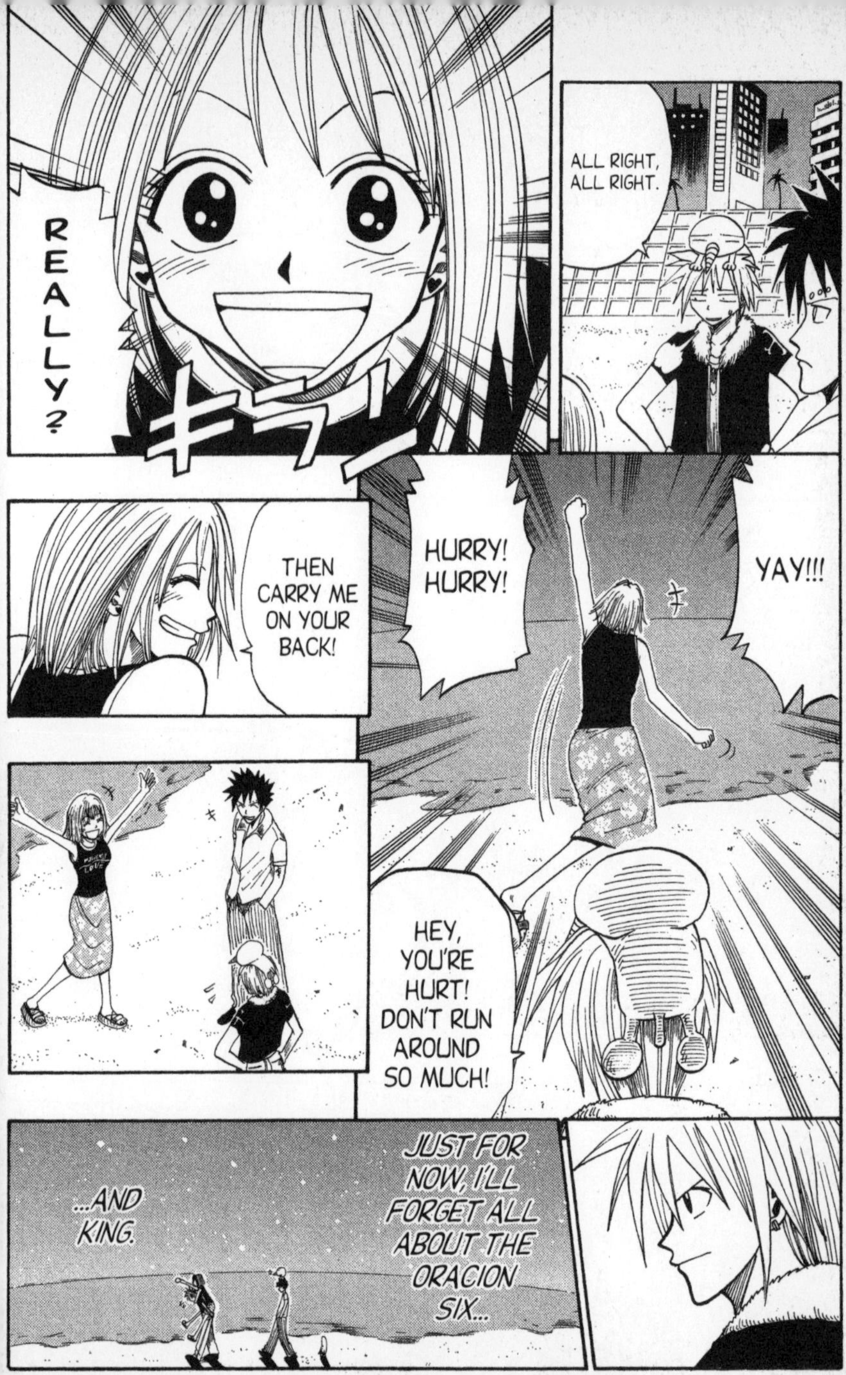
ALL RIGHT, ALL RIGHT.
REALLY?
キラー
YAY!!!
HURRY! HURRY!
キ
HEY, YOU'RE HURT! DON'T RUN AROUND SO MUCH!
THEN CARRY ME ON YOUR BACK!
JUST FOR NOW, I'LL FORGET ALL ABOUT THE ORACION SIX...
...AND KING.

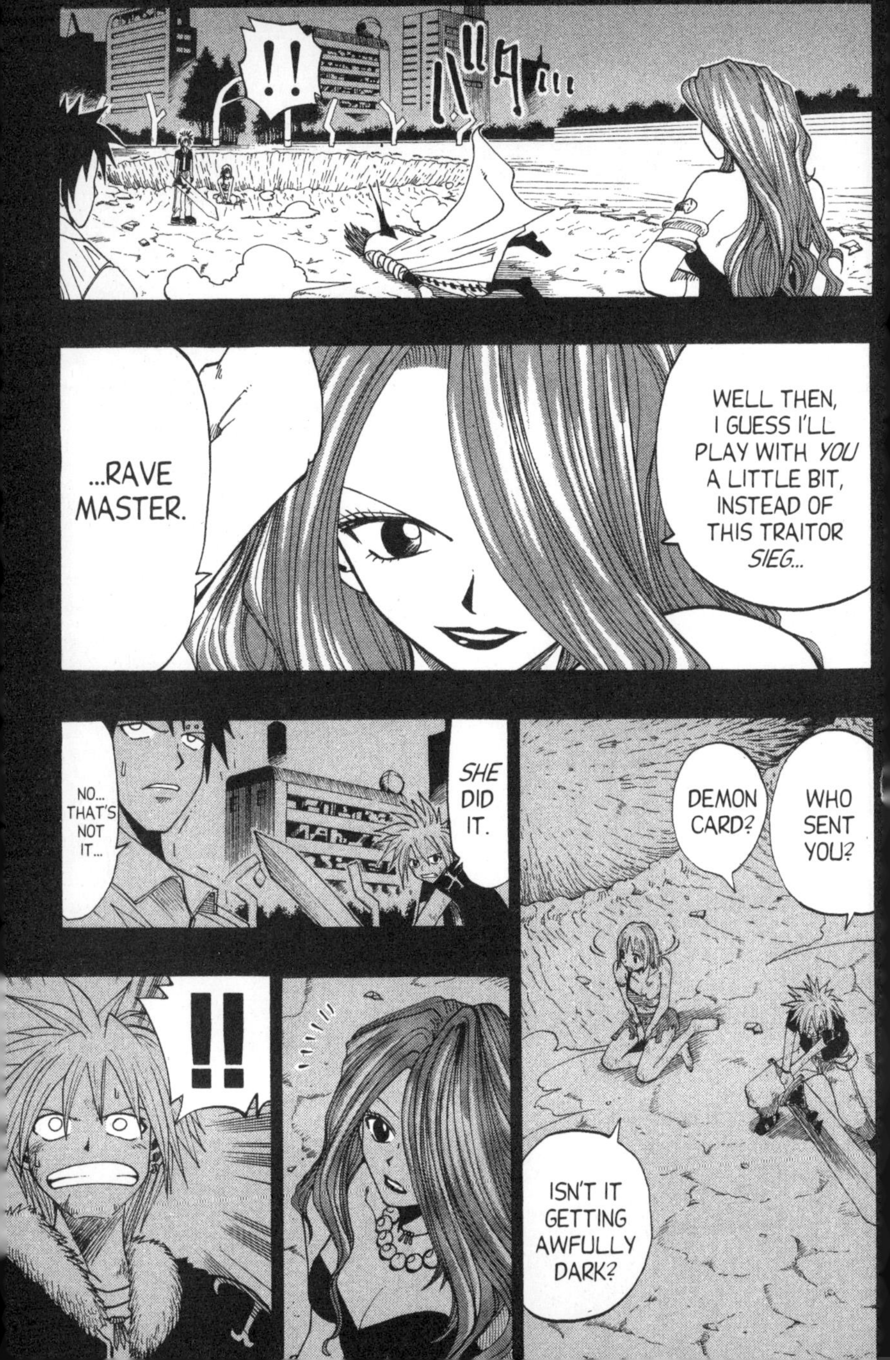
!!
WELL THEN, I GUESS I'LL PLAY WITH YOU A LITTLE BIT, INSTEAD OF THIS TRAITOR SIEG...
...RAVE MASTER.
WHO SENT YOU?
DEMON CARD?
ISN'T IT GETTING AWFULLY DARK?
SHE DID IT.
NO... THAT'S NOT IT...
!!

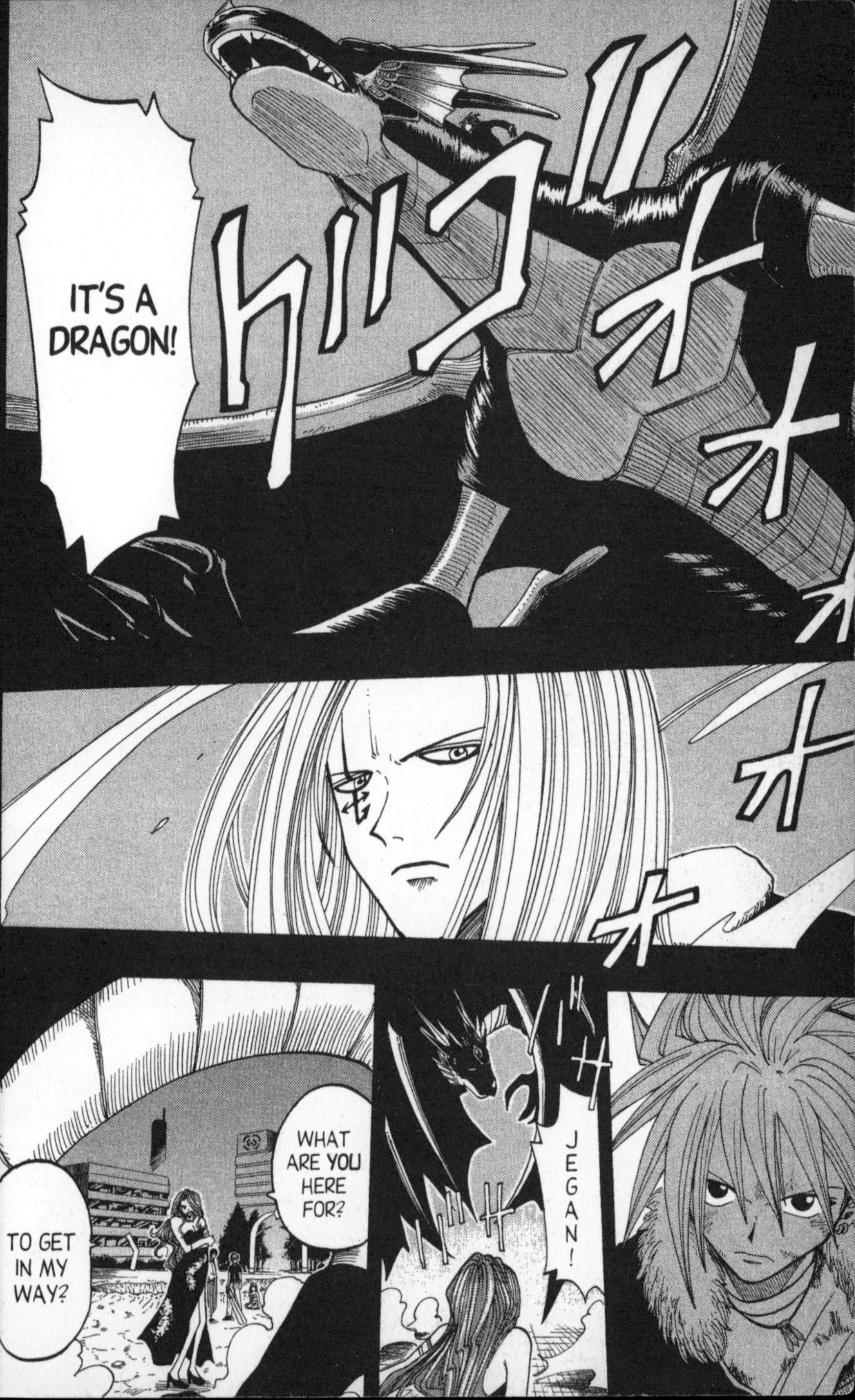
IT'S A DRAGON!
JEGAN!
WHAT ARE YOU HERE FOR?
TO GET IN MY WAY?

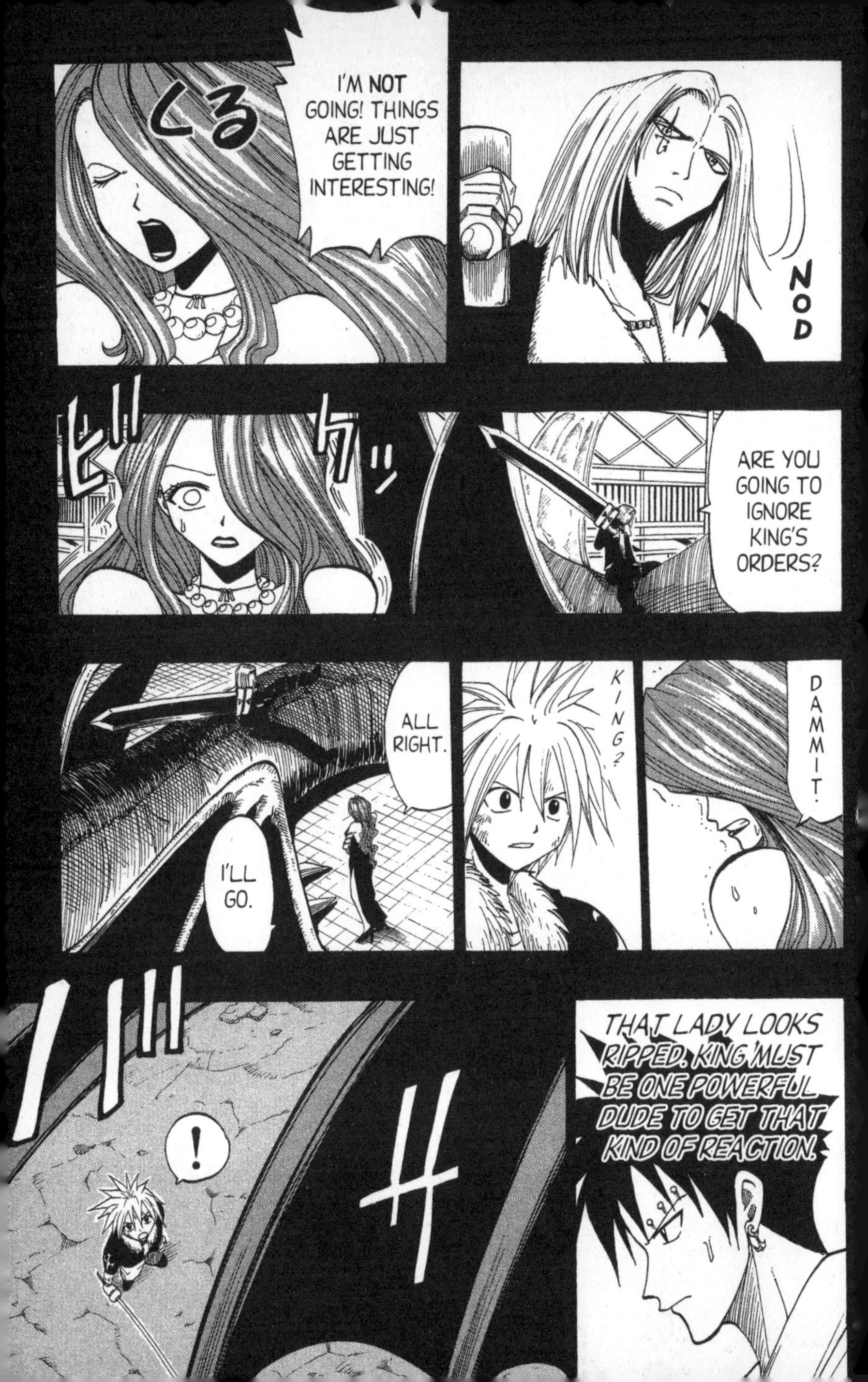
NOD
くる
I'M NOT GOING! THINGS ARE JUST GETTING INTERESTING!
ARE YOU GOING TO IGNORE KING'S ORDERS?
DAMMIT!
KING?
ALL RIGHT.
I'LL GO.
THAT LADY LOOKS RIPPED. KING MUST BE ONE POWERFUL DUDE TO GET THAT KIND OF REACTION.
!

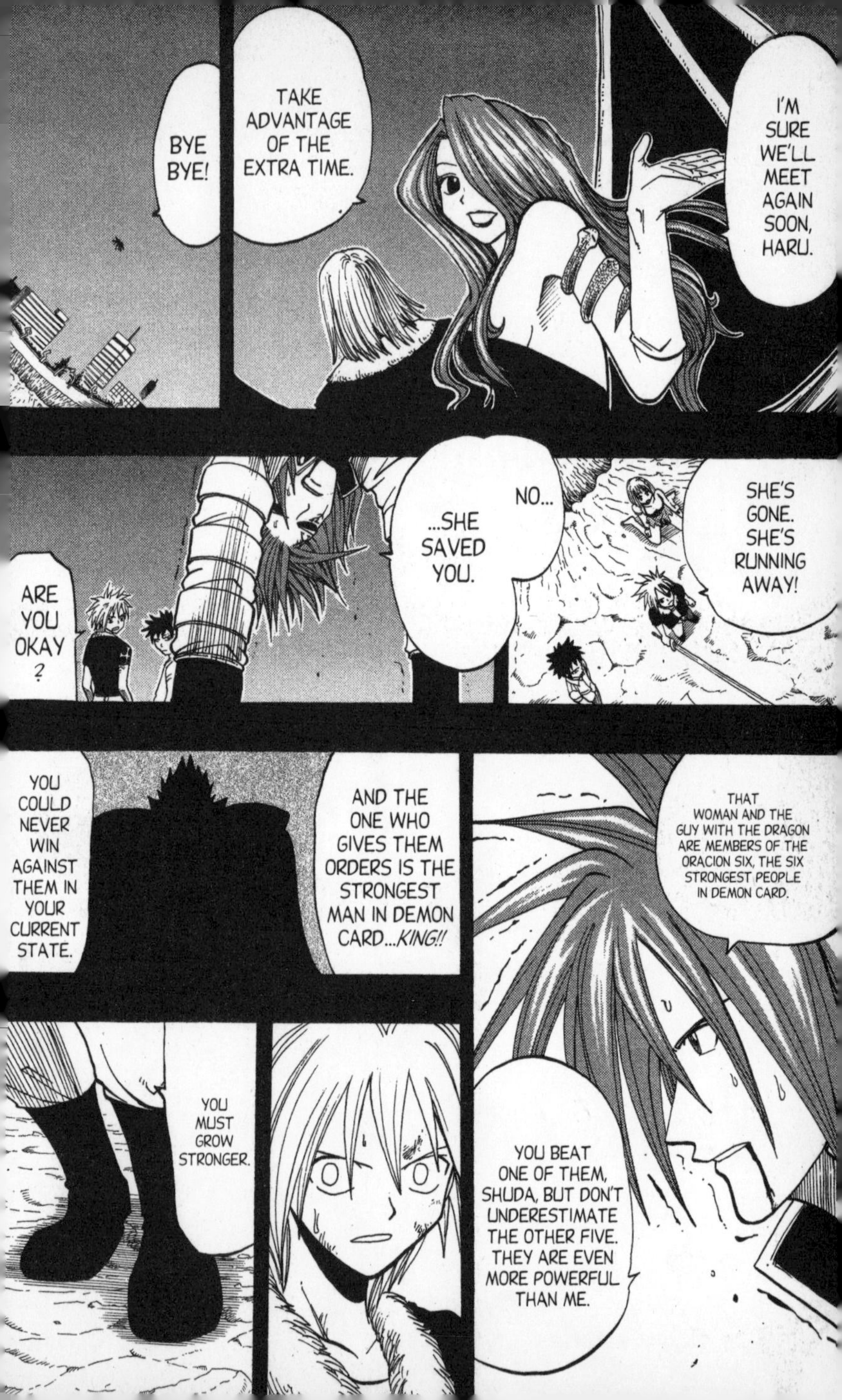
I'M SURE WE'LL MEET AGAIN SOON, HARU.
TAKE ADVANTAGE OF THE EXTRA TIME.
BYE BYE!
SHE'S GONE. SHE'S RUNNING AWAY!
NO...
...SHE SAVED YOU.
ARE YOU OKAY?
THAT WOMAN AND THE GUY WITH THE DRAGON ARE MEMBERS OF THE ORACION SIX, THE SIX STRONGEST PEOPLE IN DEMON CARD.
YOU BEAT ONE OF THEM, SHUDA, BUT DON'T UNDERESTIMATE THE OTHER FIVE. THEY ARE EVEN MORE POWERFUL THAN ME.
AND THE ONE WHO GIVES THEM ORDERS IS THE STRONGEST MAN IN DEMON CARD...*KING!!*
YOU COULD NEVER WIN AGAINST THEM IN YOUR CURRENT STATE.
YOU MUST GROW STRONGER.

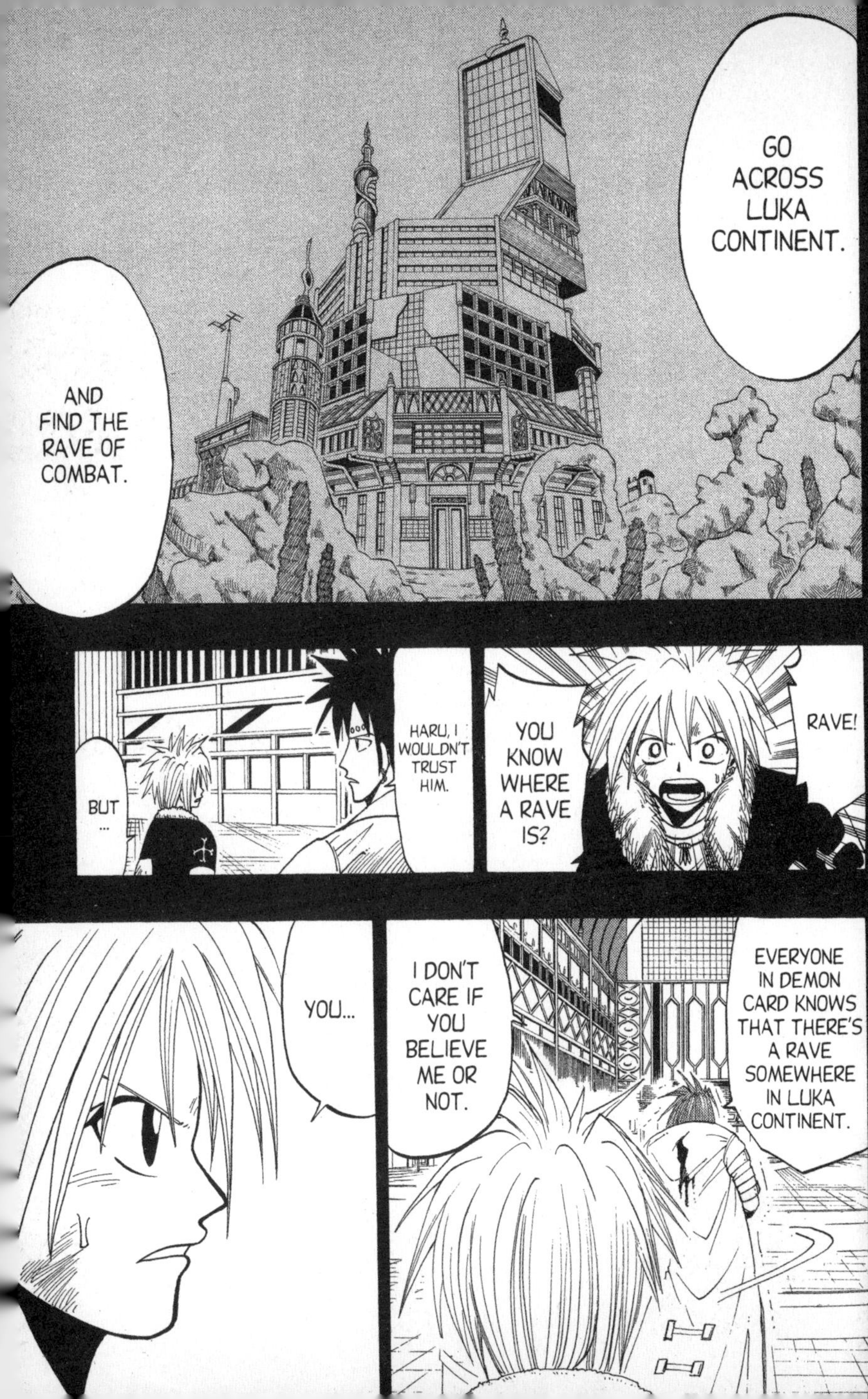
GO ACROSS LUKA CONTINENT.
AND FIND THE RAVE OF COMBAT.
RAVE!
YOU KNOW WHERE A RAVE IS?
HARU, I WOULDN'T TRUST HIM.
BUT ...
EVERYONE IN DEMON CARD KNOWS THAT THERE'S A RAVE SOMEWHERE IN LUKA CONTINENT.
I DON'T CARE IF YOU BELIEVE ME OR NOT.
YOU...

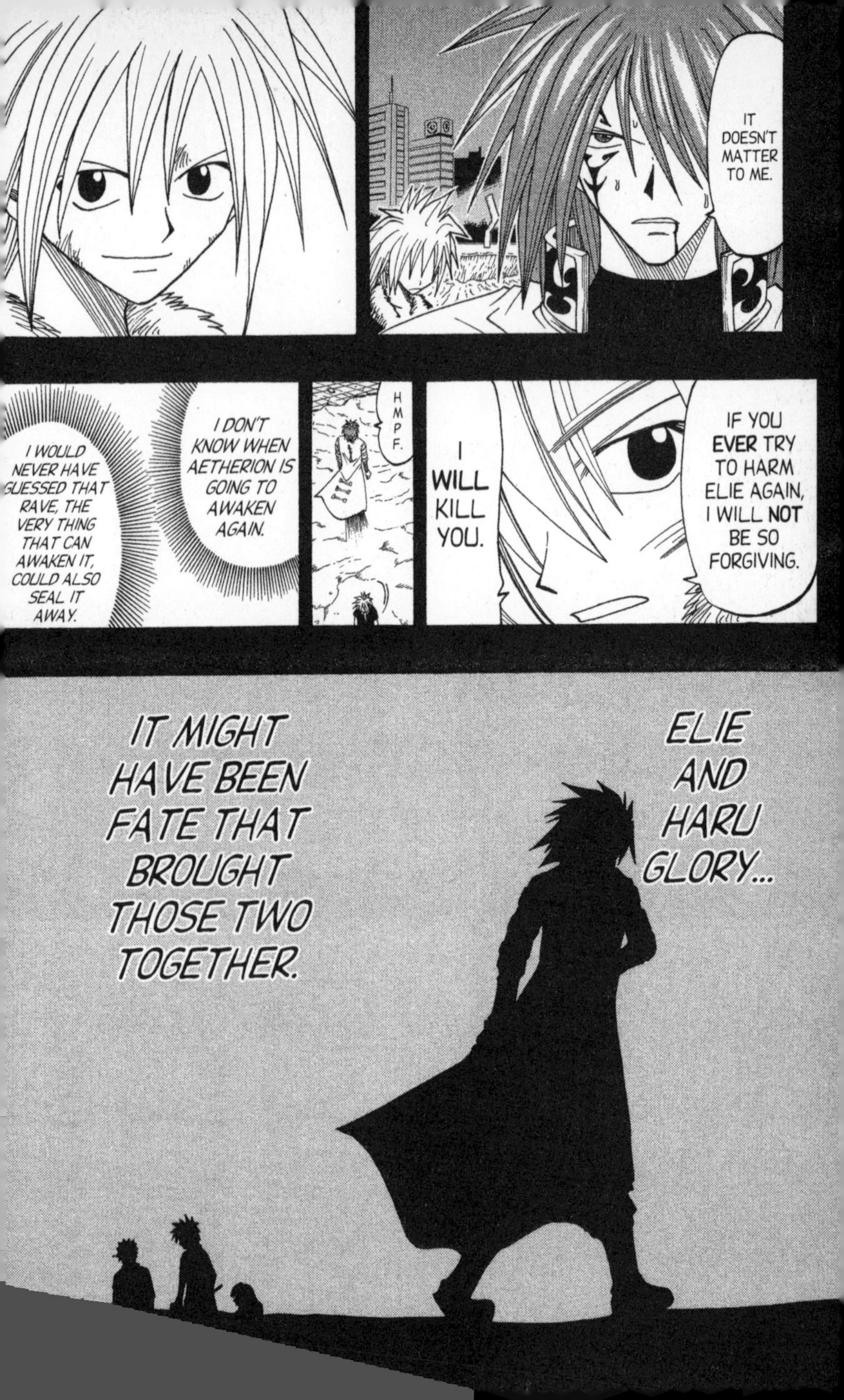
IT DOESN'T MATTER TO ME.
IF YOU EVER TRY TO HARM ELIE AGAIN, I WILL NOT BE SO FORGIVING.
I WILL KILL YOU.
HMPF.
I DON'T KNOW WHEN AETHERION IS GOING TO AWAKEN AGAIN.
I WOULD NEVER HAVE GUESSED THAT RAVE, THE VERY THING THAT CAN AWAKEN IT, COULD ALSO SEAL IT AWAY.
ELIE AND HARU GLORY...
IT MIGHT HAVE BEEN FATE THAT BROUGHT THOSE TWO TOGETHER.

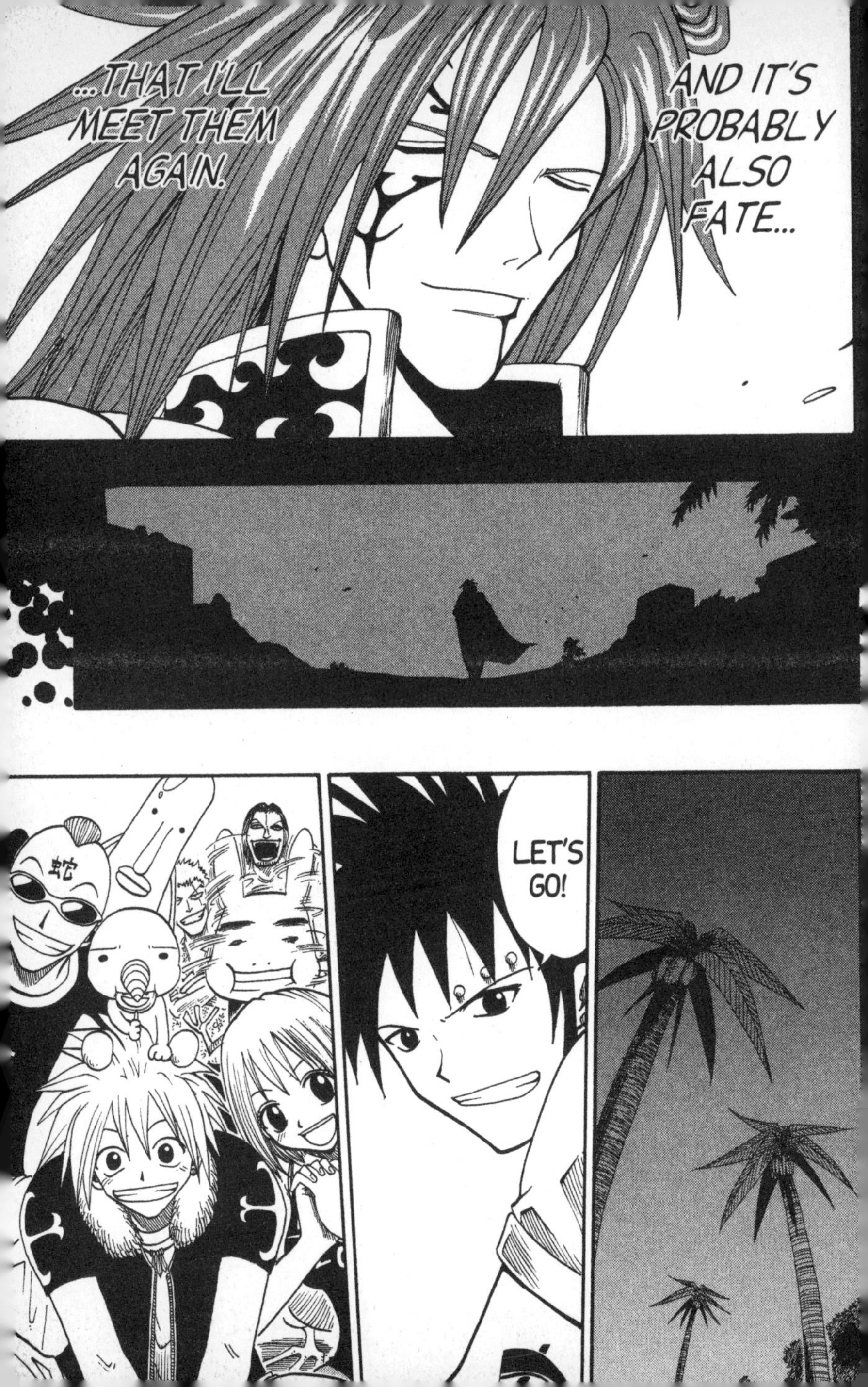
AND IT'S PROBABLY ALSO FATE...
...THAT I'LL MEET THEM AGAIN.
LET'S GO!
蛇

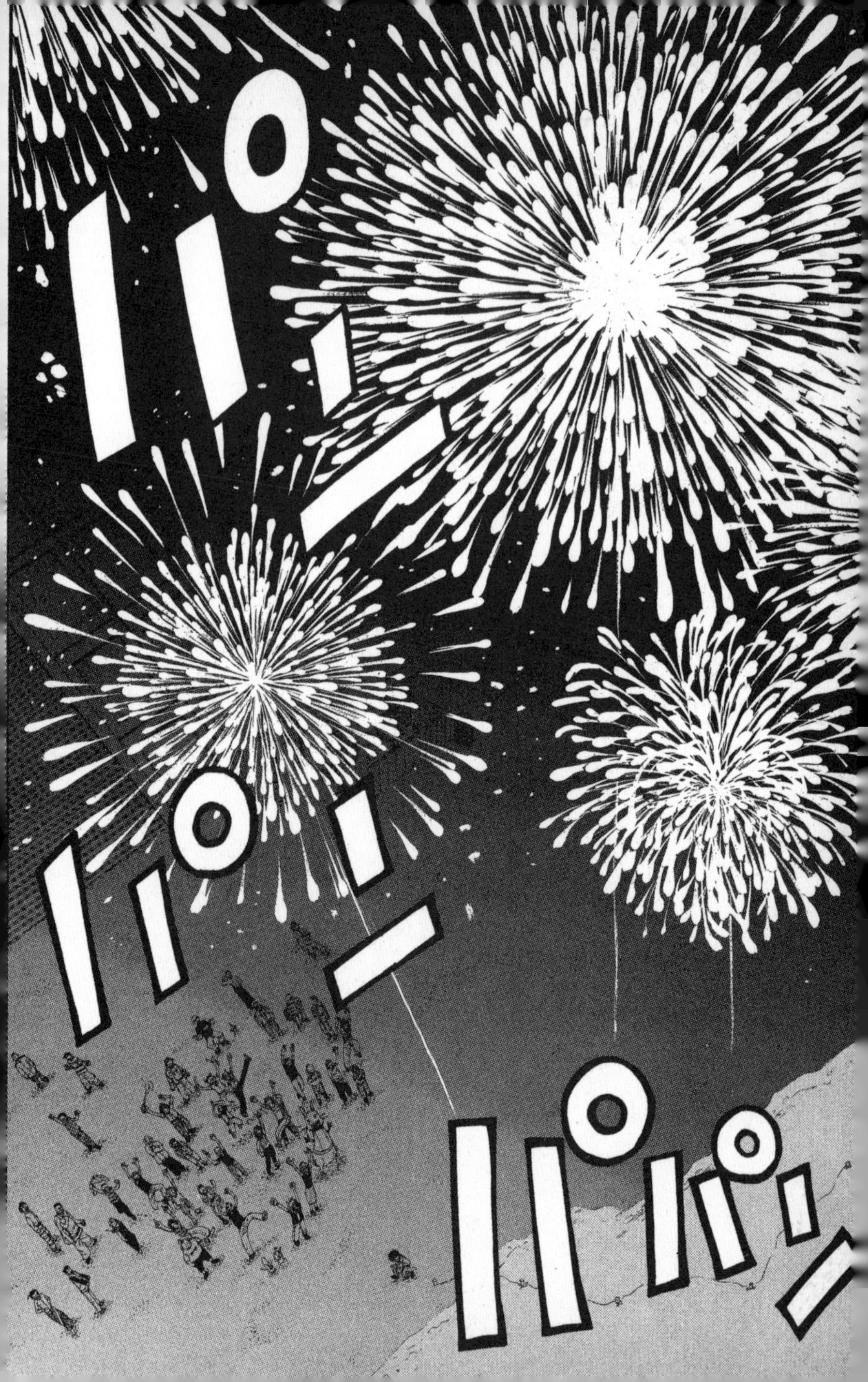
パン
パン
パパン

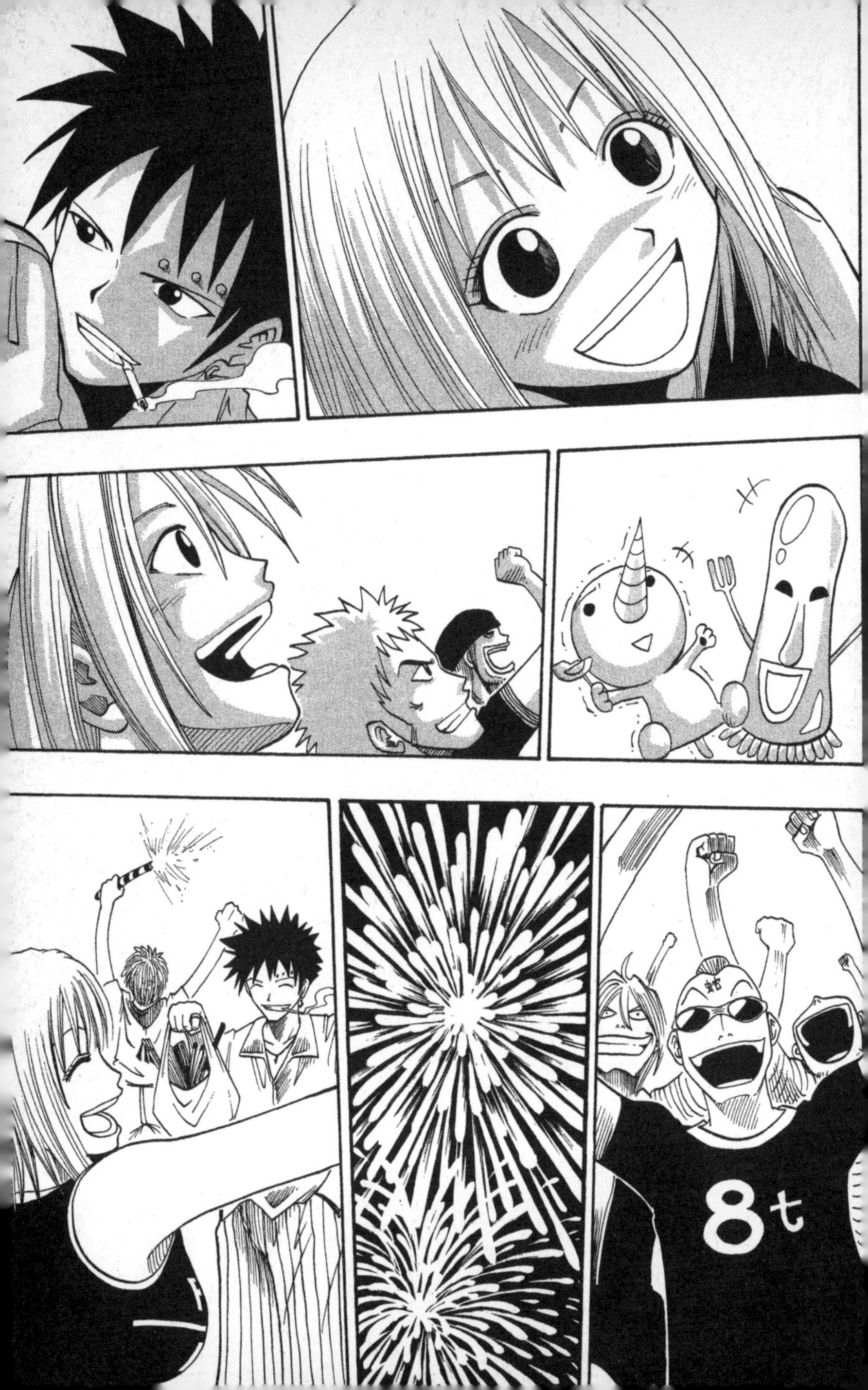
8t

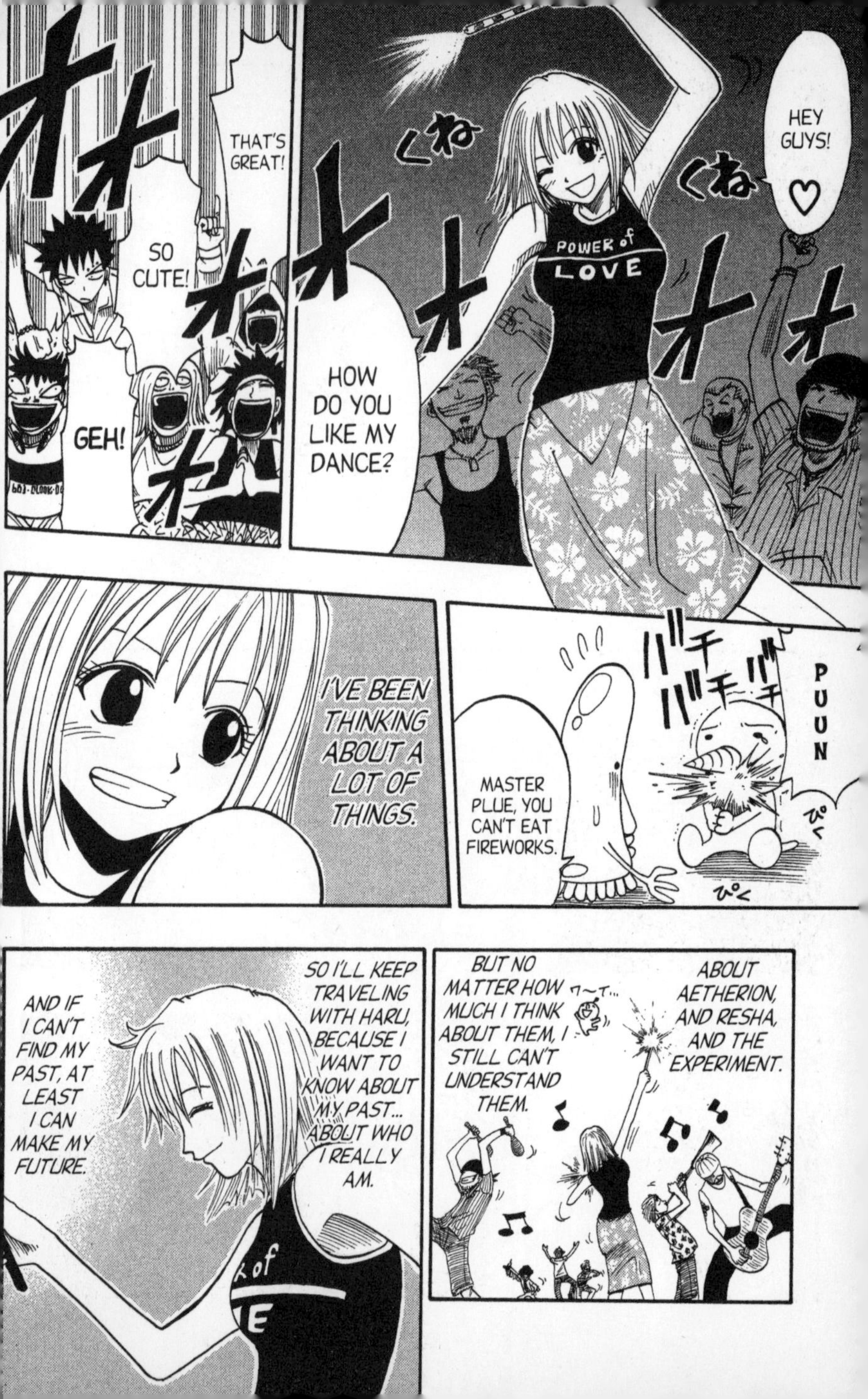
HEY GUYS! ♡
くね くね
HOW DO YOU LIKE MY DANCE?
THAT'S GREAT!
SO CUTE!
GEH!
PUUN
MASTER PLUE, YOU CAN'T EAT FIREWORKS.
ぴく ぴく
I'VE BEEN THINKING ABOUT A LOT OF THINGS.
ABOUT AETHERION, AND RESHA, AND THE EXPERIMENT.
BUT NO MATTER HOW MUCH I THINK ABOUT THEM, I STILL CAN'T UNDERSTAND THEM.
SO I'LL KEEP TRAVELING WITH HARU, BECAUSE I WANT TO KNOW ABOUT MY PAST... ABOUT WHO I REALLY AM.
AND IF I CAN'T FIND MY PAST, AT LEAST I CAN MAKE MY FUTURE.

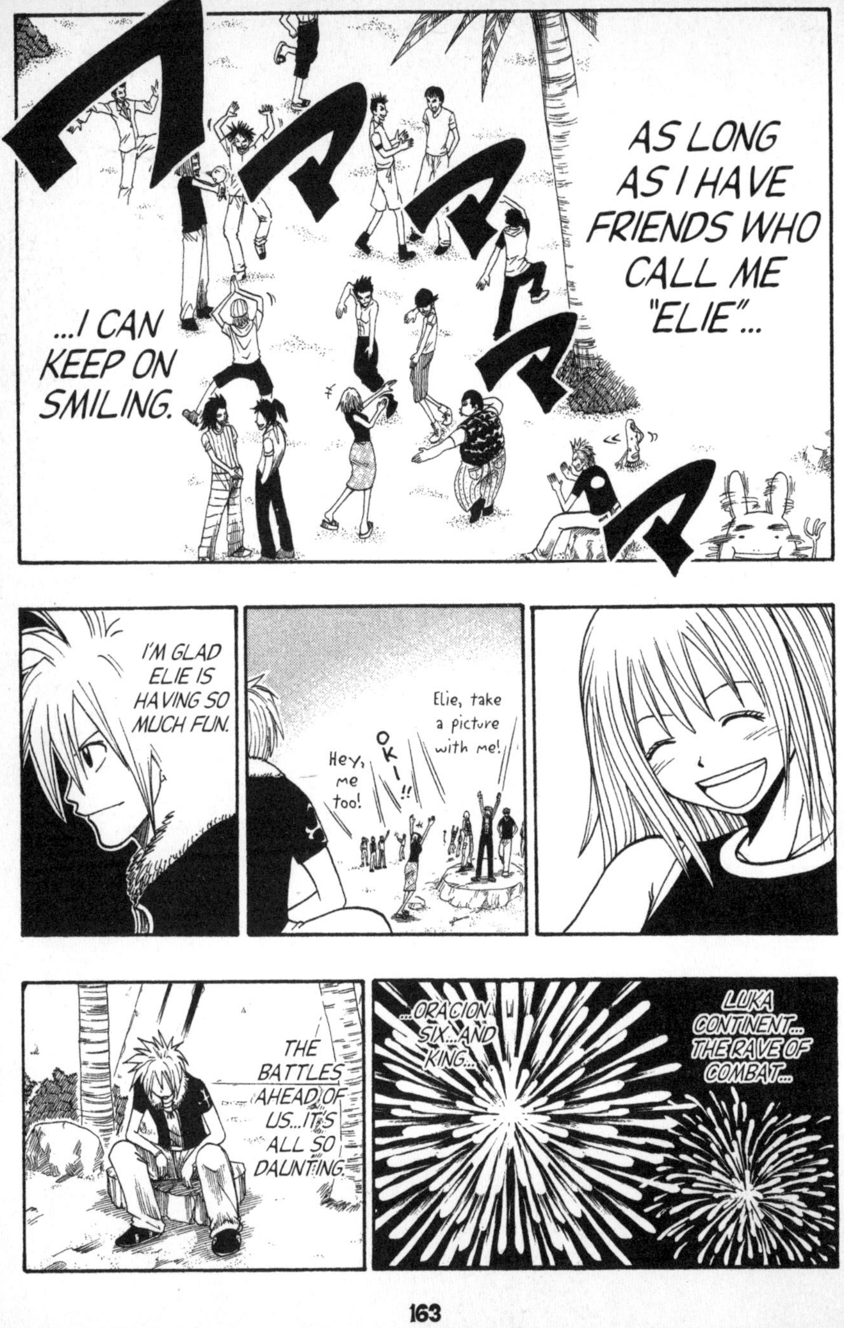
AS LONG AS I HAVE FRIENDS WHO CALL ME "ELIE"...
...I CAN KEEP ON SMILING.
Elie, take a picture with me!
OK!!
Hey, me too!
I'M GLAD ELIE IS HAVING SO MUCH FUN.
LUKA CONTINENT... THE RAVE OF COMBAT...
...ORACION SIX... AND KING...
THE BATTLES AHEAD OF US... IT'S ALL SO DAUNTING.

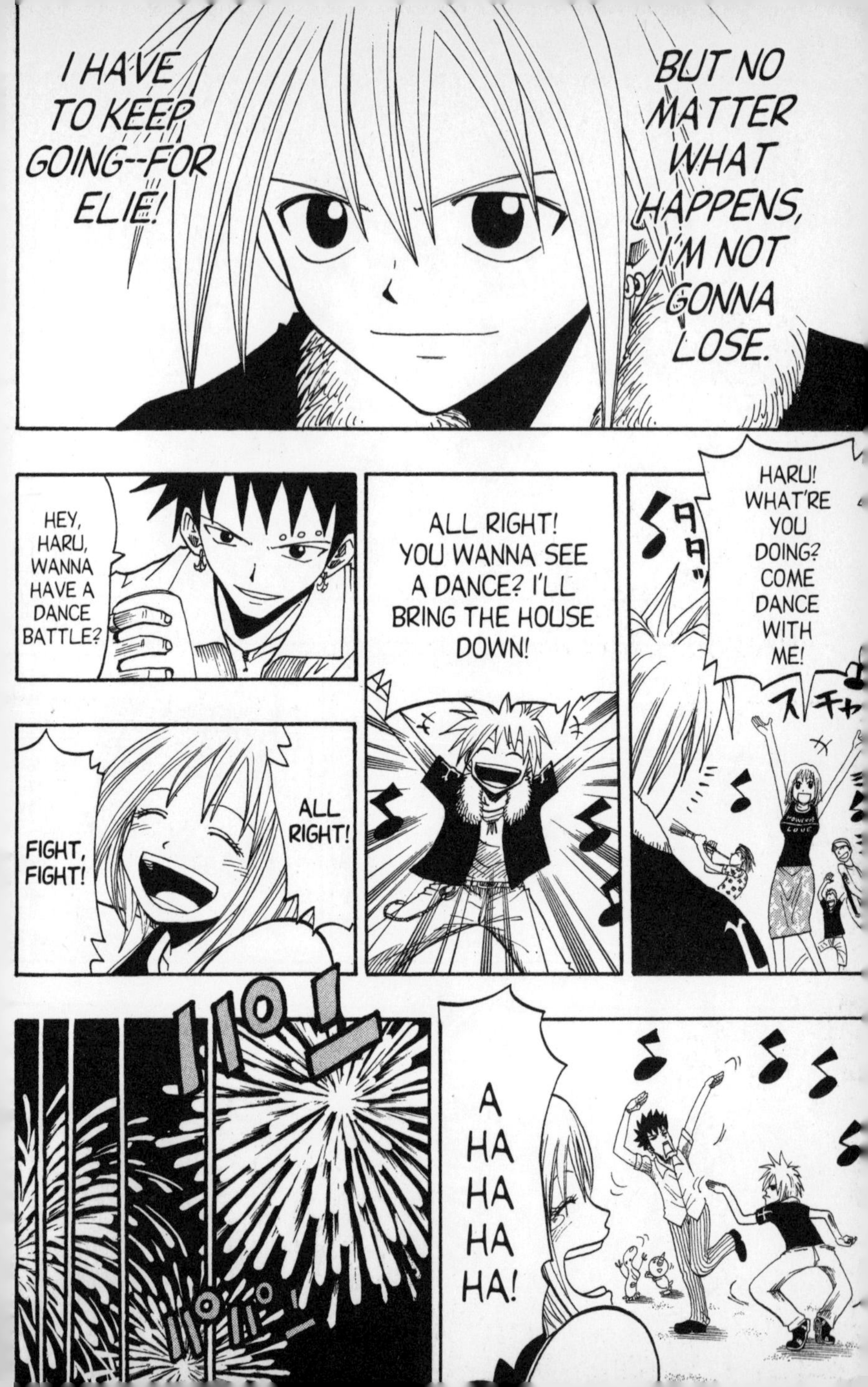
BUT NO MATTER WHAT HAPPENS, I'M NOT GONNA LOSE.
I HAVE TO KEEP GOING--FOR ELIE!
タタッ
HARU! WHAT'RE YOU DOING? COME DANCE WITH ME!
スチャ
ALL RIGHT! YOU WANNA SEE A DANCE? I'LL BRING THE HOUSE DOWN!
HEY, HARU, WANNA HAVE A DANCE BATTLE?
ALL RIGHT!
FIGHT, FIGHT!
A HA HA HA HA HA!

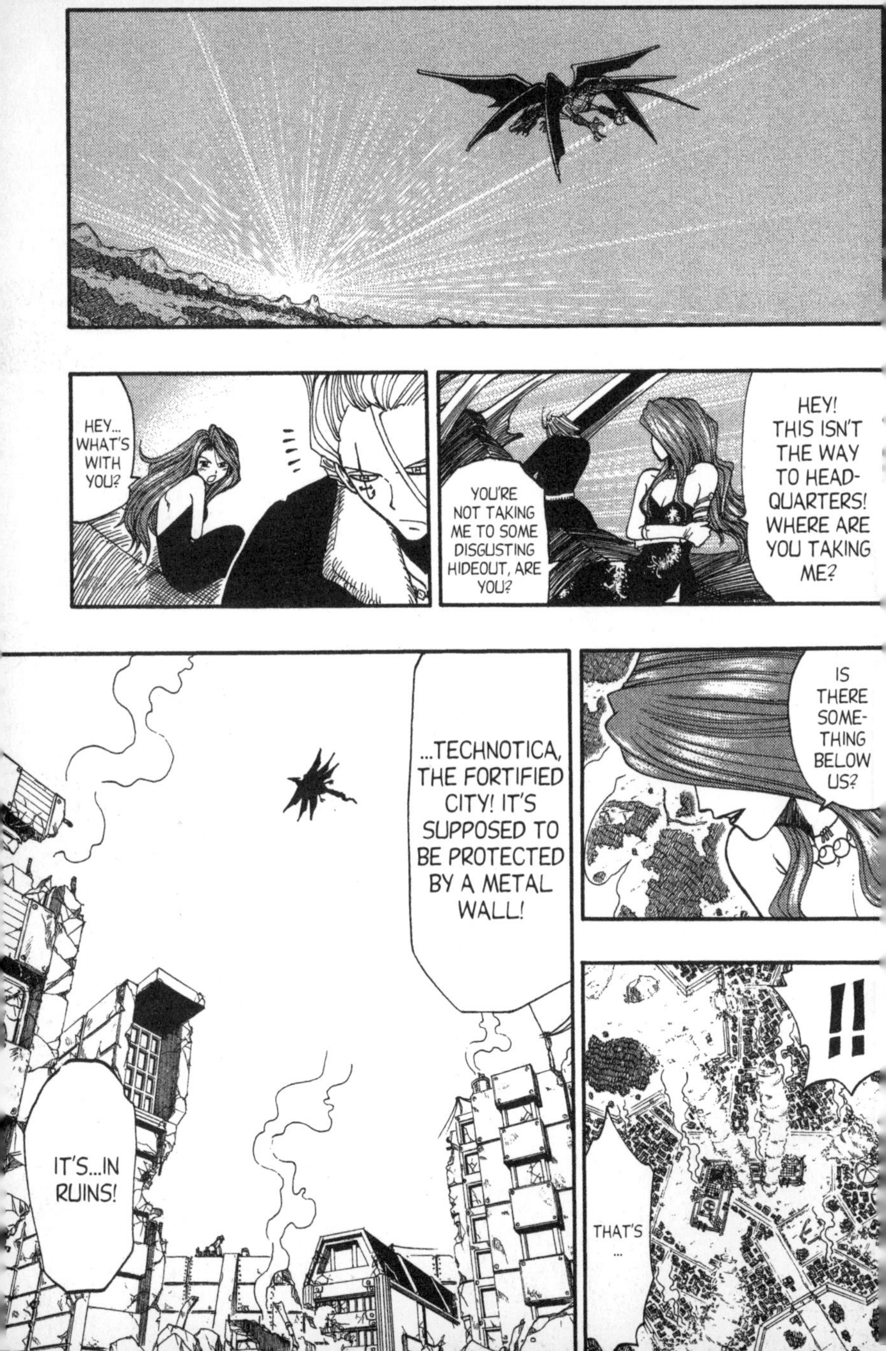
HEY! THIS ISN'T THE WAY TO HEAD-QUARTERS! WHERE ARE YOU TAKING ME?
YOU'RE NOT TAKING ME TO SOME DISGUSTING HIDEOUT, ARE YOU?
HEY... WHAT'S WITH YOU?
IS THERE SOME-THING BELOW US?
!!
THAT'S ...
...TECHNOTICA, THE FORTIFIED CITY! IT'S SUPPOSED TO BE PROTECTED BY A METAL WALL!
IT'S...IN RUINS!

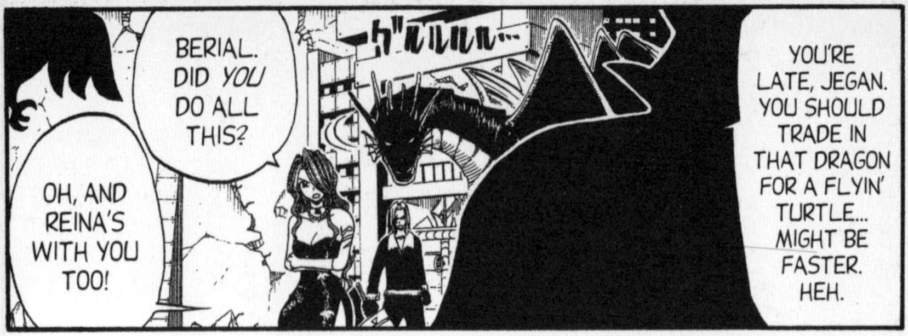
YOU'RE LATE, JEGAN. YOU SHOULD TRADE IN THAT DRAGON FOR A FLYIN' TURTLE... MIGHT BE FASTER. HEH.
BERIAL. DID *YOU* DO ALL THIS?
OH, AND REINA'S WITH YOU TOO!

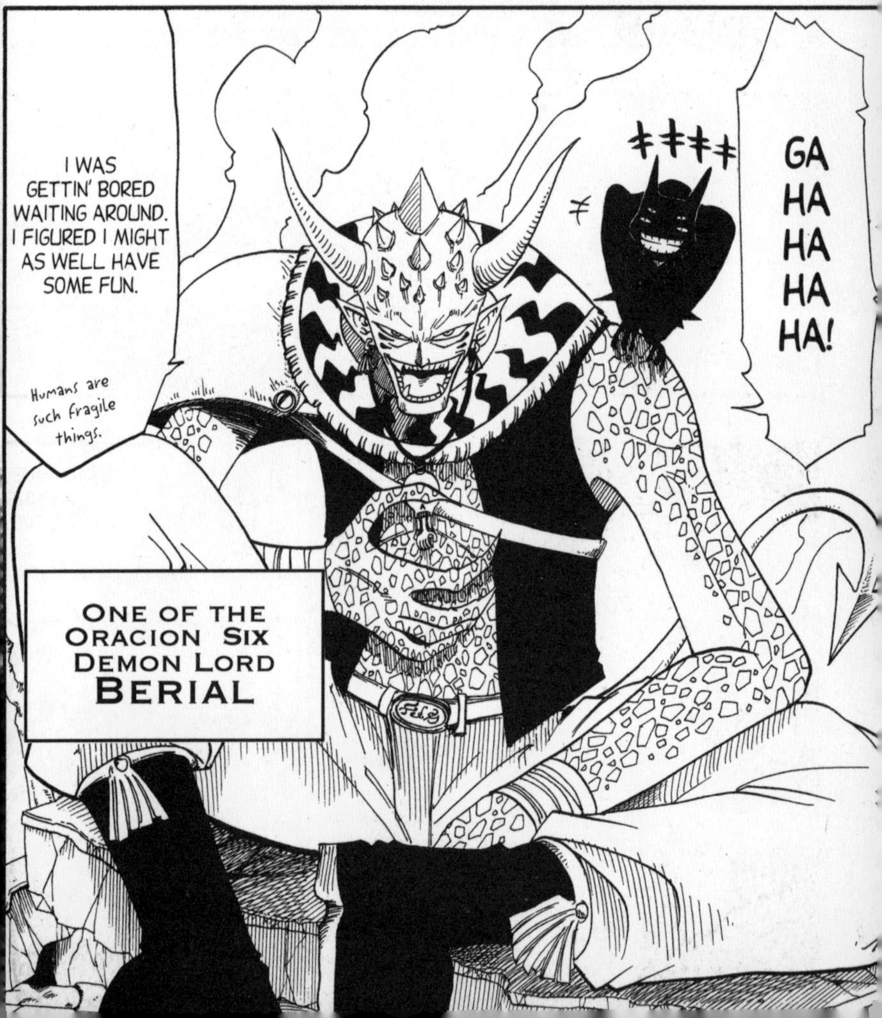
GA HA HA HA HA!
I WAS GETTIN' BORED WAITING AROUND. I FIGURED I MIGHT AS WELL HAVE SOME FUN.
Humans are such fragile things.
ONE OF THE ORACION SIX DEMON LORD BERIAL

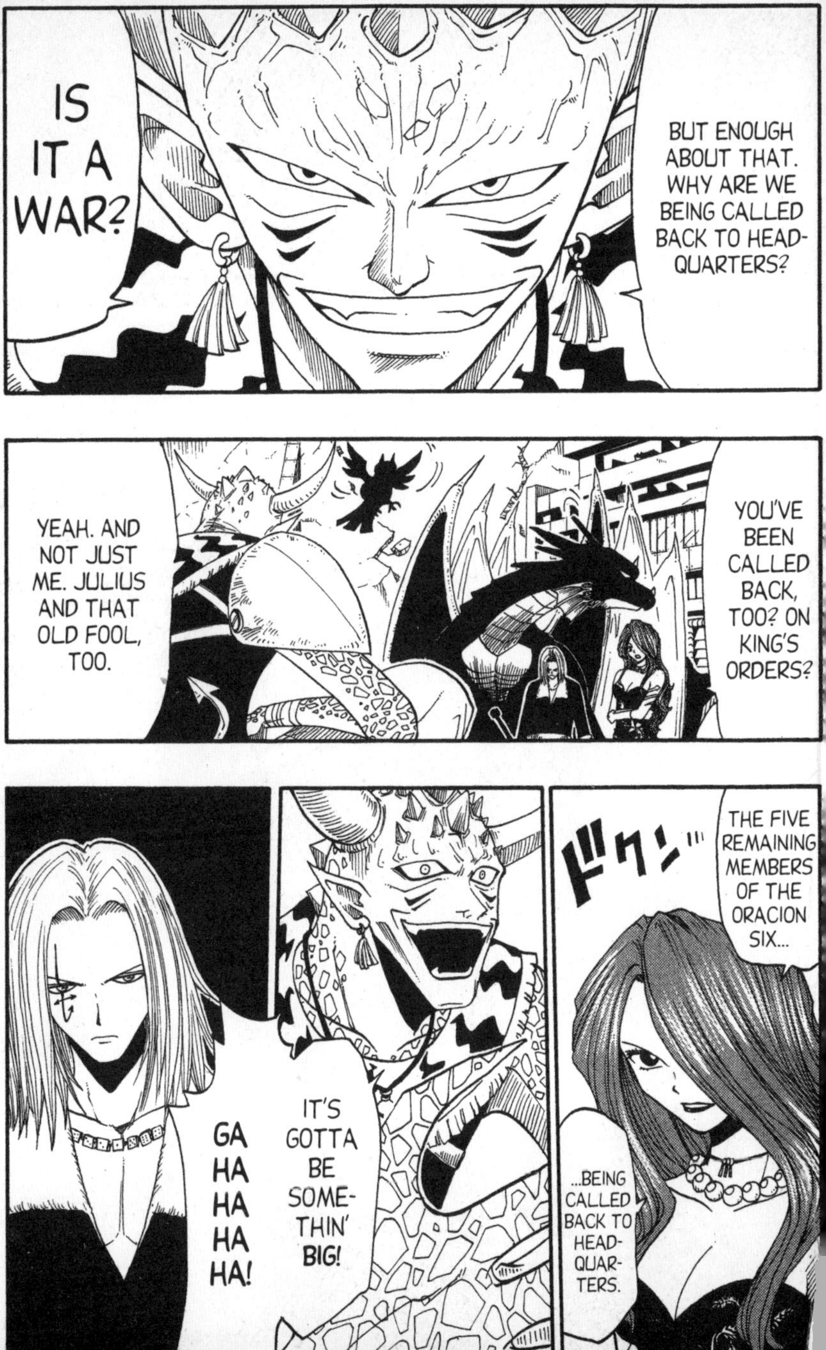
BUT ENOUGH ABOUT THAT. WHY ARE WE BEING CALLED BACK TO HEAD-QUARTERS?
IS IT A WAR?
YOU'VE BEEN CALLED BACK, TOO? ON KING'S ORDERS?
YEAH. AND NOT JUST ME. JULIUS AND THAT OLD FOOL, TOO.
ドクン
THE FIVE REMAINING MEMBERS OF THE ORACION SIX...
...BEING CALLED BACK TO HEAD-QUAR-TERS.
IT'S GOTTA BE SOME-THIN' BIG!
GA HA HA HA HA HA!

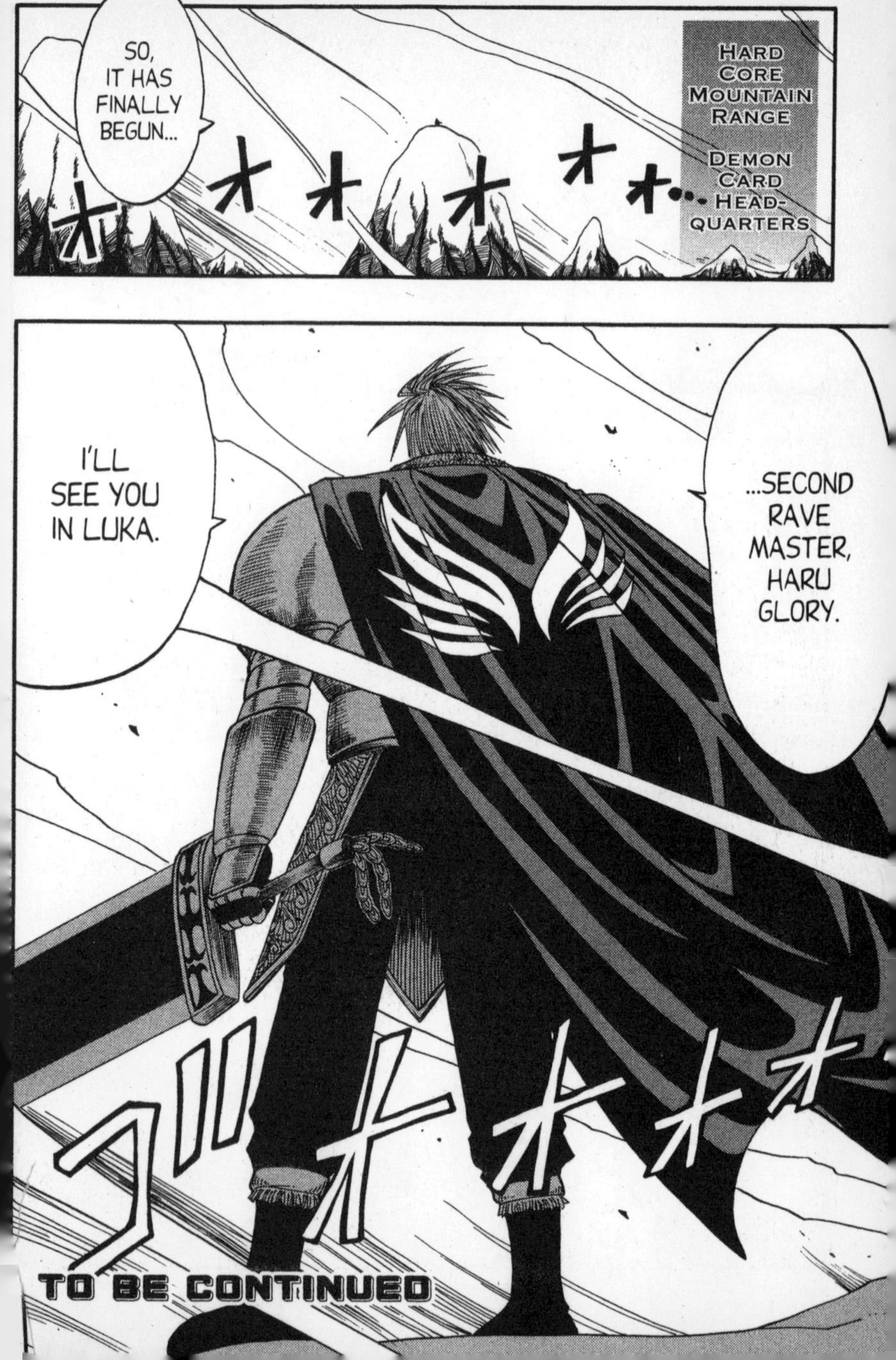

Hard Core Mountain Range
Demon Card Headquarters
オオオオオオ…
So, it has finally begun...
...Second Rave Master, Haru Glory.
I'll see you in Luka.
ゴオオオ
TO BE CONTINUED

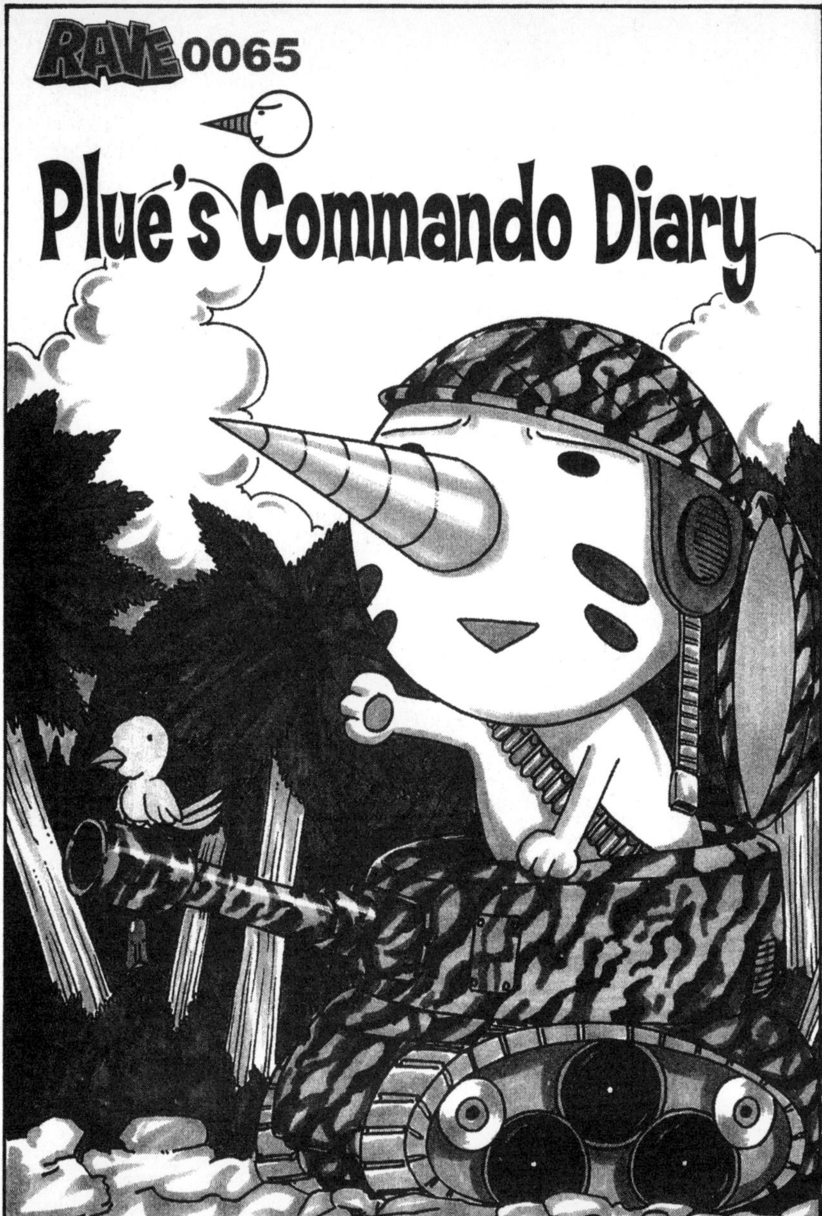
RAVE 0065
Plue's Commando Diary

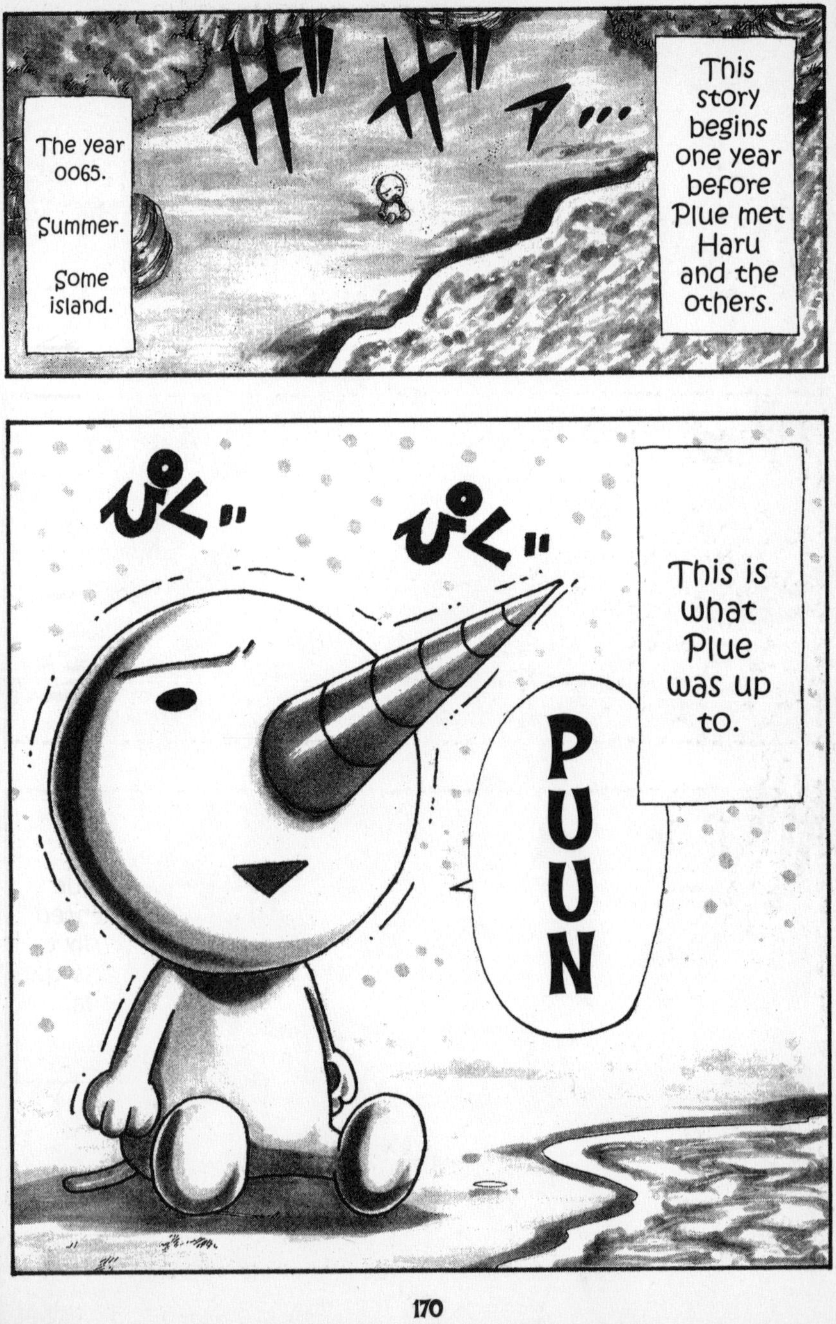
This story begins one year before Plue met Haru and the others.
ザザァ…
The year 0065.
Summer.
Some island.
This is what Plue was up to.
ぴく
ぴく
PUUN

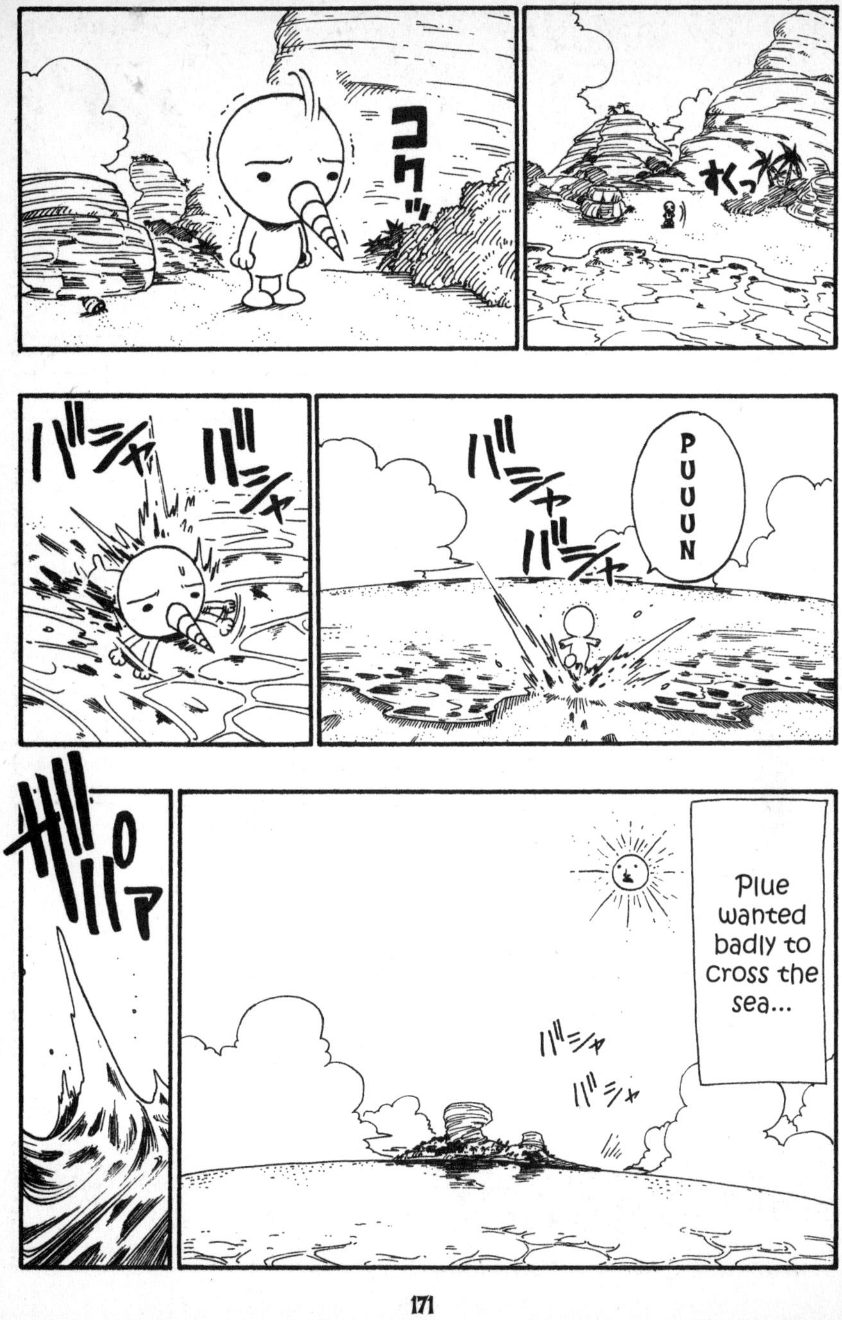
すくっ
コクッ
PUUUN
バシャ
バシャ
バシャ
バシャ
Plue wanted badly to cross the sea...
バシャ
バシャ
ザパァ

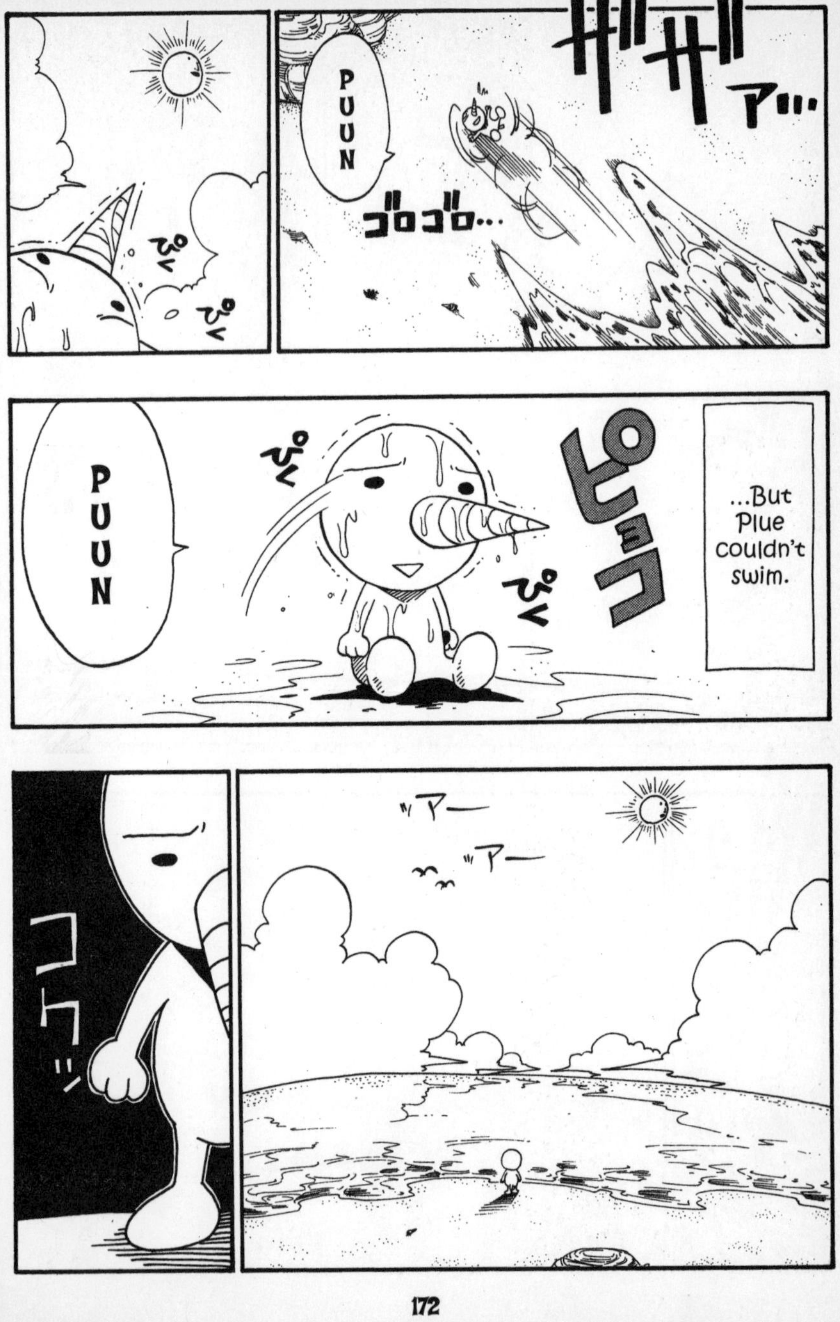
ザザアッ
PUUN
ゴロゴロ…
ぴく
ぴく
...But Plue couldn't swim.
ピョコ
ぴく
ぴく
PUUN
ッアー
ッアー
コクッ

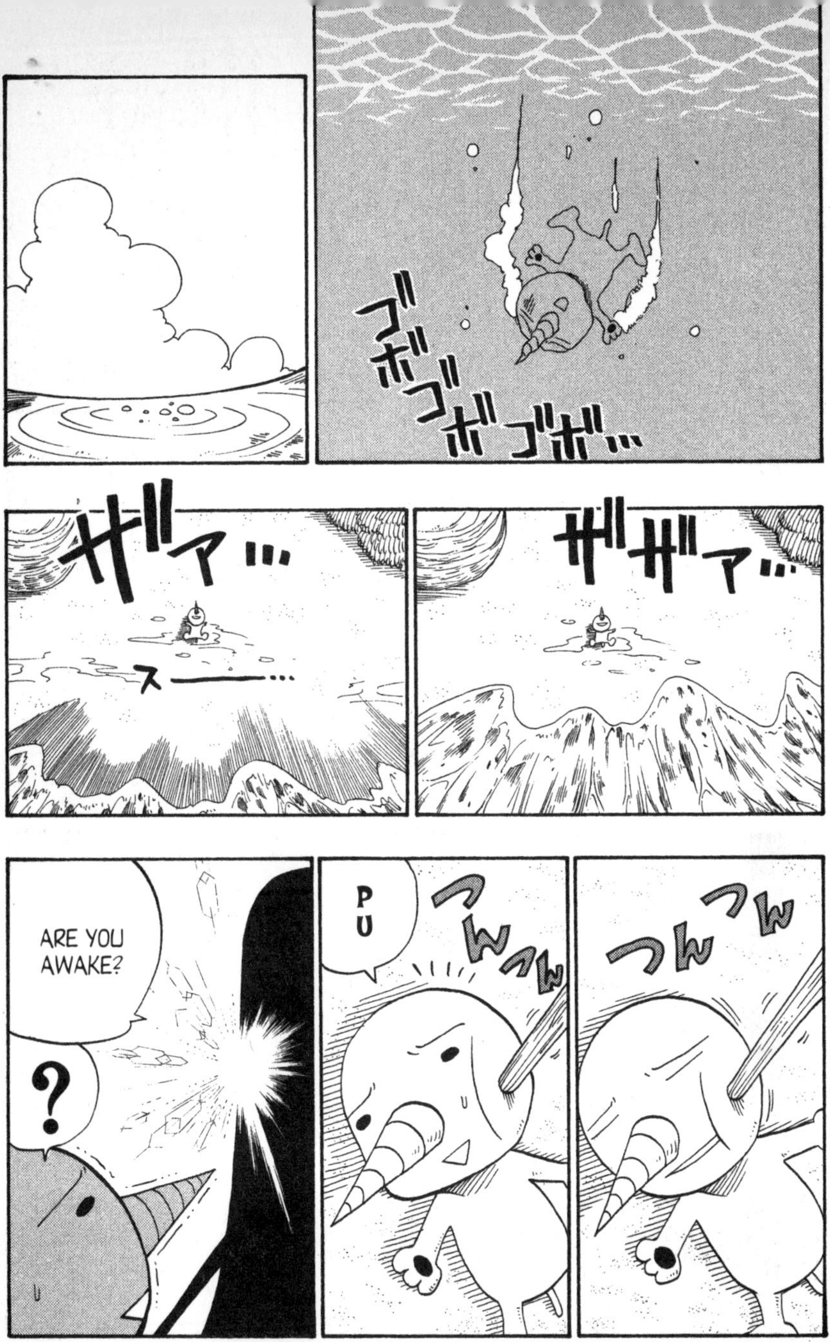
ゴボゴボゴボゴボ…
ザザァ…
ザァ…
スー……
PU
ふんふん
ふんふん
ARE YOU AWAKE?
?

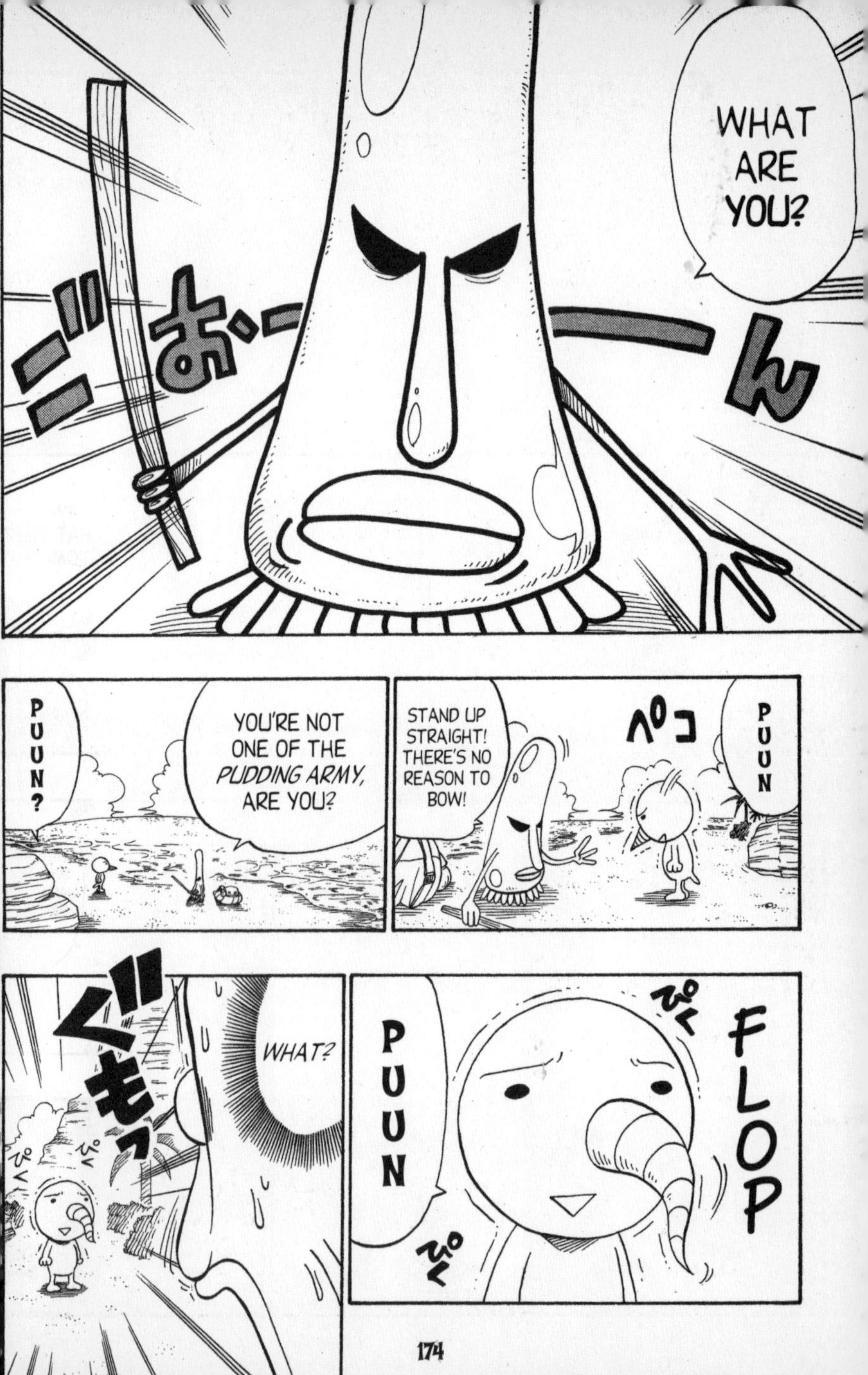

WHAT ARE YOU?
ごおーーーん
PUUN
ペコ
STAND UP STRAIGHT! THERE'S NO REASON TO BOW!
YOU'RE NOT ONE OF THE *PUDDING ARMY,* ARE YOU?
PUUN?
ぴく
FLOP
PUUN
ぴく
WHAT?
ぐもっ
ぴく
ぴく

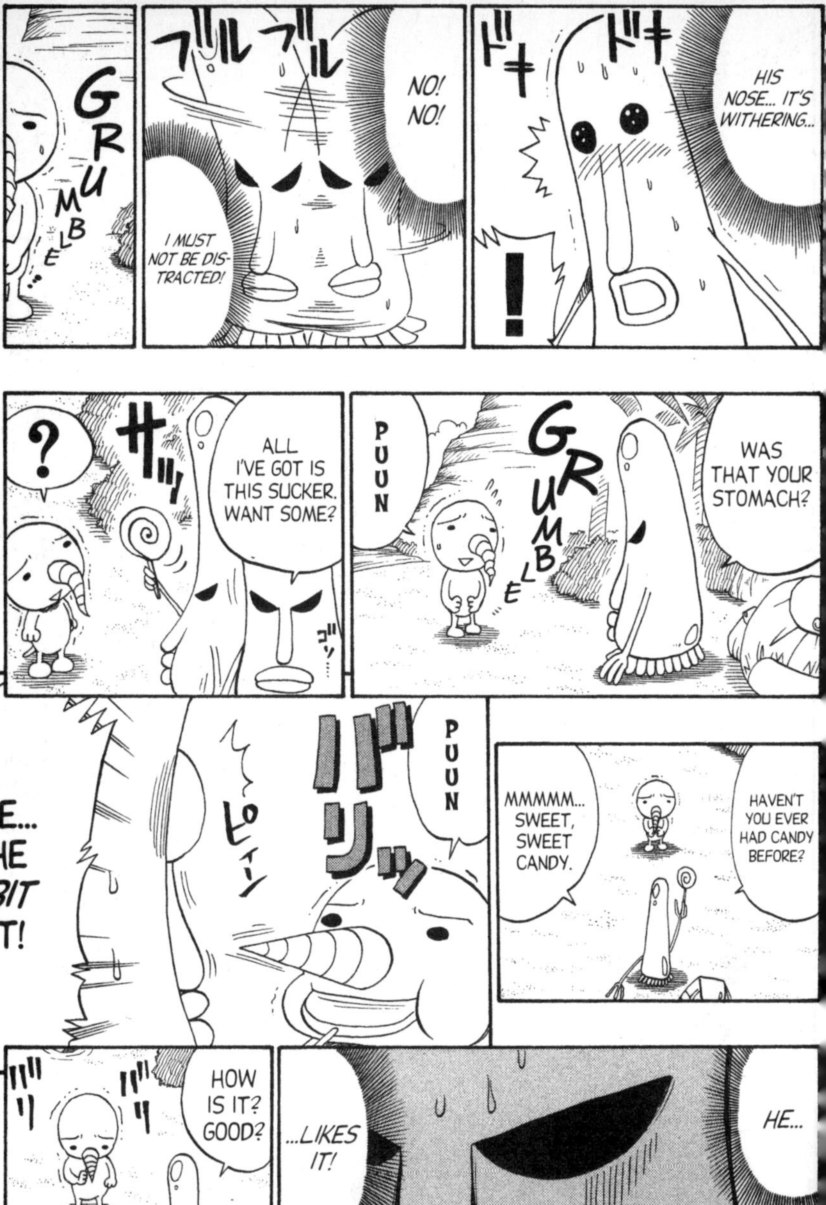
ドキ ドキ
HIS NOSE... IT'S WITHERING...
!
ブルブル
NO! NO!
I MUST NOT BE DIS-TRACTED!
GRUMBLE
WAS THAT YOUR STOMACH?
GRUMBLE
PUUN
ALL I'VE GOT IS THIS SUCKER. WANT SOME?
サッ
?
HAVEN'T YOU EVER HAD CANDY BEFORE?
MMMMM... SWEET, SWEET CANDY.
PUUN
バリッ
ピイーン
HE... HE BIT IT!
HE...
...LIKES IT!
HOW IS IT? GOOD?
バリ
バリ

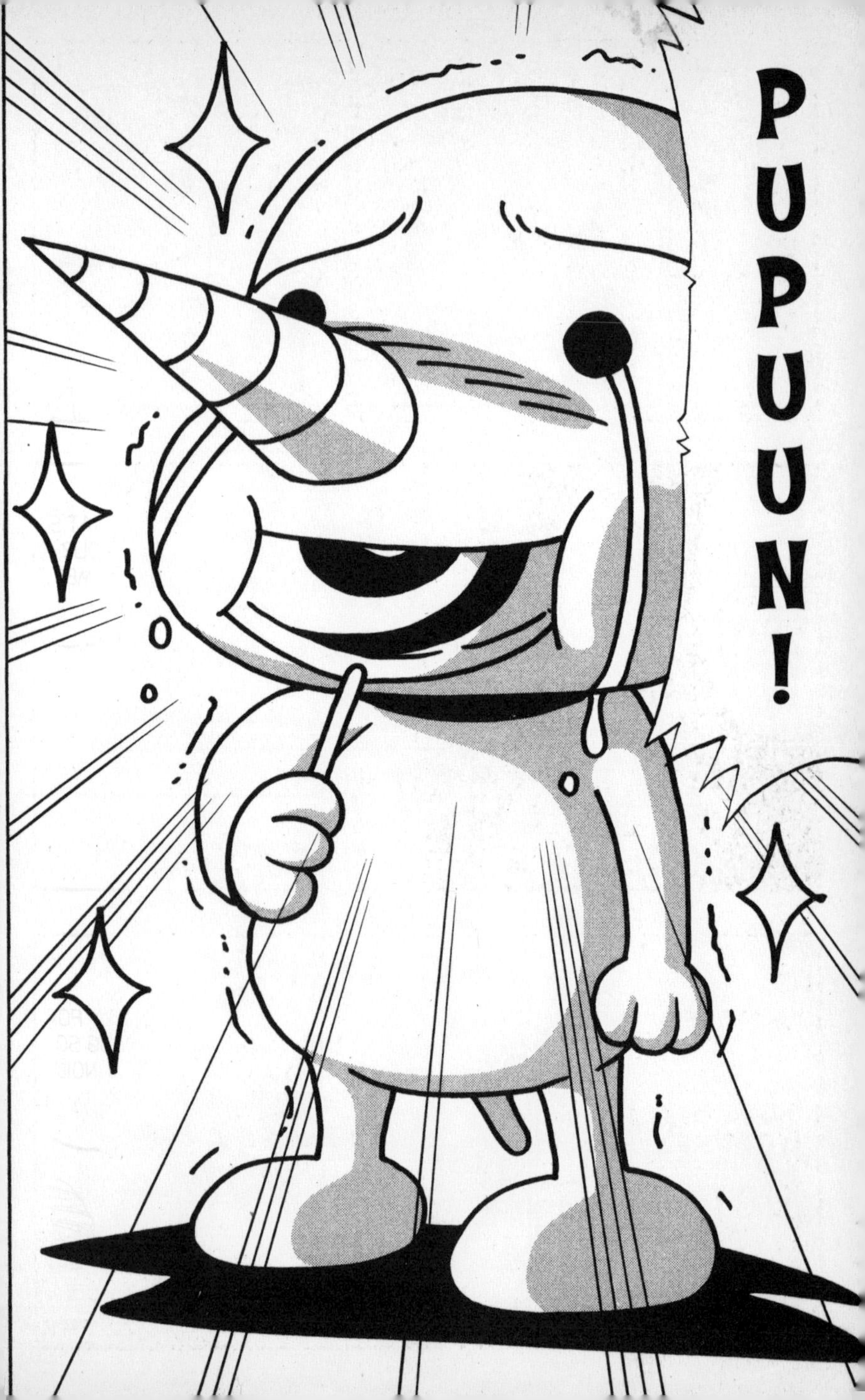
PUPUN!

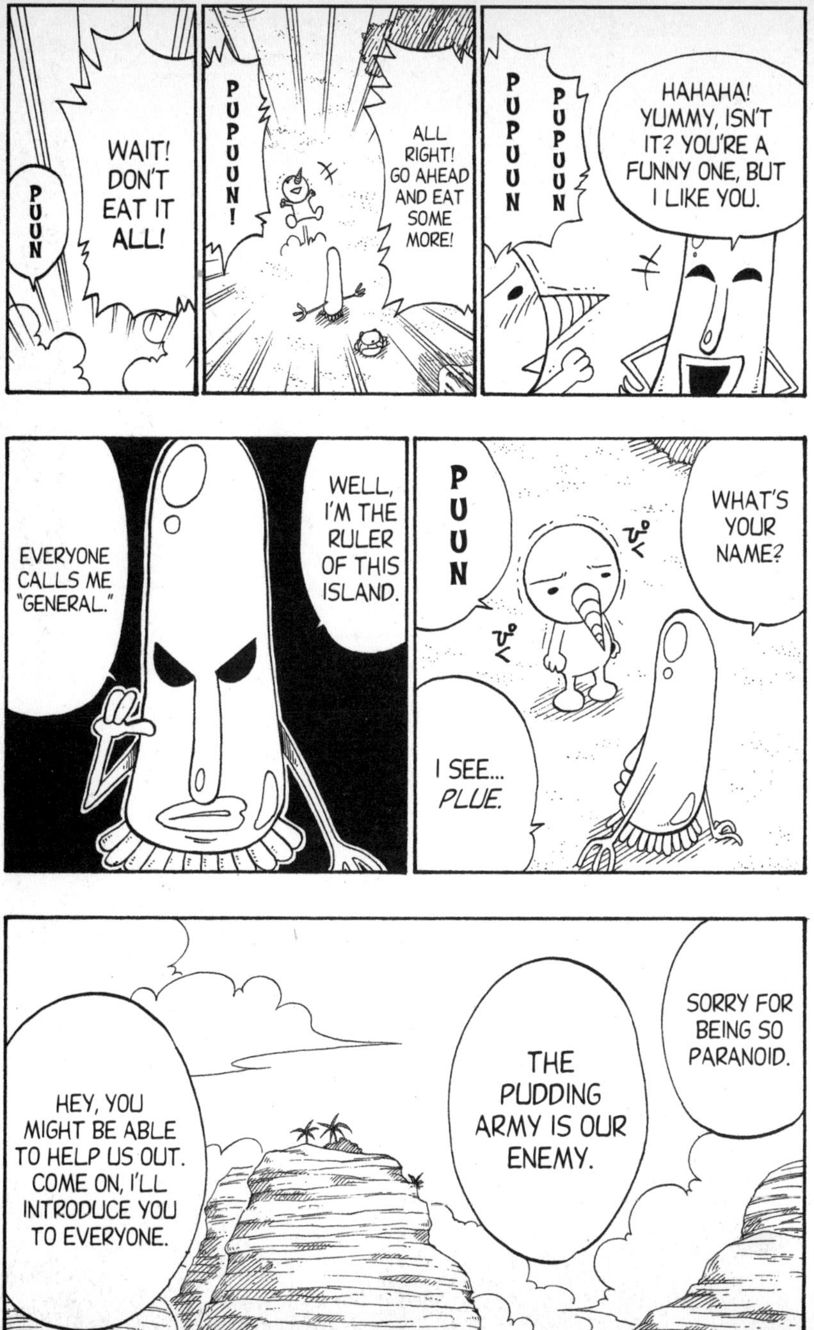
HAHAHA! YUMMY, ISN'T IT? YOU'RE A FUNNY ONE, BUT I LIKE YOU.
PUPUUN
PUPUUN
ALL RIGHT! GO AHEAD AND EAT SOME MORE!
PUPUUN!
WAIT! DON'T EAT IT ALL!
PUUN
WHAT'S YOUR NAME?
PUUN
ぴく
ぴく
I SEE... *PLUE.*
WELL, I'M THE RULER OF THIS ISLAND.
EVERYONE CALLS ME "GENERAL."
SORRY FOR BEING SO PARANOID.
THE PUDDING ARMY IS OUR ENEMY.
HEY, YOU MIGHT BE ABLE TO HELP US OUT. COME ON, I'LL INTRODUCE YOU TO EVERYONE.

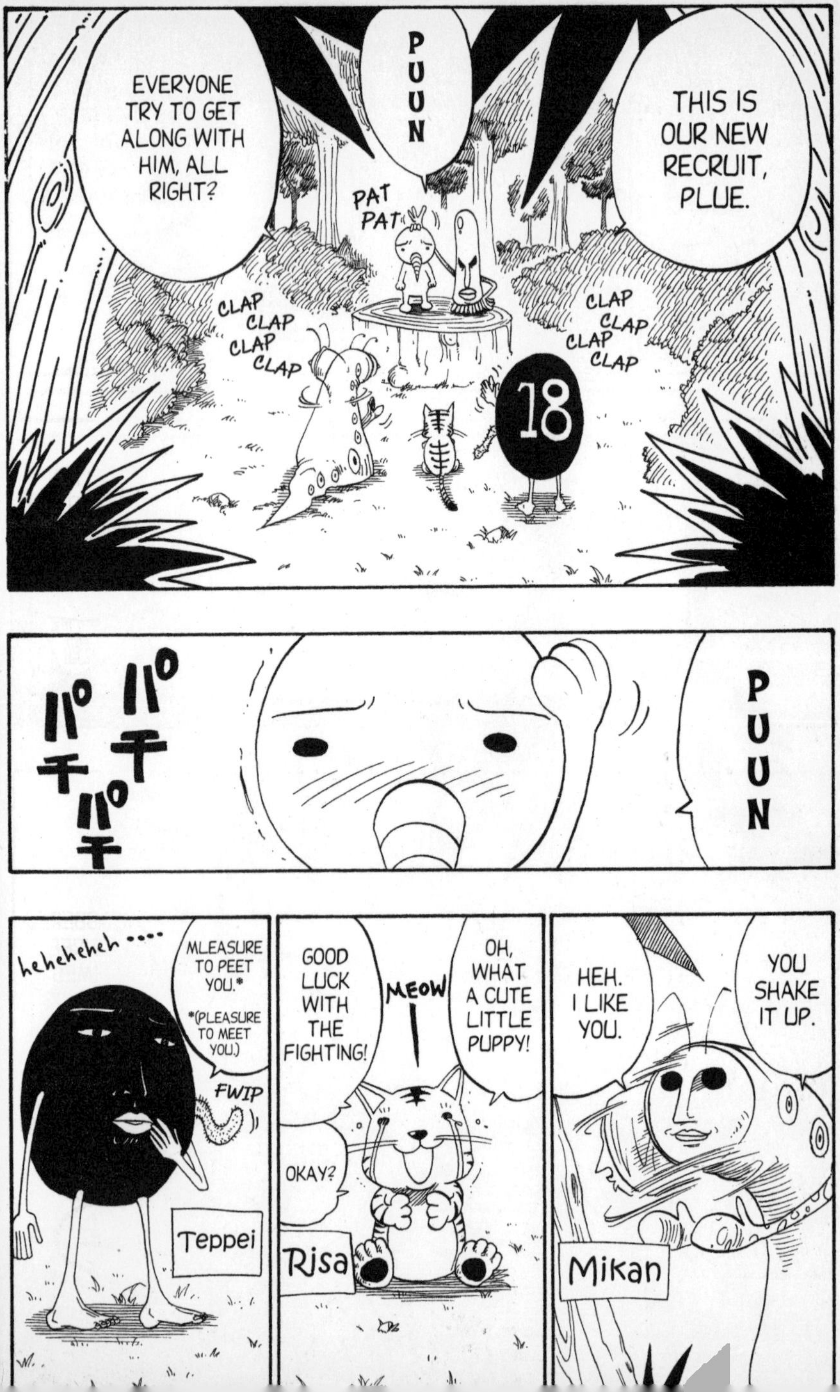
THIS IS OUR NEW RECRUIT, PLUE.
PUUN
EVERYONE TRY TO GET ALONG WITH HIM, ALL RIGHT?
PAT PAT
CLAP CLAP CLAP CLAP
CLAP CLAP CLAP CLAP
18
PUUN
パチ パチ パチ
YOU SHAKE IT UP.
HEH. I LIKE YOU.
Mikan
OH, WHAT A CUTE LITTLE PUPPY!
MEOW
GOOD LUCK WITH THE FIGHTING!
OKAY?
Risa
MLEASURE TO PEET YOU.*
*(PLEASURE TO MEET YOU.)
FWIP
heheheheh....
Teppei

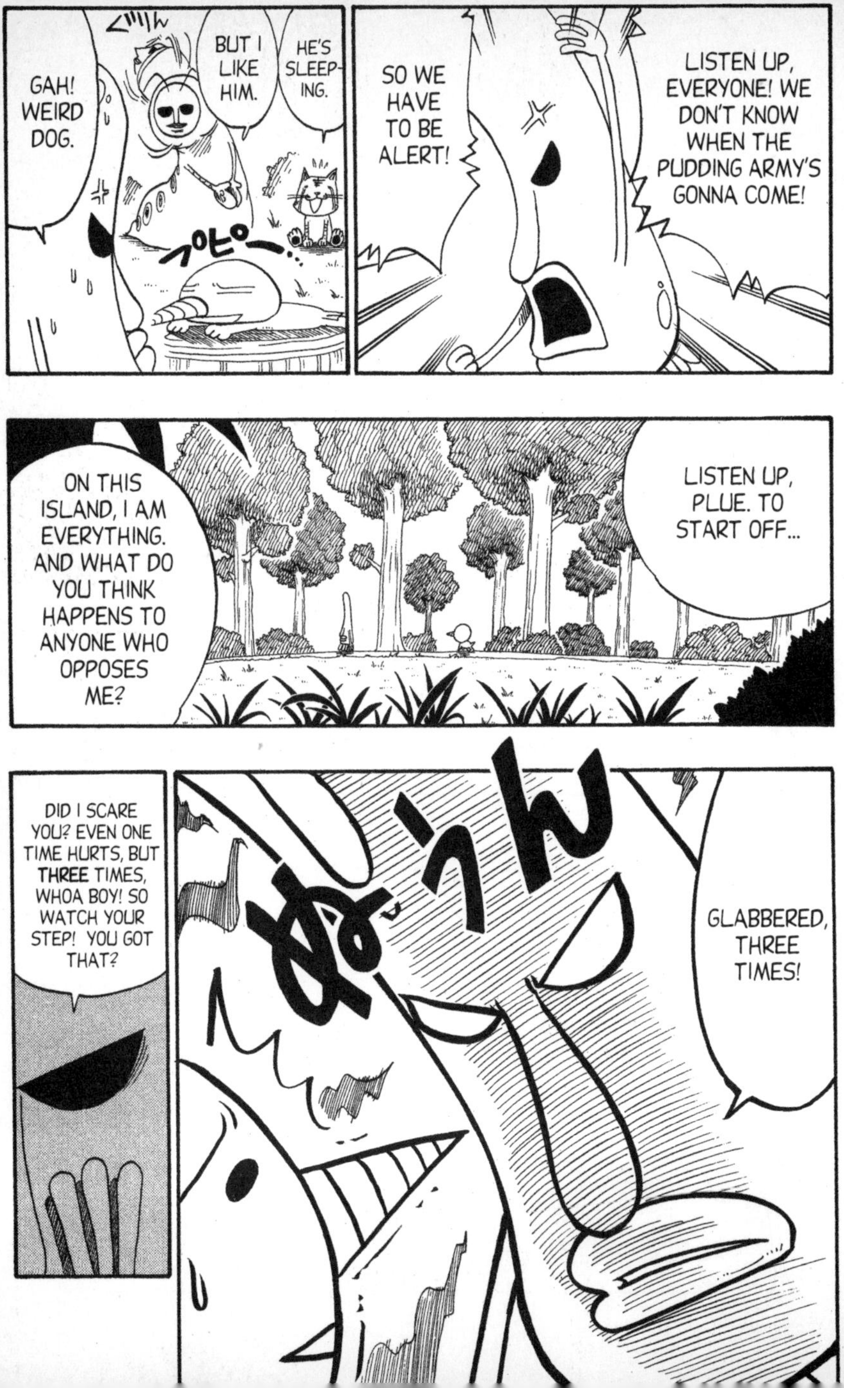
LISTEN UP, EVERYONE! WE DON'T KNOW WHEN THE PUDDING ARMY'S GONNA COME!
SO WE HAVE TO BE ALERT!
HE'S SLEEP-ING.
BUT I LIKE HIM.
GAH! WEIRD DOG.
LISTEN UP, PLUE. TO START OFF...
ON THIS ISLAND, I AM EVERYTHING. AND WHAT DO YOU THINK HAPPENS TO ANYONE WHO OPPOSES ME?
GLABBERED, THREE TIMES!
ぬうん
DID I SCARE YOU? EVEN ONE TIME HURTS, BUT **THREE** TIMES, WHOA BOY! SO WATCH YOUR STEP! YOU GOT THAT?

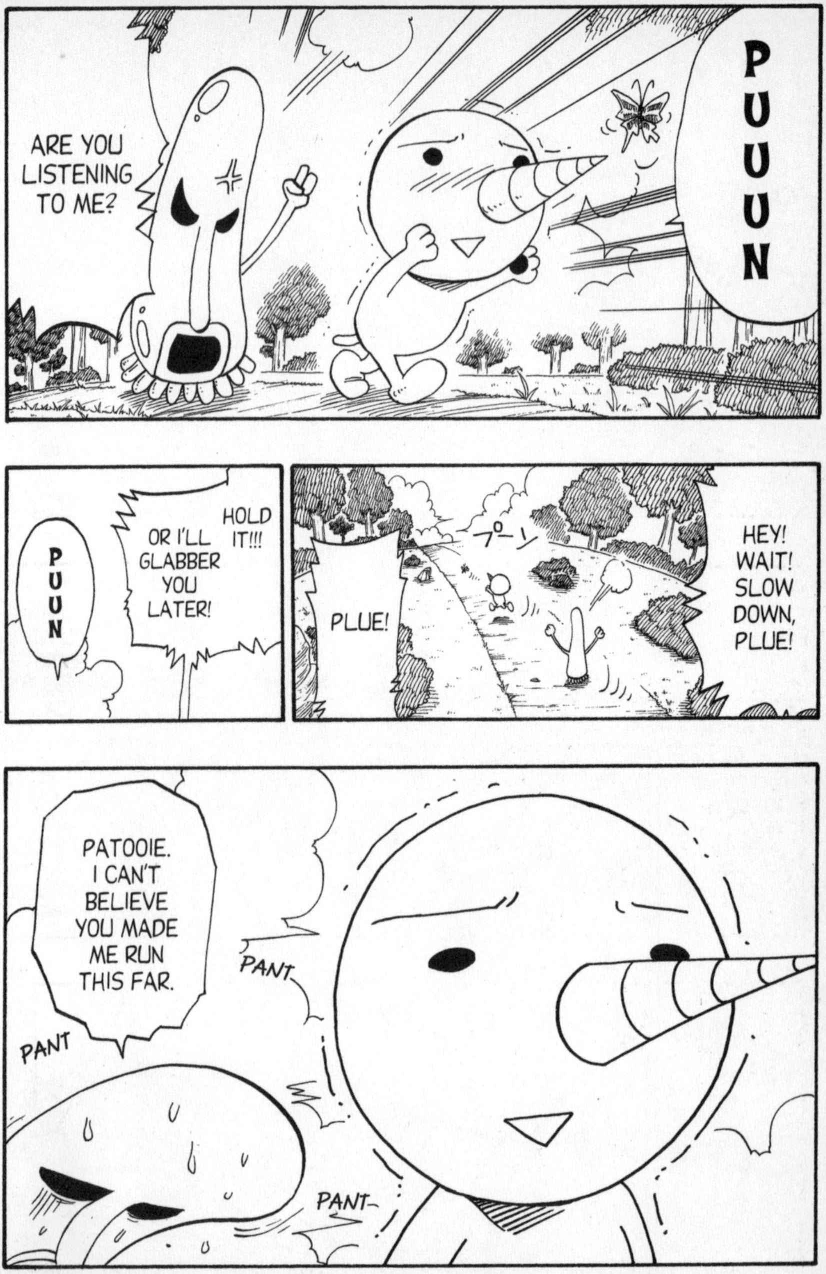
PUUUN
ARE YOU LISTENING TO ME?
HEY! WAIT! SLOW DOWN, PLUE!
PLUE!
HOLD IT!!!
OR I'LL GLABBER YOU LATER!
PUUN
PATOOIE. I CAN'T BELIEVE YOU MADE ME RUN THIS FAR.
PANT
PANT
PANT

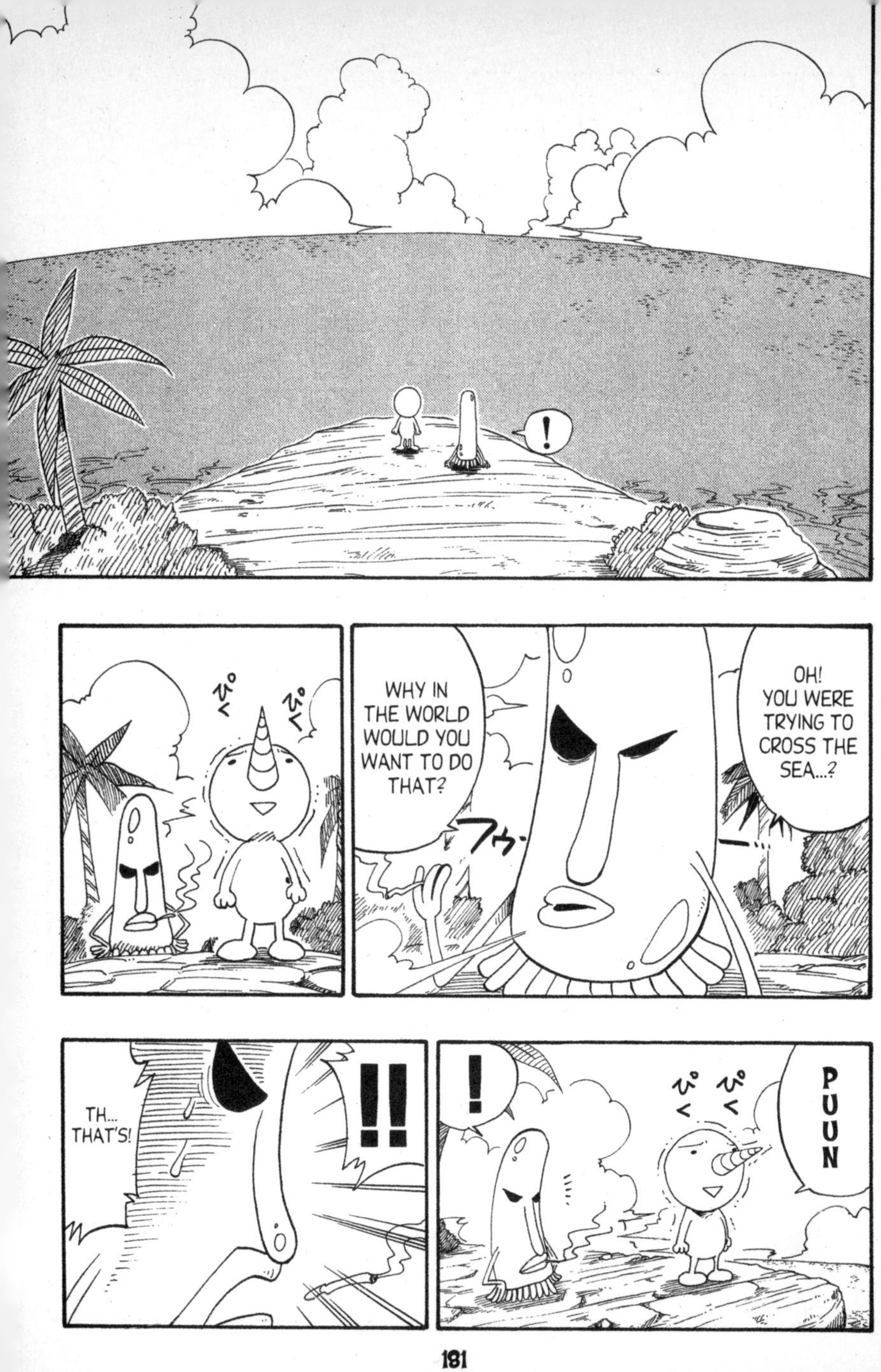
!
OH! YOU WERE TRYING TO CROSS THE SEA...?
WHY IN THE WORLD WOULD YOU WANT TO DO THAT?
フゥー
ぴく ぴく
!
ぴく ぴく
PUUN
!!
TH... THAT'S!

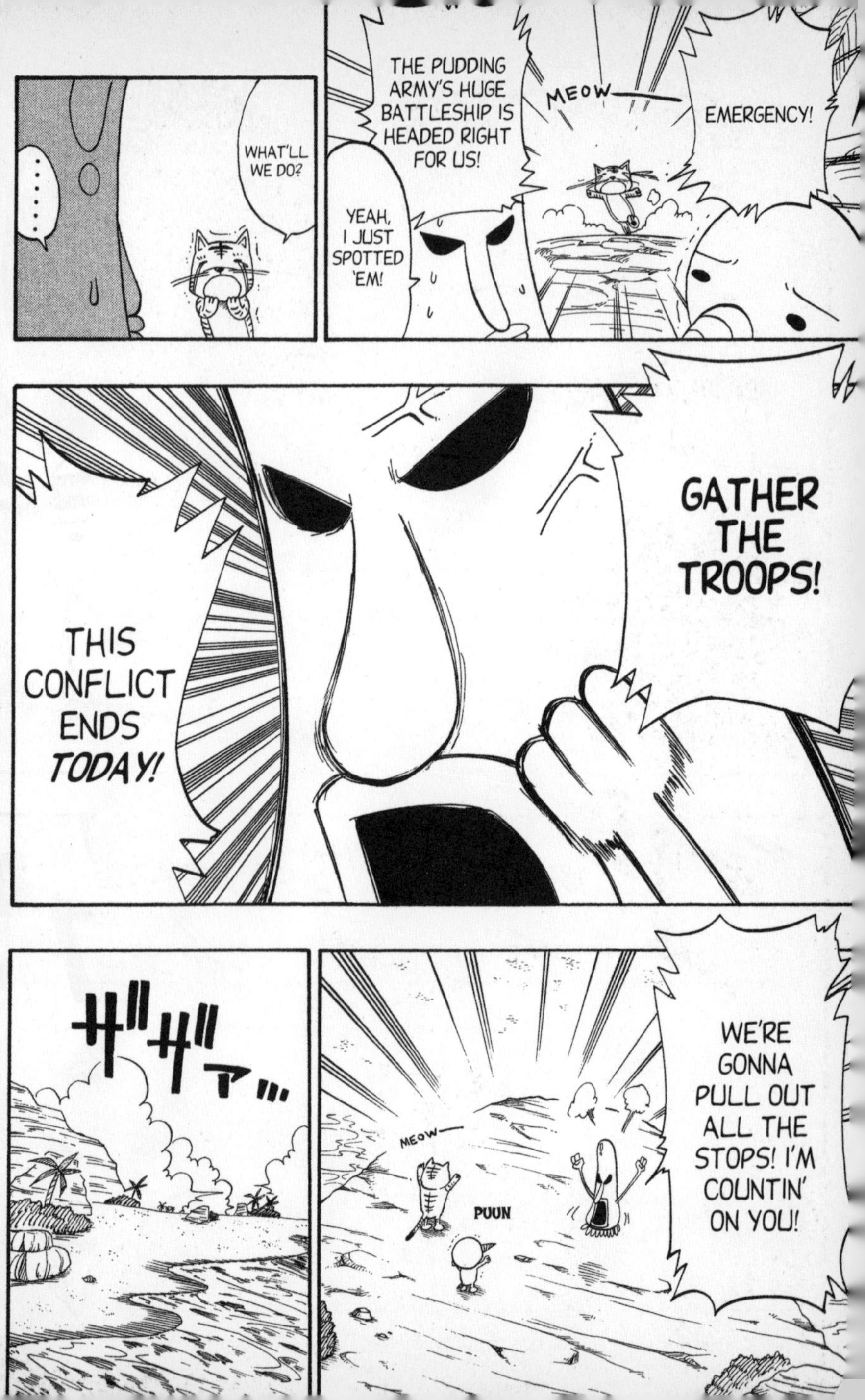
EMERGENCY!
MEOW—
THE PUDDING ARMY'S HUGE BATTLESHIP IS HEADED RIGHT FOR US!
YEAH, I JUST SPOTTED 'EM!
WHAT'LL WE DO?
......
GATHER THE TROOPS!
THIS CONFLICT ENDS *TODAY!*
WE'RE GONNA PULL OUT ALL THE STOPS! I'M COUNTIN' ON YOU!
MEOW—
PUUN
ザザァッ

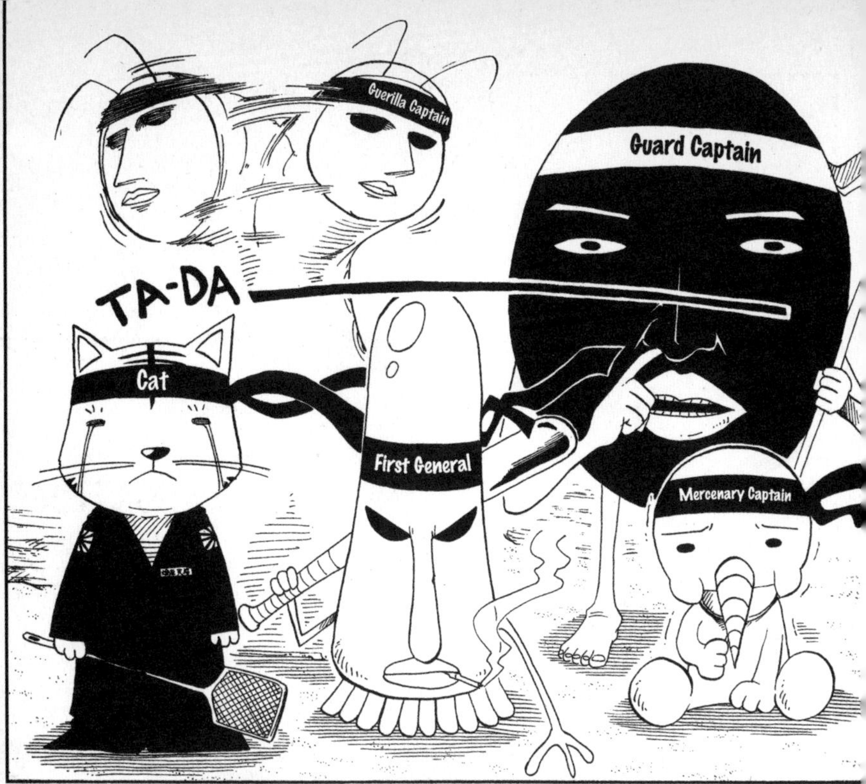
Guard Captain
Guerilla Captain
Mercenary Captain
First General
TA-DA
Cat
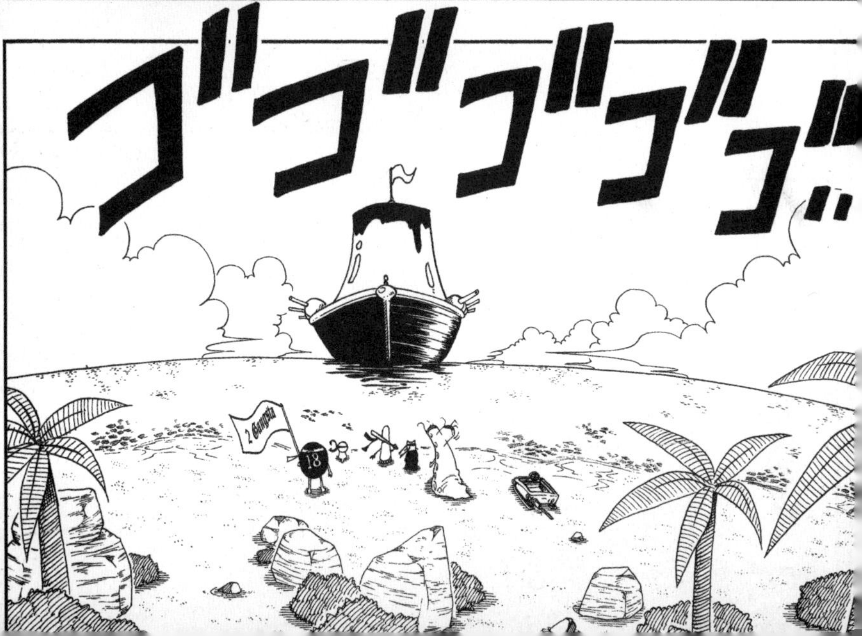
ゴゴゴゴ

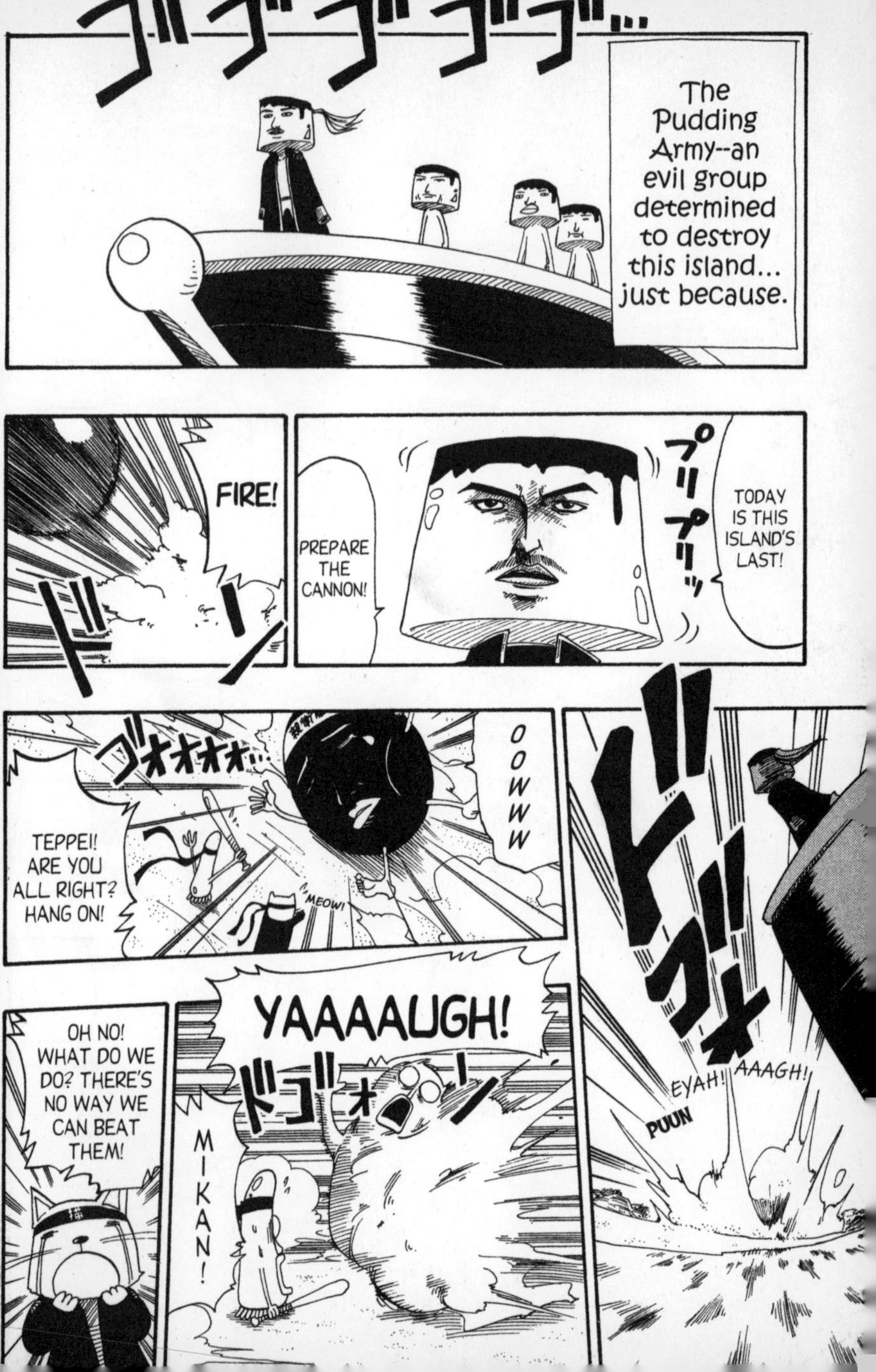
The Pudding Army--an evil group determined to destroy this island... just because.
TODAY IS THIS ISLAND'S LAST!
PREPARE THE CANNON!
FIRE!
EYAH!
AAAGH!
PUUN
OOWWW
MEOW!
TEPPEI! ARE YOU ALL RIGHT? HANG ON!
YAAAAUGH!
MIKAN!
OH NO! WHAT DO WE DO? THERE'S NO WAY WE CAN BEAT THEM!

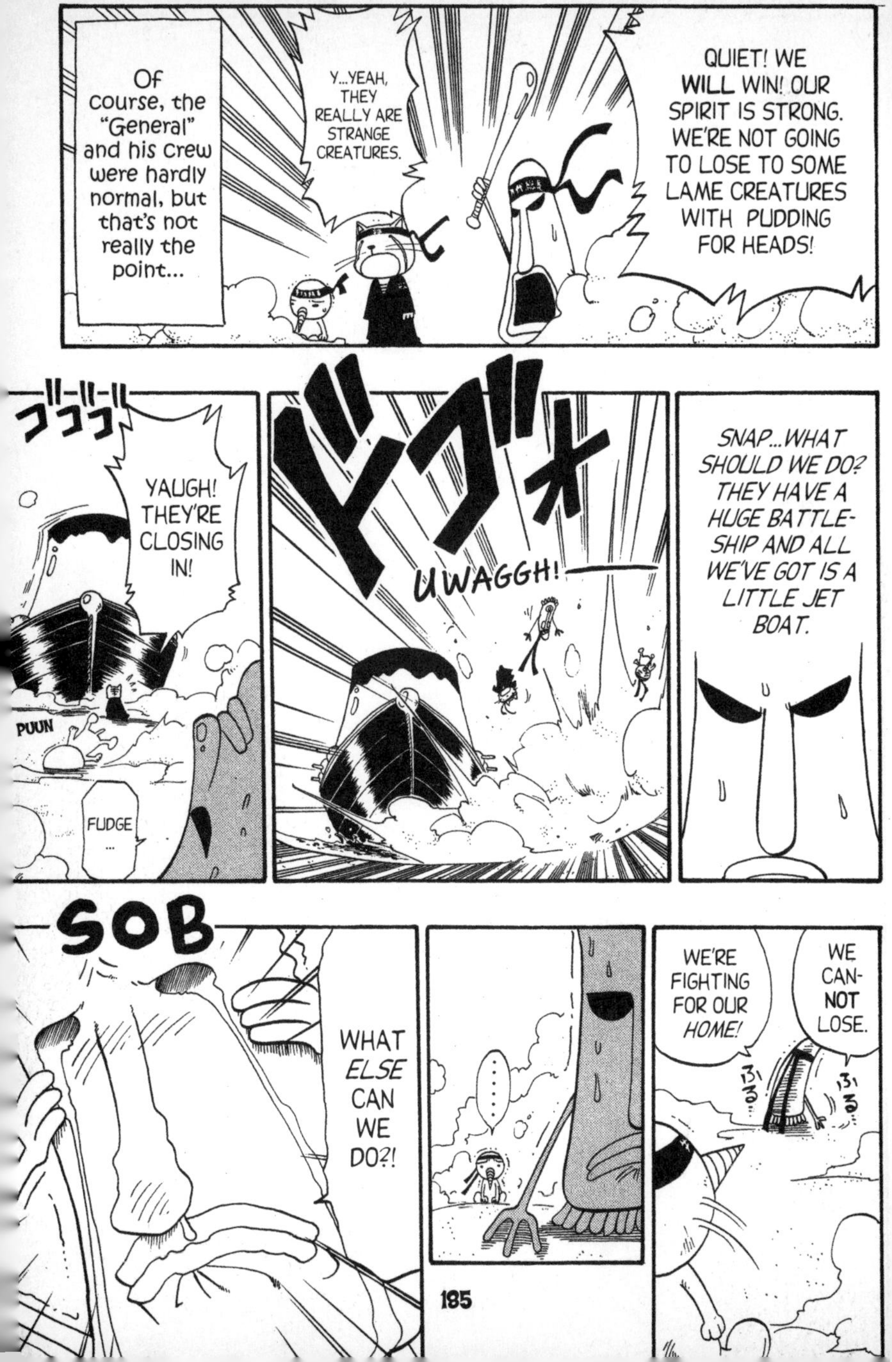
QUIET! WE WILL WIN! OUR SPIRIT IS STRONG. WE'RE NOT GOING TO LOSE TO SOME LAME CREATURES WITH PUDDING FOR HEADS!
Y...YEAH, THEY REALLY ARE STRANGE CREATURES.
Of course, the "General" and his crew were hardly normal, but that's not really the point...
SNAP...WHAT SHOULD WE DO? THEY HAVE A HUGE BATTLE-SHIP AND ALL WE'VE GOT IS A LITTLE JET BOAT.
ドゴォ
UWAGGH!
ゴゴゴ
YAUGH! THEY'RE CLOSING IN!
PUUN
FUDGE...
WE CAN-NOT LOSE.
WE'RE FIGHTING FOR OUR HOME!
ふるふる
ふるふる
......
SOB
WHAT ELSE CAN WE DO?!

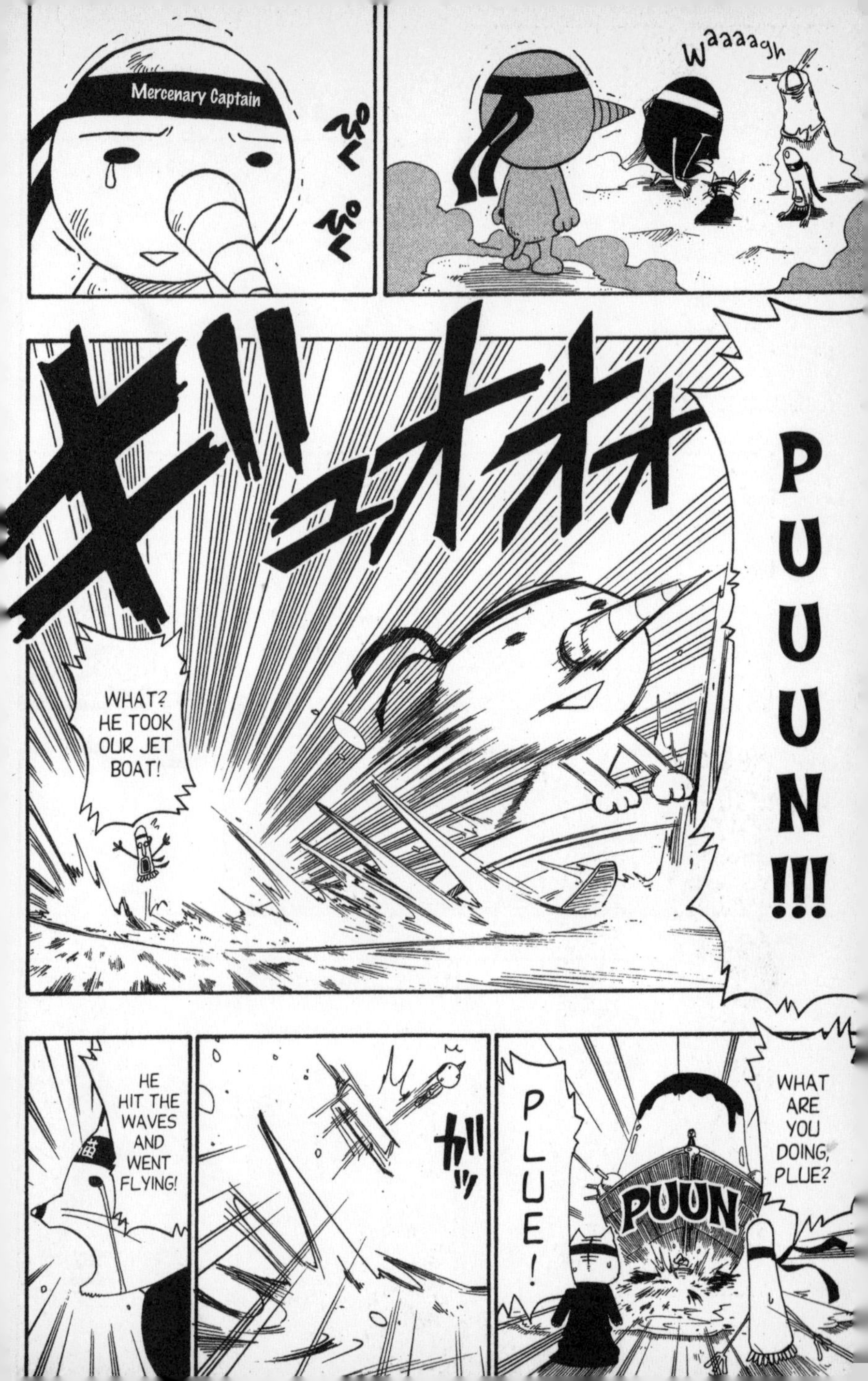
Waaaagh
Mercenary Captain
ぴく ぴく
ギュオオオ
PUUUN!!!
WHAT? HE TOOK OUR JET BOAT!
WHAT ARE YOU DOING, PLUE?
PLUE!
PUUN
ガッ
HE HIT THE WAVES AND WENT FLYING!

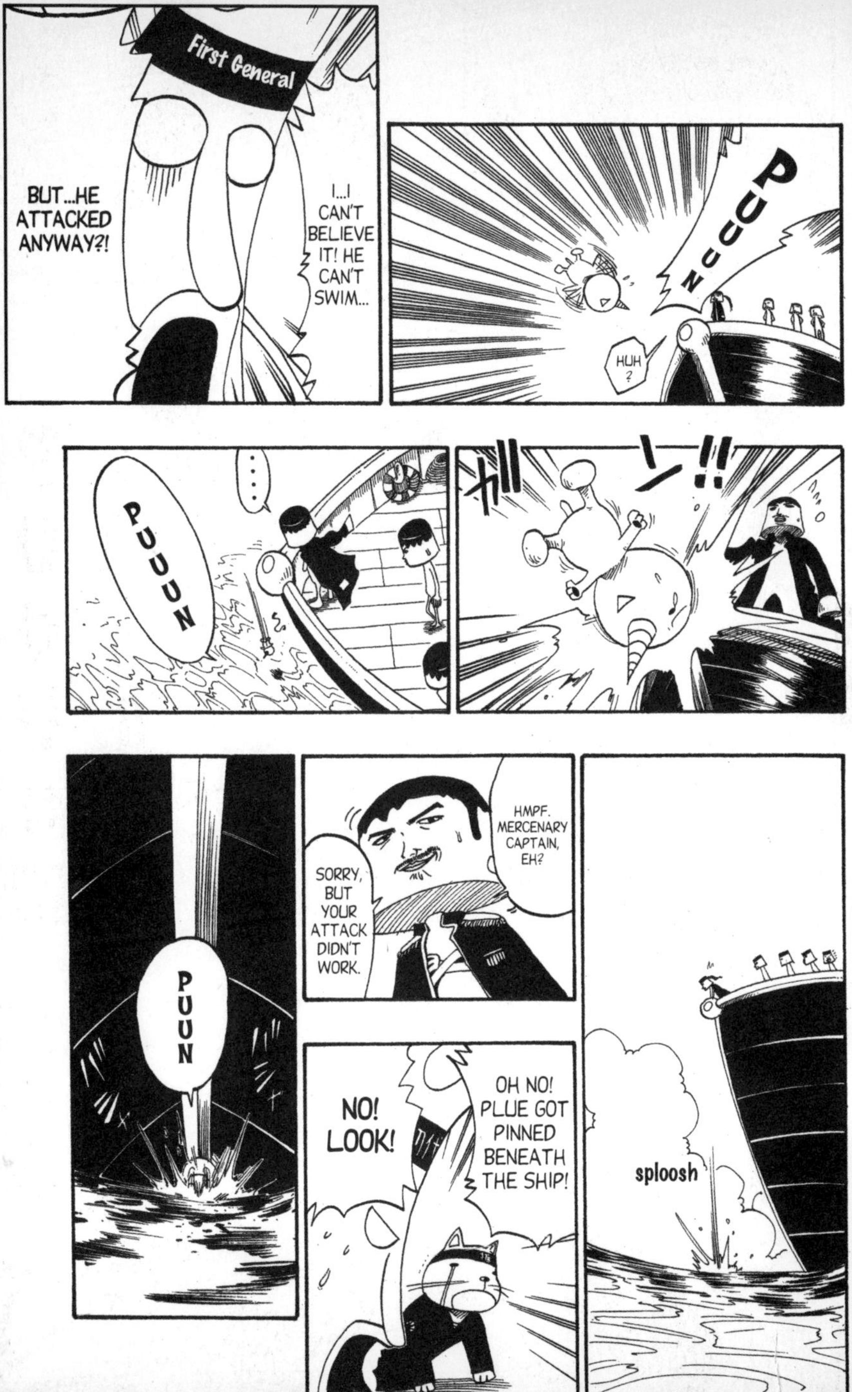
PUUUN
HUH?
First General
I...I CAN'T BELIEVE IT! HE CAN'T SWIM...
BUT...HE ATTACKED ANYWAY?!
....
PUUUN
sploosh
HMPF. MERCENARY CAPTAIN, EH?
SORRY, BUT YOUR ATTACK DIDN'T WORK.
OH NO! PLUE GOT PINNED BENEATH THE SHIP!
NO! LOOK!
PUUN

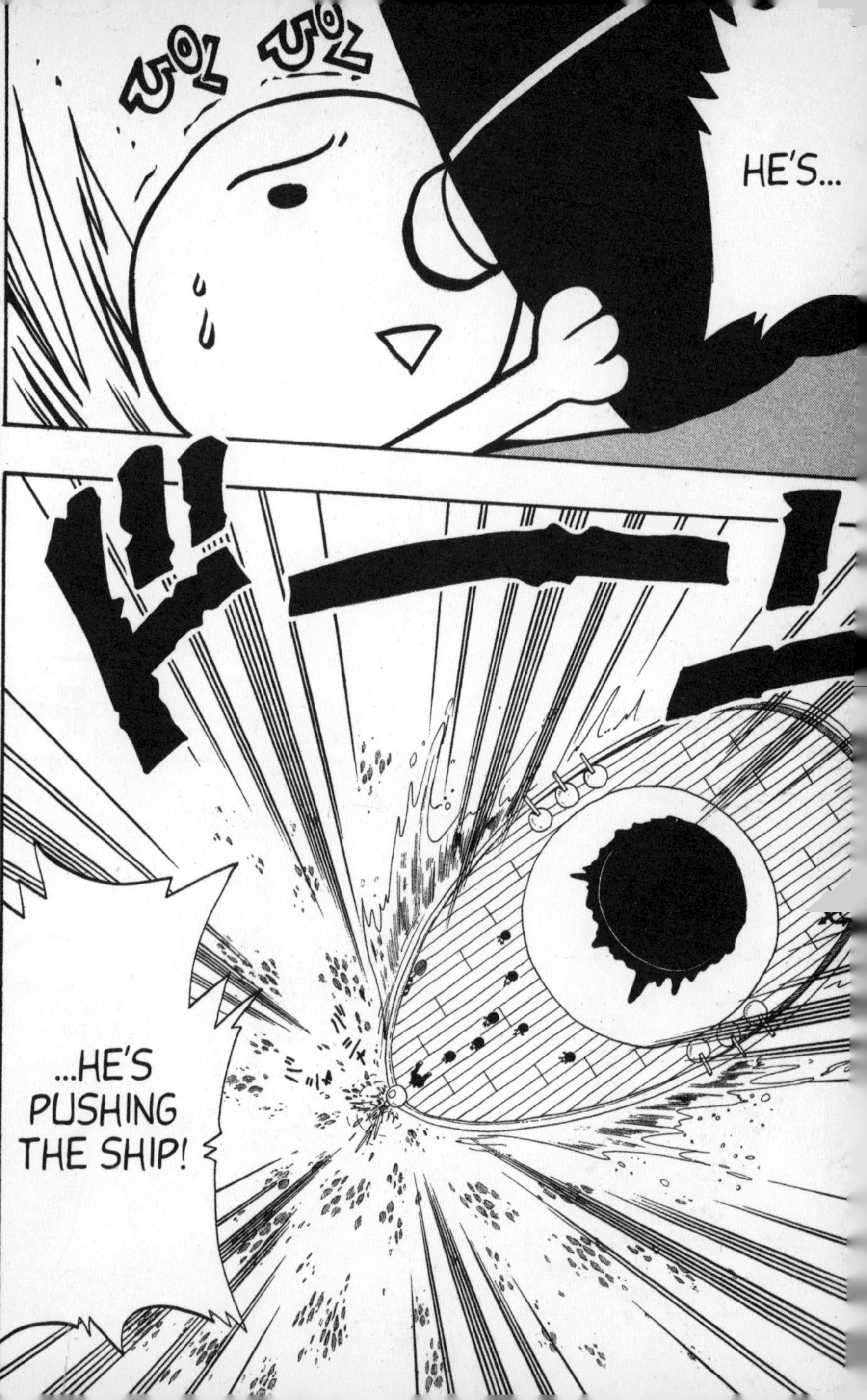
HE'S...
...HE'S PUSHING THE SHIP!

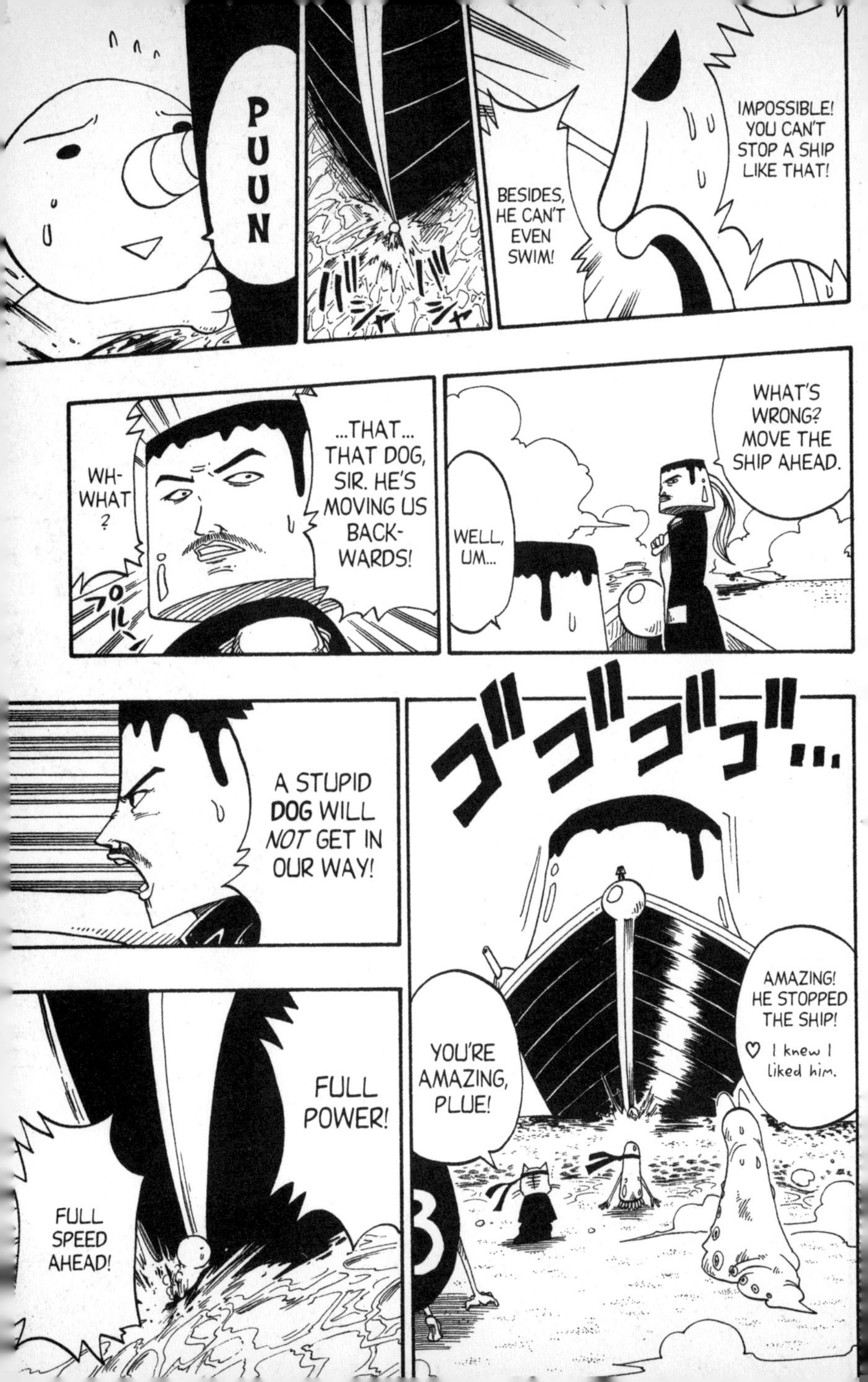
IMPOSSIBLE! YOU CAN'T STOP A SHIP LIKE THAT!
BESIDES, HE CAN'T EVEN SWIM!
バシャ バシャ
PUUN
WHAT'S WRONG? MOVE THE SHIP AHEAD.
WELL, UM...
...THAT... THAT DOG, SIR. HE'S MOVING US BACKWARDS!
WH-WHAT?
ゴゴゴゴ...
AMAZING! HE STOPPED THE SHIP!
♡ I knew I liked him.
YOU'RE AMAZING, PLUE!
A STUPID DOG WILL *NOT* GET IN OUR WAY!
FULL POWER!
FULL SPEED AHEAD!

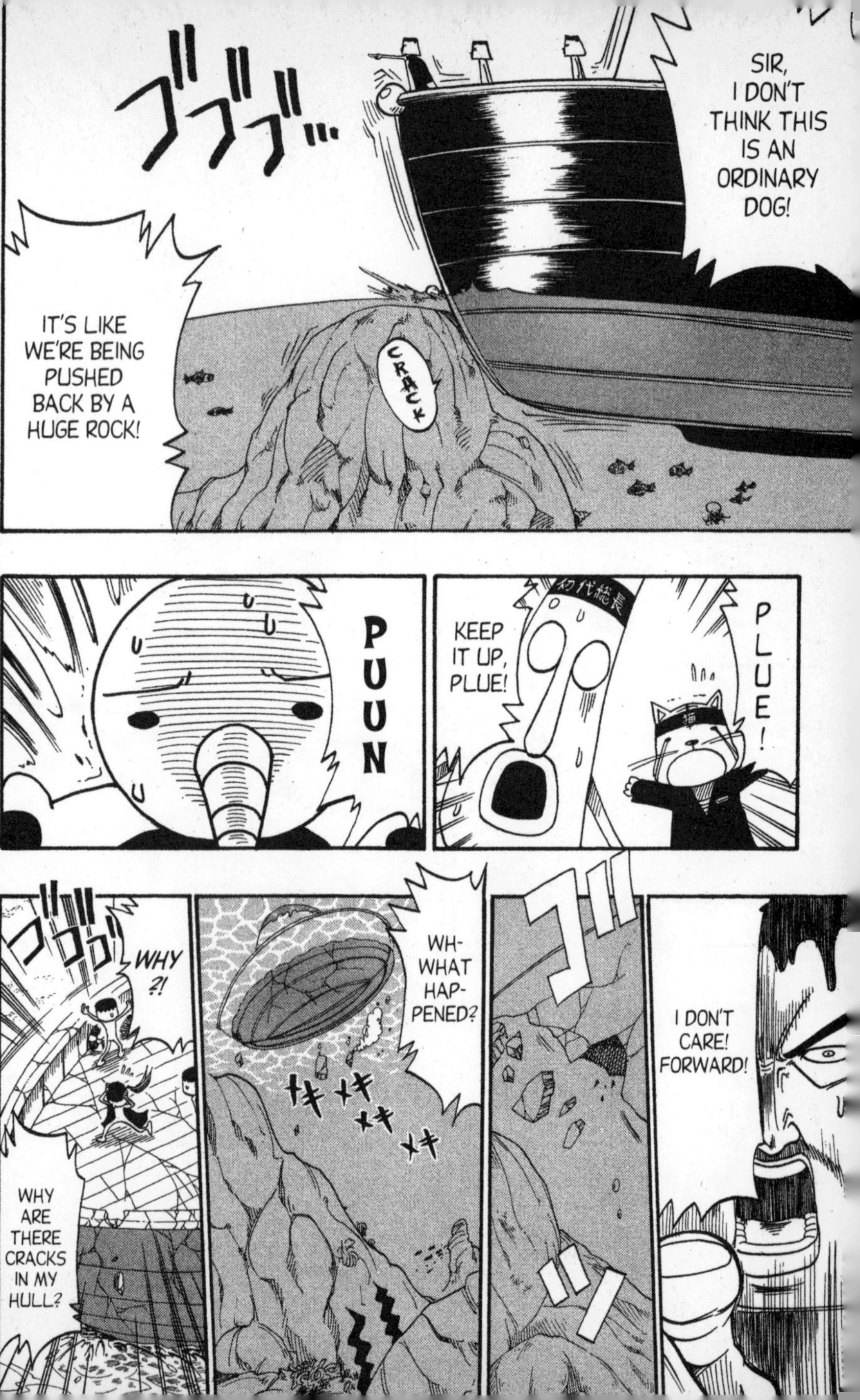
SIR, I DON'T THINK THIS IS AN ORDINARY DOG!
CRACK
IT'S LIKE WE'RE BEING PUSHED BACK BY A HUGE ROCK!
PLUE!
KEEP IT UP, PLUE!
PUUN
I DON'T CARE! FORWARD!
WH-WHAT HAPPENED?
WHY?!
WHY ARE THERE CRACKS IN MY HULL?

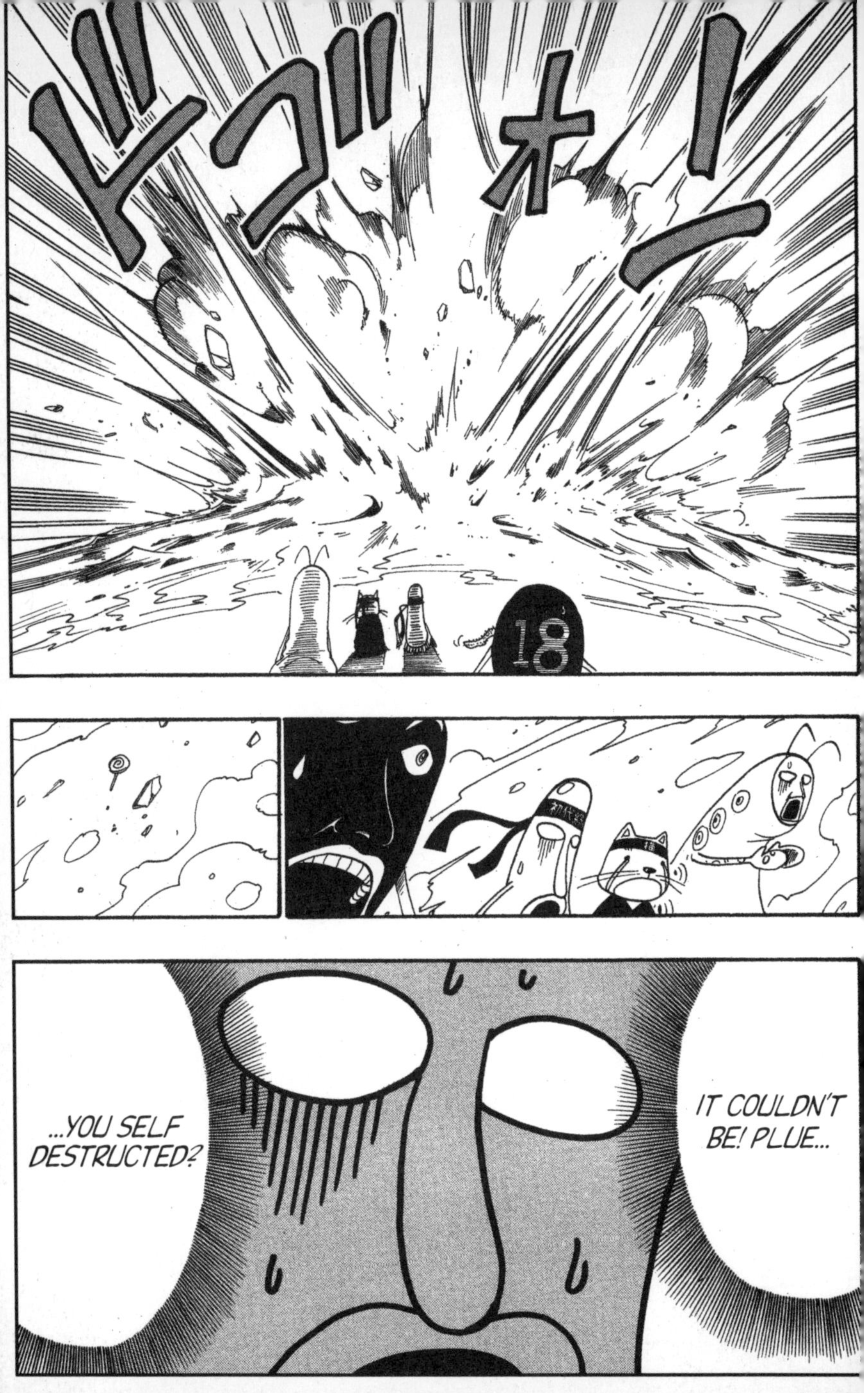
ドゴオン
18
IT COULDN'T BE! PLUE...
...YOU SELF DESTRUCTED?

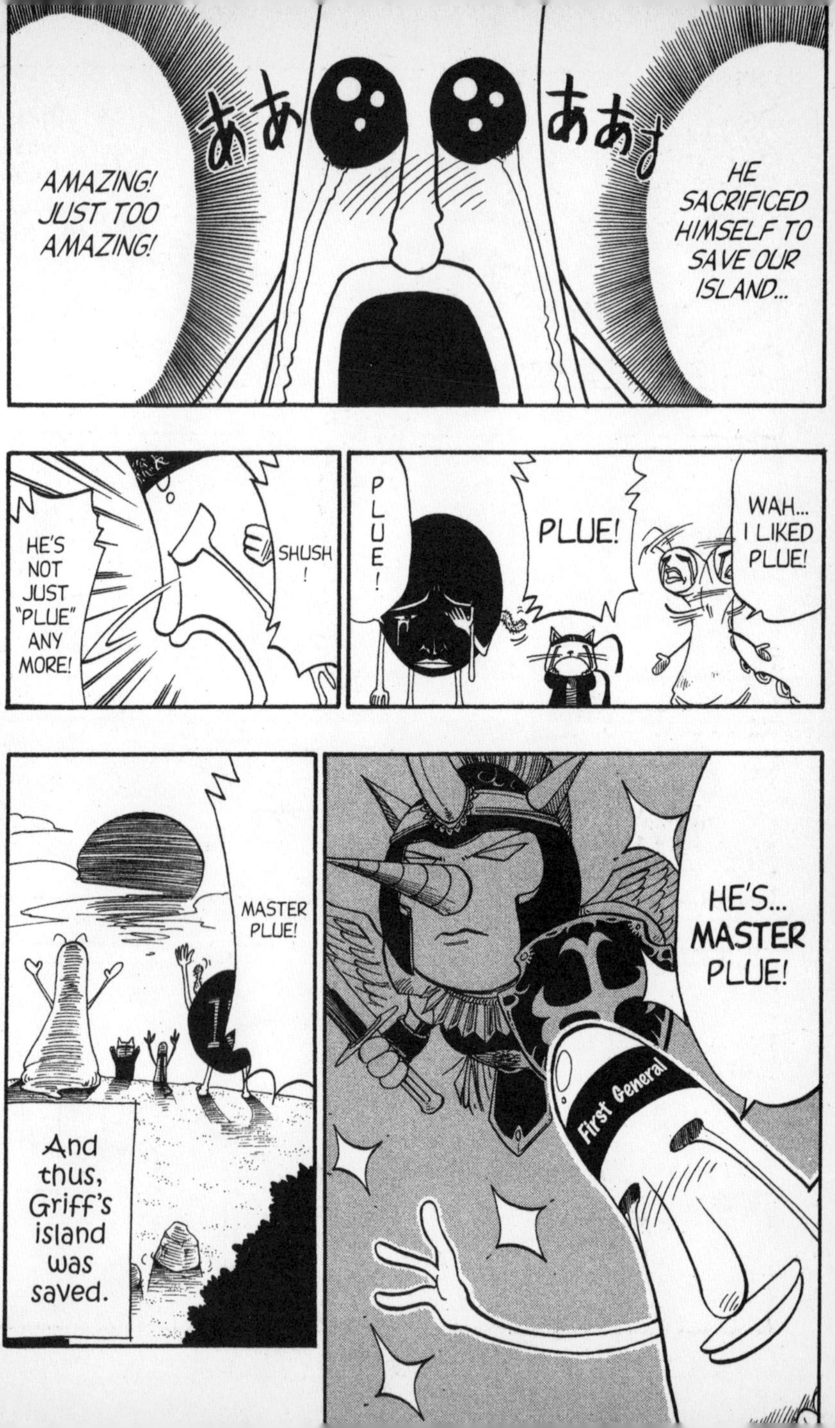
ああぁ
ああ
HE SACRIFICED HIMSELF TO SAVE OUR ISLAND...
AMAZING! JUST TOO AMAZING!
WAH... I LIKED PLUE!
PLUE!
PLUE!
SHUSH!
HE'S NOT JUST "PLUE" ANY MORE!
HE'S... MASTER PLUE!
First General
MASTER PLUE!
And thus, Griff's island was saved.

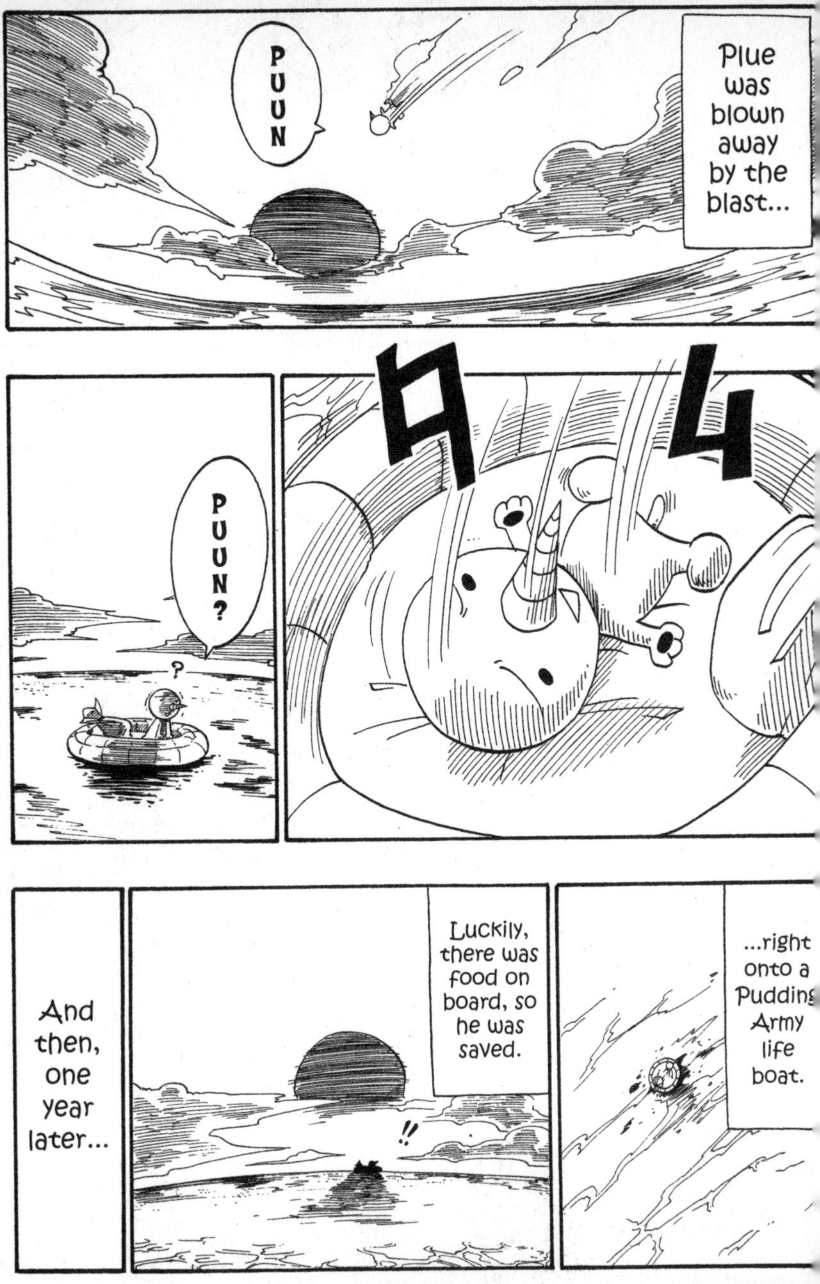
Plue was blown away by the blast...
PUUN
PUUN?
?
...right onto a Pudding Army life boat.
Luckily, there was food on board, so he was saved.
!!
And then, one year later...

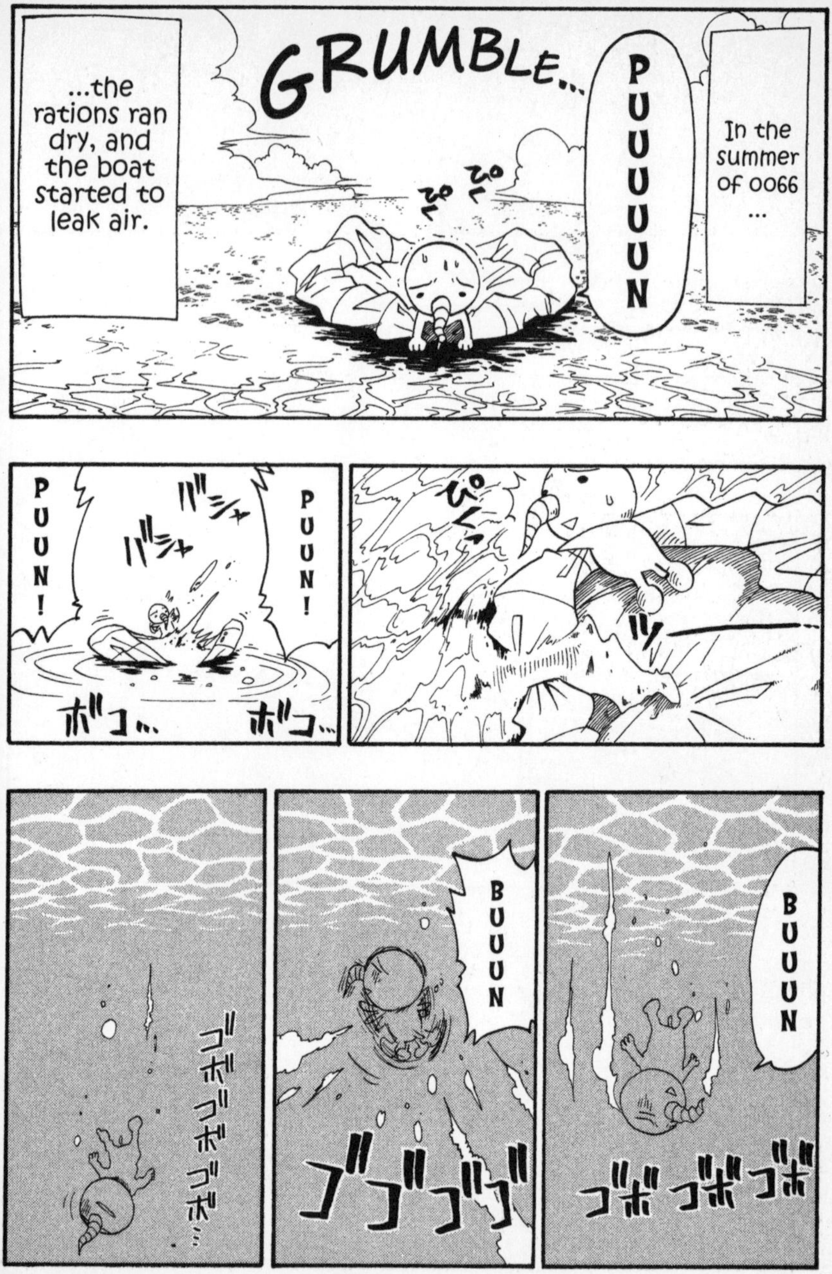

In the summer of 0066 ...
PUUUUUN
GRUMBLE...
ぴく ぴく
...the rations ran dry, and the boat started to leak air.
ぴくっ
ッ—
PUUN!
バシャ バシャ
PUUN!
ボコ… ボコ…
BUUUN
ゴボゴボゴボ
BUUUN
ゴゴゴゴ
ゴボゴボゴボ…

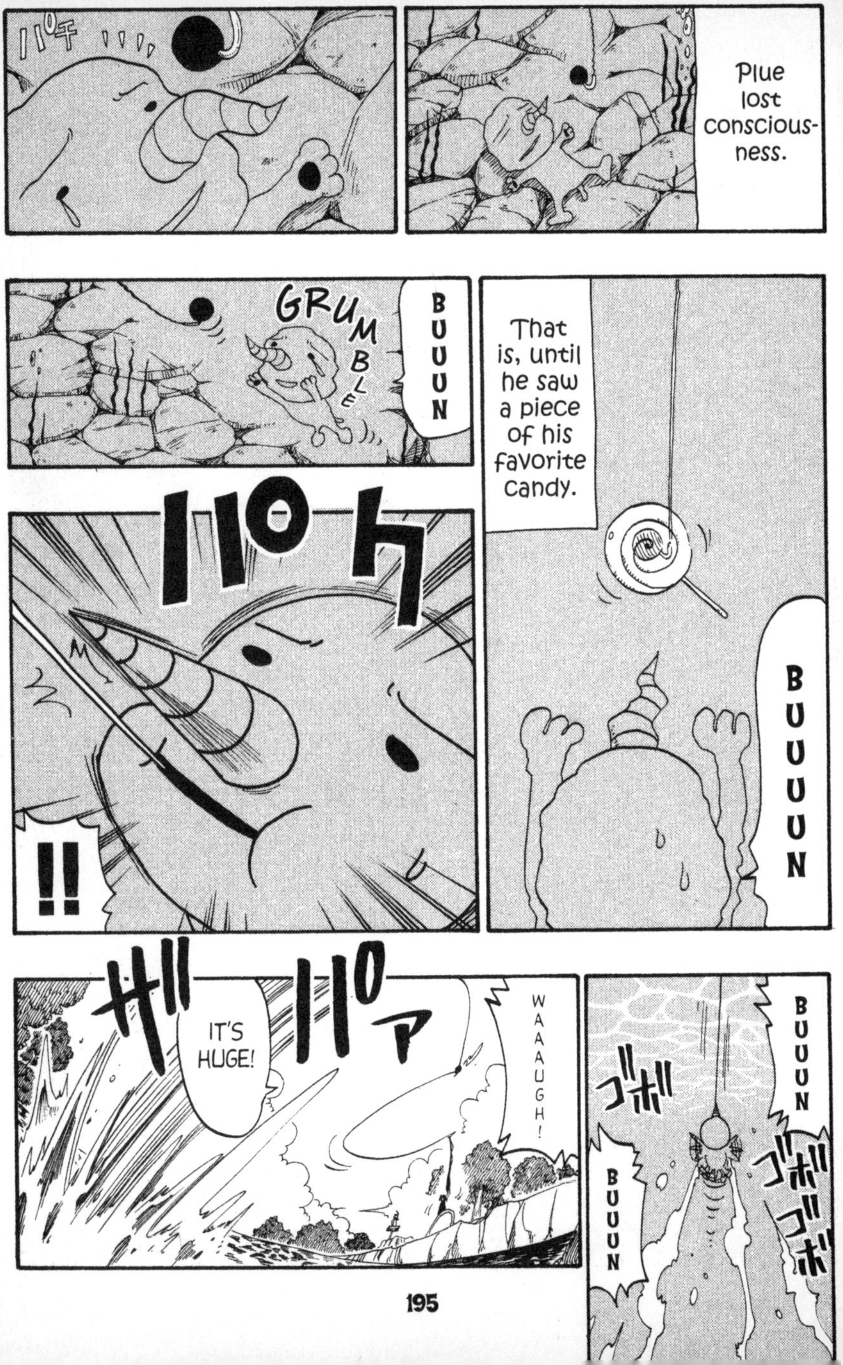
Plue lost consciousness.
パチ
That is, until he saw a piece of his favorite candy.
BUUUUN
GRUMBLE
BUUUN
パク
!!
BUUUN
ゴボ
BUUUN
ゴボゴボ
ザパァ
IT'S HUGE!
WAAAAUGH!

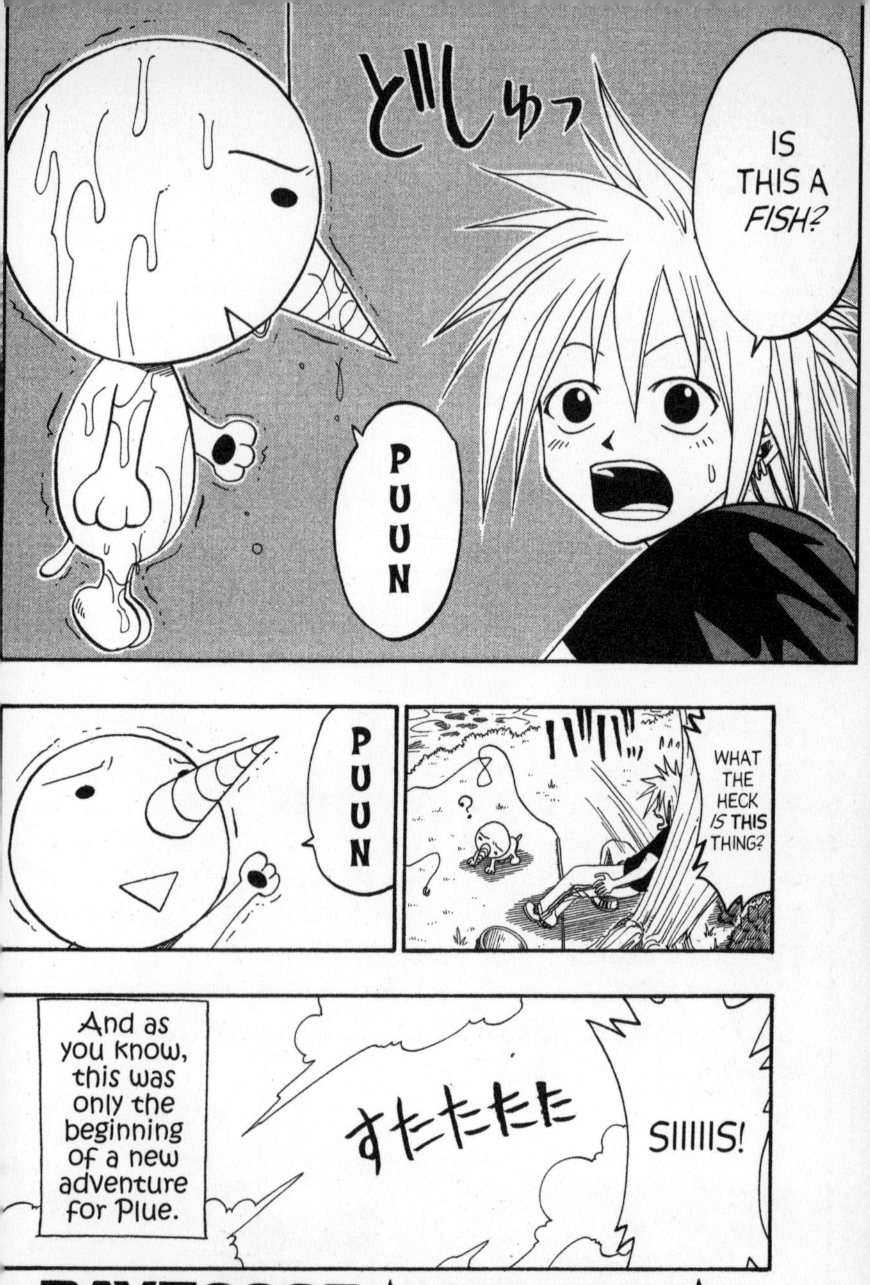
IS THIS A FISH?
どしゅっ
PUUN
ババッ
WHAT THE HECK IS THIS THING?
PUUN
SIIIIS!
すたたたた
And as you know, this was only the beginning of a new adventure for Plue.

RAVE0065★THE END★

About Rave 0065: Plue's Mercenary Diary

I WONDER IF I SHOULD'VE WRITTEN SUCH A SILLY STORY...
I CAN'T BELIEVE THIS STORY WAS IN A MAGAZINE. AMAZING, ISN'T
IT? A LOT OF READERS WANTED ME TO PUT IT IN ONE OF THE
GRAPHIC NOVELS, SO I PUT IT IN VOLUME 6. TO TELL THE TRUTH,
I'M THE KIND OF MANGA-KA WHO WRITES THESE KINDS OF SILLY
STORIES. SO I THINK THIS EXTRA PLUE STORY WAS A LOT LIKE
ME. IT WAS FUN TO DRAW. THERE ARE A LOT OF OTHER EXTRA
STORIES I WANT TO DRAW, BUT IF I HAVE THE CHANCE, I WANT
TO DRAW ANOTHER RAVE EXTRA STORY. EDITOR! PLEASE LET ME
DRAW ANOTHER ONE!

THE STORY BEHIND THE CHARACTERS (OR SHOULD I SAY CREA-
TURES?) FIRST UP, MIKAN. I ENDED UP PATTERNING HIM AFTER
TANCHIMO. LIKE THE MOVEMENT OF HIS HEAD AND STUFF...
MAN...I REGRET IT NOW. BY THE WAY, HE'S A POTATO BUG. RISA'S
A CAT. A CRYBABY CAT. TEPPEI IS A MYSTERY. EVEN I DON'T
REALLY KNOW WHAT HE IS. I CAME UP WITH THE PUDDING ARMY
LEADER CHARACTER WHEN I WAS EATING PUDDING. I THOUGHT,
"IT'D BE KIND OF SCARY IF I PUT AN OLD MAN'S FACE ON THIS
PUDDING..." I REALLY LIKE DRAWING STRANGE CHARACTERS. IT
MAKES ME HAPPY.

PUUN   Meow   wiggle   jiggle   WHAT'S THIS?

PLUE   GRIFF   RISA   MIKAN   TANCHIMO   TEPPEI   PUDDING ARMY LEADE

THE GUARDIAN OF TIME: SIEG HART

WEAPONS: MAGIC (ELEMENTAL)
BIRTHDAY / AGE: UNKNOWN / UNKNOWN
HEIGHT / WEIGHT / BLOOD TYPE:
181 CM / 63 KG / AB
BIRTHPLACE: UNKNOWN
HOBBIES: STARING AT CLOCKS
SPECIAL SKILLS: MAGIC
LIKES: THE TIME CONTINUUM
HATES: RUNE SAVE

SOME OF YOU MAY HAVE ALREADY NOTICED,
BUT HIS NAME COMES FROM SIEGFRIED, THE
LEGENDARY HERO OF THE GERMAN STORY "THE
NIBELUNGENLIED." HE SEEMS TO BE REALLY
POPULAR. I'M GLAD! HE'S ONE OF THE CHARAC-
TERS I THOUGHT UP BEFORE RAVE MASTER WAS
PUBLISHED, AND I WAS ALWAYS WORRIED ABOUT
WHEN I WOULD FINALLY BE ABLE TO USE HIM.
SIEG'S CHARACTER IS TOO SERIOUS. HE ALWAYS
SEEMS TO BE GOING AROUND IN CIRCLES (LAUGH).

THIS IS WHAT THE
MARK (CREST) ABOVE
HIS EYE LOOKS LIKE.

ONE OF THE ORACION SIX: REINA

WEAPONS: DARK BRING (WHITE KISS)
BIRTHDAY / AGE: FEBRUARY 14, 0043 / 23
HEIGHT / WEIGHT / BLOOD TYPE:
170 CM / 51 KG / A
BIRTHPLACE: THE CAPITAL OF BEAUTY, EL NADIA
HOBBIES: LISTENING TO MUSIC IN THE BATH
SPECIAL SKILLS: FLIRTING, BEING SCOUTED
LIKES: EMERALDS, WINE
HATES: LOOSE MEN, STUBBORN MEN,
          FILTHY MEN, QUIET MEN (JEGAN)

I GOT A LOT OF LETTERS BEGGING ME TO PUT REINA'S
PROFILE IN THE GRAPHIC NOVEL, SO I DID. HER STORY'S
ENDED FOR THE MOMENT, BUT I'LL MAKE AN EXCEPTION
THIS TIME. (LAUGH) SINCE HER STORY ISN'T OVER YET,
I'LL ONLY EXPLAIN WHAT YOU SHOULD KNOW UP UNTIL
THIS POINT. THE NAME OF HER DARK BRING HASN'T
BEEN MENTIONED IN THE MAIN STORY YET, BUT IT'S
MY FAVORITE DARK BRING. IT HAS A CERTAIN SPECIAL
POWER, SO LOOK FORWARD TO SEEING IT! BY THE
WAY, THE ORACION SIX, SIEG, AND KING WERE ALL
CHARACTERS I CAME UP WITH BEFORE RAVE MASTER
WAS PUBLISHED. OF COURSE, I'VE MADE SOME
CHANGES TO THE DETAILS OF THEIR CHARACTERS,
BUT REINA IS STILL THE SAME AS WHEN I FIRST
CREATED HER. I DIDN'T MAKE ANY CHANGES TO HER.

THE TEN-FORM SWORD: TEN POWERS PART 2

3. THE SONIC SWORD: SILFARION

SILFARION

WHEN THE TEN POWERS IS IN THIS FORM, THE WIELDER CAN MAKE ATTACKS AT HIGH SPEED. BUT IT DOESN'T HAVE ENOUGH POWER TO KILL IN ONE ATTACK, SO IT'S BEST FOR USING AGAINST SMALL FRIES.

IT'S WEAK POINT IS THAT IT'S VERY LIGHT. THE WIELDER HIMSELF BECOMES LIGHT AS WELL, SO YOU HAVE TO BE CAREFUL ABOUT THAT.

BY THE WAY, "SONIC" MEANS AT THE SPEED OF SOUND (ABOUT 340 M/S), BUT THIS SWORD CAN'T ACTUALLY REACH THAT KIND OF SPEED. IF IT ACTUALLY COULD GO THAT FAST, IT'D BE REALLY DANGEROUS!

4. THE SEALING SWORD: RUNE SAVE

RUNE SAVE

A DEFENSIVE SWORD. IT CAN'T CUT OBJECTS OR PEOPLE, BUT IT CAN CUT FLAMES, WATER, SMOKE, AND OTHER THINGS THAT USUALLY CAN'T BE CUT WITH A SWORD. AND JUST LIKE IT'S NAME SUGGESTS, IT CAN ALSO SEAL MAGIC. THIS SWORD IS MEANT ONLY FOR DEFENSE.

HARU SEALED ELIE'S AETHERION WITH THIS SWORD, BUT IT'S STILL UNKNOWN WHETHER IT WAS SEALED WITHIN THE SWORD, OR IN ELIE'S BODY.

RAVE0077 Levin Minds the House Number 5: Gol

NOTE: "GOL" ISN'T ACTUALLY A REAL WORD...

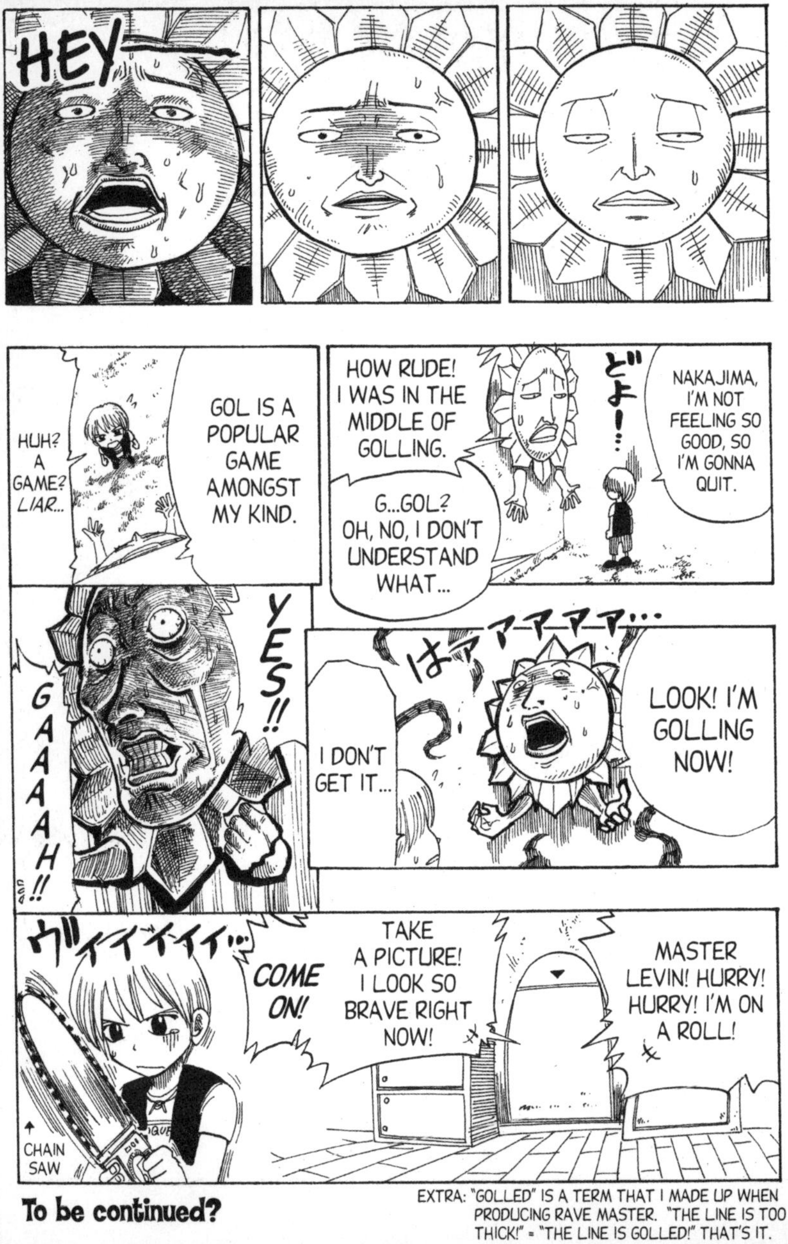
HEY—
NAKAJIMA, I'M NOT FEELING SO GOOD, SO I'M GONNA QUIT.
どよ!..
HOW RUDE! I WAS IN THE MIDDLE OF GOLLING.
G...GOL? OH, NO, I DON'T UNDERSTAND WHAT...
GOL IS A POPULAR GAME AMONGST MY KIND.
HUH? A GAME? LIAR...
LOOK! I'M GOLLING NOW!
はアアアアア...
I DON'T GET IT...
YES!!
GAAAAAH!!
MASTER LEVIN! HURRY! HURRY! I'M ON A ROLL!
TAKE A PICTURE! I LOOK SO BRAVE RIGHT NOW!
COME ON!
ヴィイイイイ...
CHAIN SAW

To be continued?

EXTRA: "GOLLED" IS A TERM THAT I MADE UP WHEN PRODUCING RAVE MASTER. "THE LINE IS TOO THICK!" = "THE LINE IS GOLLED!" THAT'S IT.

Afterword

YEAH! MY FAVORITE PART OF THE STORY SO FAR, THE AETHERION SAGA! I'VE BEEN WARMING UP FOR IT. REALLY!
ACTUALLY, IN VOLUME ONE, PAGE 37, SECOND PANEL, I WROTE "AETHERION" IN ENGLISH. SO I'VE BEEN WARMING UP FOR IT FOR A LOOOONG TIME. SO OF COURSE, THIS ISN'T THE LAST YOU'LL SEE OF THE AETHERION SAGA. I'M ONLY ABOUT HALF WAY, NO, 1/3RD OF THE WAY THROUGH. THE KEY POINTS FROM HERE ON WILL BE ELIE AND AETHERION, AND SIEG HART. PROBABLY. (I'M STILL PLOTTING IT OUT.) I WANT ALL OF THE READERS TO BE SURPRISED WHEN ELIE'S PAST IS REVEALED.

I JUST REALIZED THIS, BUT I'M PRETTY FOND OF MAGIC USERS. OF COURSE, MY DEBUT WAS A STORY CALLED "MAGICIAN." AND THE STORY I JUST FINISHED READING, "MAGIC PARTY," IS ABOUT MAGIC USERS TOO.

AND NOW THE MAGIC USER SIEG IS APPEARING IN RAVE MASTER.

I REALLY LIKE THEM. HEY, HAVEN'T YOU EVER DREAMED ABOUT BEING A MAGICIAN? IT'D BE REALLY COOL IF THERE REALLY WERE MAGICIANS LIKE YOU SEE IN RPGS. THEY CAN EVEN BRING YOU BACK TO LIFE. (LAUGH)

...AND WELL, VOLUME 6 ENDED SAFELY.

HMM, I STILL HAVE SOME SPACE LEFT. WHAT SHOULD I SAY... HMM... EVER SINCE I CAN REMEMBER, I'VE BEEN BAD AT WRITING. REALLY. WHAT I WRITE IN THIS SECTION EACH VOLUME MUST BE PAINFUL TO READ, BUT I'M REALLY GIVING IT MY ALL. PLEASE FORGIVE ME!

SEE YOU LATER, EVERYONE!

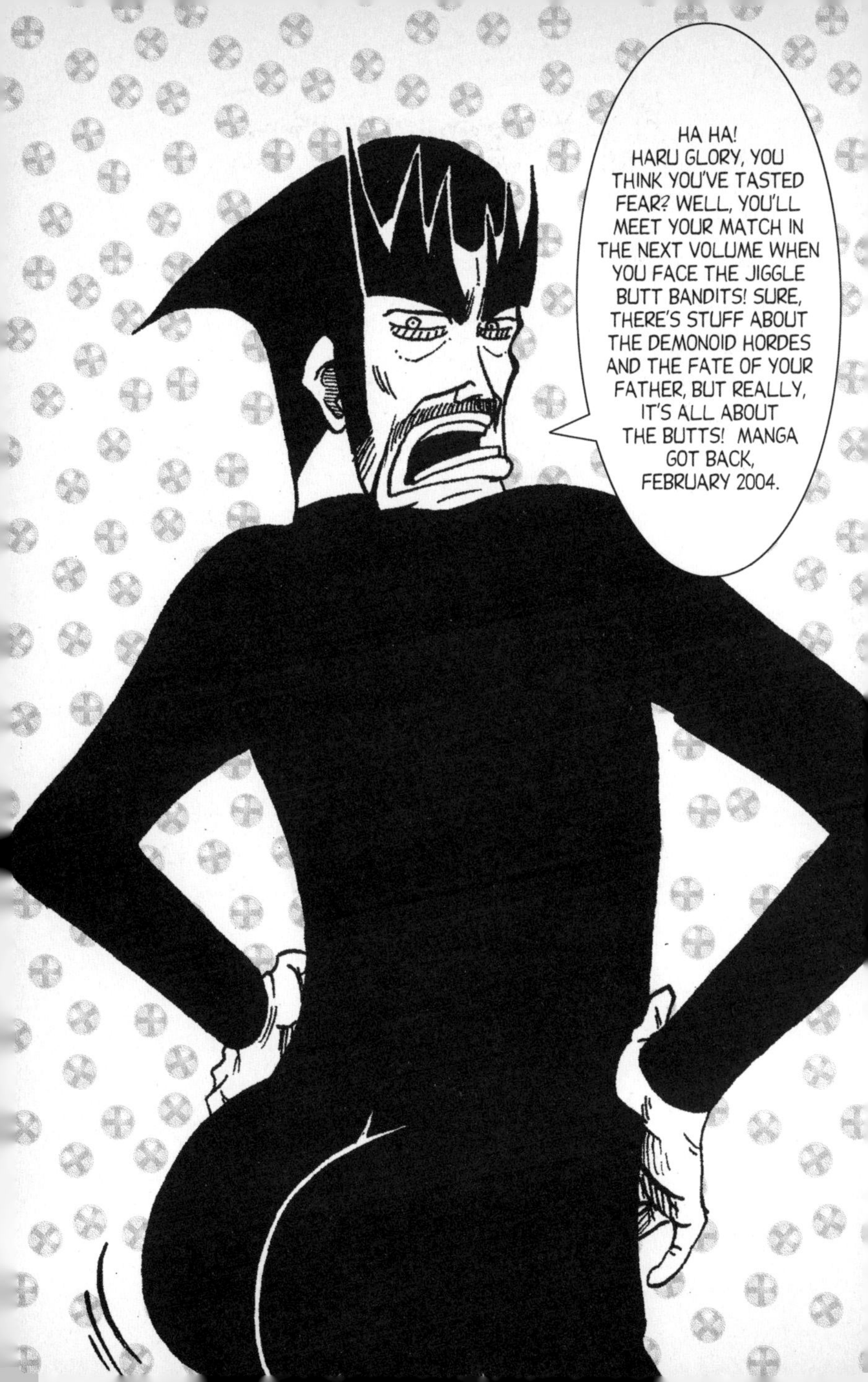
HA HA! HARU GLORY, YOU THINK YOU'VE TASTED FEAR? WELL, YOU'LL MEET YOUR MATCH IN THE NEXT VOLUME WHEN YOU FACE THE JIGGLE BUTT BANDITS! SURE, THERE'S STUFF ABOUT THE DEMONOID HORDES AND THE FATE OF YOUR FATHER, BUT REALLY, IT'S ALL ABOUT THE BUTTS! MANGA GOT BACK, FEBRUARY 2004.

THE FOLLOWING IS A PAID ADVERTISEMENT

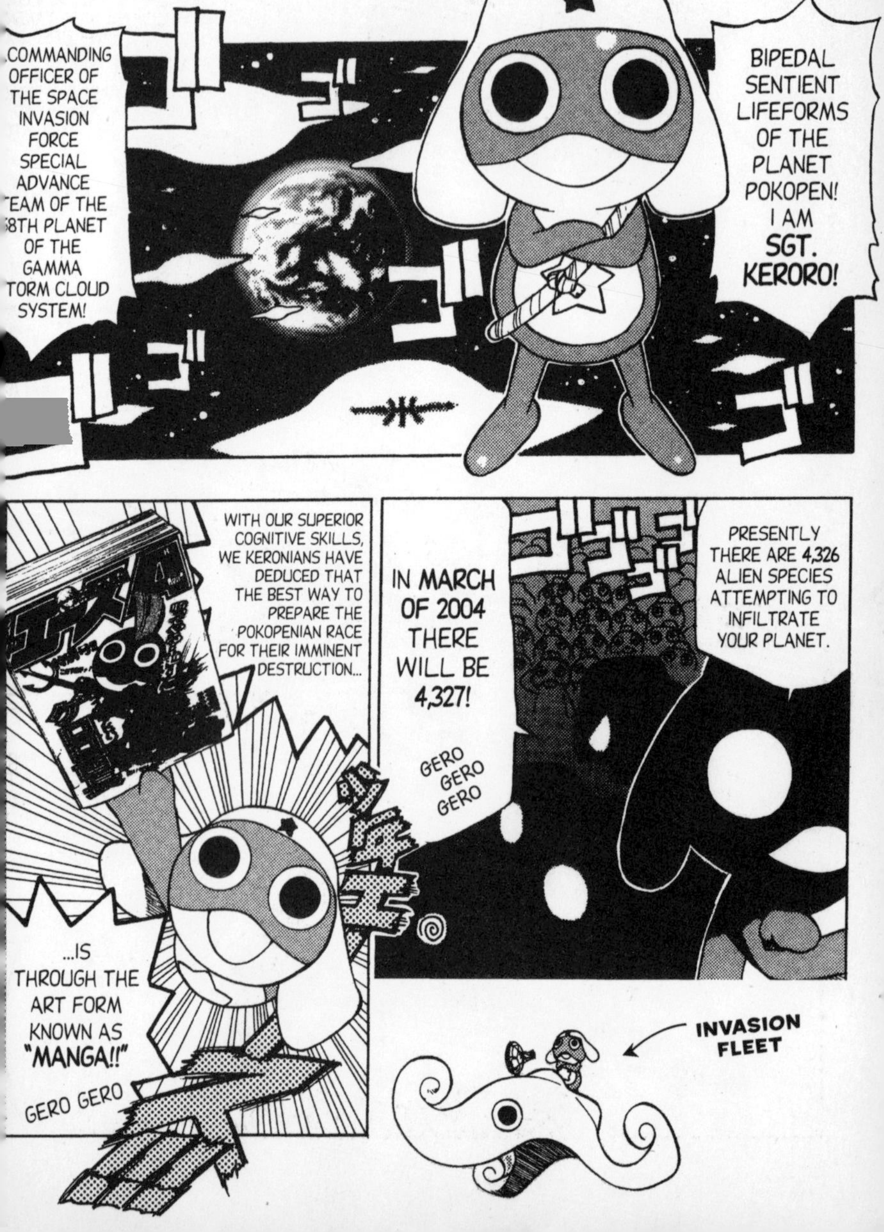
BIPEDAL SENTIENT LIFEFORMS OF THE PLANET POKOPEN! I AM SGT. KERORO!
COMMANDING OFFICER OF THE SPACE INVASION FORCE SPECIAL ADVANCE EAM OF THE 8TH PLANET OF THE GAMMA TORM CLOUD SYSTEM!
PRESENTLY THERE ARE 4,326 ALIEN SPECIES ATTEMPTING TO INFILTRATE YOUR PLANET.
IN MARCH OF 2004 THERE WILL BE 4,327!
GERO GERO GERO
INVASION FLEET
WITH OUR SUPERIOR COGNITIVE SKILLS, WE KERONIANS HAVE DEDUCED THAT THE BEST WAY TO PREPARE THE POKOPENIAN RACE FOR THEIR IMMINENT DESTRUCTION...
...IS THROUGH THE ART FORM KNOWN AS "MANGA!!"
GERO GERO

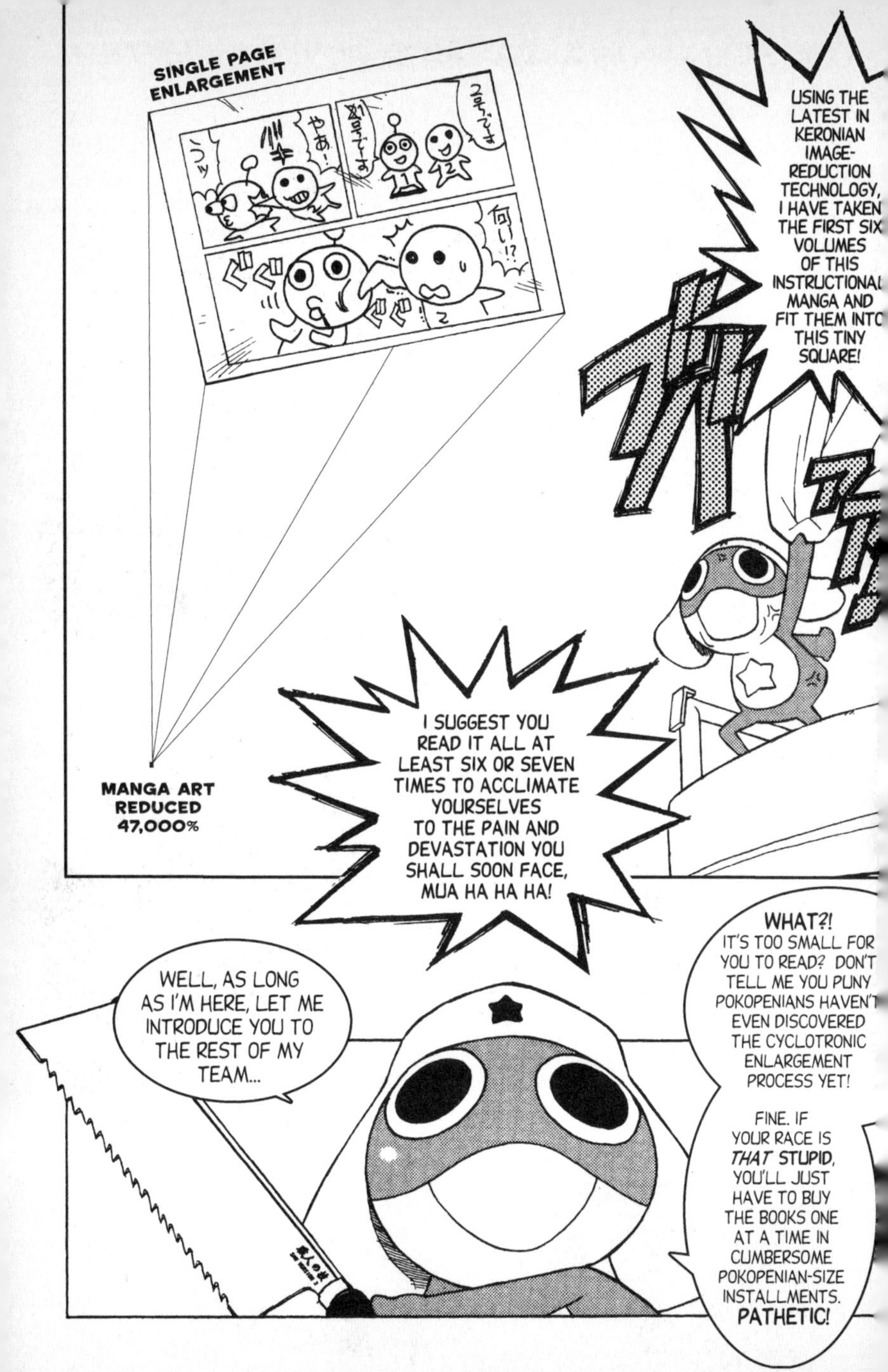
USING THE LATEST IN KERONIAN IMAGE-REDUCTION TECHNOLOGY, I HAVE TAKEN THE FIRST SIX VOLUMES OF THIS INSTRUCTIONAL MANGA AND FIT THEM INTO THIS TINY SQUARE!
SINGLE PAGE ENLARGEMENT
I SUGGEST YOU READ IT ALL AT LEAST SIX OR SEVEN TIMES TO ACCLIMATE YOURSELVES TO THE PAIN AND DEVASTATION YOU SHALL SOON FACE, MUA HA HA HA!
MANGA ART REDUCED 47,000%
WHAT?! IT'S TOO SMALL FOR YOU TO READ? DON'T TELL ME YOU PUNY POKOPENIANS HAVEN'T EVEN DISCOVERED THE CYCLOTRONIC ENLARGEMENT PROCESS YET!
FINE. IF YOUR RACE IS *THAT* **STUPID**, YOU'LL JUST HAVE TO BUY THE BOOKS ONE AT A TIME IN CUMBERSOME POKOPENIAN-SIZE INSTALLMENTS. **PATHETIC!**
WELL, AS LONG AS I'M HERE, LET ME INTRODUCE YOU TO THE REST OF MY TEAM...

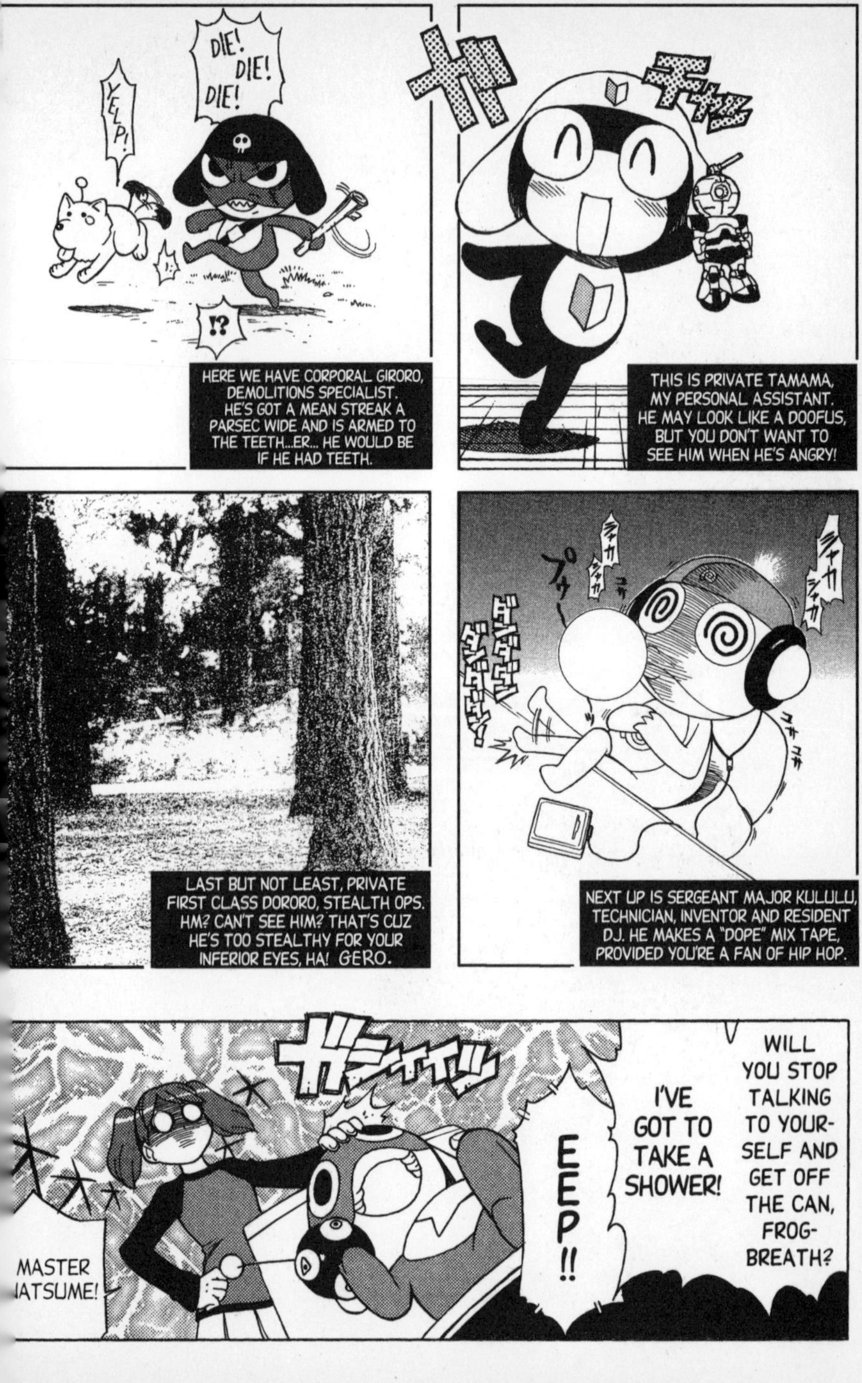
THIS IS PRIVATE TAMAMA, MY PERSONAL ASSISTANT. HE MAY LOOK LIKE A DOOFUS, BUT YOU DON'T WANT TO SEE HIM WHEN HE'S ANGRY!
DIE! DIE! DIE!
YELP!
!?
HERE WE HAVE CORPORAL GIRORO, DEMOLITIONS SPECIALIST. HE'S GOT A MEAN STREAK A PARSEC WIDE AND IS ARMED TO THE TEETH...ER... HE WOULD BE IF HE HAD TEETH.
NEXT UP IS SERGEANT MAJOR KULULU, TECHNICIAN, INVENTOR AND RESIDENT DJ. HE MAKES A "DOPE" MIX TAPE, PROVIDED YOU'RE A FAN OF HIP HOP.
LAST BUT NOT LEAST, PRIVATE FIRST CLASS DORORO, STEALTH OPS. HM? CAN'T SEE HIM? THAT'S CUZ HE'S TOO STEALTHY FOR YOUR INFERIOR EYES, HA! GERO.
WILL YOU STOP TALKING TO YOURSELF AND GET OFF THE CAN, FROG-BREATH?
I'VE GOT TO TAKE A SHOWER!
EEP!!
MASTER NATSUME!

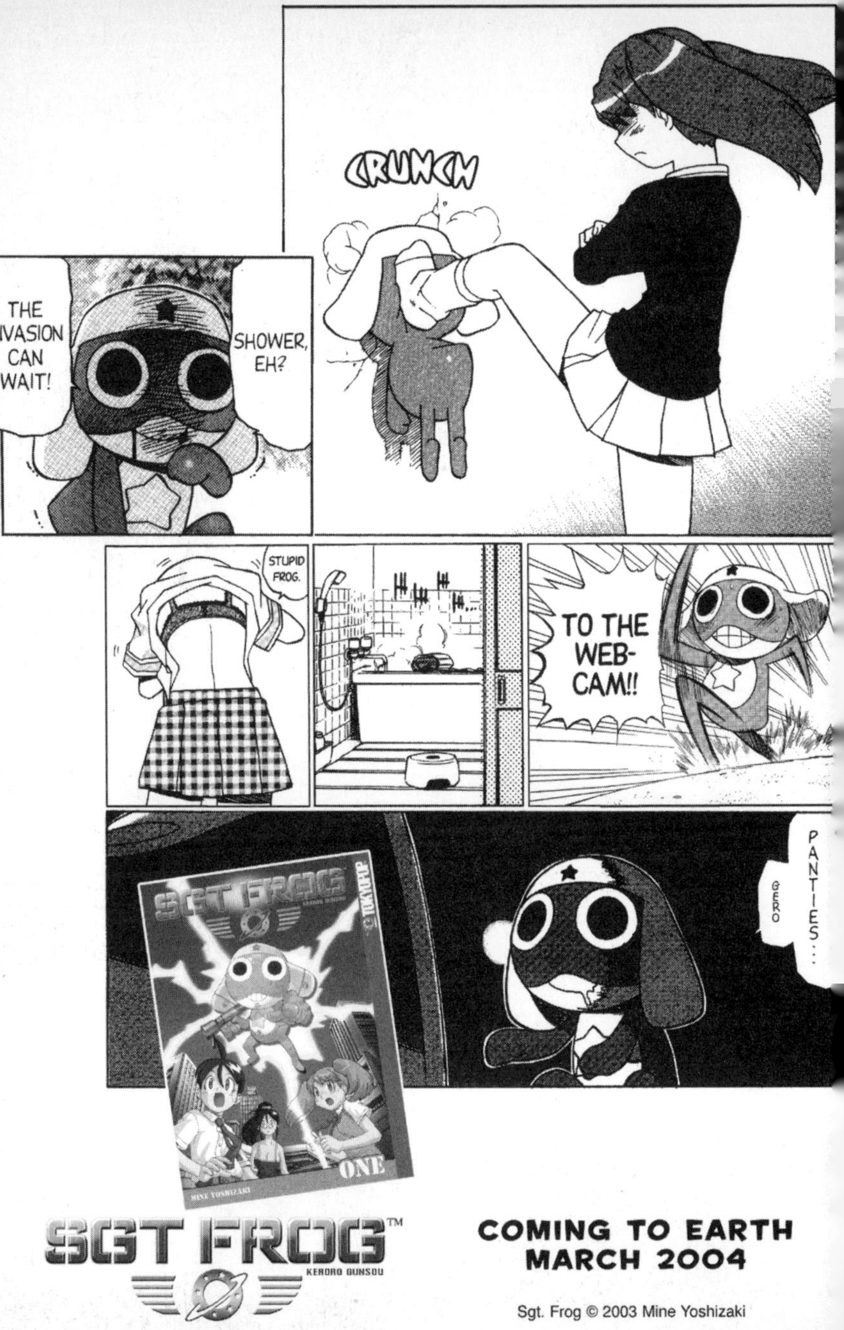
CRUNCH
SHOWER, EH?
THE INVASION CAN WAIT!
TO THE WEB-CAM!!
STUPID FROG.
PANTIES...
GERO
SGT FROG
ONE
MINE YOSHIZAKI

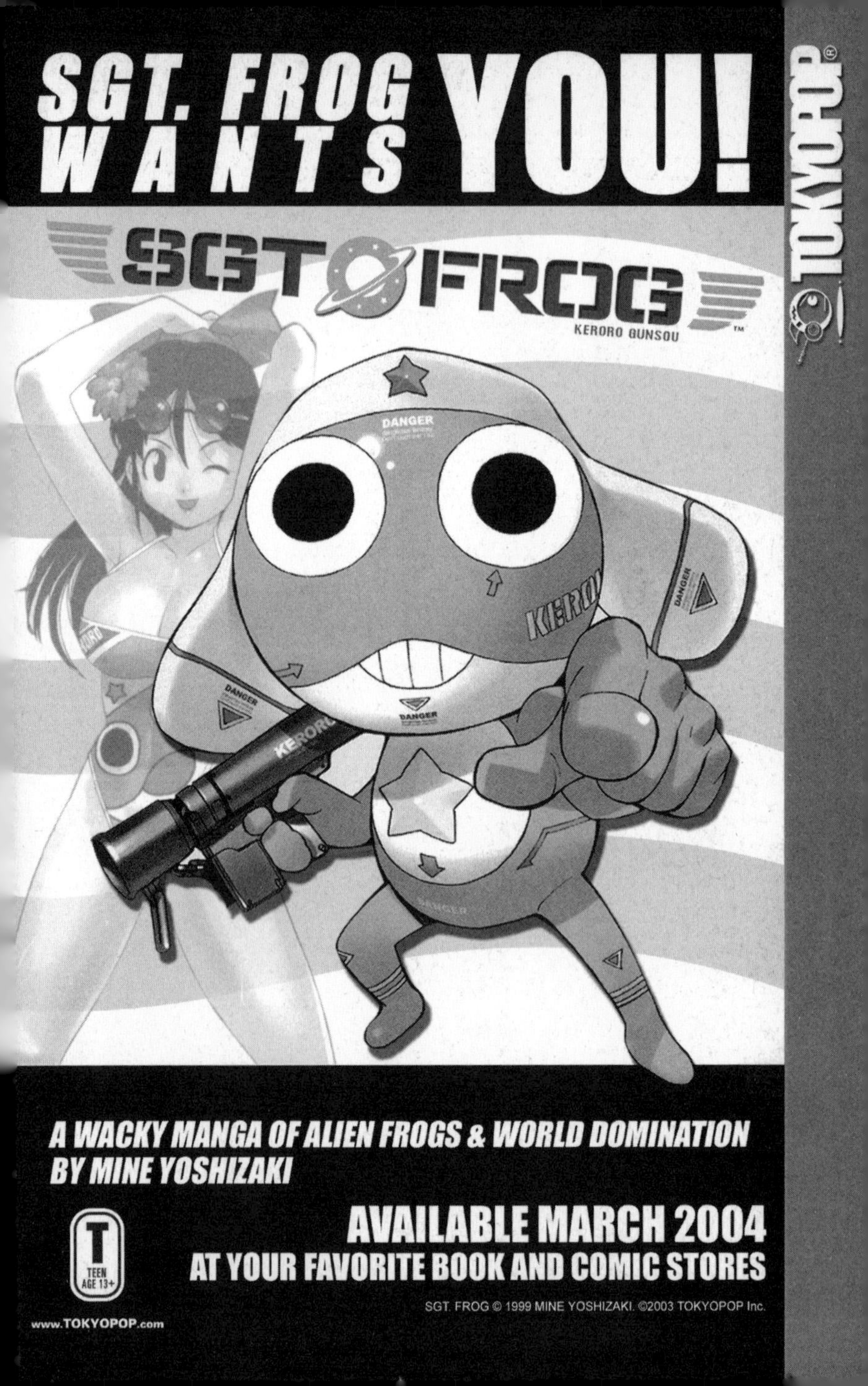
SGT. FROG WANTS YOU!
TOKYOPOP®
SGT FROG
KERORO GUNSOU™
DANGER
KERORO
DANGER
DANGER
KERORO
DANGER
A WACKY MANGA OF ALIEN FROGS & WORLD DOMINATION
BY MINE YOSHIZAKI
T TEEN AGE 13+
AVAILABLE MARCH 2004
AT YOUR FAVORITE BOOK AND COMIC STORES
SGT. FROG © 1999 MINE YOSHIZAKI. ©2003 TOKYOPOP Inc.
www.TOKYOPOP.com

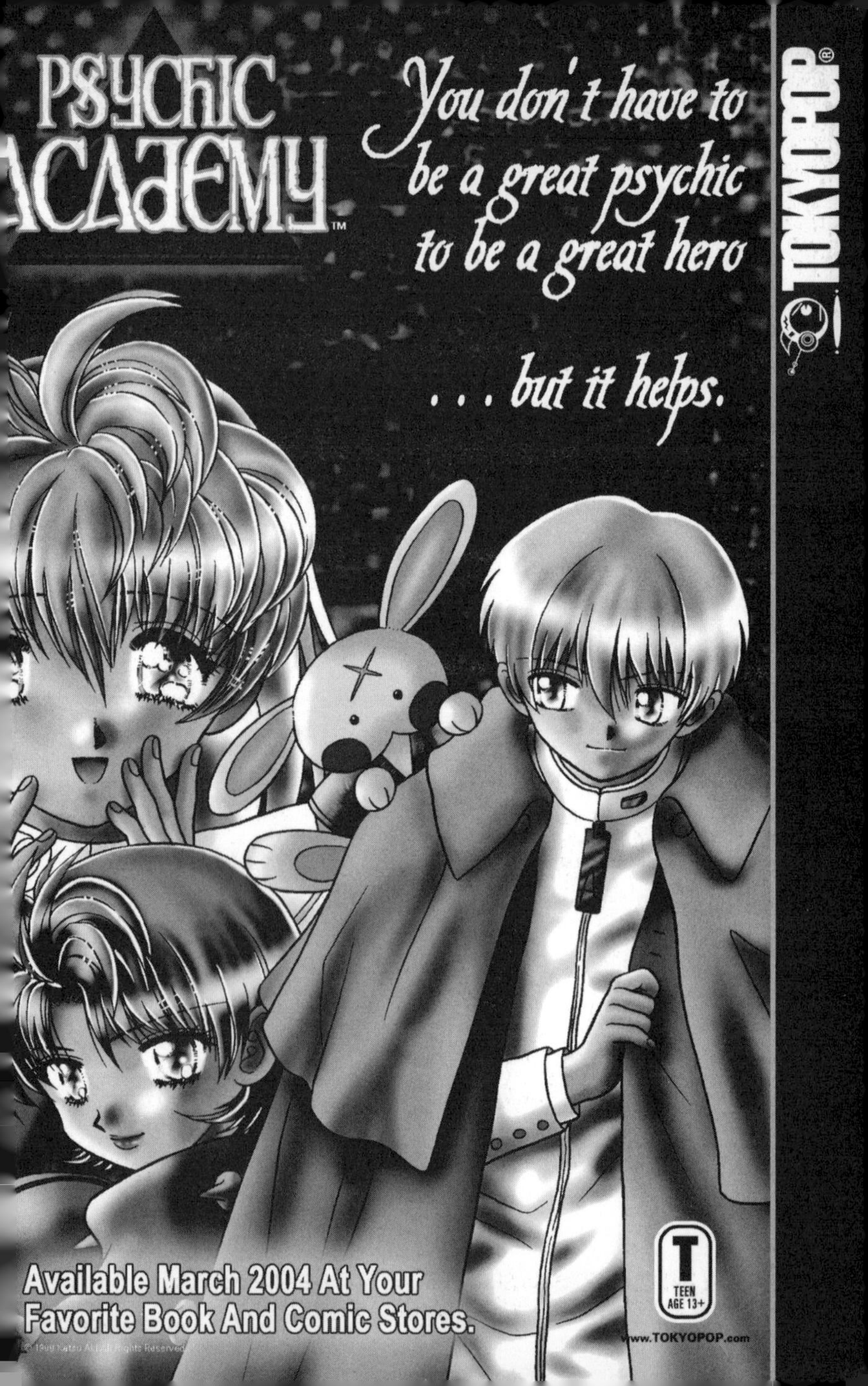
PSYCHIC ACADEMY™
You don't have to be a great psychic to be a great hero
. . . but it helps.
TOKYOPOP®
T TEEN AGE 13+
Available March 2004 At Your Favorite Book And Comic Stores.
www.TOKYOPOP.com